30 July, 2011

DEAREST EMMA,

May your commune of Bard, Belle, and your own dear self lead to wonder, joy, and comfort of soul, more even than you now imagine.

Your colleagues in Amherst with Emily,

All our love,

Kirk Granddad

Clare Grace

Emily Dickinson's Shakespeare

EMILY

DICKINSON'S SHAKESPEARE

Páraic Finnerty

University of Massachusetts Press *Amherst and Boston*

Printed in the United States of America

LC 2005052870
ISBN 1-55849-517-7

Designed by Dennis Anderson
Set in Adobe Caslon
Printed and bound by The Maple-Vail Book Manufacturing Group, Inc.

Library of Congress Cataloging-in-Publication Data

Finnerty, Páraic, 1974–
Emily Dickinson's Shakespeare / Páraic Finnerty.
p. cm.
Includes bibliographical references (p.) and index.
ISBN 1-55849-517-7 (alk. paper)
1. Dickinson, Emily, 1830–1886—Knowledge—Literature. 2. Shakespeare, William, 1564–1616—Appreciation—United States. 3. Shakespeare, William, 1564–1616—Influence. 4. Shakespeare, William, 1564–1616—Allusions. 5. American poetry—English influences. I. Title.
PS1541.Z5F56 2006
811'.4–dc22

2005052870

British Library Cataloguing in Publication data are available.

CONTENTS

ACKNOWLEDGMENTS

THIS BOOK could not have been written without the generous support of a number of individuals and awarding bodies. To begin, I thank Guy Reynolds, Sasha Roberts, Domhnall Mitchell, and Mary Loeffelholz for their advice, guidance, and enthusiasm; they have shaped this book in important and invaluable ways, and I am indebted to them for their comments and suggestions. I also acknowledge the encouragement of two early teachers, Kathleen Stanley and Maria Stuart, who stimulated my love for and interest in Dickinson's poetry. I am grateful for a Colyer-Fergusson award from the University of Kent, a grant from the Kent English Speaking Union, and the hospitality of Bobby O'Brien, all of which facilitated my initial research trip to America in April 1999. I wish also to express my gratitude to the board of the Emily Dickinson International Society for making me the first recipient of its Rogosa Scholar in Amherst Award in 2001 and to Amherst College's Copeland Committee and Karen Sanchez-Eppler (my sponsor) for selecting me as a Copeland Fellow in 2004. These awards allowed me to conduct further research in Amherst and Boston and to complete this book.

I also thank the staff and students of the School of English at the University of Kent and, in particular, the school's community of part-time teachers. I thank the staff at the Templeman Library, University of Kent, especially those at the Special Collections and Inter-library loan section, and the staff of the British Library. I am also indebted to Cindy Dickinson, Betty Bernhard, and the staff at the Emily Dickinson Museum, Amherst; Daria D'Arienzo and the staff of the Archives and Special Collections Rooms at the Frost Library, Amherst College; Tevis Kimball, Kate Boyle, and Daniel Lombardo (formerly) of the Special Collections at the Jones Public Library, Amherst; Roger Stoddard, Susan Halpert, and the staff at the Houghton Reading Room at Harvard University; Kimberly Nusco and the staff at the Massachusetts Historical Society, Boston; Eric Frazier and the staff at the Rare Books and Manuscripts Department of Boston Public Library; the staff at the Archives and Special Collections, Mount Holyoke Library; and Arthur Kinney and the staff at Massachusetts Center for Renaissance Studies, Amherst. I wish also to express my gratitude to Bruce Wilcox, Carol Betsch, and their colleagues at the University of Massachusetts Press, and to Archibald Hobson for his copyediting.

I thank all the very kind people I met during my visits to Amherst; the supportive and generous staff at Amherst College, especially those at the English Department and the Frost Library; and the other Copeland Fellows. I am very grateful to my friends in Ireland and the UK for their inspiration, influence, and encouragement, and to my new colleagues at the University of Portsmouth for their very warm welcome. Finally, I want to express my gratitude to my parents, Elizabeth and Patrick Finnerty, and my two sisters, Máire and Eilís, for their generosity, encouragement and love, without which I could not have written this book.

AN EARLIER version of chaper 8, "'We think of Others Possessing you with the throes of Othello': Dickinson Playing Othello, Race and Tommaso Salvini," appeared in *The Emily Dickinson Journal* 11, no. 1 (2002): 81–90, and is used here by permission of Johns Hopkins University Press.

Emily Dickinson's Shakespeare

INTRODUCTION

"Whose Pencil - here and there - / Had notched the place that pleased Him"

In the Emily Dickinson Room at the Houghton Library at Harvard is the Dickinson household's eight-volume pictorial and national edition of Shakespeare, edited by Charles Knight; Edward Dickinson purchased this for his family in 1857.[1] The Dickinsons, like many of their contemporaries, marked their books, and this edition of Shakespeare is no exception.[2] The contents page of the incredibly fragile fifth volume contains crosses beside *Romeo and Juliet*, *Hamlet*, and *Othello*, and between *Timon of Athens* and *King Lear*. Curiously, fourteen of the sixteen other pencil markings in the rest of the edition are found beside various lines from *Othello*. Eight sections of that play are marked with a notch on their right side, five are marked on the left, and one is marked on both left and right.[3] The lack of consistency might indicate marking on different occasions, perhaps by different hands. We are reminded of Dickinson's poem about the marginalia of a dear absent friend, "Whose Pencil - here and there - / Had notched the place that pleased Him - " (F640).[4] A note at the beginning of the catalogue for the Emily Dickinson Room warns the impetuous scholar that after years of searching for "annotation in the handwriting of Emily Dickinson" no single mark has been "positively assigned to her."[5] Nevertheless, critics continue to interpret the markings in books from the Dickinson library as the poet's.[6] While discovering the certain origin and meaning of these markings is impossible, at the very least they are the remnants of reading, and reveal that key scenes in *Othello* pleased members of the Dickinson household in some way.[7]

It is very suggestive that these marks accompany the Shakespeare play Dickinson refers to most often in her letters. The first mark in *Othello* occurs on the right side of Brabantio's reluctant parting with his daughter, where he tells Othello, "I here do give thee that with all my heart, / Which, but thou hast already, with all my heart / I would keep from thee." (I iii 193–95). Dickinson refers to this scene in four letters; in two, she actually quotes these lines. Thus, in an 1878 letter to her friend Maria Whitney, she precedes an exact quotation with the remark, "To relieve the irreparable degrades it. Brabantio's resignation is the only one -" (L538).[8] This letter, whose manuscript is lost, appears to refer to the recent death of Whitney's and the poet's mutual friend, Samuel Bowles, the editor of the *Springfield Republican.* Dickinson equates their shared loss with Brabantio's loss of his daughter. Unwillingness and endured suffering must accompany such an unalterable privation; to say otherwise would insult their shared love of Bowles. This allusion tells us much about how Dickinson read this scene. Shakespeare's lines confirm that loss, renunciation, and deprivation are "piercing Virtues" (F782); destitution and abstemiousness are self-empowering and self-affirming strategies, as well as self-destructive ones.[9] Further, this scene, where a father relinquishes his daughter, must have had a special significance for a woman who, unlike Desdemona, never married, and in 1869 told her literary preceptor, Thomas Wentworth Higginson, "I do not cross my Father's ground to any House or town" (L330).

Her letters do not refer to any of the other lines marked in this play. Jay Leyda, however, offers "He that is robb'd, not wanting what is stolen, / Let him not know 't, and he's not robb'd at all" (III iii 342–43), which has marks on both sides, as an example of Dickinson's marginalia.[10] These lines, spoken by Othello, contradict the sentiments of the letter to Whitney; robbery has no significance for a person who is unaware he has been robbed. This suggests that two different readers, or Dickinson herself, found and chose to emphasize contradictory impulses and ideas. If Brabantio is an emblem of unwilling resignation and terrible sorrow, Othello represents someone unconscious of loss. Whoever made them, both these markings reflect Dickinson's interest in themes of theft and robbery.[11] Intriguingly, while most of the other markings in this play are faint, neat strokes, the vertical notch to the right of Othello's line "Certain, men should be what they seem" is particularly heavy and distinctive. Both this line and the previous one, spoken by Iago, "Or, those that be not 'would they might seem none!" also have a lighter mark on their left side (III iii 127–28). If the same marker made these, he or she appears to be commenting on the ideal nature of Othello's remark, but marking differently to indicate Iago's duplicity. Dickinson, or someone in her inner circle, identified with Shakespeare's story of an ill-fated love affair and false friendship, involving betrayal and jealousy; certainly, these topics are frequently explored in her writings.[12] These lines may be marked because they express universal truths about human nature and/or represent crucial points in interpreting the play; alternatively, they may have a more complex and private significance.

That Dickinson may have elaborately marked *Othello* will surprise few of her scholars and critics: the poet manifested her great love of Shakespeare in numerous references to his plays. Moreover, the usually equivocal poet made her devotion to Shakespeare very clear—as if it were something she wanted her contemporaries, and perhaps posterity, to know about her. During and after her period of eye trouble in 1864–65, she told Louise Norcross, Joseph Lyman, and Thomas Wentworth Higginson that Shakespeare was the first author she chose to read, and that she regarded him as the only necessary author.[13] Although Shakespeare's omnipresence in the poet's life is recognized, and some provocative literary connections exist, they tell us only part of this complex story.[14] The tendency to accept Shakespeare's significance for Dickinson without fully exploring its biographical importance, probably reflects the fact that her remarks about Shakespeare sound, on one level, to be literary clichés, symptoms of nineteenth-century bardolatry.[15] Similarly, her many references to his works merely conform to middle-class epistolary practice of the time.

This book aims to go beyond what might be regarded as cultural truisms to discover the central and constitutive role reading Shakespeare had in Dickinson's life. Theorists of the new field of the history of the book, particularly those interested in determining reading practices and habits in a time and place, offer the procedures necessary for this project,[16] which will also draw on current scholarship on the multifaceted reception of Shakespeare in nineteenth-century America.[17] Accordingly, this book reconstructs the social and cultural milieu in which Dickinson read Shakespeare in order to clarify her actual references to reading him and so as to speculate further on her attitude toward her preferred author. From the outset, we must acknowledge difficulties and unanswered questions and confront the many gaps in the available information. This examination approaches one of the most reclusive and hidden of poets through looking at the practice of reading, which is, by its very nature, private and ephemeral. Even if Dickinson's reading of Shakespeare was, to an extent, determined by certain identifiable historical factors, these do not "cancel out the creative and inventive force" of reading or the individual freedom, fluidity, and variability it allows.[18] What emerges is the story of the predominant, often contradictory, ideas and concerns that most likely molded and affected Dickinson's understanding and reading of Shakespeare; this "horizon of expectation," however, is often unsettled by Dickinson's choices as a reader.[19]

For historians of reading, such an investigation begins with an examination of the materials through which readers are presented with texts.[20] Throughout this book, the Shakespeare Dickinson is believed to have used will be a primary resource; along with its provocative marginalia, Knight's edition provides insight into how its editor conceived of the competencies and expectations of his readers. His readers were provided with introductions and annotations that discuss the stage history, sources, and social, historical, and political background of each play, as well as the key critical debates that surrounded them. These were supplemented by Knight's biography of Shakespeare, contained in the seventh volume, and his own work of criticism on the plays, in the eighth. This final volume elaborated and extended Knight's introductions to each play, as well as surveying Shakespeare criticism from John Milton to Charles Lamb. The edition was also pictorial, offering a visual understanding of scenes and characters from the plays and the historical figures associated with them, as well as illustrations of life, manners, and clothing in Shakespeare's England. In other words, Knight sought to popularize the study of Shakespeare by offering the reader a multifaceted and intricate experience, while at the same time providing up-to-date, historical information.[21]

Like Knight's edition, another important text in this study is Dickinson's one poem that mentions Shakespeare, "Drama's Vitallest Expression is the Common Day" (F776).

Drama's Vitallest Expression is the Common Day
That arise and set about Us -
Other Tragedy

Perish in the Recitation -
This - the best enact
When the Audience is scattered
And the Boxes shut -

"Hamlet" to Himself were Hamlet -
Had not Shakespeare wrote -
Though the "Romeo" left no Record
Of his Juliet,

It were infinite enacted
In the Human Heart -
Only Theatre recorded
Owner cannot shut -
(F776)

5 best enact] more exert   10 left] leave
12 infinite] tenderer - 15] Never yet was shut -

In contrast to Dickinson's elaborate praise of Shakespeare, this poem argues that the infinite and internal dramas of everyday lives are more "Vital" than staged tragedies, which perish in recitation and end when the theater shuts; it will be read and reread in a number of different interpretative contexts.

Chapter 1 examines the ideals and assumptions about reading Shakespeare found in women's journals and advice manuals; Amherst College student literary magazines; details of an attempted act of censorship at the local Shakespeare Club, which Dickinson attended; school textbooks; the public lectures of Richard Henry Dana Sr.; and contemporary letters and diaries.[22] These demonstrate that Dickinson read Shakespeare at a time when he was regarded by some as "wicked" and to be expurgated, by others as highly moral and literary, to be acquired as a sign of education and cultivation. Although his works scandalized many conservative elements within Dickinson's reading community, Shakespeare was one of a small group of sacred texts, along with the Bible, that inspired intensive reading. Like most readers of Shakespeare in her era (and today), Dickinson kept returning to his plays and poems throughout her life, presumably changing her mind about his characters and lines, and finding new significance in his art.[23] Despite their disputed status, Shakespeare's works were also explicated to support long-established social and literary hierarchies against new and threatening cultural values.[24] Chapter 2 focuses on the importance of how and where Dickinson's reading of Shakespeare occurred.[25] In her era, reading the bard was a silent, solitary, and domestic activity, but also a public, social practice that involved skill. Reading Shakespeare aloud was a feature of Dickinson's rhetoric lessons and Shakespeare Club activities, and a form of entertainment popularized by Shakespeare readers, like Fanny Kemble and Mary Frances Scott-Siddons. For many in Dickinson's era, hearing Shakespeare read aloud and participating in readings were always different from watching his works performed; this preference is connected with class and a still apparent antitheatrical prejudice, and Dickinson's Shakespeare was not primarily the dramatist who dominated the nineteenth-century American stage and was an inextricable part of popular entertainment. Next, chapter 3 examines the presuppositions American Shakespeare critics had about, and role they ascribed to, readers, as seen in the practical guidance they offered for interpreting the plays.[26] Articles on Shakespeare were ubiquitous in the journals Dickinson read—*Harper's New Monthly, Atlantic Monthly,* and *Scribner's Monthly;* each presumed its erudite, middle-class readers to be interested in every facet of information about the man and his works. In Dickinson's community of readers Shakespeare and his plays were matters of debate, in which a nonspecialist could express his or her informed opinions. Moreover, these critics provided "knowledge" about Shakespeare from an American perspective, claimed Shakespeare as an American intellectual possession, differentiated themselves—at times radically—from English critics, and even attempted to separate Shakespeare from his English origins. Dickinson read Shakespeare when Americans had become his critics, his editors, and his collectors, and such involvement with him was a sign of American civility and cultivation.[27]

Historians of the book emphasize the importance of investigating "the network of practices and rules of reading" specific to diverse groups of readers; such concrete interpretative procedures may reveal the distinct ways each group member will approach a text.[28] Throughout this study, cultural and social categories such as gender, religious belief, education, race, class, sexuality, and nationality will be fundamental to understanding how Dickinson read Shakespeare.[29] Accordingly, chapters 4 and 5 examine readers who shared group-specific expectations, interests, and conventions with the poet. Chapter 4 positions Dickinson among her contemporaries Ralph Waldo Emerson, Herman Melville, and Walt Whitman, who, as American cultural nationalists and democrats, held ambiguous attitudes toward the English and proaristocratic bard. These writers reacted to the way conservative and antidemocratic critics, like Richard Henry Dana Sr., had made Shakespeare unsurpassable, unapproachable, unrivaled. This chapter considers whether Dickinson shared the views of the conservatives or the sentiments of Emerson and his contemporaries, and what this might reveal about her attitude regarding a distinctively American creativity. Chapter 5 places Dickinson among American women writers and readers in a period when women had, and were encouraged to have, a special relationship with Shakespeare.[30] It connects Dickinson with an emergent female tradition of Shakespeare criticism, in which women critics deferentially claimed their roles as literary professionals through work on Shakespeare. It examines the work of the American critics Henrietta Lee Palmer and Mary Preston—their modesty about their achievements and their obvious competitiveness with other (female) critics, as well as their emphasis on the exceptional knowledge and special ability they had as women in discussing Shakespeare's plays and, particularly, his heroines. This encouraged and legitimized the comparable involvement of women readers, like Dickinson, with Shakespeare's works. The chapter also connects Dickinson with other American writers, such as Margaret Fuller, Harriet Beecher Stowe, and Louisa May Alcott, who read and appropriated Shakespeare, feminizing and domesticating his texts through close study of his characters, particularly his heroines.

The next four chapters focus on the many quotations from and allusions to Shakespeare lines in Dickinson's writing. These afford not only glimpses into how she read Shakespeare, but also into her views on authorship, literary immortality, death, friendship, and love. In chapter 6 I consider her Shakespearean allusions in relation to nineteenth-century conventions expecting a display of familiarity with Shakespeare—in a time when his writings were parodied and burlesqued as a prominent form of American humor, quoted in newspapers, advertisements, and novels, and alluded to in private letters. Despite Shakespeare's supreme cultural authority, which Dickinson so frequently acknowledges, her letters demonstrate that like other readers she made his texts her own. They become sources for her imaginative fancy, for the unexpected use and interpretative variety to which she put Shakespeare; his works are not merely to be interpreted, but to be applied to suit private and individual circumstances, often by reading them against the grain.[31] Elaborating on this theme, chapter 7 investigates Dickinson's references to *Antony and Cleopatra* in light of the play's stage and critical reception. It asks why she chose one of Shakespeare's most provocative plays, with its immoral central protagonists, as her favorite. It also suggests that Cleopatra was her prototype of female elusiveness and seductiveness. Chapter 8 inspects Dickinson's suggestive identification with the character Othello in letters, linking this with Lavinia's attendance at a performance of *Othello* in 1851, questions of race, and the Italian actor Tommaso Salvini. Chapter 9 scrutinizes her references to other Shakespeare tragedies, specifically to the death scenes of his most famous protagonists; it connects her allusions to Shakespeare's tragic heroes with Charlotte Cushman's performances of these parts in antebellum America, and with two burlesques, of *Hamlet* and *Romeo and Juliet,* performed by the Amherst College Senior Dramatic Company in the early 1880s.

"Congratulate the Doctor on his growing Fame. 'Stratford on Avon' - accept us all"

To demonstrate the method of this book and introduce some aspects of Shakespeare's reception in Dickinson's culture, I begin by examining one of her most expressive statements about Shakespeare. In 1877, she told her lifelong friend Elizabeth Holland, "Congratulate the Doctor on his growing Fame. 'Stratford on Avon' - accept us all!" (L487). According to Theodora Van Wagenen Ward, the Hollands' granddaughter, this remark may refer to an actual invitation Josiah Holland had received to be present at Stratford when the cornerstone of the Shakespeare Memorial Theatre was being laid on 23 April 1877.[32] If Ward is correct, Dickinson is celebrating Holland's recognition by this emblematic site;[33] acceptance by Stratford is a result of his "growing fame": his success as a novelist, poet, public lecturer, and editor of the *Scribner's Monthly.* Although we do not know if Holland went to Stratford, his enthusiasm for Shakespeare is definite; it would seem that the bard was Holland's own model for the successful writer.[34] In a section on "Culture" from his *Every-Day Topics; a Book of Briefs* (1876), Holland writes, "the sympathy of humanity was strong in Shakespeare, and it was given to him to weave at once his own crown and that of the language in which he wrote." In a later section on "Literature and Literary Men," he praises Shakespeare as a practical man who "meant business," making money through art for himself and his family, yet wrote "wonderful plays."[35] Mrs. Holland shared her husband's enthusiasm. In fact, Dickinson seems to have regarded her as a great lover of Shakespeare; the majority of the poet's known references to Shakespeare occur in letters to this correspondent.

Dickinson presents Shakespeare as a god whose birthplace is a heaven for the worthiest and greatest of writers.[36] Her prayer, plea, even demand that this emblematic site accept "all" expresses a nineteenth-century need of Americans to measure and define themselves against the cultural standards and achievements of England.[37] This complicated Shakespeare's American reception, for he was both the sign of culture and the symbol of English culture. America sought Shakespeare as part of its cultural inheritance, integrating him into its educational, social, theatrical, and political institutions. But it also viewed him as a representative of "English" culture who stifled America's literary identity and insulted its political and social ideals. In 1837 Emerson famously told the Phi Beta Kappa Society at Harvard, "We have listened too long to the courtly muses of Europe. The spirit of the American freeman is already suspected to be timid, imitative, tame."[38] Emerson was explicit about Shakespeare's symbolic role in this: "Genius is always sufficiently the enemy of genius by over-influence. The literature of every nation bear me witness. The English dramatic poets have Shakspearized now for two hundred years" (I 57). In this context, Dickinson's remark may have been discordant.

By 1877, although she had written some of her most important poems, ten of which had been published, Dickinson was unknown. In other letters to Mrs. Holland, the poet discusses household matters and family and spiritual affairs, as well as openly disclosing her poetic vocation and aspirations.[39] She might be read as here asserting her creative ambition;[40] in this letter, she is concerned with posterity: she hopes that Mrs. Holland will live to see her asleep in her "personal Grave"; she concludes, "With love for your sweet Descendants - and the wish for yourself, I am / Emily -." Dickinson conflates literary and personal immortality. Additionally, the poet refers to her friend as the "Doctor's 'Child Wife,'" but counteracts this by praising the "prowess" of Mrs. Holland's own writing at a time when her eyes were weak, and her friend's "sweetness" to the poet's brother, Austin. Dickinson appears to be arguing that Mrs. Holland deserves acknowledgment as much as her husband does. From Dr. Holland's perspective, women, like his "Child Wife," should gain admiration through domestic kindness and service, not through literary and social aspirations.[41] Dickinson is calling subtly for public recognition of the private achievements of women like Holland and herself, which because antithetical to the idea of "fame" go unnoticed. Dickinson may also in celebrating a more public male figure's achievement by revealing a level of envy, or even resentment, as a private poet not appreciated.[42]

Despite the sentiments of writers like Emerson, Stratford was one of the main attractions in England for visiting Americans, who accounted for a large proportion of its yearly visitors.[43] In the year of Dickinson's letter to Mrs.

Holland, the eminent American Shakespeare critic Richard Grant White was informed by an English railway companion that "all 'Americans' go to Stratford" as if this were a universal law.[44] When two of Dickinson's friends were visiting Europe, the poet evoked Shakespeare's birthplace as a place she expected them to go, presenting their visits as pilgrimages to a sacred shrine. In early June of 1878, she told Higginson, who was in Europe at the time, "To have seen Stratford on Avon - and the Dresden Madonna, must be almost Peace - " (L553); in 1885, she asked Mabel Loomis Todd to "Touch Shakespeare" for her (L1004). If such friends did not tell Dickinson what Stratford was like, the periodicals the poet read offered devotees tours, complete with illustrations, of all the locations associated with Shakespeare: his birthplace, the grammar school, Anne Hathaway's cottage, Charlecote Hall, the remains of New Place, and his grave at Holy Trinity Church.[45] James G. Wilson's "Stratford-Upon-Avon" (1861) and William Winter's "Stratford-Upon-Avon" (1879) provide *Harper's New Monthly* readers with stories, anecdotes, and legends about Shakespeare and each site; clearly, they sought to attract visitors to Stratford and meet each reader's implied demand for information about Shakespeare.[46] Wilson states that the birthplace affords the "great privilege of standing beneath the roof that gave birth to the immortal dramatist," and that Holy Trinity Church possesses an interest that "does not belong to any other spot on the habitable globe" (436, 441). Winter announces that "to visit Stratford is to tread with affectionate veneration in the footsteps of the poet. To write about Stratford is to write about Shakespeare" (865).

Although these articles mirror Dickinson's conception of Stratford as a quasi-divine and essentially English literary shrine, their "tours" emphasize American connections with Stratford. To write about Stratford, for an American, is to write about America's affiliation with and claim to Shakespeare. Referring to the many signatures on the walls of Shakespeare's birth chamber, Wilson notes two short poems that poked fun at the others. One of these, parodying the inscription on Shakespeare's grave, pleads "Good friend, for Jesus' sake forbear / Thy wit or lore to scribble here / Blessed are they that rightly con him / And curs'd be they that comment on him" (438).[47] Wilson notes that such poems "belong to this side of the Atlantic"; American visitors are detached and ironic observers of such devotional practice. But, such skepticism is coupled with an American need to appropriate Shakespeare, as seen in the story of "an enthusiastic young American lady" who cut a piece from the manteltree in the room where Shakespeare was born, while her companion distracted the proprietor (437). Winter offers the extreme example of P. T. Barnum, who attempted to buy "the Shakspeare house and convey it to America." As a result of incidents like this, "the literary enthusiasm of Great Britain was made to take a practical shape; and this venerated and inestimable relic became, in 1847, a national possession" (867–68). Barnum, of course, a shrewd publicist and promoter of cultural novelties and oddities, had been seeking fame and fortune for himself by exploiting Shakespeare's reputation in both England and America.[48]

In addition, both articles emulate Washington Irving's celebrated visit to Shakespeare's birthplace, recorded in his *Sketch-Book* (1820), and, in the process, mythologize and venerate Irving.[49] Although he quotes the American writer's assessment that "the mind refuses to dwell on any thing not connected with Shakspeare," Wilson continually returns to Irving. When he visits Holy Trinity Church and asks the sexton if he may examine Irving's signature among the autographs of visitors, he is told that "the book containing [Irving's name] as well as those of two of our greatest poets, *had been stolen by a countryman of ours*" (443). This anecdote does not merely reflect an American need to acquire English culture; it establishes the value and status of American writers like Irving. At the Red Horse Inn, where Irving stayed, one room is named in his honor; American guests, like Wilson and Winter, are shown "a shovel, next a poker, and lastly a pair of tongs, all bright and apparently new," which the landlady claims were used by him.[50] In each of these articles Irving, "the pioneer of American worshippers at the shrine of Shakespeare," is "consecrated" along with the places and objects associated with Shakespeare.[51]

Yet Stratford is also associated with crude literary appropriation and exploitation. Like Irving, both writers present the town as a place where belief and unbelief coexist, and contradictions are tolerated. Wilson quotes a long passage recording Irving's skepticism about the authenticity of a chair said to have belonged to Shakespeare, and his remark that "such was the fervent zeal of devotees that it had to be new-bottomed at least once in three years" (438); but he omits Irving's important later paragraph that supports credulity:

> I am always of easy faith in such matters, and am ever willing to be deceived, where the deceit is pleasant and costs nothing. I am therefore a ready believer in relics, legends, and local anecdotes of goblins and great men; and would advise all travellers who travel for their gratification to be the same. What is it to us, whether these stories are true or false, so long as we can persuade ourselves into the belief of them, and enjoy all the charm of the reality?[52]

Like Irving, both writers encourage visitors to accept the courting chair of Shakespeare and Anne Hathaway, Shakespeare's christening font, and Shakespeare's desk, purse, glove, and ring, because, as Wilson notes, "skeptical persons are not met by bold assertions of [their] genuineness, while all credulous and nothing-doubting individuals are allowed the full benefit of faith" (444).

Wilson's faith in these objects is undisturbed until it becomes "considerably shaken" when a guide in Anne Hathaway's cottage presents him with a dog-eared Bible supposedly used by Anne and Shakespeare—printed in 1676. For Winter, these relics are tolerable substitutes for real knowledge about Shakespeare. He cautions his readers, however, that Shakespeare's father owned two houses, one at Henley Street and another in Greenhill Street, and that Shakespeare could have been born in either place. The possibility "that several generations of the poet's worshippers have been dilating with emotion in the wrong place," underlines, for Winter, the fact that Shakespeare led a "vague and shadowy life" (870). Worshipers do not even have a portrait of this writer, because "in his personality, no less than in the fathomless resources of his genius, he baffles all scrutiny, and stands forever alone" (882). Winter calls the Shakespeare Memorial Hall, to whose foundation-laying Josiah Holland may had been invited, a "depository of Shakespearean relics." He also offers an illustration of the finished museum, which consisted of a library, a theater, and a picture gallery. Noting that it has been built with financial contributions from Americans, he predicts that this building will become as venerated as other Stratford antiquities:

> The same air of poetic mystery which rests now upon his cottage and his grave will diffuse itself around his Memorial; and a remote posterity, looking back to the men and ideas of to-day, will remember with grateful pride that English-speaking people of the nineteenth-century, though they could confer no honor upon the great name of Shakespeare, yet honored themselves in consecrating this beautiful temple to his memory. (886)

This epitomizes America's need to participate in the story and history of Shakespeare and thus establish itself at the forefront of "English-speaking" culture. Yet this Anglo-American collaboration is not simply a temple to Shakespeare's memory, but also a means by which these American investors (as well as their British counterparts) can "honor" and immortalize themselves. The Wilson and Winter articles, thus depict American pilgrims as participating (knowingly) in perpetuating myth and unauthenticated associations. Stratford provides fabricated information and artifacts to a public demanding connection with its idol, and exploits such worship for financial or cultural profit.[53]

In 1863, the "enticing" Nathaniel Hawthorne gives his own diagnosis of Stratford and its attraction to Americans for *Atlantic Monthly* readers like Dickinson.[54] He offers details about the town, Shakespeare's grave, and the whitewashed and new walls of Shakespeare's birth chamber as antidotes to Americans' "excessive predilection for antique residences," advising them not to spend so much time repining for the historic features of England, an impulse that derives from "English habits of thought" (47, 58). From Hawthorne's point of view, Stratford should not "accept us all"; instead, he calls on American philosophers and poets to see and write what is "best" and "beautifullest" in "the kind of life we must lead," free from the tyranny of an English idea of tradition. At Holy Trinity Church, Shakespeare's renown becomes a threatening and tyrannical force that "suffers nothing else to be recognized within the scope of its material presence, unless illuminated by some side-ray from himself" (50). On hearing that people are no longer buried there, Hawthorne comments that "a person of delicate individuality" who is "desirous of six feet of earth alone, could never endure to lie buried near Shakspeare" and would leave "rather than sleep in the shadow of so stupendous a memory." At the birthplace, Hawthorne is appalled by the way desperate devotees write their names on the walls, seeking "to immortalize themselves" through Shakespeare, although such thrusting "forward into the dazzle of a great renown," if noticed, "cannot but be deemed impertinent" (47). He mildly admires the "respectable lady" who makes a "handsome profit" by selling memorabilia, "prints, views of houses and scenes connected with Shakspeare's memory, together with editions of his works and local publications" to the bard's foolish devotees.

For Hawthorne, visiting Stratford brings disappointment. Shakespeare's birthplace is a "humbler house than any description can prepare the visitor to expect," and he feels "conscious of not the slightest emotion while viewing [the birth chamber], nor any quickening of the imagination." Moreover, although he gains a better appreciation of Shakespeare's triumph over a stifling background, Hawthorne is not quite certain that "this power of realization is altogether desirable in reference to a great poet." His reader is warned of the dangers of peeping too curiously into Shakespeare's mysterious life because this may reveal "the shadow of an ugly doubt" whether the "flesh and blood individual," the "burgher of Stratford" about whom many impious stories and anecdotes exist, is reconcilable with Shakespeare, the great poet. Even the "ruddy English complexion" of Shakespeare's bust in the church lacks the nobility of Hawthorne's mental pictures of his "beautiful, lofty-browed, and noble" face (49). Such inquisitiveness about the "grimy actualities" of a writer's life, and his "perishing earthliness," makes great men, like Shakespeare, "in a certain lower sense, very much the same kind of men as the rest of us, and often a little worse" (48). Moreover, it compromises the standing of the "imperishable and divine" writings he left humanity, leading to "moral bewilderment and even intellectual loss."

Although Dickinson was interested in the private lives of her favorite authors, she must have wholeheartedly agreed with Hawthorne's views on inquisitiveness, especially with reference to herself. She asked Emily Fowler Ford "if it did not make [her] shiver to hear a great many people talk—they took 'all the clothes off their souls'";[55] in 1885, after George Eliot's biography was published, she told Higginson, "Biography first convinces us of the fleeing of the Biographied -" (L972). Her niece Martha Dickinson Bianchi recalled Dickinson's hatred of publicity, her "horror to have realized the idle curiosity about her and her private affairs," and her "uncompromising conviction, that her life was sacred and of no legitimate concern to the public."[56] Certainly, what Bianchi called the poet's "instinctive reserve" was central to her work; Dickinson might almost have been referring to the Shakespeare phenomenon when she wrote:

> The right to perish might be thought
> An undisputed right
> Attempt it, and the Universe
> Upon the opposite
> Will concentrate it's officers -
> You cannot even die
> But nature and mankind must pause
> To pay you scrutiny -
> (F1726)

Wilson and Winter present Stratford as one of the greatest examples of nineteenth-century commercialization and commodification.[57] Shakespeare's town is a dissatisfying sham, an emblem of obsession with renown, a disconcerting and moneymaking tourist attraction, home to America's claim to Shakespeare and to its dependency on English cultural standards.[58] It seems certain that Dickinson would have been appalled to be "accepted" by this embodiment of her worst fears about literary renown. Shakespeare is fetishized into a "consummate saint or martyr"; his birthplace and its contents, as well as his manuscripts, are icons to his worshipers.[59] Might she be slyly imagining Josiah Holland's "growing fame" as leading to his acceptance by such a place? While apparently uninterested in the "futile Diadem" (F481) of fame and aware of the transience of worldly success, she may yet have sought acceptance by Stratford as the sign of literary honor, shorn of the crudities of celebrity.[60] In some of her poems Dickinson presents the idea of literary fame in a "posthumous Sun," (F1707), referring to Shakespeare's *Sonnets* and their celebration of the immortalizing powers of poetry.[61]

Stratford is also preeminently the location of Shakespeare's absence, elusiveness, mystery, and fascination. Such ideas converge in Henry James's short story "The Birthplace" (1903); although this never mentions Shakespeare's name, it presents the birthplace's curator, Morris Gedge, as someone who no longer believes the unsubstantiated facts he tells visitors.[62] Gedge is split between his public role as "the showman, the priest of the idol" and his private identity as a "poor, unsuccessful honest man" (127). Afraid of losing his job, he continues his "first-rate show," accompanied by busts, relics, old prints, old editions, old objects, furniture, "autographs of celebrated worshippers," "the extraneous, preposterous stuffing" of an "empty shell" (121–23). An American couple, the Hayeses, encourage him to "keep it up," after recognizing the cynicism he hints at (138–39). Afterwards, Gedge offers visitors elaborate falsifications of the facts, hoping that some, like the Hayeses, will recognize a level of skepticism in his tone. When the Hayeses return, it is not to see the shrine, but "the queer case of the priest"; they tell him that he is admired by many Americans and has become famous for his subtly derisive performance (146–47). The story ends with Gedge having his salary doubled by his superior, Grant-Jackson, and the birthplace making a profit because of his performance. That the American couple offers Gedge sympathetic support is significant; it is as if American visitors to Stratford preserve and perpetuate the Shakespeare legend, regardless of its veracity, because it is exemplary of Anglo-American mythmaking: Stratford is a magnet for human creativity.[63] Perhaps Dickinson viewed it this way rather than as a factual place.

Considering her concerns with privacy and reputation, perhaps she admired Shakespeare as the author who, as Gedge says, "covered his tracks as no other human being has ever done" (129). Henry James stated in 1907 that Shakespeare is the "secret that baffles," a puzzle that torments, and a mysterious man of a thousand masks, hidden within the plays.[64] Like James, the riddle-loving Dickinson may have been more struck by the ways the "small hard facts of the Shakespeare house at Stratford" "resist their pressure of reference than with their affecting us as below their fortune," because "they are naught—deeply depressing, in fact, to any impulse to reconstitute [them]."[65] Place and man become part of what James called "the exquisite melancholy of everything unuttered."[66] For Dickinson as part of a middle-class community anxious about female creativity, self-assertion, self-expression, and egoism, Shakespeare and Stratford may have been emblems appropriate to her own task as a writer: to achieve literary renown but also authorial disappearance.[67]

CHAPTER ONE

"There's nothing wicked in Shakespeare, and if there is I don't want to know it"

Advising Women Readers, Amherst's Shakespeare Club, and Richard Henry Dana Sr.

THE POET'S SISTER, Lavinia Dickinson, in 1851 kept a diary that offers much information about the sisters' social activities in Amherst. One important part was a "reading circle" that convened on the evening of March 21 and had its final meeting on July 25.[1] Based on information supplied by the diary, the circle most likely included Amherst College tutors Henry Luther Edwards, William Howland, and William Cowper Dickinson; Amherst College students John Elliot Sanford, Richard Salter Storrs, Charles Fowler, and Milan C. Stebbins; the then principal of Amherst Academy, John Laurens Spencer; and a former Amherst student who worked at Edward Dickinson's law firm, Elbridge Gridley Bowdoin. The other female members of the club were probably Susan Gilbert, the poet's future sister-in-law; Martha Gilbert, Sue's sister; Mary Warner, the daughter of the professor of rhetoric at Amherst College; and Emily Fowler, the granddaughter of lexicographer Noah Webster. The club emerged out of local friendships and romantic attachments that involved exchanges of letters and valentines. Although Lavinia was romantically attached to William Howland, she refers to him and many of the other male members of the club as "tutors," suggesting that behind its social aspect this club was driven by an instructive impetus. The club is representative of a wider societal commitment to women's education and the cultivation of local women through reading and literary discussion.

Dickinson's brother, Austin, also belonged to the club, and on June 22, when he was in Boston teaching, Dickinson informs him:

> Our Reading Club still is, and becomes now very pleasant - *Stebbins* comes in to read now, and *Spencer* - t'would not be so if *you* were here - the *last* time *Charles* came in when we had finished reading, and we broke up with a *dance* - make your own reflections at the story I just told you - the Tutors come after us, and walk home with us - we *enjoy that!* (L44)

Dickinson appears to be implying that Austin played a key role in the (literary) direction of the group, and that without him it had changed. Perhaps Austin was a particularly good reader, and in his absence Stebbins and Spencer had grown less intimidated; the dancing and the fact the scholars "enjoyed" their tutors walking them home suggest a new dynamic. It seems likely that among this well-educated circle of friends Dickinson read the literature of the day, the work of Charles Dickens, Walter Scott, Edgar Allan Poe, Washington Irving, and Nathaniel Hawthorne, as well as of older writers.[2]

In Emily Fowler Ford's reminiscence of Dickinson, this reading circle is a "Shakespeare Club"; she recorded the following information for Mabel Loomis Todd's *Letters of Emily Dickinson* (1894):

> We had a Shakespeare Club—a rare thing in those days,—and one of the tutors proposed to take all the copies of all the members and mark out the questionable passages. This plan was negatived at the first meeting, as far as "the girls" spoke, who said they did not want the strange things emphasized, nor their books spoiled with marks. Finally we told the men to do as they liked—"we shall read everything." I remember the lofty air with which Emily took her departure, saying, "There's nothing wicked in Shakespeare, and if there is I don't want to know it." The men read for perhaps three meetings from their expurgated editions, and then gave up their plan, and the whole text was read out boldly.[3]

Two entries in Lavinia's diary may identify the time this attempted censorship occurred. On June 10 Lavinia says, "Howland called, attended reading society, Did not enjoy it *at all,* Howland came home with me"; three days later she writes, "Emilie Fowler spent morning reading Shakespeare here."[4] On the fifteenth, Dickinson tells Austin, "The Reading club seems lonely - perhaps it weeps for you" (L43), suggesting a feeling of isolation without her intellectual ally, and perhaps dismay at the atmosphere in the club, which might change if Austin were present.[5]

Few critics have discussed the significance of this club and event; those who have misrepresent Ford's reminiscence. Jay Leyda omits the sentence, "This plan was negatived at the first meeting, as far as 'the girls' spoke, who said they did not want the strange things emphasized, nor their books spoiled with marks" (Leyda II 478), eliminating the girls' awareness that certain aspects of Shakespeare were "strange" and that this form of censorship "emphasized" what was objectionable. Leyda's excerpt ends with Dickinson making her dramatic exit, and leaves out the male tutors reading their "expurgated" editions for three meetings without the female readers they sought to protect. This also excludes the final triumph of the girls when Shakespeare is "read out boldly"; instead, Leyda stresses Dickinson's personal rebellion. Similarly, Jack Capps leaves out the phrase "the strange things emphasized," presenting the whole episode as being about the girls' pristine books, and Dickinson as the only one aware that marking such passages highlighted that which was wicked.[6] Capps also misquotes Ford by suggesting that the passages were "objectionable" rather than "questionable," which draws immediate attention to their moral threat. Finally, he leaves out the all-important sentence: "we told the men to do as they liked—'we shall read everything.'" Like the tutors, both critics attempt to alter the reading of a text, and fail to represent Dickinson's defiant departure as part of a collective female rejection of bowdlerization.

Three days later Emily Fowler spent the morning at the Dickinsons' reading Shakespeare—avoiding any attempt at surveillance by the male tutors. Interestingly, the tutors appear to have been less concerned about this hazardous activity and more centrally troubled by the idea of reading Shakespeare's "questionable" passages aloud during club meetings. The two women may not have been searching for the "wickedness" in Shakespeare, but they were knowingly ignoring the tutors' warnings, and taking the chance of unleashing the impiety latent in Shakespeare's texts. Dickinson and her friends may have presented themselves as not believing that, or wanting to "know" which, Shakespeare passages were immoral, but, they were probably well aware of what was objectionable.[7] This "wickedness" may even have made Shakespeare attractive as a basis for rebellion against male authority, a source of dangerous, bawdy, and blasphemous knowledge.[8]

"On no account could I consent to your reading them, unless it were under the direction of some judicious friend"

This incident illustrates how Shakespeare was in Dickinson's culture at one moment a figure regarded with moral suspicion, at the next a great author, his texts knowledge expected of all "civilized" people. Anxiety about women reading Shakespeare was part of a much wider unease about what and how women read; while promoting female cultivation, Dickinson's society sought to preserve female respectability, morality, and purity above all else, especially as such virtues were integral to domestic and social stability.[9] Consequently, novels, periodicals, newspapers, and advice manuals sought to control and direct women's reading.[10] Two such manuals in the Dickinson library throw light on the Amherst tutors' concerns: the Rev. John Bennett's *Letters to a Young Lady on Useful and Interesting Subjects* (1824), belonging to the poet's mother, and William B. Sprague's *Letters on Practical Subjects to a Daughter* (1851), given to Dickinson by her father in 1852.[11] These stress the important and extensive influence reading practice and book choice has on women's virtue, character, and feelings, and on their future lives and immortal souls.[12] Women's greater capacity for sympathy and emotional response requires that they regulate their reading practices; daughters are advised to take an active role in reading so that it involves solid reflection and meditation, and is done in moderation, with a definite object in mind.[13] Both authors recommend the Bible and Christian discourses, and staunchly condemn novels; Bennett and Sprague, however, disagree on the issue of reading Shakespeare.[14]

Bennett advises his daughter not to develop a passion for poetry because it is "dangerous to a woman": like novels, poetry heightens a woman's "natural sensibility to an extravagant degree" and inspires "a romantic turn of mind," that is "utterly inconsistent with the solid duties and proprieties of life" (I 204). Poetry leads women into unreal worlds of fantasy, appealing as it does to the heart and the passions through poetic language and beautiful imagery. Although Bennett does not want his daughter to have a passion for poetry (or become a poet), he wants her to be acquainted with the great poets, who will refine her tastes. In this context, he calls Shakespeare "the first genius of the world," noting that "some of his dramatic works, whilst they astonish, will give you a useful fund of historical information" (I 207).[15] This "historical information" exonerates the "poetry" from having a detrimental influence, although the question remains what Bennett means by "astonish." He may be hinting at certain shocking, immoral aspects in Shakespeare, or merely alluding to what he later calls Shakespeare's "*profound* knowledge and genius," which combines beauty and simplicity (II 145, 39). Some of Bennett's final remarks re-emphasize his own love of Shakespeare: "The Avon, which runs through this city [Bath], filled me with great ideas. Shakespeare, Stratford, the Jubilee, immortal talents and immortal fame, rushed into my mind, as often as I saw its soft flowing stream roll silently along" (II 263).

Unlike this Englishman who holds Shakespeare an immortal poet, Sprague, an American, regards him as an immoral dramatist, and refers to him in warning of the risks of this genre for women. Although Shakespeare's plays are the "finest specimen of dramatic genius which the English language preserves,"

> It cannot be denied that they exhibit human life and manner with great power and beauty, and effect; but it is equally unquestionable that there is much in them to call into exercise the worst passions of human nature, to tarnish the purity of the mind, and to beget a kind of profane familiarity with things of high and sacred import. I should expect, therefore, that the loss you would sustain from reading them, in point of moral feeling, would be greater than any advantage you would gain in respect to intellectual improvement. (60)

He concludes, "on no account could I consent to your reading them, unless it were under the direction of some judicious friend, who would select for you the parts which are most unexceptionable."

Many contemporary journals directed toward women, like *The Ladies Repository,* further illustrate a widespread anxiety about women reading Shakespeare.[16] Although the Dickinson household did not subscribe to this Methodist journal, it explicates the perils of Shakespeare from a religious perspective shared by many in their community. An 1844 article, "Hints to Youthful Readers," by the editor, the Rev. E. Thomson, makes little distinction between a novelist and Shakespeare: both promote impure thoughts; they may offer a moment's amusement, but afterwards "cost unspeakable anguish." Shakespeare is one of a group of "horrid spectres" who drive the human soul away from hopes of mercy, and the salvation of God, into the very terrors of hell.[17] He is a moral and spiritual peril, a satanic influence who takes readers away from "every stanza of Zion, and every verse of the Bible." E. W. Gray's 1847 article "Books and Reading" advises women to avoid Shakespeare because he led a disreputable life; although this self-denial will "keep out of the mind some rare and happy thoughts," it "will keep out of the heart an unholy influence."[18] Similarly, the Rev. A. Stevens's 1846 article on "The Domestic Library," and his subsequent article "The Family Library," suggest that all men should be acquainted with Shakespeare, but, he is unsuitable for children and youths because "There is scarcely a page that is not marred by filthy vulgarity, or more filthy obscenity."[19] Consequently, the Christian family should turn Shakespeare "neck and heel" out of the library, for although he is the "archangel of the mind," it is the case that "archangels have been turned out of heaven" and parents must be ever vigilant about their children's purity. The Rev W. C. Hoyt's 1846 article "Shakspeare" laments that the bard failed to remove "indelicate allusions, and bawdy passages."[20] Yet "with suitable guards, and at a proper time of life" Shakespeare ought to be read; Hoyt adds, "At all events, *he will be read.* But in reading him we should do as the disciples did, when they had inclosed a great draught of fishes—gather the good and cast the bad away." Couched in religious imagery and biblical language, these articles reveal Shakespeare's threat to the home and domestic sphere, despite his greatness and popularity. Hoyt's "suitable guards," Sprague's "judicious friend," and Dickinson's tutors function to protect by mediating women's reading.

Another form of protection took the form of expurgated and child-oriented versions of Shakespeare, like the anonymously published *The Family Shakespeare* (1807) and Charles and Mary Lamb's *Tales from Shakespeare* (also 1807). Two women, Henrietta Bowdler and Mary Lamb, endangered their own purity to offer their readers, as Bowdler put it, "the various beauties of this writer, unmixed with any thing that can raise a blush on the cheek of modesty."[21] Mary Lamb described the *Tales* as having a function similar to that of older brothers who have immediate access to Shakespeare's "manly book" and initiate their sisters in Shakespeare, taking care to select passages appropriate for their ears.[22] These two volumes instigated a "purity market" in publishing, based on creating versions of Shakespeare appropriate for his assimilation by women and children. The first of many American expurgated editions was *The Shakspearian Reader* (1849); its editor, John W. Hows, sought to give readers "a severe revision of [Shakespeare's] language, beyond that adopted in any similar undertaking—'Bowdler's Family Shakspeare' not even excepted—and simply because I know the impossibility of introducing Shakspeare as a Class Book, or as a satisfactory Reading Book for Families, without this precautionary revision." Going further than its English counterpart, Bowdler, Hows's edition sought to bring Shakespeare's "profound moral and intellectual teachings to bear upon the early mental training of the young, and to extend his genial influence around the Domestic Hearth."[23] If arbitrated in some way, Shakespeare's "genial influence" is both intellectual and, perhaps surprisingly for some, moral.[24]

Like these advisers, Edward Dickinson appears to have worried about, and sought to influence, his daughter's reading. In 1870, Emily told Higginson that her father "did not wish [his children] to read anything but the Bible" (L342b) and that Henry Wadsworth Longfellow's *Kavanagh* and Lydia Maria Child's writings had to be smuggled into the household. In earlier letters, she records that her father bought her "many Books," but begged her not to read them "because he fears they joggle the Mind" (L261), and that he once reprimanded her "trifling" letter-writing style, blaming the influence of "'Uncle Tom' and 'Charles Dickens' and these 'modern Literati'" (L113).[25] However, there is no evidence to suggest that he had any concerns about his daughter reading Shakespeare: the Dickinson library contained, not censored copies of the plays, but Knight's unexpurgated edition.[26] Moreover, Shakespeare appears to have been a favorite of Edward Dickinson himself, and was probably the sort of writer he regarded as above the "modern Literati." In July 1851, Emily told Austin how impressed their father was by the latter's wit: "Father says your letters are altogether before Shakespeare, and he will have them published to put in our library" (L46). Among Edward Dickinson's papers at the Houghton is an album of passages by various authors that he collected in his youth, and Shakespeare is one of the poets included in this common "Place-Book."[27] In addition, in a letter to his future wife, dated 15 May 1826, Edward (mis)quotes a line from *As You Like It* to express the beauty of the world, "Sermons in stones, books in running brooks," / "And good in every thing" (II i 16–17).[28] Presumably he expected his future wife, Emily Norcross, to be sufficiently acquainted with Shakespeare to recognize this and be impressed.

"Shakspeare as he is, is not a fit book for the family reading. What Christian father, or virtuous mother, would allow him, if he were now alive, to come into a blooming circle of sons and daughters"

Expurgated editions of Shakespeare played a central role in his integration into American education over Emily Dickinson's lifetime, although in the years that followed her own schooling.[29] For most Americans educated in the 1840s, the study of Shakespeare was regarded as an extracurricular activity, and at Amherst Academy (1840–47) and Mount Holyoke (1847–48), Dickinson encountered Shakespeare's—often unidentified—lines in books designed for teaching rhetoric and oratory.[30] At these institutions, all disciplines were extensions of religious learning and sought to instill in students the correct attitude towards all things.[31] Isaac Watts's *Improvement of the Mind,* used at both schools, makes this very clear:[32]

> In all our studies and pursuits of knowledge, let us remember, that virtue and vice, sin and holiness, and the conformation of our hearts and lives to the duties of true religion and morality, are things of far more consequence, than all the furniture of our understandings, and the richest treasures of mere speculative knowledge. (69)

Watts's handbook for improving the young mind proposes a confrontational and critical reading practice, involving a reader's assessment of the faults, truth, falsity, and morality of "the most learned men, the wisest and best of mankind" (41). Readers are advised, "Where the author is obscure, enlighten him; where he is imperfect, supply his deficiencies; where he is too brief and concise, amplify a little, and set his notion in a fairer view; where he is redundant mark those paragraphs to be retrenched" (63–64).[33] Such advice, along with her gender and nationality, may have impelled Dickinson's competitive rewritings and transformations of her favorite authors.[34] With reference to Milton's overly sympathetic representation of Satan in *Paradise Lost,* Watts warns readers against praising an author excessively, with the result that they become unable to see certain weaknesses or blemishes in his works (70, 83). Although he does not mention Shakespeare, he clearly encourages readers to severely criticize immorality, bawdy language, violations of genre, lack of realism, and, especially, infringements of the neoclassical rules of time, space, and action. Joseph Emerson, who edited the edition of Watts that Dickinson used "for the edification of his women students," provides questions to direct the pupils' attention to the most important points of instruction.[35] Emerson was a great influence on Mary Lyon, the founder of Mount Holyoke. In his section on reading poetry, he asked: "Poetic character of Shakspeare, Dryden and Byron? / Answer: They are justly ranked among the greatest poets that ever lived." / Grand objection to their poems? / That from their immoral tendency, they are likely to do more harm than good, at least to some" (71).

The prefaces to the rhetoric books Dickinson studied at her schools, Ebenezer Porter's *The Rhetorical Reader* and Samuel Phillips Newman's *A Practical System of Rhetoric,* emphasize that the moral sentiments of the passages used were as important a criterion for selection as their virtues as rhetoric lessons.[36] Both Porter and Newman appear uncertain about whether Shakespeare's works are "esteemed models of excellence in literature," that give "grateful exercise to the imagination and refinement to the taste."[37] Porter's extracts come from the Bible, Milton, and Edward Young, and although he quotes or refers to *Julius Caesar* four times and prints an extract from *Hamlet,* Shakespeare's name is only mentioned once. Porter may be assuming his reader's familiarity with Shakespeare's works, but might also want to avoid the moral ambiguity conjured up by the bard's name. In a similar manner, Newman recommends writers like Joseph Addison, Jonathan Swift, John Milton, Oliver Goldsmith, John Locke, Edmund Burke, and Washington Irving, but refers to Shakespeare's works only twice. Using a quote from *Othello,* "Perdition seize thee, but I do love thee," Newman demonstrates that sometimes redundant words increase the vivacity of an expression (174). In addition, Milton's comparison of Oliver Cromwell to Othello—"He does nought in hate, but all in honor. He kisses the beautiful deceiver before he destroys her"—is quoted (96). Newman comments, "This allusion is to the Othello of Shakspeare; and such is the rank and antiquity of his writings, that allusions to passages found in them, are regarded much in the same manner as classical allusions." Shakespeare is one of "our English classical writers" who has outlived his century and whose "preëminence, may be supposed to be familiarly known by every English scholar." It is "lawful to make allusions to those whose works should be known; and such allusions, when happily introduced, will please us in the same manner and degree, as those made to the ancient classics." Regardless of the appropriateness of quoting, and recognizing quotations from, his works as a sign of education, Newman, like Porter, refers to Shakespeare sparsely, and both rhetoricians seem to regard his name as unsettling.[38]

Shakespeare and his name do play a fundamental role, however, in another book Dickinson used at school and throughout her life: Noah Webster's *An American Dictionary of the English Language.*[39] Although Webster deliberately utilizes American writers to illustrate many words, he refers to Shakespeare's lines to define others and give examples of their usage. Dickinson's letters refer to four of Webster's examples of Shakespearean terms; she may have clarified her Shakespeare allusions in Webster, or she may have found in his dictionary appropriate Shakespearean phrases. Webster employs "Sweet wife, my honor is at pawn—Shak." to define *pawn,* and Dickinson used the phrase "Honor is it's own pawn - " twice in her letters (L 250, 260). In addition, *remainder* is defined using "Remainder's biscuit—Shak.," a phrase alluded to by the poet in two of her letters (L545, 882). Webster coins *princelike* as "becoming like a prince—Shak.," and Dickinson draws on this word in a remark about *Hamlet.*[40] Finally, Webster's definition of *throe* refers "to put in agony—Shak.," and the poet employs this word in her description of Othello (L506).

Shakespeare's minimal role in Dickinson's early schooling seems almost inevitable considering he was condemned by two presidents of Amherst College, Heman Humphrey (1823–45), and Edward Hitchcock (1845–54).[41] These authoritative figures in Dickinson's community reflected and contributed to the character of Amherst orthodoxy. Relations between the college and the Dickinson household were especially close: her grandfather, Samuel Fowler Dickinson, was centrally involved in its founding, and, beginning in 1835, her father and later her brother were treasurers for the institution.[42] In 1834, Humphrey's *Discourses and Reviews* condemned "the Prince of English Dramatists" as one of the genius poets who "throw their richest drapery around the most seductive forms of sensuality": they varnish over the "haggard ugliness of vice" with "the mellifluous witchery of their verse." Humphrey concludes that Shakespeare, "perhaps placed by the general voice of critics and readers above all his contemporaries, will have more than almost any other poet to answer for, on the score of impurity, as well as impiety."[43] In 1840, in Humphrey's guide for parents on the education of their children, *Domestic Education,* he advises, "strike off at one heavy dash, all the cart-loads and ship-loads of plays, novels and romances which offend openly . . . against piety, morality and virtue."[44] Amid warnings to parents to be ever watchful of "seductive" and "corrupting" influences, he attacks the "Immortal Bard of Avon," whom he claims to admire "exceedingly," commenting, "to speak frankly under the pains and penalties of the highest literary tribunals in the world, I am sorry that most of his plays were ever written" (94). They cause "more harm than good" because:

> Shakspeare as he is, is not a fit book for the *family* reading. What Christian father, or virtuous mother, would allow him, if he were now alive, to come into a blooming circle of sons and daughters and recite his plays, just as they stand in the best editions. It is scarcely possible they should pass through the youthful mind and imagination, without leaving a stain behind them. (94–95)

Expurgated editions are advocated, and although they will not be "Shakspeare," still, "what would be left, would be worth vastly more in a rising family, than the whole, as it came from the pen of the author." In contrast, in his earlier essay, Humphrey is less positive about ridding the text of objectionable passages, because they are so much a part of the "fabric of his verse, as to make it nearly, or quite impossible, to separate the precious from the vile." In spite of all this disapproval, however, Humphrey openly expresses his admiration for Shakespeare and perceives that his moral objections are becoming anachronistic.

In his 1845 inaugural address to the college, however, Humphrey's successor, Edward Hitchcock argued that literature was detrimental to religion because so many of the great literary men were intemperate, immoral, and licentious antagonists of Christianity.[45] Echoing Humphrey, Hitchcock argues that their poison is "so interwoven with those fascinations of style, or thought, characteristics of genius, as to be unnoticed by the youthful mind, delighted with smartness and brilliancy." Dramatists are specifically attacked as "decidedly worse than the noble tragic poetry of antiquity," and even Shakespeare, despite all "his splendid moral sentiments," was "undoubtedly a libertine in principle and practice."[46] Interestingly, Hitchcock's daughter Jane, who was Lavinia's best friend in Amherst in the 1850s and is frequently mentioned in her diary, may have also been a member of the Shakespeare Club (Leyda I 202–3). In fact, on June 12, two days after Lavinia did not enjoy the meeting of the reading society, she recorded in her diary, "called at Jennies." Perhaps her wary father condoned Jane's attendance at the Shakespeare Club because college tutors supervised it. Implicit in all this vigilance, whether derived from moral or religious convictions, is the fear that Shakespeare's language is powerfully seductive. If it can gain the reluctant admiration of wary men like Humphrey and Hitchcock, how much more susceptible would the daughters of Amherst be? Attacks on Shakespeare were part of a larger Puritan debate about the nature of poetic language and its tendency to obscure the truth.[47]

By 1856, two years after his own inauguration, the fourth president (1854–76) of Amherst College, William Augustus Stearns, wholeheartedly and publicly recommends Shakespeare, especially for the "moral principles" of his tragedies.[48] The front page of the local newspaper, *The Hampshire and Franklin Express,* on Friday, 11 January 1856, published an excerpt from Stearns's lecture in Northampton, Massachusetts, titled "Reading." Here, the president suggests that Shakespeare was "written in sweet pure Saxon" and had a "prodigious influence on the English mind."[49] His wonderful creations "deserve all the praises which have been bestowed upon them"; he is "the prince of drama, among all times and languages," and the "mightiest of human intellects." Although Shakespeare has his faults, and his language is at times "highly exceptionable," Stearns considers these matters superficial, part of his age and the medium through which he worked:

> I have no commendations to bestow on the theatre, school of immorality as it usually is; but Hamlet, Macbeth, Othello, what works of power. In a moral respect the writings of Shakespeare have been rarely appreciated, especially by religious people. They have been looked upon as mere plays, while his tragedies, at least, are developments each one of them of some great moral principle.

Stearns proceeds to praise the moral lessons *Hamlet* and *The Merchant of Venice* teach, concluding "He who reads Shakespeare judiciously must be elevated by his reading." Stearns is probably imagining a male reader, and perhaps would not have extended this proposition to include a female, like Dickinson; he places the onus on the reader to proceed "judiciously." Stearns differentiates Shakespeare from the immoral theater, for him to be acceptable his associations with the theater must be understated or ignored.[50]

There is no evidence to suggest that all the efforts of this morally and religiously strict community restricted Dickinson's reading habits. In fact, she appropriates the language of earnest counsel to comic effect in some of her letters. In December 1847, writing Austin from Mount Holyoke, she advises him, "Cultivate your other powers in proportion as you allow Imagination to captivate you!" and then, asks sarcastically, "Am not I a very wise *young lady?*" (L19). In an 1853 letter to the Hollands, she writes, "Monday, I solemnly resolved I would be *sensible,* so I wore thick shoes, and thought of Dr Humphrey, and the Moral Law. One glimpse of *The Republican* makes me break things again - I read in it every night" (L133). She has yielded to the temptation to read "sprightly-written," sensationalist accounts of accidents, in clear defiance of Humphrey's sensible instructions.[51] In a January 1850 letter to Abiah Root, she concocts an ornate story of a cold that has come to New England from the Alps and is her constant, overbearing companion. She then breaks off to remind her correspondent that this is a "wicked story," full of "vain imaginations to lead astray foolish young women" (L31). Although she warns Abiah that these "are flowers of speech, they both *make,* and *tell* deliberate falsehoods, avoid them as the snake," she also expresses her love of those "little green" snakes of satanic fiction. She closes by telling Root how much she misses her and about "*several* somethings which have happened since" they last saw each other, but that she will "put [her] treasures away till 'we two meet again.'" Her reference here to the first line of *Macbeth* clearly aligns her story and these "treasures" with this play's mischievous and malevolent witches. Abiah's "very sincere and *wicked* friend" may be hinting that she has begun to write, with Shakespeare's rhyming witches as her sponsors.

These letters put Dickinson in league with "sensationalist" tempters, like Shakespeare, against the conservative reading community of Amherst. Prescriptions on how and what to read could be rejected, publicly or privately, and reading could become the sort of subversive and liberating pastime moral advisors feared. Two of Dickinson's poems concur: one suggests, "There is no Frigate like a Book / To take us Lands away" (F1286); the other says "this Bequest of Wings / Was but a Book - What Liberty / A loosened Spirit brings -" (F1593). Further, the cultural requirement that she read a "wicked" Shakespeare exposed the poet to an erotically charged and bawdy language that, in turn, may have influenced her own use of sexual metaphors and allusions.[52] Nevertheless, Dickinson, to some extent, must have internalized the conservative value system of her father and other male authority figures.[53] In 1862, for instance, she told T. W. Higginson, "You speak of Mr Whitman - I never read his Book - but was told that he was disgraceful - " (L261). This could have been for Higginson's benefit, but the predominantly conservative books she read suggest that she may have shared some of the traditional "Whiggish" views of her peers.[54] Although reading Shakespeare may have been a rebellion, it was simultaneously evidence of learning and cultivation. Shakespeare's emerging status in Dickinson's culture as required reading is connected with the appropriation of his texts to support traditionalist political and social views.[55]

"It is a privilege for one to read Shakespeare"

Shakespeare's standing as the epitome of literary genius and morality was not in any way in question for the students at Amherst College in the 1850s. Close links between the college and the Dickinsons make student activities another important context for understanding Dickinson's Shakespeare. Moreover, the tutors at the Shakespeare Club, many of Dickinson's teachers at Amherst Academy, and her male friends were all Amherst College graduates. Despite, and maybe because of, the disapproval of Humphrey and Hitchcock, the college's students, under the influence of Romantic critics like Samuel Taylor Coleridge and William Hazlitt, made Shakespeare an important part of their lives.[56] For these students, he was an all-sympathetic genius who presented that which is universal and timeless in life; his immorality was justified as an attempt to compassionately represent all aspects of humanity.[57] This is very apparent in *Remembrance of Amherst: An Undergraduate's Diary 1846–48* by William Gardiner Hammond, who entered the sophomore class in 1846 and knew many of Dickinson's friends, including Mary Warner, Emily Fowler, and Catherine Hitchcock.[58] During the winter term of 1847, Hammond mentions a debate in his composition class about immorality in literature: one group of students condemns Byron's drama *Cain* as immoral, while the other praises its representation of evil as "introducing such themes" that have "the authority of [the Bible,] Shakespeare and Milton" (58). Siding with the first group, their tutor draws attention to the fact that authors are responsible for what they have written and that Byron fails to "follow Shakespeare and Milton in making the evil he introduced hateful." Hammond later reflects that Shakespeare's immorality is "redeeming" because he uses it as a means to present "unsophisticated," but never "wanton" aspects of human nature (83).

This diary also provides us with a fascinating insight into the role Shakespeare may have played in Dickinson's own life. For instance, later in the same year, Hammond and a fellow student stayed up all night reading and discussing Shakespeare, finding it "delightful to select beautiful or striking passages and make mutual comments." Hammond was "never so forcibly struck by Shakespeare's *wit* before"; it pervades all save "his most solemn pages." The range of Shakespeare's genius impresses Hammond, as does the way he "puts in no words to fill out the ideas; every sentence *tells* and would make a page of modern poetry." The friends go on to compare Homer and Shakespeare, agreeing that "Homer treats man as a great whole," while Shakespeare examines the diversity in humanity through "all his Proteus shapes" (84). Shakespeare presents "the educated, crafty man; tracks him in all his writings, exposes all his tracks, unravels his mysteries, gives a clue through all the labyrinths of his nature." Most likely, Dickinson and her female coterie read, marked, discussed, and praised Shakespeare in this way, and were just as aware as Hammond of Romantic criticism of Shakespeare.

In the fall term of 1847, Hammond set out to read all of Shakespeare's comedies; although Dickinson left no similar record, she may have attempted, perhaps in conjunction with the Shakespeare Club, to read the plays in a systematic way (194–97). Hammond begins with *The Tempest,* praising its plot, supernatural agencies, exquisite love scenes between Ferdinand and Miranda, and excellent comic scenes between Caliban and the two drunkards, Stefano and Trinculo. The next day, he reads *Love's Labour's Lost,* finding its irregular plot inferior to *The Tempest*'s. Days later, he reads and prefers *Much Ado About Nothing,* a play with "the best of *broad humor* so plentifully found in Shakespeare," and then *The Merchant of Venice,* "one of Shakespeare's masterpieces." Although Shakespeare was predominantly an extracurricular activity, Hammond writes an essay on the character of Bassanio for his composition class, praising the play's "general truth to nature and skill of design" rather than its "strongly marked" characters. Hammond goes on to read *As You Like It,* the long poem *Venus and Adonis,* and *Hamlet.* Of the latter, he writes, "I will not attempt weak panegyric here, but methinks I never knew one half of Shakespeare's greatness. That one noble tragedy of his contains the germ of innumerable volumes of small poetry and prose that have been written since" (227).

Although Dickinson's quotations allude chiefly to Shakespeare's tragedies, the poet may have shared Hammond's love of the comedies. Certainly, she refers to *As You Like It, The Merchant of Venice,* and *The Tempest,* and her own droll wit suggests she may have similarly appreciated Shakespeare's humor.

Hammond's diary provides a good indication of the kind of topics the Amherst College tutors and their tutees addressed during Shakespeare Club meetings; also illuminating are the frequent articles on Shakespeare and his plays published in two student magazines, *The Indicator* and *Amherst Collegiate Magazine,* which Dickinson is associated with, and presumably read.[59] George Gould was a member of the editorial staff of *The Indicator* and a friend and classmate of Austin; he is mentioned in Lavinia's 1851 diary and may have been a member of the Shakespeare Club (Leyda I 207). He probably wrote the "Prolegomena" to the first issue of this magazine, promising readers that it would "indicate the literary taste, spirit, and acquirements, of the undergraduates of Amherst College."[60] Although the magazine may not uncover a "new Shakespeare," the author is confident that "there exist in college germs of true poetic feeling, which need only to be fostered, by the very means now offered, to produce abundant and delicious fruits." The magazine will become a "memorial" of their "youth" and "the pleasant days of college life"; the author hopes it will appeal to their "fathers, mothers, sisters, brothers, cousins and *particular* friends, we trust they [meaning their productions] will be scarcely less interesting as *indicators* of the thoughts and feelings of the Absent." Considering the magazine had a potential audience of entire families, it is fascinating to examine what ideas about Shakespeare and his plays these young men chose to communicate to their parents and siblings, ideas they believed were "the thoughts and feelings of the Absent."

An article in the January 1850 edition, "Thoughts on Novel Reading," acknowledges the "great evils which result undeniably from excessive novel reading," yet defends novels against such reproach by openly acknowledging that they share their indecorous and inappropriate features with Shakespeare's plays. The essayist counters criticism of the way novels present "scenes and characters which never had any real existence" by arguing that a book's power derives from its ability to allow us to "forget ourselves and everything around us," until "its scenes and events have become a part of our own personal recollections." Readers are advised to listen to "Sweetest" Shakespeare, "Fancy's child" and discover

> how it feels to let your soul thrill to his great thoughts, you must forget all rules, you must be no longer critic, cavilling about the dramatic unities. With an

implicit faith even in the existence of Bohemian seaports, you must be for the time as simple-hearted and credulous as a little child.[61]

While some felt that similarities between Shakespeare and novelists condemned both equally, this essayist saw Shakespeare's literary status as affording an argument for reevaluating the novel. He advises his readers, some of them female friends and family members, to read Shakespeare for the very reasons others have so ardently condemned him. Shakespeare's faults (of style and morality) are redeemed through reference to the reader's own childlike imagination. The incident of attempted censorship at the Shakespeare Club would have derived from a clash between this type of blind idealism and the practicalities of reading Shakespeare's often troubling texts.

In the same issue, an essay on "Desdemona" reminds readers that no American will regret that "he speaks the language of Shakspeare"; like many other essays in both student magazines, this one presents Shakespeare's heroines as paragons of femininity.[62] Desdemona is "a maiden of beauty and fortune and high birth" whose love for Othello is pure, deep, and earnest, unlike the fickle and sensuous love of Romeo and Juliet (176). Moreover, Desdemona remains constant to her husband despite his cruelties, and even her last words exonerate him for murdering her.[63] The essayist is not convinced that this exemplary heroine immodestly encouraged Othello, or that "Jane Eyre-like, [she] popped the question [of marriage] herself," which "sounds to[o] like the 'encouragement' given by 'sweet girls' now-a-days" (179). He argues that "A true woman may indeed unguardedly betray her love in a thousand ways; but she will ever seek to guard it. Beautiful is the struggle between native frankness and guilelessness, and innate shrinking modesty." Such advocacy of an acquiescent and loving Desdemona in contrast to the more forthright and self-determined Jane Eyre must have struck readers who, like Dickinson, admired Charlotte Brontë's novel. The poet first read *Jane Eyre* in 1849, when it was given to her by Elbridge G. Bowdoin, and in letters she describes it as "electric," and was certainly very aware of its unorthodoxy (L475, 28). In fact, Dickinson may have identified with Brontë's self-reliant heroine, and there are very suggestive parallels between the novel and her own life and writings.[64] Although an earlier article in *The Indicator* defended the novel, many writers of the day used Shakespeare's heroines to ratify and exemplify "The Cult of True Womanhood" in the face of more radical and unsettling notions of womanhood emerging in contemporary novels.[65] Perhaps the fact that in her letters Dickinson appears less interested in the worthiness of Shakespeare's heroines is a reaction to such prescription and moralizing. In the month this essay was published, she told Jane Humphrey that the path of female duty "looks very ugly" and described herself as a "villain unparalleled," reaching for satanic flowers, who refuses opportunities for "cultivating meekness - and patience - and submission - and for turning [her] back to this sinful, and wicked world" (L30).

The essayist also employs Desdemona to attack the women's rights movement, and, perhaps more pertinently for Dickinson, the worldly ambition of women writers. Unlike these women, Desdemona's "whole soul shrinks back from moving a hair's breadth from her sphere." Ever-humble, she is connected with an ideal of female authorship, whereby if a woman is "gifted with a brilliant imagination,"

> that Gothic window of the mind that turns the light of common day to softest tints of beauty, they will play only around her quiet home. [She is] endowed with that true fire from heaven, the poetry of heart which is thrillingly alive to every great and generous sentiment, and worships, with whole-souled devotion, the nobleness of self-denial. (180)

The author remarks that literary ladies and social reformists "would pounce upon us, if they only thought us worthy of their notice." Many traditionalists, including Edward Dickinson, also believed that woman writers should occupy an unobtrusive place within American society.[66] Of course, at this time, Emily had been hinting in letters to her female friends about recent literary experiments: in April 1850, she tells Jane Humphrey of her daring to do "strange things - bold things" and heeding "beautiful tempters, yet do not think I am wrong" (L35). Despite these early sentiments, though, she chose eventually to preserve her powers, for the most part, within the parameters and according to the dominant ideals of femininity and the domestic sphere;[67] as this student advised, she settled for self-denial and let her powers of imagination "play around her quiet home."

Surely Dickinson had a particular interest in the February edition of *The Indicator*, where a valentine she sent to Gould became her first publication.[68] In this issue is an essay on "Shakespeare's Women" that begins by asserting, "It is a privilege for one to read Shakespeare" and place "ourselves in the focus of his genius, and follow with the eye the rays of light which penetrate mysteries and illume beauties, and reveal deformities in nature and humanity."[69] The writer goes on to reprimand critics who have underrated the variety and individuality of Shakespeare's heroines, who are "old familiar friends" approached "almost with prayer and fasting, as the knights of old prepared for a [j]ourney for the fame and the beauty of their lady-loves" (210). These heroines are praised for their transparency of character, which allows readers to "enter into their heart of hearts" and perfectly understand them. "Is not this true of all rightly trained women, who have been carefully shielded from this evil and cold world?" (211–12). Their beauty is increased by their "power of sustaining the purity and dignity of their characters under all circumstances, even the most adverse." Accordingly, the heroines Shakespeare intended for us to "love and honor" show consistency and constancy in their characters and affections: they "trust at once and entirely"; they walk "through a baptism of fire, and come out whiter as clothed in garments of amianthus." This essayist employs Shakespeare's heroines, once again, as models of femininity, against which to measure and reprove his female friends and family members. The one thing this young man does not want is a self-conscious woman who speculates about her own existence; he is grateful that "there are no female Hamlets."

But a female Hamlet, whose later choice of white garments may have represented her own baptism of fire, had her nontransparent, inconsistent, speculative, and contemplative "Valentine Eve" published a few pages after this article. Dickinson's text is a very self-conscious, humorous parody of romantic love that teases a male lover by proposing an interview, mentions where, when, and what clothes should be worn for the meeting, but is unspecific enough to make an actual encounter improbable. The speaker imagines herself as a man meeting another man (David or Jonathan; Damon or Pythias) and later as Judith, the heroine who cut off Holofernes's head. She mocks Transcendentalism and the reform movement, asserts female assurance, and ends with the Biblical "Hallelujah" and the "all hail" of *Macbeth*'s witches.[70] Commenting on the poem, the editor, Henry Shipley, wishes he knew the author and could talk to her, although he does not believe "her mouth has any corners, perhaps 'like a rose leaf torn.'" He thinks, "she must have some spell, by which she quickened the imagination, and causes the high blood 'run frolic through the veins.'" Like one of *Macbeth*'s witches, Dickinson puts a spell on her excited male reader, who praises her "frenzy built edifice" and admires her intellect, humor, "analytic spirit," and "very ingenious affair." He suggests that if "it is not *true,* it is at any rate philosophical," and that "the author, however, has not (it is plain to see) told the half of her feelings. It were impossible!" Such admiration for qualities that deviate from the ideal traits of Shakespeare's heroines is striking; conceivably, this valentine is one of the "treasures" Dickinson had mentioned a few days earlier, in her January 29 letter to Abiah Root.

Dickinson was also a friend of Henry V. Emmons, the founder of the other magazine produced by Amherst students, *The Amherst Collegiate Magazine* (Leyda I 283).[71] This published many articles on Shakespeare that reiterated topics and themes of its predecessor.[72] One of the essayists, E. D. Gardner, is very self-conscious about this, noting in 1858, "it would indeed be difficult to write an original essay upon the beauties of Shakspeare." He declares that

"There is perhaps no author whose works are more read and studied than those of Shakspeare. Our constant companion from youth to old age, they have a place in our affections second only to that of the Bible, in the minds of some even that yields to their magic sway." Without any sense of contradiction, Gardner calls Shakespeare the "King of English literature" who unites America: his power is "felt by all the classes and dwelt upon with fond enthusiasm by the coldest and most impassable critics."[73] Shakespeare's image in American culture is altered; once skeptical Puritans are embracing and celebrating him in a way previously reserved for the Bible alone. Gardner's comments suggest the way Romanticism inverted the positions of sacred and secular writing.[74] By 1868, student fascination with Shakespeare was such that an "official" Shakespeare Club was established at Amherst College, and essays on the bard and his characters proliferated in the college newspaper, the *Amherst Student.*[75]

"Woman attempting to discharge the duties of men must have care that she does not come out like Nick Bottom in the Midsummer Night's Dream, capped with an Ass's head"

In September 1850, one of the lecturers principally responsible for popularizing the Romantics' reevaluation of Shakespeare, Richard Henry Dana Sr., was invited to Amherst to give a series of eight talks.[76] The "Local Items" section of the *Hampshire and Franklin Express* for 20 September 1850 noted that these lectures have been "received with marked approbation" across America and that "No one should neglect the opportunity of hearing them."[77] In fact, Dana had first given the series in 1838, establishing Shakespeare as central to the educational and cultivating function of the Lyceum movement. His influence on the reception of Shakespeare in America was vast, and is very evident in the Amherst College magazine articles.[78] Like the student authors, Dana used the plays to examine social, political, and religious issues. Dana, however, was an Anglophile and a member of the traditionalist and conservative "Old America" party in Boston. His Shakespeare was embroiled in a critique of American society, with its false ideals of equality and democracy that led to materialism, greed, and conformity.[79] His sentiments certainly reiterated the anxiety of Dickinson's class in a materialistic culture in flux, in which traditional hierarchies were breaking down under the pressure of economic, social, and cultural mobility. Dana's defense of monarchy, social hierarchy, and hereditary classes might have appealed to Dickinson, especially in light of certain elitist sentiments in her writings that may hint at her own ambiguous feelings toward American social and political ideals.[80] Like Dana, who became in his later years a virtual recluse, Dickinson may have sought to distance herself from a society in which she felt isolated. Certainly, she shared his view that "to be a social creature" it was necessary for a man "to be the creature of seclusion for the larger portion of his time; so that what makes him to differ from other men, and constitutes his individuality, may be allowed to expand and strengthen from its own living energy."[81]

Most probably, Dana's lectures were an impetus for the creation of the later Shakespeare Club, and, presumably Dickinson and other future members attended some, or all, of them.[82] They may have prepared in advance of going; on October 14, Lavinia asks Austin, "Can you spare your Shakespeare to us for a day or so? We want to read Hamlet before the lecture. If willing, please send it by the Stage, this afternoon."[83] In her essay "Society at Amherst," Sue regarded the lectures as important enough to recall:

> The poet Dana, father of Richard Dana gave a course of six lectures on poetry in the old College chapel. They were exquisite [sic], subtle, most poetic but rather over the heads of sweet-sixteen and the college boys. But these, as all our lectures not strictly in the college course, were given in the evening, affording a delightful sort of time, as we were invited by the gentlemen friends; strolling slowly up the long hill under their escort, and even more slowly back, under the stars when the lecture was over.[84]

Like the meetings of the Shakespeare Club, these lectures were educational but also social or even romantic encounters, and clearly separate from the college's activities, hinting that the president, Edward Hitchcock, disapproved of Shakespeare. Sue implies that *she* understood the difficult lectures, and perhaps she and Emily discussed their scholarly content.

Dana's first lecture, titled "The Influences of Literature on our Characters and Daily Life," was given on Friday, September 20, and would have interested the recently published and fledgling writer because of its powerful defense of literature against those who believed it was immoral and illusionary, that it removed readers from the realities of life. In contrast, Dana argues that the real enjoyment of literature demands "a preparatory moral discipline and a well-regulated life" from readers; with such discipline readers could experience the "thorough and permanent influence over our moral and intellectual character" that literature offered.[85] Listeners were advised that if read in the correct way, nothing is more essential than what literature and poetry teaches: it provides access to the highest and eternal truths and strengthens the spiritual life, opposing the transitory knowledge gained from the senses. Poetry gives "expanse to our imagination, activity to our fancy"; it opens "the passages deep down into our natures, to unseal our eyes to the beauty, grandeur, and secret spiritual meanings of the outer world, and to make us feel the correspondence between the outer world, and our inner selves."[86] Undeniably, Dickinson would have agreed. In many later poems, she described the expansive powers of poetry, summarized in her term "Circumference," which she suggested was her "business" (L268).[87]

In his second lecture, on September 24, "The Condition of Society in its Influence on the Poet, and the Converse," Dana addresses one of his central themes: the hostile effect American society has upon its authors, and more particularly its "positive opposition" to the poetical.[88] Dickinson's own feelings of estrangement at this time suggest that if she heard Dana's lecture, she may have identified with the misunderstood American poet. According to Dana, such estrangement results from the lack of correspondence between poetry and everyday life; in contrast, "old English writers," like Shakespeare, wrote a poetry "so blended with life and fact" in a society "peculiarly receptive of poetic impressions."[89] He suggests that American society has forced its poets either to find solace in the natural world or to retreat into their own thoughts.[90] America's principles of democracy and equality encourage discontent and avarice, and stifle creativity; poets cannot flourish in a society that attempts to eliminate diversity, and where "The free play of the individual is checked, and his clearly marked naturalness blurred into the tame, monotonous hue of mass."[91] In addition, Dana criticizes nineteenth-century skepticism and the modern belief that "nothing can be but what may be comprehended—nothing is but what is known."[92] This has sapped vitality from contemporary poetry, especially the wonder and awe that the Elizabethans found in the natural world. In this and his fifth lecture, Dana championed Shakespeare's supernatural characters, which offer psychological insight into human emotions and behavior.[93] Dickinson's reference to *Macbeth*'s witches earlier that year, and some of her later allusions to other supernatural elements in Shakespeare's plays, make it likely she believed these fantastical features articulate and express what Dana calls the "the commonest circumstances of life."[94] Moreover, she considered herself "old-fashioned" in an incredulous world (L395); and although her seclusion from this society had many reasons, especially to do with her class and gender, Dana's second lecture offers an early explanation.[95] Others in Amherst also approved, for on September 27 the *Hampshire and Franklin Express* recorded, "Mr. Dana's Lectures at the College Chapel, of which two have already been given, are beautiful in language, rich in thought, discriminating in criticism and well calculated to improve the intellect and enrich the understanding. The third will be given tonight. The subject is 'Woman' and is considered by many the best of the course."[96]

The third lecture, delayed owing to bad weather, was given on October 1.[97] On the fourth the *Hampshire and Franklin Express* offered a full account of this talk on the "different relations existing between the sexes and their mutual fitness for and dependence on each other."[98] Dana told his audience that neither sex was perfect and that current debates about women's rights and equality of the sexes stemmed from "the infidel notions of the old French Revolution," which were too abstract and without reference to "the characteristics of either sex":

> Each [sex] had their peculiar and appropriate sphere and whenever the boundary was overstepped a sense of disgust and degradation followed. Woman aspiring to the station of man, became not manly but mannish, and man attempting a similar change, became not womanly but effeminate. Woman attempting to discharge the duties of men must have care that she does not come out like Nick Bottom in the Midsummer Night's Dream, capped with an Ass's head.[99]

Consequently, he told his listeners, "Modest and retiring, woman was not designed for, neither did she desire to be the recipient of searched attention in public as well as private." In other words, women's real power was influence in the private sphere of the home, and not the public realm of the forum; the idea of women's rights or their social aspirations went against natural order.[100] This attack was timely, echoing the views of many in Amherst; the paper mentions that the lecture was "interrupted it is true by occasional bursts of applause" and calls it a beautiful and "truthful exposition of the proper sphere of woman." Dana reminded Dickinson that by overstepping the domestic sphere into the public, male realm, she might be setting herself up for ridicule and unhappiness. Possibly Dickinson was recalling, and revising, such images in her later poetry, when she presented lower-class and rustic speakers aspiring to, and eventually achieving, a denied and recalcitrant royalty and status.[101] Thus, although the first two lectures endorsed her recent forays into poetry, and clarified her feelings of separateness from her society, this third one underlined the fraught nature of attempting to step outside naturally and socially determined gender roles.

Presumably Dana followed this lecture with one on "Woman as in the Old Dramatists—Desdemona." Here he delineates three characteristics of Shakespeare's women: their freedom in expressing affections, their use of words that would be disapproved of even for men, and their ability to blend dignity and purity with boldness.[102] He elucidates the more socially unorthodox aspects of these heroines (which might easily align them with the self-assured Jane Eyre), but reminds his audience that despite "their infirmities and faults," they obey the law of sex and remain "truly feminine."[103] Moreover, in his subsequent analysis of Desdemona, although he draws attention to her rebellious disobedience in marrying Othello, he stresses that this was a result of her passionate love for her husband. Her duty as a daughter is transformed into "her devout love [and] groveling idolatry" as a wife.[104] It is drawn to the audience's attention that even Desdemona's passions are "purified to the very height of mere human love," passing through a refining process and become "sublimated into spiritual essences."[105] Dana's Desdemona is a "modest, delicate and submissive spirit," who fulfills "the sacred relations and duties of the wife"; she is the antithesis of the "lofty and manly" Othello.[106]

After the fifth lecture, on the supernatural in the plays, the Dickinson sisters appear to have missed the sixth one, in which Dana justified Shakespeare's representation of violence and death; he argues that these excite an audience's sympathies to the point that each viewer experiences "instances of self-forgetting and beautiful devotion to others."[107] This lecture was delivered on October 11: on Monday the fourteenth, Lavinia writes to Austin, "Why did'nt you come home, Friday? We expected to see you. We did'nt hear the lecture. It was considered about like the others I believe."[108] Although we cannot be certain that Emily heard any of these lectures, this letter implies the family's keen interest in them, and perhaps their awareness of a certain degree of repetition in Dana's views. The lecture on *Macbeth* took place the day after this letter, which may suggest that the sisters did not attend it, either; they appear more interested in preparing for his final lecture, on *Hamlet.*[109] In these final lectures, Dana makes his most original contributions to Shakespeare criticism by arguing that both tragic heroes are brought to tragic ends by "the strong workings of the imagination" and their desires for imagination's "grandeur of regality, its robes of splendour, its loftily-seated throne, its voice of power."[110] This argument illuminates Dickinson's early and continuing interest in *Macbeth,* especially her attraction to its final act. Dana's Macbeth is not simply a villain, but a complex character, whose powers of imagination make him attempt to realize his personal and social possibilities:

> [Macbeth's] mind possessed not only the character of greatness, but of that undefined vastness, also, which belongs to the imaginative. . . . He craved to realize to himself what this spirit of majesty might be—to possess majesty that he might be possessed by it—might make this abstraction, living, individual consciousness within him.[111]

Macbeth's imagination "half freed" and tainted with desire becomes corrupted and immoral:

> [It] expands finite into infinite, etherealizes grosser things of sense into sublime, spiritual forms; and in the conflicts of his moral nature a meditative twilight

touches and softens the black deeds of his hand—mind, heart, soul encompass and tinge all.[112]

Although this lecture warns listeners about the dangers of the imagination, it also suggests that this faculty produces in Macbeth the most frightening images of remorse and guilt, bloody daggers and ghosts. The witches reinforce Macbeth's ambition, and through them his actions become part of fate and destiny, allowing him to see himself beyond human boundaries. Macbeth becomes "more than man" and "in union with the supernatural, the invisible and infinite, his being, as it were, expands into them and he becomes them."[113] The narrow "laws of earth and of his fellow-creatures" no longer bind him; by act V, however, he is a lonely and lost figure, meditative and somber; it is with this thoughtful, despairing, and regretful man that Dickinson later identifies. As a woman poet, Dickinson may have especially related to Macbeth as one who suffers because of his own creative powers, which doom him with dreams of ambition and exacerbate his despair.

Considering the sisters' preparations beforehand, it seems very likely they attended the lecture on *Hamlet.* The prince is the embodiment of the poetic imagination, and Emily may have recognized in Dana's description a fellow idealist, who valued the world of the imagination over and above the external world.[114] Certainly, Hamlet's symbolic status for Dickinson in her later life might have had its origin in Dana's character analysis. Even in 1850, Dickinson may have related to Hamlet, for "This world was not made for him to act in, or he formed to act in it"[115] Dana also tells his listeners that Hamlet is in love with the idea of perfect love rather than with the flesh-and-blood Ophelia, seemingly predicting Dickinson's own later need to distance herself from real-life encounters, while maintaining a purer ideal of friendship and love. Dana's Hamlet longs to experience to the fullest possibilities of the mind: for the imagination to reach the "height and depths of its being:—a finite sprung from the infinite, and striving, through the strong workings of its many affections and faculties, to realize that infinite."[116] Certainly, Dickinson's later poems engage in a similar quest to discover the "Ourself behind ourself, concealed - " (F407) and the "Columner Self" (F740). Her journeys beyond the known boundaries, "Beyond the Dip of Bell -" are reminiscent of what Dana describes as Hamlet's longing to "experience his all of being," and his need to "push every faculty and emotion to the very verge of his being."[117] Appropriately, at a time when Amherst was in the grip of religious revivals and conversions, Dana argues that Hamlet's real desire is for God and that all his actions are in accordance with divine and eternal principles. It is therefore appropriate that in his last lecture, Dana transforms Shakespeare's play into a biblical parable and sign of divine order, although such a reading may have been more problematic for the skeptical Dickinson.

The establishment of Shakespeare's universal genius is inseparable from the appropriation of his works in support of traditional gender roles, social hierarchy, and conservative views. Dana's lectures and the Shakespeare Club provided Dickinson and her female friends with more than just a safe Shakespeare. No longer explicitly associated with immorality, social anxiety, and anarchy, Dickinson's Shakespeare involved scholarship, lessons in personal morality, and instruction in proper femininity. During her lifetime, he became an instrument for the imposition of a class version of "civility" on, and Anglo-Saxon superiority over, a society formed out of disparate immigrant nationalities.[118] Many of her later remarks evidence her affiliation with Shakespeare as a sign of learning and class credentials, and as a means of establishing literary and social order in the face of uncertainty.[119] But Shakespeare remained contradictory, providing a female reader with, and prescribing, highly erotic language and ambivalent characters, like *Macbeth*'s witches, with which she might identify rather than with Shakespeare's submissive heroines.[120]

CHAPTER TWO

"I read a few words since I came home - John Talbot's parting with his son, and Margaret's with Suffolk"

Reading and Performing Shakespeare, Fanny Kemble, and the Astor Place Riot

IN 1864, from late April to November 21, and again in 1865, from April 1 to October, Emily Dickinson underwent a course of eye treatment with Henry W. Williams in Boston, during which she stayed in Cambridge with her cousins, Louise and Frances Norcross. Between these two visits, in March 1865, she wrote the following to Louise: "I read a few words since I came home - John Talbot's parting with his son, and Margaret's with Suffolk. I read them in the garret, and the rafters wept" (L304). At this time, she also told her cousins that her eyes were not worse and not better—"sometimes easy, sometimes sad" (L302). After the first sessions of this treatment, when reading was obviously difficult, it is significant that she chose to read these scenes and record the event for her cousin. Later, in her 1870 interview with Higginson, she equated being able to read Shakespeare with recovering her eyesight: it was the end of her literal and symbolic blindness. She told Higginson, "When I lost the use of my Eyes it was a comfort to think there were so few real *books* that I could easily find some one to read me all of them" (L342a), and he noted, "After long disuse of her eyes she read Shakespeare & thought why is any other book needed" (L342b). In this very calculated interview, her new appreciation of Shakespeare was something Dickinson wanted Higginson to know about his "Scholar." Of course, this hints that while she was staying with her Norcross cousins they may actually have read Shakespeare's plays for the temporarily disabled poet, causing a renewed admiration for his works as texts to be heard and read aloud.[1] Fanny and Louise were greatly interested in theater, and they attended Shakespeare readings in Boston;[2] thus, Dickinson acknowledges to Louise that she is feeling well enough to engage in an activity that her cousins enjoyed and had reintroduced her to. Why might the poet have chosen the garret for her solitary performance, and why did she choose these particular scenes?

At that time, the garret, which in 1916 was converted into a third floor with three additional rooms, was the largest space in the Dickinson mansion.[3] With windows at each end and stairs that led up to the cupola, it offered Dickinson complete privacy; access was through a staircase just outside her bedroom. Obviously, at a time when "snow-light offend[ed] them, and the house [was] bright" she decided to read in this darker space (L302). It may have been during the day, for the level of light coming from the garret windows would have suited sensitive eyes; or, she may have read in the evening, with the aid of a kerosene lamp. The size and acoustics of the garret transformed this space into Dickinson's own private home auditorium, in which she could give full expression to words and emotions, making echo and resonance central to the activity of reading. Although the letter to Louise is her only reference to reading in the garret, perhaps she often chose it to read aloud in; she may also have read nondramatic texts, or even her own poems, here. Certainly, in this letter, she is less the madwoman in the attic than a quasi-actress blurring the gap between reading and performance.[4]

John Talbot's parting with his son, from act IV of *Henry VI, part 1,* is an unusual choice, considering that this play about England's loss of France and the beginnings of the War of the Roses was one of the least popular of Shakespeare's plays in the nineteenth century.[5] It was rarely performed in England and was not staged in America until the twentieth century.[6] Most critics mentioned it only to remark its inferiority to Shakespeare's other plays and to dispute whether he wrote it.[7] Charles Knight was one of the few who believed that Shakespeare wrote this as well as the other two parts of *Henry VI.*[8] He argued that the play was the bard's earliest involvement in writing for the London theater, in which he subordinated his "aspirations as a poet" to the task of writing a piece that would appeal to the "rude popular taste" of the audience. Shakespeare's genius, though is especially visible in the play's presentation of the jealousy, hatred, and courage of its characters. While other critics were appalled by Shakespeare's depiction of Joan of Arc, Knight describes her as a "person of very rare natural endowments," demonstrating the playwright's, impartiality and tolerance in representing human events and characters.[9]

The scenes Dickinson read, which are now attributed to Shakespeare on the grounds of style, present the dauntless John Talbot, betrayed by the disputing dukes of Somerset and York and left to fight, without any chance of success, at the siege of Bordeaux.[10] His courage and virtue as a warrior are never more apparent than as he dies alongside his son, John. Knight contrasts the fierce, terrible, and, at times contemptible Talbot, who "fights onward from scene to scene as if there were nothing high in man except the power of warring against his fellows," with the father who "weeps like a lover over the fruitless gallantry of his devoted son."[11] Probably, it was the "tender natural affections" of this man who "folds his dead boy in his rough arms, even as the mother, perishing with her child, takes the cold clay of the dear one to her bosom" that appealed to the poet. In these parting scenes, son and father urge each other to escape inevitable doom; Talbot wants his son to flee so he can revenge his father's death and preserve the family name. As Knight describes it, Talbot's son "answered that it was neither honest nor natural for him to leave his father in the extreme jeopardy of his life, and that he would taste of that draught which his father and parent should assay and begin."[12] Talbot's son proves himself as heroic as his father, and both die ensuring the honor, if not the perpetuation, of the Talbot name.[13]

In this act, Talbot parts with his son three times, and it is not clear whether Dickinson's garret reading included all of these partings or only one. Two lines from the first are marked in the family Shakespeare:

> Then here I take my leave of thee, fair son,
> Born to eclipse thy life this afternoon.
> (IV v 52–53)[14]

But these are merely an initial leave-taking, for Talbot continues, "Come, side by side, together live and die, / And soul with soul from France to heaven fly." In the next scene he rescues his son and again begs him to flee, to which he receives the reply, "An if I fly I am not Talbot's son" (IV vi 51). Talbot now calls his son Icarus, bidding him to fight by his father's side and "die in pride." Dickinson may have read either or both of these partings; but, she may also be referring to the final and most poignant, when Talbot addresses the body of his dead son:

> Thou antic death, which laugh'st us here to scorn,
> Anon, from thy insulting tyranny,
> Coupled in bonds of perpetuity,
> Two Talbots, winged, through the lither sky,
> In thy despite shall 'scape mortality.
> (IV vii 18–22)

This display of fatherly affection and tenderness may explain the reaction of the rafters to Dickinson's reading. The references to Icarus, who flies too near the sun, are very apt at this time when Dickinson had extreme problems with light. Talbot's and his son's bravery would be worthy models during her days of affliction and pain.

In the same letter, the poet also writes, "I dreamed last night I heard bees fight for pond-lily stamens, and waked with a fly in my room" (L304). Perhaps she is reminding Louise not only of these scenes that center on the possibility of flying from troubles, but also of Joan of Arc's description of Talbot's dead body as merely food for flies:

> Him, that thou magnifiest with all these titles,
> Stinking, and fly-blown, lies here at our feet.
> (IV vii 75–76)

If Dickinson's fly recalls those on Talbot's body, perhaps the bees fighting over the pond lily represent the war between England and France. At the time of her reading, the American Civil War was in its last month; she may have chosen this play because it examines the events leading up to an English civil war. Talbot's parting with his son may evoke the suffering war had caused families in Amherst[15]—a representation of the "more general" sorrow in America "since the war began," when "the anguish of others helped one with one's own" (L298).

The other speech Dickinson read in the garret was Margaret's parting with Suffolk. Thomas Johnson assumes that she is reading two scenes from *Henry VI, part 1.* This is unlikely, considering that Margaret's parting with Suffolk in this play is brief and, with its numerous asides, more comic than tragic. Such a scene would hardly have caused the rafters to weep, unless Dickinson was referring to the tragic consequences of the meeting between Suffolk and Margaret—their adulterous affair, which spurred on hatred that would culminate in the Wars of the Roses. What seems more probable is that she read from act III, scene two of *Henry VI, part 2,* where Margaret parts with her now lover Suffolk, who has been banished for his part in the murder of the Duke of Gloucester. It seems strange that Dickinson should read the part of Margaret. Knight described Margaret's "aptitude for boldness and dangerous intrigue," her "passionate hatred," and the "treachery and blood shed" she causes;[16] he also, however, praised the complexity of this character who endures much personal suffering, including watching her defenseless son, Edward, butchered by the sons of York in *Henry VI, part 3.*[17] Moreover, Margaret is a warrior queen, a powerful orator and the antithesis of her weak husband, Henry VI; in fact, for Knight, the eventual defeat of the house of York in *Richard III* seems to derive from Margaret's curses in this play.[18]

Anna Jameson, the nineteenth-century critic and defender of Shakespeare's heroines, argued that Margaret lacked a woman's soul; consequently, Jameson was unconvinced that Shakespeare wrote the *Henry VI* plays.[19] Margaret is beautiful, "treacherous, haughty, dissembling, vindictive, and fierce": she possesses unwomanly malignity, bitterness, and atrocious cruelty; she has "every coarser feature of depravity and ferocity" (399–400). Unlike any of Shakespeare's other heroines, she is "without a single personal quality which would excite our interest in her bravely-endured misfortunes." Nevertheless, Jameson also noted that Shakespeare gave Margaret "some of the finest and most characteristic scenes," one of which was Margaret's "beautiful parting" scene with Suffolk in *Henry VI, part 2*. Jameson suggests that it is impossible to read this scene "without a thrill of emotion, hurried away by that power and pathos which forces us to sympathize with the eloquence of grief, yet excites not a momentary interest either for Margaret or her lover" (401).[20] Margaret expresses her "ungoverned fury" and then is

> overcome by the violence of the spirit she had herself evoked, and terrified by the vehemence of his imprecations; the transition of her mind from the extremity of rage to tears and melting fondness, have been pronounced, and justly, to be in Shakspeare's own manner. (401–2)

Dickinson most likely read the following lines, which Jameson quotes to illustrate her point:

> Go, speak not to me; even now be gone.—
> O go not yet!— Even thus two friends condemn'd
> Embrace, and kiss, and take ten thousand leaves,
> Loather a hundred times to part than die.
> Yet now farewell; and farewell life with thee!
> (III ii 352–56)

Margaret has just kissed Suffolk's hand, telling him

> "So get thee gone, that I may know my grief,
> 'T is surmis'd whilst thou art standing by,
> As one that surfeits thinking on a want.
> I will repeal thee, or, be well assur'd,
> Adventure to be banished myself:
> And banished I am, if but from thee."
> (III ii 346–51)

Finally, she asks, "Let me hear from thee; / For whereso'er thou art in this world's Globe / I'll have an Iris that shall find thee out." As he departs, she declares, "And take my heart with thee" (III ii 405–8). The American critic Henrietta Lee Palmer considers Margaret as ambitious as Lady Macbeth but "vulgar in quality," acting in ways the Scottish Queen would disdain.[21] Palmer reprimands Margaret as the "faithless wife" of a virtuous husband and a woman of "petty spites and coarse cruelty." She also argues, however, that the one situation "in which we are permitted to regard Margaret with even tolerable kindness" is her parting with Suffolk, and offers her readers much of the sorrowful dialogue.

This scene had a particular appeal for Dickinson: by 1865, she had written many poems that dealt with the sorrowful and inevitable separation of lovers and the denial of their physical union in this world.[22] These echo the themes of Margaret's tearful parting speeches, but without her explicit anger. Possibly Dickinson found in this problematic heroine words to voice rage and frustration she could articulate only covertly in her own writings. One of Dickinson's most famous renunciation poems, "I cannot live with You" (F706), echoes Suffolk's response to Margaret's parting:

> If I depart from thee I cannot live:
> And in thy sight to die, what were it else,
> But like a pleasant slumber in thy lap?
> Here could I breathe my soul into the air,
> As mild and gentle as the cradle-babe,
> Dying with mother's dug between its lips:
> Where, from thy sight, I should be raging mad,
> And cry out for thee to close up mine eyes,
> To have thee with thy lips to stop my mouth;
> So shouldst thou either turn my flying soul,
> Or should breathe it so into thy body,
> And then it liv'd in sweet Elysium.
> To die by thee were but to die in jest;
> From thee to die were torture more than death:
> O let me stay, befall what may befall.
> (III ii 388–402)

Suffolk's lines are recalled by the speaker of Dickinson's poem, who can have her beloved only by not having him or her. Both summon up the "White Sustenance - / Despair - " on which exiled lovers must be nourished, and each pictures one lover finally shutting the other's eyes. After Suffolk is killed, Margaret nurses his severed head and openly admits her love for him (IV iv 1–6). In Dickinson's "If I may have it when it's dead" (F431) the speaker lays claim to the dead body of a lover who has been confiscated from her.[23] That Dickinson should in the garret be reading Shakespeare's first examination of destructive and adulterous love is very significant, considering her later interest in such themes in *Antony and Cleopatra.* In telling of reading the speech of this notorious queen, Dickinson is announcing her interest in, and more importantly her ability to represent, forbidden passion, female strength, and self-assertion. Rather than one of Shakespeare's idealized heroines, she finds resonances for herself in the words of one described in *Henry VI, part 3* as having a "tiger's heart wrapp'd in a woman's hide" (I iv 137).[24] In her attic reading Dickinson has chosen plays in which the threat to England is embodied in powerful female figures—Joan of Arc, the Countess of Auvergne, the Duchess of Gloucester, Margaret of Anjou—each of whom defy male conventions and contravene notions of femininity.[25] In fact, one of Dickinson's earlier poems, "A Mien to move a Queen" (F254), alludes to hidden female potency in calling up Joan of Arc, "Half-Child - half Heroine - / An Orleans in the eye," to describe a wren, whose potential power is unrecognized and thus unthreatening: "Too small - to fear - / Too distant - to endear - / And so Men Compromise - / And just - revere -".

"For it may be urged, that he who attempts this, *must be, to a certain extent, an Actor"*

To understand how Dickinson read the above scenes we must examine the culture of declamation in which she lived, and the kind of training given to nineteenth-century students of rhetoric in reading aloud.[26] According to Ebenezer Porter, every intelligent father who wished his son and daughter to

> hold a respectable rank in well-bred society, will regard it among the very first of polite accomplishments, that they should be able to read well. But beyond this, the talent may be applied to many important purposes of business, of rational entertainment, and of religious duty.[27]

For although "the whole of one sex, and all but comparatively a few of the other" will never have a need for public speaking, "the ability to read in a graceful and impressive manner" will be of great value.[28] For Porter, "nearly all our youth, of both sexes, must be good readers," and he aimed to provide the oratorical principles necessary for managing the voice to convey correctly thought, emotion, and passion. The highest goal was reading that sounded natural, requiring students not merely to speak eloquently but "with all the varied intonations which sentiment requires" (16, 17). An artificial tone was to be avoided and standard punctuation and grammar subordinated to expression, as the reading "*voice must conform to sentiment*" (20). Most importantly, the reader should not merely express "the thoughts of an author, but [express] them with the force, variety, and beauty, which feeling demands" (21). It might seem that Porter, paradoxically, was offering instruction on how to speak in an unstudied way; in fact, he used examples from literary texts to demonstrate the various rhetorical principles that will improve oratory and skilled elocution, offering guidance on articulation, inflection, accent, emphasis, pause, force, time, and pitch. He advised students to use a system of notation whereby a different type of accent is placed above words depending on whether they are to be read with a falling or rising inflection.[29]

Porter suggests that "lessons should, at first, be chiefly narrative; or narrative and colloquial combined;—by which I mean, dialogue proper, or rhetorical dialogue; in which the same voice must represent two speakers or more" (22). This would justify his brief use of Shakespeare's plays, which, of course, necessitate a shift from one character to the next, from one emotional and intellectual perspective to another. His chapters on articulation, emphasis, and inflection employ *Julius Caesar* and *Hamlet;* Dickinson's instruction on how to read aloud occasionally involved training in how to perform scenes from Shakespeare. Porter demonstrates the link between declamation and hermeneutics; the interpretation of the emotional and intellectual states of Shakespeare's characters is examined with reference to rhetorical principles, and vice versa.[30] For example, Cassius's line, "You wrong me every way; you wrong me, Brutus" (*Julius Caesar* IV iii 55) is given as an example of the way in which emphatic repetition requires a falling slide (36). Porter's argument is that the second "wrong" must be read with double or triple the force of the first "wrong"; both have a dash over them to indicate a falling inflection, but the second is italicized to confirm it should be more emphasized. Brutus's earlier line "You wrong'd yourself to write in such a case" (IV iii 6) is given as an instance of relative stress (42); "yourself" is italicized, suggesting that it needs to be inflected to convey that from Brutus's perspective, although Cassius feels himself injured by some other person, it is his own fault. In this same scene, where Brutus tells Cassius, "You have done that you should be sorry for" (IV iii 65), Porter italicizes "have" and "should," because Brutus is saying, "Not only are you liable to do wrong, but you *have* done so already" and "though you are *not* sorry, you *ought* to be sorry." This is "precisely the meaning of Brutus, for he replied to a threat of Cassius, 'I *may* do that I shall be sorry for.'" Consequently, in exercises on the language of authority, of surprise, and of distress, where a falling inflection is required, students are advised to read Brutus's entire speech, beginning with the line "You have done that you should be sorry for" (IV iii 65–82).[31] Porter also interprets and explains how to read "The fault, dear Brutus, is not in our stars; / But in ourselves, that we are underlings" (I ii 140–41), arguing that it requires a rising inflection "on *stars* and the falling inflection on *ourselves*" (43). He suggests that no reader of the least taste would mistake the one for the other. To read such a speech with attention to the sentiments of the characters is to read it "naturally" yet also according to rhetorical principles.

Claudius's soliloquy from *Hamlet* that begins "Oh! My offence is rank, it smells to heaven" (III iii 36–72) is printed as a class exercise on the pathetic and delicate (129–30). Students are advised to prepare their minds "to feel the spirit of each piece, by entering fully into the circumstances of the case"; before reading this scene, they must also review an earlier section on how to express sorrow and the most pathetic sentiments (125). This informs readers that such speech requires "a modification of voice" to express an "awakened sensibility" of the soul, "that is more easily felt than described; and this constitutes the *unction* of delivery" (61). Readers must remember that "sorrow, and its kindred passions, when carried to a high pitch, suspend the voice entirely" (62). To portray the sorrow of Claudius (and by implication, of Talbot, and Margaret) a reader must be careful to avoid artificial amplification, embellishment in language or vociferation, and whining in utterance:

> The highest passion of this sort, is expressed by *silence;* and when so far moderated, as to admit of words, it speaks only in abrupt fragments of sentences. Hence it is, that all artificial *imitation,* in this case, is commonly so unlike the reality. . . . Whereas real passion intended to be imitated, if it speaks at all, speaks without ornament, in few words, and in tones that are a perfect contrast to those of declamation. This distinction arises from those laws of the human mind, by which internal emotion is connected with its external signs.

This implies that when Dickinson read the scenes from the *Henry VI* plays, she would have aimed to make her voice an external sign of the inner states of Talbot and Margaret, and would not have read these scenes unless she had studied and fully understood these complex characters. Moreover, in her attic reading, she would have subordinated punctuation and even Shakespeare's blank verse to a need to express inexpressible sorrows; in all probability she interspersed Shakespeare's words with moments of silence. Conceivably her own poetry follows Porter in deviating from standard grammar and syntax, and fragments and disjoints language to express difficult emotions and move her audience. Her voice-splitting dashes and her often abrupt endings call to mind Porter's advice that to represent "sorrow and its kindred passions" the voice may need to become silent.

Richard Whately's *Elements of Rhetoric* was hugely influential on American rhetoric books, including Porter's; Dickinson's father bought a copy in 1839.[32] In 1856, Dickinson refers to Whately in a letter to Mrs. Holland discussing rhetoric, "Your voice is sweet, dear Mrs. Holland - I wish I heard it oftener. One of the mortal musics Jupiter denies, and when indeed its gentle measures fall upon my ear, I stop the birds to listen. Perhaps you think I *have* no bird, and this is rhetoric - pray, Mr. Whately, what is *that* upon the cherry-tree?" (L182). Like Porter, Whately argues for what he calls "Natural Delivery," but places greater significance on reading aloud as communication with an audience. Consequently, he advises the reader

> to fix his mind as earnestly as possible on the [subject-]*matter,* and to strive to adopt as his *own,* and as his *own at the moment* of utterance, every sentiment

> he delivers;—and to *say* to the audience, in the manner which the occasion and subject spontaneously suggest to him who has abstracted his mind both from all consideration of *himself*, and from the consideration that he is reading. (364)

Reading means persuading an audience of one's authenticity and sincerity, and that it is being addressed personally on a subject of intimate importance. Moreover, "there certainly is a kind of moral excellence implied in the renunciation of all effort after display,—in that forgetfulness of self,—which is absolutely necessary, both in the manner of writing, and in the delivery, to give the full force of what is said" (372). This lack of egotism is an important part of the declamatory process, making it possible for female readers to engage in public display and, simultaneously, offer a self-effacing performance.[33] Thus, Dickinson may embody the passions of characters like Margaret convincingly without being herself indicted for what might be deemed reprehensible in their speeches. Whately is aware, however, that his advice raises a problem: "it may be urged, that he who attempts *this*, must be, to a certain extent, an Actor" (393). For a good reader is like "an accomplished *actor*,—possessing the *plastic* power of putting himself, in imagination, so completely into the situation of him whom he personates" (389). But Whately carefully distinguishes between the two: the reader merely expresses in the moment of reading "all the sentiments and views of that character," and this "exactly as such a person would have done, in the supposed situation," while the actor pretends to be this character, with all his or her sentiments and characteristics (389–90). This distinction, though, succeeds in reemphasizing the similarities rather than the differences between performing and reading: both clearly involve affecting the guise of genuineness and naturalness.

Whately is overt in his praise of "The first of Dramatists, who might have been perhaps the first of Orators," and he especially admires Antony's speech over Caesar's corpse, his primary example of an orator exciting an audience by expressing feelings openly while at the same time laboring to suppress his real thoughts and emotions (183–87). By indirectly describing Caesar's murder, Antony makes it all the more striking; this kind of indirection would be expected to soften what is shocking, but Antony's words produce a more vivid impression. Antony's object being "to *excite* horror, Shakspeare puts into his mouth the most *particular* expressions; 'those honourable men (not, who *killed* Caesar, but) whose *daggers* have *stabbed* Caesar'" (245). Whately also employs *Macbeth* to demonstrate where the voice should be suspended, raised, and lowered; in the witches' cave, when the spirits address him—"Macbeth! Macbeth! Macbeth!"—he answers, "Had I three ears I'd hear thee" (350). Like Porter, Whately claims that no one would dispute that the stress here is on the word "three," suggesting that, to attempt to emphasize any other would be "utterly absurd." The implication is that if one fully understands and empathizes with what one reads, one knows instinctively how to convey the words orally. This makes clear why, for Whately, the recitation of Shakespeare should not be encouraged in schools. To "make a boy deliver a Speech of Caesar, for instance, or Lear, in the natural manner" is fraught because "the learner himself will be reciting in a manner, to *him,* wholly artificial" since "the composition, the situation, and the circumstances *could not* have been his own" (394–95). The evidence from these rhetoric books supports the suggestion of many critics that Dickinson's writings are like performances, aimed at stimulating and affecting an audience.[34]

"It was done with great simplicity and naturalness, with an earnest desire to express the exact conception of the author, without any thought of herself, or the impression her reading was sure to make"

In an era when public readings played a major role in the educational and social lives of her contemporaries, and reading aloud was a skill to be judged and discussed, much evidence suggests that Dickinson was very accomplished.[35] According to Lavinia, it would seem that rhetoric lessons informed her abilities:

> Emily was herself a most charming reader. It was done with great simplicity and naturalness, with an earnest desire to express the exact conception of the author, without any thought of herself, or the impression her reading was sure to make.[36]

The poet's father, who required readers to take "pains to read distinctively—and give every word its full sound—and correct emphasis," further attested to Dickinson's skills (Leyda I 74). When Austin was away from home in the early 1850s, Edward insisted that his daughter read his letters: her talent allowed him to "relish the story more"; although he had read the letters several times himself, he made her "read them loud at the supper table again" (L44, 108).[37] Dickinson told Austin that she read his letter "very *artlessly* and unconsciously," while at the same time consciously "striking out all suspicious places" that she could not read "loud to anybody" (L53, 116). The poet had clearly mastered natural delivery, becoming a medium through which Austin's humor and wit came alive (L53). At this time, Dickinson frequently read letters among her circle of female friends, and she remained the chief reader of newspapers, poems, books, and letters in her family.[38] Her cousins, Louise Norcross and Anna Norcross Swett, attested to having heard her read her poems aloud.[39] This accomplished reader would have expected her own readers, who shared her education in rhetoric and declamation, to perform her poems and letters aloud.[40]

Dickinson and her friends in the Shakespeare Club read his plays aloud and, presumably, commented on their readings; this must have also contributed to her abilities.[41] The Amherst tutors were specifically concerned with marking "questionable" passages, so they would not be read aloud in the mixed company of the club. While Emily Fowler called the group a "rare thing in those days," Shakespeare clubs and societies proliferated throughout America from the 1860s onwards, and details of their activities help in understanding the Amherst club. It seems likely that Dickinson and her friends read the plays, scene by scene, "explaining, calling attention to beauties, asking opinions, comparing passages, and in fact throwing all possible light upon the act under consideration."[42] They probably also addressed each play through a series of questions focused, as most nineteenth-century discussion of Shakespeare was, on characters, historical period, sources, and Shakespeare's biography.[43] Critical commentaries of the day may have been used "to produce a change in the discussion that will be quite as valuable in exciting interest and in fostering study."[44] Perhaps two evenings a week were "devoted to reading a play, and then two evenings, either to answering an exhaustive list of questions, or reading original essays upon topics connected with, or suggested by the play, the subjects and writers being chosen" by the tutors.[45]

As late as June 1884, Dickinson confirmed the importance of reading Shakespeare aloud, in a message of comfort to Mrs. Holland, who had just left New York for her summer home:

> I was with you in all the loneliness, when you took your flight, for every jostling of the Spirit barbs the Loss afresh - even the coming out of the Sun after an Hour's Rain, intensifies their Absence - Ask some kind Voice to read to you Mark Antony's Oration over his playmate Caesar - I never knew a broken Heart to break itself so sweet. (L901)

Dickinson may have heard this particular speech read during her rhetoric lessons, or at meetings of the Shakespeare Club, and this scene (III ii 73–107) is marked with a pink string in the family's edition of Shakespeare. Presumably, a "kind" voice will be a skilled one able to convey Antony's sorrow. It will express this so as to articulate Mrs. Holland's loneliness and the pervasive sense of loss and absence in human life. In the same letter, Dickinson notes that "Death cannot plunder half so fast as Fervor can re-earn," indicating that for her it is the fervor of Antony's speech that reanimates Caesar, reminding the plebeian crowd of the "good" he has done before this is "interred with [his] bones" (III ii 76). By the end of Antony's cunning oration, he has altered the crowd's perception of Brutus and the other assassins, changing "honorable men" into murderers. Dickinson has chosen a speech regarded by Whately as the greatest example of Shakespeare's rhetorical powers, in which Antony uses all the strategies available to him to persuade and convince his listeners; but Dickinson seems most attracted to the moment when Antony is so moved by his own speech that he allows his real feelings to emerge. She is likely referring to the point where Antony breaks off, saying, "Bear with me / My heart is in the coffin there with Caesar, / And I must pause till it come back to me" (III ii 105–7). At this moment, from Porter's perspective, Antony perfectly represents his own sorrow; although this may be part of a strategy to influence the crowd, he is obviously also devastated by the loss of his friend. In the best spirit of natural delivery, Antony feels that which he speaks. For Dickinson, a "kind" voice will represent Antony's speech as a display of real human friendship and love in the face of death; when read aloud, it will, she hopes, transform her friend's morbid mood.

"I have heard many notedly bad readers, and a fine one would be almost a fairy surprise"

The popularity of public Shakespeare readings in the America of Dickinson's time also lay behind her interest in oral performances.[46] Perhaps she and her fellow enthusiasts in Amherst attended an elocutionary entertainment titled "An Evening with SHAKSPEARE," given by Miss Lizzie Johnson in Phoenix Hall, on Thursday, 24 June 1852. The advertisement for the event appeared in the *Hampshire and Franklin Express,* describing how Johnson would read "some of the most popular selections from the IMMORTAL BARD OF AVON."[47] In its "Local Items," the newspaper reveals that Johnson "has met with good encouragement wherever she has appeared before the public and we doubt not will abundantly satisfy all lovers of the 'Immortal bard'."[48] It also quotes the *Springfield Republican*'s assessment that Johnson has "evidently devoted much time and labor to the study and expression of the great Bard—has a good voice, good face and figure, and backed by talent and enthusiasm will we think succeed." The reading is presented as an educational and intellectual event, for which the presenter has meticulously prepared, and, at the same time, as a form of public entertainment: not only has she a "good voice," she also possesses a "good face and figure," clearly important in attracting an audience.

In a letter to Louise Norcross in late 1859, Dickinson refers to the most famous Shakespeare reader of the day:

> Do you still attend Fanny Kemble? "Aaron Burr" and father think her an "animal," but I fear zoology has few such instances. I have heard many notedly *bad* readers, and a fine one would be almost a fairy surprise. (L199)

Kemble, a member of the prestigious Kemble acting dynasty, had begun reading a survey of Shakespeare's most popular comedies, tragedies, and histories in Boston ten years earlier,[49] as a means of supporting herself financially at the end of a much publicized divorce case; Pierce Butler, a native of Philadelphia who owned the second-largest slave-owning plantation in Georgia, had sued her on grounds of desertion, and claimed custody of their two daughters.[50] When Dickinson's father called Kemble an animal, he might have been judging her skills as a reader; but he might also have been referring to her unfeminine self-display, not to mention her scandalous decision to desert her family and the domestic sphere, and the notoriety this entailed.[51] Others shared the view that Kemble had overstepped traditional boundaries. After hearing her in 1849, Herman Melville had described her as "unfemininely masculine," and suggested that "had she not, on unimpeachable authority, borne children, I should be curious to learn the result of a surgical examination of her person in private."[52] Yet despite these reservations, Kemble's readings attracted the elite of Boston, and she became a friend of Ralph Waldo Emerson, James Russell Lowell, and the Longfellows. Suggesting that the actress is beyond "zoology," Dickinson positions herself (and Louise) on Kemble's side, against her father and Aaron Warner ("Aaron Burr"), the retired professor of rhetoric at Amherst College.[53]

Throughout 1849, anticipating her arrival in its city, the *Springfield Republican* continually updated readers like Dickinson on the great popularity and financial success Kemble was having in Salem, Boston, Hartford, Albany, New York, Lenox, and Brooklyn.[54] Months before her scheduled reading in Springfield's North Congregational Church on Tuesday and Wednesday evening, May 29 and 30, the paper offered very specific details of Kemble's performance:

> The coming of the Lady was heralded by an elderly gentleman's placing a chair behind the little red-covered desk on the platform, which constituted all the stage of the performer. Two large volumes of Shakspeare were laid on the desk, and the buzz of conversation that had filled the Hall ceased. Presently, Mrs. Butler made her appearance as from a trap door near the platform, and escorted by Charles Sumner, she took her place behind the desk. She was elegantly dressed, as if for a ball, wearing a rich light silk with short sleeves and low neck; the vacuity being supplied by a superabundance of flowing lacework. Bowing with infinite grace, she put back with her hand her dark and glossy hair (which was dressed with elegant plainness,) and with slightly affected emotion said, "I have the honor to read the Merchant of Venice." Then taking her seat, and just reading the list of characters, she entered at once upon the play.[55]

Kemble's entrance escorted by Mr. Sumner, her "infinite grace," her elegant white dress, her humble prelude, and the simplicity of the staging all align her with respectable, modest, and proper femininity. Although initially concerned with her appearance, the columnist goes on to refer to her ability to captivate and is surprised that "a single human voice" by simply reading a play could produce "the beauty, the power, and the genius displayed by this woman." For "two entire hours, with but a short intermission at the middle," she kept a large audience "bound in almost breathless silence, interrupted only by spontaneous outbreaks of applause, which it was impossible to restrain."

Kemble defied social categories during her readings because of her ability to represent all of Shakespeare's characters, regardless of their gender, race, or age:

> One moment, she was the fiendish Shylock, and rage, hate and vengeance ruled in her countenance and her voice; the next, the calm, kind, Christian Antonio, submissive to his fate, was counterfeited; again she was sweet Portia, describing her lovers to her maid, acting the Judge with dignity and wisdom, and tantalizing her husband with the loss of the ring, which he had vowed to keep till death.

In her readings "every shade of character was portrayed with a faithfulness and a vigor, that showed the master-mind, the genius and the acquirements of the reader." On June 1, after her reading in Springfield, the same newspaper suggested that Mrs. Butler had revealed an important secret to "our Shakespeare loving public"—that "the most direct road to the human soul, is through the human voice."[56] It went on, "The voice is Nature's own channel of communication of mind with mind; and it is the only channel through which the conceptions of creative imagination, can transmit themselves with undiminished force, and unadulterated beauty." The columnist differentiated Kemble's abilities from those of her female listeners, who "in conversation or reading, use our good English" with "an uncultivated voice and a most weak and melting articulation," constantly misrepresenting themselves. Another columnist suggested that many of the women present did not recognize the "satirical strain in [Kemble's] voice" when she read passages that he believed had biographical import for her.[57] But during her 1849–50 tour, Kemble offered Dickinson the possibility of female self-assurance, intellectual ability, social achievement, autonomy, and empowerment through Shakespeare.[58] Ten years before her letter to Louise, Emily was probably aware of Kemble as someone who gained immense popularity while transgressing gender roles—despite her feminine appearance, her clear and eloquent reading and her authoritative voice, expressions, and gestures, demonstrated a self-confidence and ability traditionally thought of as male.

In her 1859 letter to Louise, she is alluding to Kemble's having begun a course of sixteen readings from Shakespeare at the Meionaon Tremont

Temple, Boston.[59] This received much praise in the *Boston Evening Transcript*,[60] and the *Springfield Republican* on January 15 commented how "the great passions of the human soul, love, jealousy, revenge, hate, tenderness, sorrow, in such rapid succession, live in that living face, breathe in the tragic power, the imploring pathos of that wonderful voice, is an event for a life time."[61] The columnist suggests that

> Fanny Kemble is unreservedly great. And when a woman stands before the world as an artist, with what delight, when I may utter it truly, I say "She is great." It was worth more than the price of the ticket only to see the soul flashes radiate across that most expressive face.

Possibly Dickinson has this passage in mind when she says to Louise, on the subject of female greatness,[62]

> You and I in the dining room decided to be distinguished. It's great thing to be "great" Loo, and you and I might tug for a life, and never accomplish it, but no one can stop our looking on, and you know some cannot sing, but the orchard is full of birds and we all can listen. What if we learn ourselves some day!

A year earlier, Dickinson had begun privately "distinguishing" herself as a serious poet by placing the poems she had already written into fascicles. Although she may have never heard Kemble "sing" Shakespeare's lines, the actress's example perhaps influenced her sense of herself as a poet whose business it was to "sing," even orally recite, her poetry (L269). Presumably, as with Jenny Lind, (whom she heard in Northampton on 3 July 1851 and discussed in a subsequent letter to Austin) Dickinson was primarily interested in Kemble as one of the great female performers—and icons—of her era (L46). Moreover, considering that she reported to Austin that Lind took $4,000, she may have been interested in *Springfield Republican*'s claims that Kemble received $250 to $300 per reading, making her financially independent through her own endeavors.[63] In fact, both Lind and Kemble assumed a predominantly male position in the public sphere, occupying the frightening, especially for Dickinson, new role of marketable female spectacle.[64] But Kemble, unlike Lind, had no master manager like P. T. Barnum organizing her tour and manipulating her performances from behind the scenes; she was an independent woman, in control of her own performance.

The *Republican* columnist praises Kemble's simple clothes, adding "what is more disgusting than to see a woman come before the public as an expounder of art, attired in flaunting array, with head, ears, neck, fingers, full of badges of feminine vanity?" In contrast to fashion-conscious "household women," the great artist "in her attire emulate[s] only the classic severity, the unequalled grace, of the Roman vestal, or the Grecian muse." Henry James recalled that Kemble "dressed in black velvet for *Lear* and in white satin for the comedy."[65] Perhaps Dickinson's decision to wear a simple white dress around this time further connects her with the great Shakespeare reader (and even with Lind, who also wore white during her performances).[66] Dickinson's conception and depiction of female performance and performers in her poetry may also derive from Kemble. In her attic performance, she probably imagined herself as, and expected Louise to associate her with, a performer like Kemble. In her dark garret, through Shakespeare, she ventures "out of sight, in sound" as the weeping rafters "encore [her] so" (F381).

Kemble's later readings were never as successful as those she gave during her 1849–50 tour: this was due mainly to the frequency of her readings and to the proliferation of rivals.[67] In 1871, however, the impending arrival of Mary Frances Scott-Siddons, a cousin of Fanny Kemble and an accomplished actress and noted beauty, attracted the attention of another member of the Dickinson family. On 16 March 1871, J. Leander Skinner told his wife, "I am here on business for Scott-Siddons . . . It is very funny so many people want I should save them tickets. Had to refuse Austin Dickinson today. He has arranged with Prof Mather & Mr Jenkins they are going to send two of their hired men up to secure *seven* seats, as I refused to give seven to one man" (Leyda II 172). Austin may have been one of the "leading citizens" of Amherst who, according to the *Amherst Record,* organized a special train so people from Palmer and Belchertown could attend the "inimitable and charming Recitations and readings" of the "exquisitely beautiful" Mrs. Scott-Siddons.[68] The paper's advertisement for this reading, in College Hall on Tuesday, March 21, recommends the event as perhaps "the finest entertainment of the season, Mrs Siddons being the most beautiful of readers before the public at this time." Scott-Siddons read passages from *Much Ado About Nothing, Macbeth,* and *Henry V,* as well as from works by other writers, and on March 22 the paper describes an appreciative audience enthralled by this woman:[69]

> Mrs Siddons is a beautiful woman, with such a charming grace of gesture, and majestic voice that even common sentiments, coming from her lips would be elevated into poetry. In the scene of Lady Macbeth the audience was breathless in their engrossing interest, and it was her highest achievement.

Considering her brother's key interest in Scott-Siddons performance, Dickinson probably knew of the event. If she read this review, she might have been interested in the ability of Scott-Siddons's voice to convert any words into poetry.[70] A year before, she had offered Higginson her famous definition of poetry, using very similar terms:

> If I read a book [and] it makes my whole body so cold no fire ever can warm me I know *that* is poetry. If I feel physically as if the top of my head were taken off, I know *that* is poetry. These are the only way I know it. Is there any other way. (342a)

Perhaps it is specifically reading aloud which tests whether writing is "poetry" or not. Certainly Dickinson appears to endorse Whately's description of declamation as involving readers losing their own identity, consumed by the emotions they convey.

"Reading belongs to a higher order of art than acting"

These Shakespeare readings, performed by actresses such as Kemble and Scott-Siddons, were continually differentiated from performances on the stage, and were evidently popular in part because they allowed those staunchly opposed to the theater to attend. On 1 June 1849, the *Springfield Republican* notes that for "lovers of virtue and religion" some "ten thousand corrupting and dissipating influences" always accompany theater.[71] It adds, "Reading belongs to a higher order of art than acting"; without the gaudiness of theater and the "scenery or stage clap-trap," Kemble astonishes those "most accustomed to the representations of the best actors that ever walked on a stage."[72] Another *Republican* reviewer is grateful that Kemble has chosen these readings in preference to returning to the disreputable profession of acting, noting "few or none, however pure, go on the stage now-a-days, that do not suffer from the breath of scandal."[73] Years later, the same paper declared that when Scott-Siddons read at the Opera House in Springfield her delicacy and power were "more notable without the stage accessions."[74]

In 1832, Kemble had recorded that "the happiness of reading Shakespeare's heavenly imagination is so far beyond all the excitement of acting them."[75] Later that year she wrote, "How I do loathe the stage! these wretched, tawdry, glittering rages, flung over the breathing forms of ideal loveliness . . . how I do loath my most impotent and unpoetical craft!"[76] Her readings, and her later writings, mark her determination to avoid what she regarded as a "disgusting travesty" that distorted Shakespeare's plays into a mockery. In an 1864 article, "On the Stage," in *Harper's New Monthly,* Kemble suggests that the stage is repugnant to her because of her education and her nature, and goes on to distinguish between the theatrical and the dramatic.[77] The dramatic is the instinctual power of representing emotions and passions, while the theatrical is false, self-conscious, showy display. By implication, readings are dramatic, the stage theatrical. Such views echo those of earlier commentators, such as Charles Lamb and the former American president John Quincy Adams, who lamented the inadequacies, "misconceptions," and alterations of Shakespeare's plays on the nineteenth-century stage.[78] Likewise, in an 1862 article, "Plays and Play-Acting," in the *Atlantic Monthly,* A. Dexter argues that "Shakespeare on the stage is a sad falling off from Shakespeare in the closet" because "our imaginations are not kept in check by the pitiless limits that make themselves felt in the theatre."[79]

Present research suggests that although other plays were performed in Amherst in this period, no full-length Shakespeare works were staged there during Dickinson's lifetime.[80] This almost certainly reflects a lingering anti-theatrical prejudice, and fear of Shakespeare's immorality, in this conservative town. *A History of the Town of Amherst, Massachusetts* records that "theatricals were regarded as devices of the evil one, not to be tolerated in any law-abiding community."[81] Such prejudice is also manifest in the Dickinson family. On 11 October 1851, Austin told his future wife, Sue, "I attended places of amusement, for the time lost my identity in the witchery of dazzling lights & Gay dresses—brilliant music, & the parade and glitter of the stage—but retired without the least feeling of satisfaction or sympathy with any body or thing" (Leyda I 218). Although Austin in later life attended and enjoyed the theater, this early account reflects a Puritan anxiety about "places of amusement" where one can lose one's identity.[82] Similarly, Sue, writing from Baltimore on 22 October 1851, notifies her brother Dwight Gilbert, "By the way I must write you of my dissipation—Have been to Theatre and Opera once—I was disgusted with the Theatre—never care to go again—but the Opera perfectly fascinated me" (Leyda I 221). In an 1860 letter, Emily Dickinson thanks her Norcross cousins for a cape and asks them, "Do you think I am going 'upon the boards' that I wish so smart attire? Such are my designs, though. I beg you not to disclose them! May I secure Loo for drama, and Fanny for comedy?" (L225). Obviously, she is joking, especially considering the social stigma attached to actresses and acting, despite the respectability women like Kemble and Scott-Siddons had brought to the profession.[83] Dickinson's fears about self-exposure and self-display suggest that the profession of actress was the antithesis of her "designs." Similarly, her poem "Drama's Vitallest Expression is the Common Day" (F776) argues a clear preference for the private and daily enactments of dramas over and above publicly performed, ephemeral plays. It seems likely that when she read in her attic she was replicating Kemble's readings rather than performances on the stage, and likewise that her poems about performance were dramatic but not theatrical.

Unlike plays on the stage, Shakespeare readings were presented as intellectual and educational, a "safe" way for women to engage with Shakespeare. Kemble reassured the public that "whatever her selections, they will have neither cause nor desire to complain of the manner in which she executes her part."[84] When Kemble was in New York, the *Evening Post* suggested that her readings complemented recent lectures on Shakespeare given by Dana.[85] Kemble herself wanted to bring Shakespeare to those who would not normally have read him, and lowered the price of tickets to her readings.[86] On 16 April 1849, however, the *Springfield Republican* presented her as educating only the "mere fashionables, who crowd to hear her" in New York.[87] It recorded the "rumors" that many of the elite "now listen to the Swan of Avon for the first time," have never heard of *Hamlet,* and suppose Shakespeare "to be the person who kept a tavern at the corner of Center and Chambers street." It also noted that none of these listeners would attend the "decidedly vulgar" theater. Despite Kemble's intention of widening her audience, some newspapers believed her readings cost too much and her shows were solely for the elite. On 2 February 1850 the *Daily Mail* recorded the following attack on Kemble:

> So far as the real people of Boston are concerned, she might as well have expended her breath in some airy situation on the Mill Dam. By dollar tickets, a packing box church [the Tremont Temple], and the august attendance of the Mutual Admiration Society, considerable self-glorification has been achieved; but the spirit of William Shakespeare—he who wrote "for all ages and for all time"—has been most sublimely snobbed and snubbed.[88]

In other words, Kemble's readings were for the gentry rather than in the all-inclusive "spirit of Shakespeare."[89]

Despite Edward Dickinson's reservations about Kemble, her readings would have appealed to the Dickinsons as theater could not. After all, this family was part of the New England gentry, one of the most eminent and influential in Amherst. There is no concrete evidence that Dickinson saw any plays in her lifetime, and it seems unlikely that a woman who "wore white [and] shut herself away from her race as a mark of her separation from the mass of minds," would have enjoyed the Shakespeare productions in many theaters across America.[90] As a result, her Shakespeare is unlike that of Herman Melville, who calls theatrical productions of his work an "all popularizing noise and show of broad farce and blood-besmeared tragedy" that gives the "all popular Shakespeare" most of "his mob renown."[91] Similarly, Walt Whitman's Shakespeare, experienced at New York's Bowery Theater, would not have attracted the poet. Whitman records that in the first tier of boxes were the faces of the leading authors, poets, and editors, while in the pit there were "young shipbuilders, cartmen, butchers, firemen," and mechanics, with their "slang, wit, occasional shirt sleeves, and a picturesque freedom of looks and manners, with a rude, good-nature and restless movement."[92] Whitman describes their hand-clapping as "no dainty kid-glove business, but electric force and muscle from perhaps 2000 full sinew'd men."

On 10 May 1849, between Kemble's April reading in New York and her upcoming one in Springfield, New York City's Astor Place Riot occurred, confronting Dickinson and others of her class with the literal dangers of theater. Dickinson probably read about this event in the *Springfield Republican;* she claimed to enjoy its sensational stories "every night," regarding the paper as a letter from her friends, the Hollands (L133). The *Republican* noted the rivalry between the "English Tragedian," William Macready, and "his American rival," Edwin Forrest, which led to innocent blood being spilled because of the "brutal passions of a mob." The actors had been competing on both sides of the Atlantic, and on May 7, opened in rival performances of *Macbeth*—Forrest at the more "democratic" Park Theater and Macready in the highly priced Astor Place Opera.[93] On Wednesday, May 9, the *Republican* reported the "tragical reception" of the "celebrated English tragedian" who suffered "all sorts of menagerie noises, rotten eggs, potatoes, pennies, cheers for Forrest, chairs thrown from the third tier" because of many "sympathizers of Mr. Forrest" at the play.[94] On Saturday, May 12, the paper recorded that on May 10 one "of the most shameful events which ever disgraced the history of our City" occurred.[95] Despite a police presence outside the Opera house, threats of violence were directed at those who "dared express their opinion at the English Aristocratic Opera House," and working men were told to "stand by their lawful rights." On Macready's entrance in the third scene of the first act, there was a "storm of cheers, groans and hisses," to which nine-tenths of the audience, who were favorable to Macready, responded by "waving their hats and handkerchiefs." The police intervened and removed the leaders of the disturbances, so that "one by one the rioters were taken and carried out, the greater part of the audience applauding as they disappeared." This allowed the "obnoxious actor," Macready, to perform his part with complete self-possession, until the rioters outside smashed the windows and the theater came under siege.[96] The paper reported that during the subsequent riot, fifteen people were killed and twenty-five wounded "in the name of vengeance and abhorrence." In fact, more than 1,800 people—house capacity—filled the theater, while outside a crowd of about 20,000, mainly working-class men, chanted, "Burn the damned den of the aristocracy!" and "You can't go in there without kid gloves . . . and a white vest, damn 'em."[97] During the subsequent riot, soldiers killed twenty-one and wounded one hundred fifty—according to a speech given in City Hall Park the next day, "To please the aristocracy of the city, at the expense of the lives of the inoffending citizens—to please an aristocratic Englishman, backed by a few sycophantic Americans."[98]

It was not that Shakespeare was condemned as an "English" playwright, rather that his supporters were divided along class lines that were also largely national. The elite and moneyed classes were associated with England and Englishness, while the working class exulted in "America for Americans" as part of their pride in a still relatively newly independent and democratic United States.[99] Lawrence Levine suggests that this riot was a struggle for cultural authority and "an indication of and a catalyst for the cultural changes that came to characterize the United States at the end of the century."[100] This would culminate in the establishment of Shakespeare's works as serious rather than popular; in fact, they would be held as the opposite of stage entertainment. Thus, A. A. Lipcomb's 1882 essay "Uses of Shakespeare Off the Stage," in *Harper's New Monthly,* argued that Shakespeare off the stage appeals to the intellect and the imagination, and is therefore superior to Shakespeare on the stage.[101] Prophetically, he suggested that the playwright was destined to become "the Shakespeare of the college and university, and even more the Shakespeare of private and select culture." Clearly, Dickinson's attic reading could not have been further removed from Shakespeare's position on the American stage: it was modeled on Kemble's readings, informed by her rhetoric lessons and activities at the Shakespeare Club, and involved the careful study of his texts and an engagement with Shakespeare criticism.

CHAPTER THREE

"Shakespeare was never accused of writing Bacon's Works"

American Shakespeare Criticism, Delia Bacon, James Russell Lowell, and Richard Grant White

In August 1881 Dickinson, unsatisfied with William Dean Howells's novel *A Fearful Responsibility,* which was appearing in installments in *Scribner's Monthly,* asked Mrs. Holland, the wife of its editor, "Who wrote Mr. Howells' story?" (L721). She continued, "Certainly he did not. Shakespeare was never accused of writing Bacon's works, though to have been suspected of writing his, was the most beautiful stigma of Bacon's Life - Higher, is the doom of the High." Just as to accuse Shakespeare of writing Bacon's works would be demeaning to the bard, to accuse Howells of writing his latest, less than impressive, novel would be degrading. Dickinson's awareness of this debate is hardly surprising considering its prominence. In 1856, the year the who-wrote-Shakespeare controversy began, the *Amherst Collegiate Magazine* published an article that accused "irreverential carping critics of our time" of attempting to pluck away laurels from "the prince of dramatists."[1] Such critics attempted to make him no more than "a miserable pot-house rhymer, or at best some indifferent and obscure theatrical appendage" to "contemporary master wits who were the real authors of the plays that bear his name." Likewise, the three journals the Dickinson family subscribed to, which the poet read conscientiously—the *Atlantic Monthly, Harper's New Monthly,* and *Scribner's Monthly*—all addressed what had become an issue of the day.[2]

A mutual love of humor and the whimsical, as well as a common interest in intellectual and literary activity, clearly characterized Dickinson's correspondence with Mrs. Holland. Frequently, in these letters, Dickinson emphasizes their shared reading of newspapers and journal articles, particularly those published by Josiah Holland in the *Scribner's Monthly.*[3] Although Dickinson here may refer to any of numerous sources, E. O. Vaile's 1875 *Scribner's* article "The Bacon-Shakespeare Controversy"[4] is likely. Vaile discusses the life and work of Delia Bacon, who was one of the first to claim that Shakespeare did not write the plays attributed to him. Vaile laments her "interesting and gifted mind" sacrificed to this "futile idea," her heavily condemned article and book, and her eventual mental breakdown and death. The problem Delia Bacon raised was how to account for a poorly educated boy from Stratford having the intimate knowledge of law, medicine, classical learning, French and Italian literature, the Bible, science, astrology, alchemy, and witchcraft found in the plays.[5] For Vaile, "all the circumstances of Bacon's life—and in regard to them there is no want of fullness or certainty—are as conclusive in favor of his authorship as all the circumstances of Shakespeare's life are conclusive against *his* claim" (748).[6] But, Vaile asserts that the lack of historical evidence that Shakespeare wrote the plays has little significance, because the bard "did not live in the conditions of modern life, and we must not judge him by our standards" (752). If one expects him to be "an Emerson or a Carlyle sitting by his study window," a "philosopher or man of letters," one misunderstands the age in which and the stage for which he wrote. The intention behind Dickinson's remark on Howells is clear. One of the reasons Vaile gives why Bacon probably did not write the plays was their association with the lowly theater, rather than with the dignity of science and philosophy. Thus "the familiarity with low and vulgar life displayed by Shakespeare, would be quite impossible for Bacon, as he was never thrown into fellowship with it." Finally, the frequent inaccuracies in geographical and historical information in the plays suggest that if Bacon wrote them he "affected an ignorance of things with which he must have been perfectly acquainted" (754). This is why accusing Bacon of writing Shakespeare's plays was "the most beautiful stigma of Bacon's life."

Richard Grant White's 1883 article "The Bacon-Shakespeare Craze" in the *Atlantic Monthly* calls this controversy "an infatuation, a literary bee in the bonnets of certain ladies of both sexes, which should make them the objects of tender care and sympathy." This "craze," this "mental epidemic," is associated with women, was initiated by a "loony," and degrades "the two greatest minds of modern times" in a "petty parade of piddling, perverted verbal coincidences."[7] While Dickinson may have thought Delia Bacon's idea ludicrous, she may yet have found something to admire in this woman's attempt to prove all her predecessors wrong.[8] Moreover, like Fanny Kemble and Mrs. Scott-Siddon, Delia Bacon offered the poet an example, albeit a flawed one, of female literary fame achieved through Shakespeare. At the time when Dickinson was beginning to write her poetry, Bacon presented a model—of an aspiring, displaced, intellectual American woman like herself, from a similar conservative New England background, characterized by Whig politics and Calvinism.[9] Certainly, not everyone agreed with White's assessment of Bacon; Hawthorne's "Recollections of a Gifted Woman" (1863) provided *Atlantic Monthly* readers with a staunch defense of the originator of this debate.[10] Hawthorne met Bacon in London on 26 July 1856, when he was United States consul in Liverpool; he mentions his support and assistance to her and her eventual refusal to see him because he criticized her ideas. Hawthorne's admiration derived from Bacon's symbolic status as an American laying claim to her own inheritance of the great English literary and cultural past.[11] He vehemently condemns the way American critics, reiterating the harsh views of their English contemporaries, pelted "their poor countrywoman with stolen mud." Although he describes his "sturdy unbelief" in Bacon's "erroneous" theory, he demands American recognition of this "very remarkable woman," her intellect, powers of belief, and earnestness:

> We Americans, at least, in the scanty annals of our literature, cannot afford to forget her high and conscientious exercise of noble faculties, which, indeed, if you look at the matter in one way, evolved only a miserable error, but, more fairly considered, produced a result worth almost what it cost her. (50)

Hawthorne stresses the "Americanness" of this woman and her discovery of a "deep political philosophy concealed beneath the surface of" Shakespeare's plays that has added to his reputation and greatness. This entitles her to "the distinction of being that one of all his worshippers who sought, though she knew it not, to place the richest and stateliest diadem upon his brow."

Despite his doubts about her ideas, Hawthorne esteemed Bacon's powers of imagination, reminding his readers, "Whatever you seek in [Shakespeare] you will surely discover, provided you seek truths" (51). Shakespeare's texts allow a range of interpretations: they have "surface beneath surface, to an immeasurable depth, adapted to the plummet-line of every reader; his works present many faces of truth, each with scope enough to fill a contemplative mind." The inexhaustibly "various interpretations" Shakespeare's works allow must have been one of their central attractions for Dickinson, who by 1863 had perfected her own abstruse and enigmatic writing style.

Hawthorne's Delia Bacon is no mere lunatic, but an ingenious woman who has "now entirely secluded herself from the world" because it has rejected her idea (52). She possesses the power of a great speaker, whose faith in her own beliefs may instill in her listener a "temporary faith," and a vast knowledge of Elizabethan history and literature, and of the lives of Shakespeare and Bacon. Tragically, her idea has consumed and overmastered her, substituting "itself in the place of everything that originally grew there." Almost like one of Hawthorne's own characters, she is depicted as a ghost haunting Holy Trinity Church; she believed that documents which proved her theory were found inside Shakespeare's grave. But when a kindly vicar agrees to open it for her, she becomes consumed with the fear that she will find nothing.[12] Hawthorne calls this her "lady-like feeling of propriety," her "New-England orderliness";

yet he confides to his readers that Bacon would have argued with Shakespeare himself, demanding of the man she "profanely" called the "Old Player" and "Lord Leicester's groom" that he speak truthfully about the authorship of the plays. Hawthorne's description of Bacon may have influenced T. W. Higginson's accounts of meeting Dickinson in 1870 and 1873; certainly, Higginson was reading Hawthorne's work at this time.[13] Higginson presents Dickinson as his "enigmatical," "abnormal," and "partially cracked poetess at Amherst"; she has drained his "nerve power so much" on their first meeting (L342b, 405, 481). Moreover, as in Hawthorne's experience of meeting Bacon, an instinct tells Higginson "the slightest attempt at direct cross-examination would make her withdraw into her shell."[14] On the other hand, like Bacon, Dickinson is a writer with a definitive sense of her own vocation: "*My* business is to sing" (L271, 269).

If Bacon's sense of destiny and powerful determination were exemplary for Dickinson, her fate was a warning about the severity of critical reception. A year before Hawthorne's article, Dickinson had received Higginson's initial criticism of her own poetry; he believed she should "delay 'to publish'" (L265). Although the poet claimed his "surgery" "was not so painful as [she had] supposed [it would be]," Higginson was certainly doubtful about the extent of her talent (L261). Like Bacon, however, Dickinson never compromised on the basis of judgments by Higginson or others, and the poet must have shared the controversialist's pride in her work, self-assurance, and even moments of self-doubt. Bacon may have failed, but Hawthorne refers to the emergence of new readers who have discovered truth in her work; possibly this had reverberations for Dickinson.

For Hawthorne, Delia Bacon's eventual mental breakdown was not the operation of a curse on all those who seek to violate Shakespeare's grave; instead, he argues that the bard met her and led her into the "better world," thanking her for explaining his thoughts so well to mankind, despite "certain mistaken speculations":

> This bewildered enthusiast had recognized a depth in the man whom she decried which scholars, critics, and learned societies, devoted to the elucidation of his unrivalled scenes, had never imagined to exist there. She had paid him the loftiest honor that all these ages of renown have been able to accumulate upon his memory. (56)[15]

What Hawthorne is suggesting becomes apparent on examination of Bacon's criticism. Her 1856 article, "William Shakespeare and his plays: An Inquiry concerning them," in *Putnam's Monthly* argues that modern criticism has transformed "the Stratford poacher" into a superhuman genius, "bringing with it its own laws and intuitions from some outlying region of life, not subject to our natural conditions."[16] This has been necessary to demonstrate how a man intellectually "below all other men," who did not recognize the value of his own work, should have written plays of such genius, beyond the capability of any past or future writer (5–6). The "boundless sea of negations" that surrounds Shakespeare reflects the "oblivion to which this man's time consigned him," allowing him to become "any shape or attitude which the criticism in hand may call for" (4, 8). In other words, the myth of Shakespeare's unsurpassable genius is generated and facilitated by the absence of a biography. Bacon's thesis suggests how Dickinson will become the myth of Amherst, who, as Mabel Loomis Todd noted in 1881, "no one *ever* sees" (Leyda II 357). According to Bacon, readers know only "the posthumous Shakespeare of the posthumous volume" and actually "it is only the work itself that we now know by that name—the phenomenon and not its beginning." Dickinson's "Drama's Vitallest Expression is the Common Day" (F776), written in the same year as Hawthorne's article, declares, "'Hamlet' to Himself were Hamlet - / Had not Shakespeare wrote -," echoing the radical skepticism in Bacon's criticism. Similarly, E. O. Vaile suggests that the authorship controversy does not lessen "our reverence for those inspired words called Shakespeare" (754),[17] and in James's "The Birthplace," Mr. Hayes tells Gedge, "'The play's the thing.' Let the author alone," and Gedge replies: "there *is* no author; that is for us to deal with. There are all the immoral people—*in* the work; but there's nobody else.'"[18] Dickinson, at least in this poem, regards the author as less relevant, and knowable, than his characters, who are intimately known. Perhaps she hoped for a similar fate for her own poems, telling Higginson that "When I state myself, as the Representative of the Verse - it does not mean - me - but a supposed person" (L268).

Of course, for Bacon, it is the belief that this uneducated man wrote the plays that "prevent[s] all the kind of reading and study of the plays which would have made its gross absurdity apparent" (13). She asks her American readers, "what new race of Calibans are we, that we should be called upon to worship this monstrous incongruity—this Trinculo" (7). With the myth of Shakespeare deconstructed, Bacon in her subsequent book *The Philosophy of Shakspere's Plays* (1857) demonstrates the ways in which the plays, especially *Julius Caesar, Coriolanus,* and *King Lear,* are disguised calls for reform and innovation. She presents herself as the guardian of the ideas that Francis Bacon and his group concealed within the plays—acknowledgment of the power and humanity of the lower orders and a powerful critique of the despotism, superficiality, and corruption of the Elizabethan and Jacobean court. The plays sought to teach the uneducated audience history, leading it away from the corrupt monarchy and court to the natural world, where despotism might be judged.[19] *King Lear* is the grand and social tragedy "of an unlearned human society" and Lear himself that "impersonation of absolutism—the very embodiment of pure will and tyranny in their most frantic form," but, the play anatomizes all that which is the "addition" of a king, finally presenting Lear in a new "state of things" where he no longer has his divinely anointed power (202–5). Similarly, in *Henry V*, when Henry, disguised as a commoner, declares, "I think the King is but a man as I am, the violet smells to him as it doth to me; all his senses, have but human condition," Bacon says, "His ceremonies laid by, in his nakedness he appears but a man" (194). Of course, such ideas are the antithesis of what many of Dickinson's poems propose: usually her speakers rise within monarchical or divine hierarchies to be finally, and deservedly, crowned; her girls are disguised Earls and her rustic speakers are revealed to be queens (F734, F575).[20]

Dickinson saw Bacon's theory produce a new field of study, Anti-Stratfordian criticism, which between 1856 and the poet's death generated over two hundred sixty books, pamphlets, and articles; it attracted female enthusiasts because it was rejected by predominantly male editors, academics, and critics.[21] Of similar importance was the fact that the majority of the early Anti-Stratfordians were Americans, an equally peripheral group that sought to take possession of the scrutiny of Shakespeare's texts and show all previous (European) criticism to be flawed.[22] This is implicit in Emerson's comment, on hearing that Delia Bacon had failed to find a publisher in England: "all that makes it formidable there, should make it popular here."[23] Her American publisher, Philips Sampson, said that "if she is correct, there will be great fitness in our *undeceiving* the American public, for no house has done so much to publish, and spread the name and fame of Shakspeare as ourselves."[24] Bacon herself wanted her work published in America because her ideas properly belonged to her country, and she saw the initial rejection by British publishers as an attack on her country's honor.[25] However unsettling her theory may have been, it represented a clear attempt to retrieve Shakespeare's texts from the "incorrect" and "misled" English critics and give them back to American readers; in the process, it refashioned them as upholders of American democracy. To an extent, Dickinson's brief discussion of Shakespeare and his plays in her letters derives from the same American spirit of amateur scholarship as Delia Bacon's work. Like Bacon's criticism, Dickinson's poetry in its own way subversively redefines and revises "beyond easy recognition" poetry's traditional form and content in order to find a space for her own female voice.[26]

"We write for those who are somewhat interested in this subject, and must assume that our readers are not entirely without information upon it"

The journals Dickinson read published numerous pieces on Shakespeare as part of their commitment to discussion of European culture and its central texts;[27] it seems very probable that Dickinson read at least some of these.[28] As it is surprising that the Bacon-Shakespeare debate should have become a national controversy, the variety, subject matter, and frequently erudite nature of these articles is also astonishing. Readers were offered information on Shakespeare's use of legal terms; his literary contemporaries; the history of Hamlet's presentation on the stage; the habits and manners of the people for whom he wrote; the influence of Holinshed on Shakespeare; Shakespeare's death mask; his portraits; and the spelling of his name.[29] Such articles derived from readers' desires to establish personal bonds with their favorite authors.[30] Dickinson's reaction to the authorship controversy demonstrates her own definite conception of who Shakespeare was.[31] Her interest in his characters was met by many articles on character analysis.[32] The profusion of these journal articles reflects a time when Shakespeare, whether approached historically, textually, biographically, editorially, or dramaturgically, was not the domain solely of professional academics. For readers like Dickinson Shakespeare was one of *their* concerns. Thus, between 1859 and 1861, the John Payne Collier folio controversy inspired a review and two full-length articles in the *Atlantic Monthly;* each discussed the 1632 folio, containing notes and emendations, which Collier claimed dated from the seventeenth century and were an authoritative guide for editing Shakespeare.[33] Most likely, Richard Grant White wrote all three features in the *Atlantic;* in 1853, White had proved that these emendations had no authority and, to the delight of his American readers, demonstrated the error in the proposition of the then leading British Shakespeare scholar.[34] The highly scholarly and specialized nature of all three pieces of criticism presupposes readers' interest in the minutiae of Shakespearean textual scholarship. Certainly, the review begins, "We write for those who are somewhat interested in this subject, and must assume that our readers are not entirely without information upon it."[35] The articles offer what one calls a "comprehensive view of this subject," as "nothing has appeared in this country; but several important publications have been made in London concerning it," thus, stressing this journal's position at the forefront of Shakespeare scholarship in America.[36] Moreover, although they condemn Collier's behavior, they also reprimand British critics for their "disgraceful attempts to injure a literary opponent," claiming that the behavior of neither party would be tolerated in America.[37] At one point White notes that the hostility Collier's folio has caused would be "uninteresting" to "the general reader"; he then proceeds, however, to give an exhaustive examination of this folio, its emendations and notes, and the dispute between Collier and his accusers.[38]

This is in sharp contrast to prevailing practice today, when information about Shakespeare is published in scholarly journals by specialist academics, for the perusal of other specialists. These articles and journals provided their middle-class readership with "democratic" access to the major, as well as minor, features of Shakespeare scholarship, allowing further debate. Written by some of the most influential American Shakespeare critics, they pursued the general aims of Victorian Shakespeare scholarship: to discover historical information about the man and his times; to establish his canon and its chronology; and to link biography to art.[39] They do so from a distinctly American perspective, with three central aspects: an emphasis on Shakespeare's universality that understated his "Englishness"; an often thorough rejection of or disputation with "flawed" English precursors; and a stress on the political aspects of Shakespeare's plays and their relation to American democracy.

Even articles from *Harper's,* which concentrated on publishing more accessible pieces, shared these foci. In "Mr. William Shakspeare, At Home," M. D. Conway outlines his experiences as an American in England during Shakespeare's tercentenary on 23 April 1864.[40] Conway begins by addressing his reader as a fellow "brother-in-curiosity" implying an assumed interest in Shakespeare (340). He acknowledges that this special occasion was "a strife as to who would say or do the finest thing about Shakspeare that ever was said or done," and reports that one man declared, "Pah! Paper! What's the use of a paper now? Shakspeare has written everything down beforehand." The delineation of the festivities and celebrations at Stratford, and of Conway's own Shakespeare "fever," is accompanied by his continually addressing the issue of nationality. After the grand banquet, attended chiefly by British hereditary aristocracy and a few lesser-known literary figures, an Englishman proposed the health of American poets, and although he could not name any he was sure that Shakespeare was their inspiration. Such national superiority was also apparent in a lecture given the following day by a bishop who declared that Shakespeare was "an *English* saint," and an "intensely *national* prophet and poet" (342). Conway finds such nationalism disturbing, considering the admiration for Shakespeare in Italy, Russia, Germany, and America, and all the more insulting when Charles Albert Fechter is regarded as the greatest Hamlet and Stella Colas, the finest Juliet—neither of them English. When Colas gives a performance at Ann Hathaway's cottage, it rebukes the bishop:

"These flushing cheeks and falling tears around you are the criticism of the common heart, and they declare that this Frenchwoman is the *only* Juliet now on the stage" (345). Conway calls Shakespeare's genius "a flower with hues from the sky bending over all nations, whose fragrance is the joy of the whole earth" (342). Readers are left with an image of men and women from different countries gathering around the grave and bust of Shakespeare.

Poems in these journals that celebrate Shakespeare's genius may also have interested Dickinson.[41] One of the most fascinating was written by Oliver Wendell Holmes in honor of the tercentenary, and published in the *Atlantic Monthly*.[42] In the first stanza, England inquires why Shakespeare is being claimed by "warring aliens" from "realms unknown." To this, the American nation responds that even during a period of civil war, Americans "Come with fresh lilies in our fevered hands / To wreathe his bust, and scatter purple flowers,—/ Not his the need but ours!" The poem argues that Shakespeare was "bequeathed" to Americans by their "fathers" who left England, and is a legacy of "joyous pride." It describes Shakespeare as the poet who brings "the coming of the dawn," the first pale spark of hope in "twlight's gloom," and he is "God's kingliest creature" and "Earth's clearest mirror of the light above." The worship of Shakespeare is equivalent with devotion to God, "Counting all glory, power, and wisdom Thine, - / For Thy great gift Thy greater name adore, / And praise Thee evermore!" In the last stanza, Shakespeare's gifts of beauty, wisdom, power, and love are "freshening dew," keeping "every sweet remembrance true, / Till from this blood-red sunset springs new-born / Our Nation's second morn!" Holmes's poem typifies Shakespeare worship in American culture; it also demonstrates that when Dickinson found resonances of the Civil War, in which "martyrs fall and heroes bleed," in *Henry VI, part 1*, she was participating in a broad cultural use of Shakespeare as a force of stability and reassurance at this time of national crisis.

"If a great national poet could ever avail himself of circumstances, this was the occasion,—and, fortunately, Shakespeare was equal to it"

James Russell Lowell was one of Dickinson's favorite American writers, and the editor of the *Atlantic Monthly;* his essay "Shakespeare Once More" appears in *Among My Books* (1868), which Sue owned and Dickinson quoted from in an 1878 letter (L564).[43] This essay may have especially interested Dickinson because it discussed Shakespeare primarily as a poet; surely, its opening sentence must have caught her attention:

> It may be doubted whether any language be rich enough to maintain more than one truly great poet,—and whether there be more than one period, and that

very short, in the life of a language, when such a phenomenon as a great poet is possible. (151)

Examining Shakespeare's language, Lowell suggests that it was one of the "rarest pieces of good luck" that Shakespeare, the "most rhythmic genius" with the "acutest intellect," the "profoundest imagination" and "healthiest understanding," was born when "the material in which he was to work . . . was in its freshest perfection." Shakespeare's full powers were developed when the English language was "the best result of the confusion of tongues." It had become "*modern*,—just as it had recruited itself, by fresh impressments from the Latin and Latinized languages, with new words to express the new ideas of an enlarging intelligence which printing and translation were fast making cosmopolitan" (156). Although to a certain extent "*established*," Shakespeare's English was "not yet fetlocked by dictionary and grammar mongers" (157). Such an explanation for Shakespeare's powerful—and unorthodox—language is intriguing when we consider that Higginson described Dickinson's wayward and unconventional poems as "deviant of form, measure, rhyme, and even grammar," and stated that "fracture[s] of grammar and dictionary" were key aspects of her style.[44] Later critics, such as Charles Anderson and Richard Sewall, have connected Dickinson's innovations in nineteenth-century poetry with her reading of Shakespeare, calling him her strategic model in refreshing and revitalizing the language.[45] Similarly, Brita Lindberg-Seyersted suggests that Shakespeare was Dickinson's "great model" in her use of unaccented rhymes; he was "her preceptor" in the creation of neologisms because he used words in unorthodox syntactic arrangements, and his spoken plays were exemplary for Dickinson's creation of poetry that resembles speech.[46] Dickinson's poetry might also be regarded as a conglomeration of the Anglo-Saxon colloquial and the foreign, of everyday American provincial speech with polysyllabic and Latinate words.[47]

Although Dickinson's combination of the exotic and the known corresponds to Lowell's description of Shakespeare's language, there is also a major difference. Lowell's epitome of creative genius is "a representative Englishman," with a Saxon father and Norman mother, and his language was "first the rough and ready English of his rustic mates, who knew how to make nice verbs and adjectives courtesy to their needs" (156). Shakespeare's powers are the national product of the Elizabethan milieu in which he wrote: his language was "still hot from the hearts and brains of a people" (155). His plays reflect the spirit of his country at a time of innovation, learning, and new discoveries, when English national feeling was high and the country was ruled by a wise and cultivated monarch. For Lowell, "if a great national poet could ever avail himself of circumstances, this was the occasion,—and fortunately, Shakespeare was equal to it" (154). This draws a provocative parallel with Dickinson's nineteenth-century America, which, ethnically diverse and heterogeneous, was seeking its "national" poet, whose language would be representative of its people.[48] Obviously, Lowell's Shakespeare sounds more like Walt Whitman than the reclusive and exclusive Dickinson, who in 1870 asked Higginson, "how do most people live without any thoughts. There are many people in the world (you may have noticed them in the street) How do they live. How do they get strength to put on their clothes in the morning" (L342a).

Like much American criticism on Shakespeare, Lowell's article attempts more than mere praise; he wishes to explain, and perhaps justify, Shakespeare's importance:

> The hold which Shakespeare has acquired and maintained upon minds so many and so various, in so many vital respects utterly unsympathetic and even incapable of sympathy with his own, is one of the most noteworthy phenomena in the history of literature. (166)

For Lowell, the "hold" this sixteenth-century playwright has on nineteenth-century America is a result of the fact that Shakespeare's plays were written at the beginning of the "modern" period in language; they remain relevant because they have shaped and therefore reflect contemporary life and thought. Now "there is nothing in history or politics, nothing in art or science, nothing in physics or metaphysics that is not sooner or later taxed for his illustration" (170). Yet this becomes even more threatening, for Shakespeare has penetrated the consciousness of his readers:

> the more we have familiarized ourselves with the operations of our own consciousness, the more do we find, reading [Shakespeare], that he has been beforehand with us, and that, while we have been vainly endeavouring to find the door of his being, he has searched every nook and cranny of our own. (171)

Perhaps such ideas explain and inform Dickinson's assessment of Shakespeare as the only necessary writer. Lowell's essay, however, lessens Shakespeare's threat to an American culture attempting to establish its own distinctive literature by transforming this representative English poet into a pan-European figure comparable to Dante, Cervantes, and Goethe. In fact, like these writers, and in contrast to other English writers such as Milton, Sterne, and Wordsworth, Shakespeare has left no "successful imitators" or school (181–82). Establishing a perfect and unique bond between himself and the language, he had "the privilege which only first-comers enjoy," and appears uninfluenced by his precursors and nearest contemporaries; consequently, he is superior to his contemporaries and followers "in degree," but also in "kind." Shakespeare is "thoroughly English and thoroughly cosmopolitan"; it is his "aeration of the understanding by the imagination which he had in common with all the greater poets, and which is the privilege of genius."

For Lowell, the greatest mistake of Shakespeare studies is that it makes its goal to discover the biography of this elusive, benevolent, naturelike genius without egotism who inspires the world with wonder. Going even further, Lowell's essay ends by arguing that there is an element ever greater than Shakespeare's genius:

> But higher even than the genius we rate the character of this unique man, and the grand impersonality of what he wrote. What has he told us of himself? In our self-exploiting nineteenth century, with its melancholy liver-complaint, how serene and high he seems! If he had sorrows, he has made them the woof of everlasting consolation to his kind; and if, as poets are wont to whine, the outward world was cold to him, its biting air did but trace itself in loveliest frost-work of fancy on the many windows of that self-centred and cheerful soul. (227)

Such ideas recall the American poet Jones Very's presentation of Shakespeare as a "spirit [who] seemed the antagonist of matter; whose life was as various and all-embracing as nature's; and in whom the individual seemed lost and blended with the universal. In him we have a gift not of a world of matter but one of mind; a spirit to whom time and place seemed not to adhere."[49] This understanding of Shakespeare's authorship encapsulates a prescription for female writers like Dickinson of adopting an ideology of female reticence, removing their personal identities and individual passions from their published work, whose aims were ultimately altruism and never egoism.[50] An 1870 *Scribner's Monthly* reviewer of Lowell's book commented sarcastically, "unable to ground his preference of Shakespeare's character to Shakespeare's genius on knowledge, [Lowell] grounds it on ignorance, of the man."[51] Yet this image of an impersonal, absent author may have appealed most to Dickinson. The same reviewer suggests that in his title, "Shakespeare Once More," Lowell implies "the difficulty of attracting public literary attention by saying anything new on so hackneyed a theme, and the whole essay seems to betray that uneasy effort to overtop predecessors in far-sought hyperbole of adulation."[52] Dickinson must also have been aware that many of her remarks about Shakespeare's preeminence were part of a discourse, in which it was hard to say anything new.

"Abstractly speaking he spits on democracy and treads it under his feet"

One of the striking features of American criticism of Shakespeare in Dickinson's era is its examination of his politics. Although many, including Knight and Lowell, argued that he was incapable of political partisanship, and although Delia Bacon introduced the idea that his works were "mechanism for moving and moulding the multitude" toward freedom and democracy, others found antidemocratic and monarchist sentiments in the plays.[53] In his 1863 *Harper's* article, "The Statesmanship of Shakspeare," Charles T. Congdon argues that the plays contain many passages that "would prove him to have been a Republican or a Democrat or for that matter, an atheist, a Jew, or a madman," yet, "abstractly speaking he spits on democracy and treads it under his feet."[54] Although fundamentally monarchist, Shakespeare's plays examine "the duties of the throne to the people," and even his bad kings hold to an ideal of how those with power should rule. Congdon's Shakespeare is a commonsense politician who regards fulfillment of the basic needs of ordinary people as imperative for political stability and success. Accordingly, he should not be blamed for not adopting a political idea highly unpopular in his day, nor condemned for his inaccurate representation of the rebellion against the monarchy by Jack Cade in *Henry VI, part 2;* these features of Shakespeare's texts merely reflect his natural monarchical bias.[55]

In contrast, George Wilkes, in *Shakespeare, From an American Point of View* (1877), argued that Shakespeare's plays were "the unseen source, the incessant fountain, the constant domineering influence, which had done more to continue the worship of the English people of royalty and rank, than all other agencies combined."[56] For Wilkes, Shakespeare will continue to have a prominent place in American culture, but it must condemn him as a moralist and politician because American critics, unlike the English, are not entangled in political and cultural allegiances and can treat "this mighty mortal as a man" (12). For political, rather than moral, reasons Wilkes questions the suitability of Shakespeare for family reading, or as a textbook in schools and colleges. He is horrified that American audiences, "in the face of their democratic principles, uproariously applaud the patrician despot [Coriolanus]" and endorse a play against "human rights and popular liberty" (294–95). Shakespeare is guilty of consistent servility to royalty and rank, deficient in tenderness toward those of his own social status, and without generosity toward popular liberty. As for Delia Bacon, the central problem for Wilkes is that an uneducated boy from Stratford wrote the plays; yet Wilkes finds it difficult to understand how Shakespeare could prefer to be "the parasite of the rich and noble, and seldom, if ever, permits the humble to escape him without a derisive jest or sneer."[57]

> [This] genius of the life-giving order who was born in comparative humbleness never betray[ed] one emotion, for or exhibited a single sympathy with the downtrodden classes, whose degradation and miseries must have constantly intruded upon his subtle comprehension. (11)

For Wilkes, Shakespeare appeased the interests of the nobles and kings, although "surely the [common] people endured wrongs enough during the whole of this turbulent period to enlist some slight sympathy from the great genius" (183). Throughout his book, Shakespeare's plays are presented as demeaning the "mechanical and labouring classes," which in America are "esteemed to be not the least honest, virtuous and patriotic of the community" (112). The treatment of Bottom in *A Midsummer's Night's Dream* by Puck, the servant of the King and Queen, is condemned, as is Shakespeare's falsification or obfuscation of liberal ideas and popular suffrage, evident in his maligning of a dead patriot, Jack Cade, in the interests of the powerful nobles. Wilkes suggests that it would be a "positive relief" to be able to suggest that Bacon, rather than Shakespeare, had written these plays (254).

An 1877 review of Wilkes's book published in the *Atlantic Monthly* is far from positive: it praises his repudiation of "Miss Bacon's book," yet maintains that Wilkes does not possess a clear understanding of Elizabethan history or of the religious disputes of that time.[58] His arguments simplistically and unconvincingly connect America with Protestantism and Puritanism, aiming to defend America against a "Romanist" dramatist who disrespected Puritanism. Wilkes omits to inform his readers how Shakespeare was supposed to write his plays and how readers are supposed to engage properly with Shakespeare's works now. Finally, the reviewer agrees only with Wilkes's sentiment that "the works of this 'money-making' man, this incarnation of 'toadyism and venality,' this 'beaming epicure,' are still 'the richest inheritance of the intellectual world'." It is unlikely that if Dickinson read Wilkes she would have approved of his views. In fact, she probably admired Shakespeare for the very reasons that Wilkes abhorred him. Not only did she choose to read, and perhaps identify with, the sorrows of Talbot and Queen Margaret, her writings appropriate a Shakespearean vocabulary of hierarchy, crowns, earls, jewels, kings, queens, and court, a language that in Wilkes's view was inappropriate for America.[59] Benjamin Lease argues that this language derives from Dickinson's knowledge of Shakespeare's history plays, and he notes the way she drew "repeatedly on Shakespeare's conception of sacred royalty to represent in her poems a lover's—and her own—sacred suffering and transcendent triumph."[60] Lease identifies *Richard II* as having a special significance for her, as its protagonist presented himself as Christ delivered by his enemies to his "sour cross" (IV i 240–41). To add to Lease's speculation, it may be noted that many of the illustrations of the kings of England in Knight's edition, including the portraits of Richard II in the Jerusalem Chamber, and of the crowned Henry V and Henry VI, present them as quite androgynous figures.[61]

"Throw the commentators and the editors to the dogs.
Don't read any man's notes, or essays, or introductions,
aesthetical, historical, philosophical, or philological.
Don't read mine. Read the plays themselves"

Dickinson was probably aware of Richard Grant White, the most celebrated American Shakespeare critic and editor in her era, and frequent commentator in the *Atlantic Monthly.*[62] In 1859, James Russell Lowell praised White as having "in larger proportion than any editor" the ability to meet the demands that a perfect editor of Shakespeare must. Lowell commends White's "glossological knowledge of the English language contemporary with Shakspeare"; his "metaphysical training"; his preference for Shakespeare's ideas over his own; his sensitivity to Shakespeare's versification; and his "familiarity with the workings of the imaginative faculty in general and of its peculiar operation in the mind of Shakspeare."[63] In direct contrast to Wilkes, White was a lifelong Anglophile, and his tireless work derived from the fact that he regarded himself and his fellow Americans as "coheirs [of Shakespeare] and equals with our blood brethren in Great Britain."[64] While others critics downplay Shakespeare's Englishness, White stresses it as a means of connecting Americans with what he called their "Englishhood." Unlike most of his contemporaries, White had a real impact on Shakespeare studies: not only was he the first to expose Collier's forgery, but his work was praised, admired, and even, on occasion, plagiarized by British scholars.[65] For readers like Dickinson White validated and popularized American scholarship, although he may himself have been more interested in recognition as a scholar than as an American. Problematically for Dickinson, White attacked Shakespeare worshipers.[66] Instead of rejecting, criticizing, or ignoring this poorly educated man from Stratford, White emphasized known and often less favorable facts about him as a means of critiquing contemporary Shakespeare scholarship.

In 1884, White published a series of four articles, titled "The Anatomizing of William Shakespeare," in the *Atlantic,* summarizing his most important ideas about the playwright.[67] Shakespeare emerges as an imperfect genius and no saint: his origin, his lack of formal education, and his profession as an actor, meant he was coarse and vulgar, which explains his carelessness and recklessness as a writer, and his deficient literary knowledge. White attacks the "squeamish objection" to his annotation in his 1884 Riverside edition for certain words "not quite readable aloud in mixed company"; these demonstrate that Shakespeare, although he often represented the loveliest and sweetest aspects of human nature, was also "often gross for grossness' sake" to please the groundlings.[68] Without appearing to justify it, White informs his readers about Shakespeare's frequent borrowing from literary predecessors; but he does acknowledge the bard's power of transformation, which he calls "the most nearly miraculous manifestation of the all-forming power that the earth has ever seen."[69] Despite his talents, White emphasizes that Shakespeare wrote without intellectual, moral, social, or religious aim, instead seeking only social advancement.[70] Other information about the man is even more unsettling, particularly that about his business dealings; in these, like Wilkes, White finds that this great genius of the world was an opportunist and materialist who through thrift and flattery gained social position.[71] (Unlike Wilkes, however, White respectfully notes that the proudest day of Shakespeare's life came when he saw himself described in a law document as "William Shakespeare, of Stratford-on-Avon in the county of Warwick, Gentleman.")[72] Moreover, so great was Shakespeare's desire for money that he would have burnt *King Lear, Hamlet* and *Othello* and promised never to rewrite them had Southampton offered to give him one thousand pounds.[73] This kind of information was certainly available to Dickinson, although it is impossible to know, considering her reverence for Shakespeare, how she would have responded to it.[74] She may have preferred the version of Shakespeare that Knight presented in his biography, which, as Samuel Schoenbaum notes, offers "nothing about Shakespeare and his family that would challenge the sensibility of a morally righteous and liberally orientated middle-class reader of the Victorian era."[75] Knight's Shakespeare is from a prosperous, middle-class family; he is well educated, and through his imagination and genius, he raises the lowly theater, not out of greed for money but from poetic ability. One of the pages in Dickinson's copy of this biography has a large dog-ear in a section titled "Solitary Hours." On both sides of this page, Knight emphasizes Shakespeare's observations and appreciation of the natural world, noting his "wonderful power of assimilation which perceives all the subtile and delicate relations between the moral and the physical worlds, and thus raises the objects of sense into a companionship with the loftiest things that belong to the fancy and the reason."[76]

For White, although there is much to admire in Shakespeare there is "nothing to worship"; yet he is not attacking Shakespeare, rather those who have turned him into a religion and made themselves into prophets, scribes, Pharisees, priests, and professional incense burners at his altar.[77] They anatomize Shakespeare, glorifying in his mystery, making his blemishes beautiful, and parasitically establishing their own literary reputations as Shakespeare guides and experts.[78] Such "criticism" consists of cries of praise, "O wonderful Shakespeare! O mysterious! O divine! protracted sometimes through hundreds of pages, or philosophic systems of Shakespeare's art which are hardly more than formulated folly."[79] White's own criticism focuses on the discovery of historical and social information about Shakespeare and his culture rather than such adulation. He argues that despite all their proselytizing, these writers' "revolutionary" views are actually reiteration of ideas about the plays already in circulation.[80] What White specifically objects to is that they try to appoint themselves mediators between Shakespeare and his readers, who he advises to "Throw the commentators and the editors to the dogs. Don't read any man's notes, or essays, or introductions, aesthetical, historical, philosophical, or philological. Don't read mine. Read the plays themselves."[81] A contemporary American reader is capable of engaging with Shakespeare and his texts as long as a skilled editor has accurately prepared them. Intelligent readers of today have the same power of apprehension as playgoers in Shakespeare's day. Like Bacon, Wilkes, and Lowell, White wants to remove Shakespeare from the purview of traditional criticism and biography, and celebrates the imaginative powers of ordinary readers and amateur scholars.

Dickinson's rejection of the idea that Francis Bacon wrote Shakespeare's plays (L721), her continual use of Shakespeare as a moral and literary oracle in her letters, and her use of his hierarchical language in her own poems suggest that she did not see him as Bacon, White, or Wilkes did. Her weaving of Shakespeare into her letters indicates a belief in his universality, morality, and wisdom; this aligns her most closely with Lowell. She probably agreed with him that "among the most alien races [Shakespeare] is as solidly at home as a mountain seen from different sides by many lands, itself superbly soliltary, yet the companion of all thoughts and domesticated in all imaginations" (184).

CHAPTER FOUR

"He has had his Future who has found Shakespeare"

American Nationalism and the English Dramatist

IN REPLY TO a letter from Franklin B. Sanborn that probably gave her information about recent books and asked for a literary contribution, Dickinson wrote, "Thank you, Mr Sanborn. I am glad there are Books. They are better than Heaven for that is unavoidable while one may miss these. Had I a trait you would accept I should be most proud, though he has had his Future who has found Shakespeare" (L 402). Johnson has dated the letter "about 1873," and by this time Sanborn was no longer the resident editor of the *Springfield Republican* and had returned with his family to Concord.[1] He continued to have a regular column in the paper as the correspondent from Boston and Concord, and was responsible for book notices.[2] Sanborn knew of Dickinson's writings either through her friend—and his boss—Samuel Bowles, or because seven of her poems had already been published in the paper.[3] But she contrasts her level of creativity with Shakespeare's overachieving accomplishments. Her reluctance to submit a poem is framed as a confirmation that Shakespeare supersedes all prospective authors, herself included. Dickinson's poems are like the hypothetical books too easily missed.

While Dickinson may feel ambiguity toward publishing, more significantly she is here placing herself in opposition to many of her contemporaries, who sought a different future for American literature—as a literature distinct from its English counterpart. Sanborn's autobiography, *Recollections of Seventy Years,* proclaims his great love of Shakespeare. He recalls that at eight he found odd volumes of *Henry VI, Richard III,* and *Henry VIII* and learnt these plays by heart; at twelve, he obtained Shakespeare's complete works.[4] In fact, he begins his recollections by differentiating his feelings at seventy-eight from those of Mortimer in *Henry VI, part 2,* who reflects disdainfully on his life to his young nephew, Richard, the ambitious Duke of York.[5] Yet despite his obvious love of Shakespeare, Sanborn throughout his recollections stresses his much stronger affiliations with American writers, especially Hawthorne, Emerson, and Thoreau. Moreover, Dickinson's remark quoted above is in sharp contrast to the sentiments of an 1852 letter by Ariana Smith Walker, who in August 1854 became Sanborn's wife:

> I do not like the boastful comparisons which Americans sometimes make, of their own merits with those of other countries; but I think it unjust that America should not calmly and wisely acknowledge the genius and talent which she has, and which is enough to enable her to hold up her head among the nations, and have no need to blush. She is a child still, it is true; and we cannot expect of a child what we demand of the strong man; but if she is a child she is no weak, puny babe, but an infant Hercules who can strangle some serpents which would crush many a grown man.[6]

For Walker, America's own literature must be regarded as pivotal, and although only in its infancy will in time be the world's most powerful writing. Walker goes on to praise American poets, like Emerson, Whittier, and Lowell, and novelists, among them Stowe, Hawthorne, Sedgwick, and Cooper. She condemns Americans who do not appreciate the great writers they have, noting that because of Emerson Americans "may stand up erect among the thinking men of England and France and Germany, and not be ashamed."[7] When Ariana died, eight days after they were married, Sanborn became anxious that no restoration should be performed on his New Hampshire homestead because he remembered there reading Shakespeare to Ariana "under a bright moon through many a splendid summer evening."[8] Although both Sanborn and his wife shared Dickinson's love of Shakespeare, it is unlikely either of them would have agreed with her declaration. In the year Sanborn received Dickinson's letter, he was living in the house of Thoreau's sister and busy editing a manuscript by William Ellery Channing;[9] the result was one of the first biographies of Thoreau: *Thoreau: the Poet Naturalist, with Memorial Verses* (1873), and Sanborn would go on to write or edit biographies of leading American literary figures: Thoreau (1882); John Brown (1885 with later editions); Bronson Alcott (1893); and Emerson (1901). In this context, Dickinson's statement seems out of place;[10] at the very least, she is a cultural provocateur, using the debate about Shakespeare and American literature to excuse refusing to submit a poem for publication.

"If it is not national, it is nothing"

Although recent Dickinson criticism has placed the poet and her poems firmly within her nineteenth-century American culture, her association with the promotion of a distinctively American literature remains tenuous. Most critics, if they mention her in relation to cultural nationalism, merely note the unusualness of Dickinson's lack of concern with an issue that provoked such potent responses from most of her contemporaries.[11] Robert Weisbuch argues that American literature emerged as in part a defensive drive in the face of overwhelming British literary achievement.[12] For him, there is no evidence that Dickinson shared the enmity and anxiety that American writers felt toward their British contemporaries. He does acknowledge, however, that certain traces of hostility manifest themselves in the language of some of her poems.[13] These traces seem inevitable considering the American history of conscious promotion of native literature. It was a frequent topic at Lyceum lectures; her brother, Austin, delivered an Amherst commencement oration entitled "The Elements of our National Literature" in August 1850, a month before Dana's lectures on Shakespeare (Leyda I 178–79). In 1855–56, the *Amherst Collegiate Magazine* published articles warning Americans of the dangers of servile imitation of English authors and arguing the inevitable and impending arrival of a distinctive American literature.[14] Such high ideals are manifest in the editorial policies of the American journals Dickinson read and in the condemnation of publications that popularized British writers in favor of American ones.[15] Dickinson's favorite journals published many of her contemporaries, among them Emerson, Melville, Whitman, Poe, Hawthorne, Longfellow, Cooper, James, Stowe, and Alcott. Similarly, gift books and anthologies that promoted American writing and achievement flooded the American market, culminating in E. A. and G. L. Duyckinck's two-volume *Cyclopaedia of American Literature* (1855), which sampled two centuries of American literature and was governed by a general design "to exhibit and illustrate the products of the pen on American soil."[16]

American novels also addressed the issue of a national literature, including one of Dickinson's favorites, Henry Wadsworth Longfellow's *Kavanagh* (1849).[17] In chapter 20, Mr. Hathaway, who is about to establish a magazine called *The Niagara* to promote American literature, explains his plan and the prospects for such a venture to Mr. Churchill, a writer. This is followed by Hathaway's account of how American literature was, at the time, generally understood:

> I think, Mr. Churchill . . . that we want a national literature commensurate with our mountains and rivers,—commensurate with Niagara, and the Alleghanies, and the Great Lakes . . . We want a national epic that shall correspond to the size of the country . . . We want a national drama in which scope enough shall be given to our gigantic ideas, and to the unparalleled activity and progress of our people! . . . In a word, we want a national literature altogether shaggy and unshorn, that shall shake the earth, like a herd of buffaloes, thundering over the prairies.[18]

Churchill disagrees with this and argues that literature is tied to the spiritual, not to the physical; for him, where a poet writes will not make his poetry distinctive or superior. In response, Hathaway declares, "If it is not national, it is nothing" (367). Churchill goes on to explain that what is more important than a national literature is a literature that is universal, that speaks to all men. For him, American literature is a continuation of its English counterpart, "we are very like the English,—are, in fact, English under a different sky—I do not see how our literature can be very different from theirs" (367–68). When asked by Hathaway for a contribution to his magazine, Churchill remarks, in a manner that echoes Dickinson's refusal to Sanborn, "my writings are too insignificant" (371). Yet finally, by appealing to his "personal vanity," Hathaway persuades Churchill to offer something to his American magazine.

The man Dickinson chose as her "Preceptor," Thomas Wentworth Higginson, appears to have shared Churchill's view.[19] The relationship began in April 1862 when she read Higginson's essay "Letter to a Young Contributor" in the *Atlantic Monthly,* in which he encouraged the journal's readers to become "Atlantic contributors."[20] He told readers that "American literature is now thoroughly out of leading-strings" and that "to the previous traditions and associations of the English tongue we add resources of contemporary life such as England cannot rival" (406). The American audience that was the first to appreciate recent British authors, such as the Brownings, Tennyson, and Carlyle, "can certainly trust its own literary instincts." He refers to the unique political, educational, and industrial features of American life, and the fact that the "mixture of nationalities" is constantly rejuvenating the language and mental costume of American thought. He warns of the powerful mystique of English authors: "Keats and Lamb seem to our young people to be existences as remote and legendary as Homer" (409). Readers are reminded, "'To-Day is a king in disguise,' and . . . this American literature of ours will be just as classic a thing, if we do our part, as any which the past has treasured." Nevertheless, Higginson praises British writers throughout this article and when he asked Dickinson about her favorite writers, despite her more assorted tastes, she chose the authors he had commended (L261).[21] His 1867 *Atlantic* article "A Plea for Culture" is more explicit in its suggestion that high culture is British and classical.[22] By contrast, "American literature is not yet copious, American scholarship not profound, American society not highly intellectual, and the American style of execution, in all high arts, yet hasty and superficial" (33). He calls on America to "recognize as a nation, the value of all culture and resolutely organize it into our institutions." To "be ranked among the productive nations in literature," America needs a climate open to all things of intellectual and cultural significance rather than one obsessed with native literature (37).[23] Consequently, American literature's "full harvest" must be postponed but is sure to ripen:

> Everything is here, between these Atlantic and Pacific shores, save only the perfected utterance that comes with years. Between Shakespeare in his cradle and Shakespeare in Hamlet there was needed but an interval of time, and the same sublime condition is all that lies between the America of toil and the America of art.

The futurity of American literary achievement is definite; but there is also the caution that "any misconceived patronage—to call anything art merely because it interests us as American—must react against us in the end." Unfortunately, "neither man nor nation can develop by defying traditions"; they must first master and remold "the fine arts." After reading this article, and to reestablish their lapsed correspondence, Dickinson wrote Higginson, "Bringing still my 'plea for Culture,' Would it teach me now?" (L323). Although she may have originally written him because she agreed to some extent with his emphasis on the "intrinsic worth" of literature as a civilizing medium, she perhaps shared his view that "British" literature was superior to its fledging American counterpart.[24]

In her one poem that explicitly addresses nationality, "The Robin's my Criterion for Tune -" (F256), Dickinson's speaker argues that poetic perspective depends on place, declaring that she sees "New Englandly." Although seeming to identify her subject matter and perspective as American, she concludes by noting the relative nature of all outlooks: "The Queen, discerns like me - / Provincially -." Dickinson's letters praise and refer to American and English authors without making any distinction between the two.[25] Thus, as Higginson expressed it, "Art is higher than nations, older than many centuries; its code includes no local or partial provisions."[26] Moreover, when Dickinson tells Sanborn that the "Future" of literature is Shakespeare, she is speaking of his universality, not his nationality. Perhaps, like many of her contemporaries, she regarded Shakespeare as not threatening but benign, honor-bestowing.[27] Probably, she agreed with James Fenimore Cooper that "The authors, previously to the revolution, are common property, and it is quite idle to say that the American has not just as good a right to claim Milton, and Shakespeare, and all the old masters of the language, for his countrymen, as an Englishman."[28] Like the reviewer of Lowell's essay on Shakespeare, she may have believed that "Shakespeare's solidity of understanding kept him thoroughly national as an Englishman, while his gift of imagination, qualifying that, put him in effective sympathy with all men of every race; that this temperament belongs to great poets generally, and is indeed the prerogative of genius."[29]

The Astor Place Riot, however, and Wilkes's critique of Shakespeare's politics, suggest that his reception in nineteenth-century America was more complex. As Thomas Cartelli demonstrates, the interpretation of Shakespeare as the personification of Englishness and English aristocratic ideals caused "admittedly exceptional, but recurring, voices" of dissent and opposition.[30] An instance appears in an April 1846 review of Carlyle by Edgar Allan Poe, in the *Democratic Review,* in which he attacks those who place Shakespeare above all other authors:

> Your Shakspeare worshippers, for example—what do they know about Shakspeare? They worship him—rant about him—lecture about him—about *him, him,* and nothing else. . . . They have arrived at an idea of his greatness from the pertinacity with which men have called him great.[31]

This indicates how the "worship" of Shakespeare was regarded by an American writer like Poe despite his own great love for and thorough involvement with Shakespeare's plays.[32] This conflict was intensified by Shakespeare's appropriation by conservative and antidemocratic critics who, like Dana, put his unrivaled genius up against what they regarded as an infinitely inferior and stifled American literature. Along with Dana, one of the most influential of these was the editor and critic Henry Norman Hudson, a High Church Episcopalian minister and a member of the "Old America" party of Boston.[33] Having dedicated his *Lectures on Shakspeare* (1848) to Dana, Hudson unequivocally declares, "Shakspeare, by general concession, is the greatest name in literature. Such various, and, at the same time, such exalted powers, probably never met together in the mind of any other human being. Whether we regard the kind or the degree of his faculties, he not only is, but is everywhere allowed to be, the prodigy of our race."[34] In his later work, *Shakespeare: His Life, Art and Characters* (1872), Hudson affirms that "Shakespeare's poetry will stand the test of [moral] principles better than any other writing we have outside the Bible."[35] Throughout his criticism, Hudson champions hierarchy, monarchy, and tradition against the flawed ideals of equality and individualism in American society and politics.[36] For her to choose Shakespeare as her favorite author and the "future" of literature might mean that Dickinson shared Hudson's views and the social and political values that lay beneath them. Dana and Hudson may be among the conservative intellectuals who, according to Domhnall Mitchell, influenced her preference, especially in later life, for British authors, like Shakespeare, over Americans. If so, Dickinson stands away from contemporaries like Emerson, Melville, and Whitman, whose public remarks on Shakespeare are inseparable from their articulation of their commitment to American literature, and who attack those who advocate Shakespeare as a genius unrivaled and unsurpassable in human history. Yet though they opposed the idea that Shakespeare was the "future" of literature, their attitudes were ambiguous, and they shared in and even at times exceeded

Dickinson's praise of him. Might she, in turn, have shared their skepticism about Shakespeare?

"Climes beyond the solar road probably call this planet not Earth but Shakespeare"

Emerson was one of the most passionate spokesmen for American cultural independence. Most famously in his "The American Scholar" lecture (1837), he attacked those who endorsed the idea that, "The book, the college, the school of art, the institution of any kind, stop with some past utterance of genius. This is good say they,—let us hold by this. They pin me down. They look backwards and not forward."[37] Instead, Emerson proposes that "Every age, it is found, must write its own books . . . the books of an older period will not fit this" and that books are "for nothing but to inspire" (I 56). Many of the remarks in his journals and essays, though, unequivocally record Emerson's great love for Shakespeare; he calls him a god, and praises his penetrating insights into human nature, his translation of nature into universal truths, and his impartiality.[38] In 1838, Emerson writes in his journal, "Yet . . . not I, or any man, or all men, produce any thing comparable to one scene in Hamlet or Lear. With all my admiration for this life-like picture,—set me to producing a match for it, and I should instantly depart into mouthing rhetoric."[39] In 1859, he says, "I delight in the persons who clearly perceive the transcendent superiority of Shakspeare to all other writers."[40] His feelings were also apparent when he played a key role in the tercentennial celebration of Shakespeare's birth for the Saturday Club, on 24 April 1864;[41] he is recorded as having said, "The climes beyond the solar road probably call this planet not Earth but Shakespeare."[42] In the manuscript of his lecture to the club, he calls Shakespeare, "the first poet of the world," praising his "transcendent reach" of thought that dwarfs "all writers without a solitary exception."[43] Shakespeare is superior to men of all "other nations and other times" and is equated with nature; both console "our mortal condition." In fact, Emerson's speech ends, "the Pilgrims came to Plymouth in 1620. The plays of Shakespeare's were not published until three years later. Had they been published earlier, our forefathers, or the most poetical among them, might have stayed at home to read them."[44] The temptation of these dramatic works would have prevented even some antitheatrical Puritans from leaving England, and halted the colonization of America itself.[45]

But the complexity of Emerson's response to Shakespeare is evident in his essay "Shakespeare or the Poet," first given as a lecture in 1846 and published in *Representative Men* (1850). Dickinson called this volume "a little Granite Book you can lean upon" (L481), and must have read this most renowned and influential essay on Shakespeare.[46] Lowell's 1868 essay on Shakespeare (see chapter 3) is very derivative of Emerson's, although his discussion centers on language, whereas Emerson addresses Shakespeare's originality. Emerson begins by defending the bard against those who criticize his borrowings from other writers; in the process, he redefines creativity. "Great men are more distinguished by range and extent, than by originality," and "The greatest genius is the most indebted man" (IV 109). Genius is receptiveness and indebtedness to all that is in an artist's literary and social environment, and Shakespeare is the "great poet, who appears in illiterate times, absorbs into his sphere all the light which is anywhere radiating" (IV 113). Like Thomas Carlyle's Shakespeare, Emerson's is a "bringer of light"; he becomes Emerson's representative poet, however, because his "heart [was] in unison with his time and country" and "The rude warm blood of the living England circulated in the play[s]" (IV 109, 111).[47] Shakespeare wrote when "a great body of stage plays" existed and were treated "with more or less skill, by every playwright" until it was "no longer possible to say who wrote them first," as they were the property of the theater itself and appropriated by all. Like the Bible, Shakespeare's plays were "no man's work, but came by wide social labour, when a thousand wrought like one, sharing the same impulse" (IV 114–15). How might Dickinson have reacted to the idea that art was not the product of unique private experiences, rather of moments of collaboration with her society? Certainly, she was concerned with her own originality and aware of her status as "the only Kangaroo among the Beauty" (L268). In December 1873, during their second meeting, she told Higginson that "there is always one thing to be grateful for—that one is one's self & not somebody else" (L405). Yet in one of her assertions of her own unique creativity she is attentive to the possibility of indebtedness: "I marked a line in One Verse - because I met it after I made it - and never consciously touch a paint, mixed by another. I do not let it go because it is mine" (L271). In fact, she appears to have been very interested in the ways in which ideas and thoughts are shared. Emerson's Shakespeare sounds very like Dickinson's own definition of the poet as someone who "Distills amazing sense / From Ordinary Meanings - " that is, "From the familiar species / That perished by the Door - "; this poem, of course, is written from the perspective of an envious reader who wonders why "it was not Ourselves / Arrested it - before - " (F446). Like Emerson, she suggests that the ingredients out of which a poem is produced are somehow available to all, although it is the renowned poet who appropriates and transforms them. And there are examples of Dickinson transforming the works of other writers. As Higginson, one of her victims, noted after reading her rewriting of his poem "Decoration," "It is the condensed essence of [my poem] & so far finer."[48] In many other poems Dickinson presents poetry as a collaboration between poets—who "light but Lamps," offering "Each Age a Lens" and disseminating their "Circumference"—and later readers, who are inspired and "stimulate[d]," if these poems offer "vital Light," to go on to create new works of art (F930).[49]

Although the poet's lamps may "inhere as do the Suns," the poets "Themselves - go out." Similarly, Emerson's Shakespeare has "no discoverable egotism" and he draws "up the ladder after him," leaving no history (IV 121, 119). Consequently, "whatever scraps of information concerning his conditions these researches may have rescued, they can shed no light upon the infinite invention which is the concealed magnet of his attraction for us" (IV 118). Emerson goes on to articulate what might almost be the manifesto for Dickinson's poetry: "It is the essence of poetry to spring, like the rainbow daughter of Wonder, from the invisible, to abolish the past, and refuse all history." For an unknown, like Dickinson, Emerson encouragingly emphasizes that Shakespeare, the "popular player," was not suspected of being the "poet of the human race"; his age "lets pass without a single valuable note the founder of another dynasty, which alone will cause the Tudor dynasty to be remembered" (IV 116). To Dickinson, Shakespeare might thus be the greatest example of the undervalued poet who finally gains a posthumous recognition, despite the indifference of his contemporaries and his own carelessness with his manuscripts.[50] By contrasting the indifference of the Elizabethans to Shakespeare with the modern obsession with him, Emerson implies that genius is not absolute but relative to circumstances: it cannot be assumed or projected with certainty into the future.

Nevertheless, "Now literature, philosophy, and thought are Shakspearized," and Shakespeare is involved in questions of morality, manners, economy, philosophy, religion, taste, and the conduct of life:

> He wrote the text of modern life; of manners; he drew the man of England and Europe; the father of the man in America: he drew the man, and described the day, and what is done in it: he read the hearts of men and women, their probity, and their second thoughts and wiles; the wiles of innocence, and the transitions by which virtues and vices slide into their contraries (IV 121).

Shakespeare is doubly the "representative" poet: his works are collaborations with the spirit of his Elizabethan age, and yet they are also the origin of modernity and modern human consciousness. Emerson's Shakespeare is the medium through which modern life is conducted.[51] He is "like some saint whose history is to be rendered into all languages," and "the occasion which gave the saint's meaning . . . is immaterial, compared with the universality of its application"

(IV 120). It is not only Shakespeare's debts "in all directions" and his impersonality that prevent his pervasive influence from being ominous for an American writer; Emerson suggests that his origin is irrelevant in light of his relevance today. The most indebted man becomes a most suitable writer for an American society anxious about its own many cultural debts—including Shakespeare's texts themselves. America and Shakespeare become almost equivalent, for both transform their cultural inheritance.[52] Shakespeare clarifies how the representative American poet should assimilate the many voices of American culture.[53]

From this point of high praise, Emerson's ends with dissatisfaction, that Shakespeare led "an obscure and profane life, using his genius for the public amusement" and sharing "the halfness and imperfection of humanity" (IV 125, 124). "The world," he declares, "still wants its poet-priest, a reconciler who shall not trifle, with Shakspeare the player, nor shall grope in graves, with Swedenborg the mourner, but who shall see, speak and act, with equal inspiration." Although this may simply reflect Emerson's antitheatrical prejudice, his dismissal of Shakespeare on moral grounds is inseparable from the bard's problematic status in relation to the promotion of a specifically American literature. Thus when Emerson says that Shakespeare is the man whose thoughts "the foremost people of the world are now for some ages to be nourished," this is not the same as what Dickinson wrote to Sanborn. As Emerson declares in "The Poet" (1844), "America is a poem in our eyes; its ample geography dazzles the imagination and it will not wait long for metres" (III 22). He recalls the awe he has experienced in the presence of a young poet who has written "under this very roof, by your side," saying, "We sat in the aurora of a sunrise which was to put out all the stars. Boston seemed to be at twice the distance it had the night before, or was much farther than that. Rome,—what was Rome? Plutarch and Shakspeare were in the yellow leaf" (III 7). Compared with the fresh power of American writing and inspiration, Shakespeare's plays are dated and stale. The power of his works "resemble[s] a mirror carried through the street, ready to render an image of every created thing": his literary supremacy depends on his ability to be representative (III 23). Yet Shakespeare becomes a more intimidating figure in Emerson's *Nature* (1836); here he possesses, beyond all other poets, the power of "subordinating nature for the purposes of expression. His imperial muse tosses the creation like a bauble from hand to hand, and uses it to embody any capricious shade of thought that is uppermost in his mind" (I 31–32). Comparing him to *The Tempest*'s Prospero, Emerson presents Shakespeare as the all-powerful artist who is able to appropriate all objects, and to make connections between the remotest things: all material objects are transfigured through his "passion" as a poet. The bard animates nature "like a creator, with his own thoughts." Through the power of his poetry, Shakespeare is "magnify[ing] the small" and "micrify[ing] the great."

"I fancy that this moment Shakspeare in heaven ranks with Gabriel Raphael and Michael. And if another Messiah ever comes twill be in Shakspeare's person"

There is no evidence that Dickinson read Herman Melville, or that she shared the views of the "Young America" movement and the Democratic Party, with which Melville was associated (L285).[54] This movement's unflinching defense of all things American largely shaped Melville's response to Shakespeare; yet his engagement with the bard offers interesting parallels with Dickinson's own. In a 24 February 1849 letter to Everet A. Duyckinck, one of the founders of "Young America," Melville records his own rediscovery of Shakespeare:[55]

> Dolt & and ass that I am I have lived more than 29 years, & until a few days ago, never made close acquaintance with divine William. Ah, he's full of sermons-on-the-mount, and gentle, aye, almost as Jesus. I take such men to be inspired. I fancy that this moment Shakspeare in heaven ranks with Gabriel Raphael and Michael. And if another Messiah ever comes twill be in Shakspeare's person.[56]

Melville here makes the commonplace deification of Shakespeare even more blasphemous.[57] While Dickinson merely presents him as the "future" of literature, Melville has him replacing Christ at the Second Coming, the future savior of the human race. In his next letter to Duyckinck, on March 3, Melville has to defend his remarks because he has been teased or even reprimanded:

> To one of your habits of thought, I confess that in my last, I seemed, but only *seemed* irreverent. And do not think, my boy, that because I, impulsively broke forth in jubillations over Shakspeare, that, therefore, I am of the number of the *snobs* who burn their tuns of rancid fat at his shrine. No, I would stand afar off & alone, & burn some pure Palm oil, the product of some overtopping trunk.— I would to God Shakspeare had lived later, & promenaded in Broadway. Not that I might have had the pleasure of leaving my card for him at the Astor, or made merry with him over a bowl of the fine Duyckinck punch; but that the muzzle which all men wore on their souls in the Elizabethan day, might not have intercepted Shakspeare full articulation. Now I hold it a verity, that even Shakspeare, was not a frank man to the uttermost. And, indeed, who in this intolerable Universe is, or can be? But the Declaration of Independence makes a difference. (122)

Dickinson probably never had to defend her worship of Shakespeare in this way; her allusions to Shakespeare and his works may express precisely the upper-class affiliations Melville wants to avoid. He attempts to make his engagement with Shakespeare personal, presenting himself as "afar off & alone" in a reverence that has nothing to do with public displays at shrines, or class condescension, but is simply a result of Shakespeare's greatness. Possibly, like Melville, Dickinson regarded her love of Shakespeare as beyond what it might connote politically and socially. Yet Melville regrets that Shakespeare was not born in America and has not "promenaded in Broadway," which would remove the "muzzle which all men wore on their souls in the Elizabethan day." While all writers are restricted to some extent in their expression, he concludes that being American alters this. The "Declaration of Independence makes a difference"; the implication is that Shakespeare would have been superior writer had he been an American.

In his review "Hawthorne and His Mosses," printed in *Literary World* (1850), Melville celebrates a writer who has equaled Shakespeare, but is unrecognized for his achievement by American critics.[58] He attacks those who lavish "blind, unbridled admiration" on Shakespeare and would denounce the comparison: "They may say, that if an illustration were needed, a lesser light might have sufficed to elucidate this Hawthorne, this small man of yesterday."[59] But "There are hardly five critics in America; and several of them are asleep," and Melville reprimands those who when they look "forward to the coming of a great literary genius among us, they somehow fancy he will come in the costume of Queen Elizabeth's day; be a writer of dramas founded upon old English history, or the tales of Boccaccio."[60] He accuses these critics of what he himself had proposed earlier, calling it "Anglo-Saxon superstition," which teaches "all noble-souled aspirants that there is no hope for them" and that we must "pronounce Shakspeare absolutely unapproachable."[61] This unapproachability does not take into account the fact that, according to Melville, "men not very much inferior to Shakspeare, are this day being born on the banks of the Ohio." Whereas Emerson makes Shakespeare a model for the democratic poet, Melville presents all the people of a democratic America as potential Shakespeares. Like Emerson, he argues that poets must be "parts of the times; they themselves are the times"; and that if Shakespeare "has not been equalled, give the world time and he is sure to be surpassed, in one hemisphere or the other."[62] Nature has not yet been fully "ransacked by our progenitors, so that no new charms and mysteries remain for this latter generation to find," and "The trillionth part has not yet been said; and all that has been said, but multiplies the avenues to what remains to be said." For Melville, the difference between Shakespeare and Hawthorne is "by no means immeasurable. Not a very great deal more, and Nathaniel were verily William." Going further, he argues for a "republican progressiveness" in life and literature: "let America first praise mediocrity even, in her own children, before she praises . . . the best excellence in the children of any other land."[63] Dickinson would probably have disagreed with the standards Melville is proposing, and with his equating Hawthorne with Shakespeare.[64] But Melville is not attacking Shakespeare, only his American reception, and he proceeds to aspects of the bard to which Dickinson was probably greatly attracted.

First, his is not the Shakespeare of the "tricky stage"—the "mere man of Richard-the-third humps, and Macbeth daggers."[65] Moreover, the "infinite obscure" of Shakespeare's elusive character is the background from which he fashions his "grandest conceits, the things that have made for Shakspeare his loftiest, but most circumscribed renown, as the profoundest of thinkers." Shakespeare's life does not limit the meaning of his works, and, his words include "those occasional flashings-forth of the intuitive Truth," and "short, quick probings at the very axis of reality." Like the "blackness" of innate sin and depravity in Hawthorne's works, Shakespeare's own "power of blackness" fascinates Melville, although it is not discerned by most readers, who have not read him "deeply" and certainly do not extol him for this aspect of his work. Dickinson, who sought a reader with the "rare Ear" or "rewarding person" that might understand her, would certainly have appreciated Melville's distinction between types of reader (F945).[66] There are meanings in Shakespeare that evade most readers, stagegoers, and conservative critics, which manifest themselves in his "dark characters" Hamlet, Timon, Lear, and Iago. Through their mouths, Shakespeare "craftily says, or sometimes insinuates the things which we feel to be so terrifically true, that it were all but madness for any good man, in his own proper character, to utter, or even hint of them." Lear tears off his mask and "speaks the sane madness of vital truth"; and like Hawthorne, Shakespeare, in a world of lies where Truth "is forced to fly like a scared white doe," reveals his true meaning only in "cunning glimpses." Shakespeare is one of the masters of "the great Art of Telling the Truth" about darker and most unsettling aspects of humanity. Although others discovered morality and traditional Christian teachings in the plays, Dickinson, like Melville, may have been attracted to the "Innate Depravity" that Shakespeare's plays explore. Her poetry's examination of various terrifying psychological states, human depravity, and near madness probably owed much to her intense interest in Shakespeare's tragedies.[67] In a January 1895 letter, replying to distortions about Emily's life that had arisen from autobiographical readings of some poems, Lavinia was adamant that her sister's "intense verses were no more personal experiences than Shakespeare's tragedies."[68] Certainly Dickinson, as a middle-class nineteenth-century woman, was adept at the craft of telling the truth in a "slanted" manner, imitating Shakespeare's ability to allow darker truths to "dazzle gradually / Or every man be blind -" (F1263).

Although he suggests that "no American writer should write like an Englishman," Melville's own appropriations of Shakespeare were seen even by his early reviewers.[69] Some commended his abilities at characterization and his depths of pathos as Shakespearean, comparing *Pierre* (1852) with *Hamlet* and *The Confidence Man* (1857) with *Timon of Athens.*[70] Developing such insights, Charles Olson has explored the Shakespearean themes, images, and characters found in Melville's prose, particularly in *Moby-Dick,* suggesting that "the Crew is where what America stands for got into *Moby-Dick.* They're what we *imagine* democracy to be. They're Melville's addition to tragedy as he took it from Shakespeare."[71] F. O. Matthiessen, identifying echoes and allusions in Melville's work, writes, "Shakespeare's conception of tragedy had so grown into the fibre of Melville's thought that much of his mature work became a re-creation of its themes in modern terms"[72]; he suggests that Melville was trying to offer America a story about whaling to satisfy the groundlings together with a study of Ahab's tragic character and a metaphysical approach to the "Whiteness of the Whale" for more intellectual readers.[73] Melville's creative engagement with the "darker" aspects of Shakespeare represents both an effort to make the Elizabethan more suitable for American democracy, and his need, like Shakespeare's, to appeal to two distinguishable audiences.[74]

"The great poems, Shakspere included, are poisonous to the idea of the pride and dignity of the common people, the life-blood of democracy"

Although Dickinson did not assert that Walt Whitman was "disgraceful"—rather, she was told he was—there is no evidence that she read his works (L261).[75] Unlike Emerson, Melville, and many of her other contemporaries, she probably disagreed with Whitman's declaration that "The New World (America) is the region of the future; its poetry must be spiritual and democratic."[76] The Amherst poet would also have disliked the severity of Whitman's critique of Shakespeare's politics. In 1871, in *Democratic Vistas,* he argued that Shakespeare's "[great] poems are poisonous to the idea of the pride and dignity of the common people, the life-blood of democracy. The models of our literature, as we get it from other lands, ultramarine, have their births in courts, and bask'd and grown in castle sunshine; all smells of princes' favors" (II 388). In Whitman's writings, Shakespeare is frequently associated with tyranny, superstition, and "that principle of caste which we Americans have come to destroy" (II 476). In "A Thought on Shakespeare" (1886), Whitman, like George Wilkes (see chapter 3), criticizes the playwright's representations of the lower class:

> The low characters, mechanics, even the loyal henchmen—all in themselves nothing—serve as capital foils to the aristocracy. The comedies (exquisite as they certainly are) bringing in admirably portray'd common characters, have the unmistakable hue of plays, portraits, made for the divertisement only of the élite of the castle, and from its point of view. The comedies are altogether non-acceptable to America and Democracy. (II 558)

For Whitman, although Shakespeare is "the loftiest of singers life has yet given voice to," his works "belong in America just about as much as the persons and institutions they depict" (II 720–21).

Whitman acknowledges, however, the power of Shakespeare's characters, which perform "a service incalculably precious to our America": our authors can "popularize and enlarge, and present again in our own growths" his "perfect *personnel*" (II 476). Thus, the individualism and "interiority" of Shakespeare's characters offer models for writers like Dickinson: Whitman says that these "splendid personalizations" are "formulated on the largest, freest, most heroic, most artistic mould," providing precious models for democracy (II 565). Moreover, Whitman's essay "What Lurks Behind Shakspeare's Historical Plays" (1884) argues that the history plays rather than the "dramas of the passions" are "greater than anything else in recorded literature" (II 554). Following the theory of Delia Bacon, Whitman argues that in Shakespeare's plays there is "an *essentially controlling plan*":

> Will it not indeed be strange if the author of "Othello" and "Hamlet" is destin'd to live in America, in a generation or two, less as the cunning draughtsman of the passions, and more as putting on record the first full exposé—and by far the most vivid one, immeasurably ahead of doctrinaires and economists—of the political theory and result, or the reason-why and necessity for them which America has come on earth to abnegate and replace? (II 556)

Particularly in the history plays, readers can discern "the scientific inauguration of Modern Democracy" that demonstrates the bankruptcy of aristocracy. Although it is a "secondary consideration," Whitman ends this essay by saying that Shakespeare's critique of feudalism was a "more or less conscious" artistic decision.

According to Richard Clarence Harrison, an "actuating motive" and "one of the springs of" Whitman's poetry was his belief that he was the poet of democracy, Shakespeare the poet of feudalism.[77] In fact, Whitman was a great lover of Shakespeare and a regular theatergoer, and was especially influenced by the interaction between audience and performers that was a central part of Shakespearean theater in that day.[78] As a reader, he cut up cheap secondhand copies of the plays, pasting them into personal notebooks; he also recited Shakespeare's lines on Broadway stagecoaches and after bathing at Coney Island.[79] Assimilating Shakespeare's works, he carried them over into his own prose and poems.[80] In 1890, a contemporary reviewer, Jonathan Trumbull, asked readers of *Poet-Lore* if there was room in America for both Shakespeare, a royalist, and Whitman, a democrat.[81] A year later, Whitman informed Trumbull that poetry was an evolutionary process in which Shakespeare marked an important stage, but that "the New World (America) is the region of the future, and its poetry must be spiritual and democratic" (II 675).[82] Throughout his writings, Whitman like his contemporaries attempts to determine how American writers should work with "the old hereditaments, legends, poems, theologies, and even customs, with fitting respect and toleration, and at the same time clearly understand and justify, and be devoted to and exploit our own day" (II 667). In fact, he names Shakespeare as among the poetic "heirlooms," without which he could not himself have written. As Trumbull observes, though, Whitman saw "an insufficiency in Shakespeare," a "difference and gap between the poetry which we of America need and the poetry of Shakespeare."[83] Might Dickinson also have expressed this sense?

"Drama's Vitallest Expression is the Common Day"

Dickinson's one explicit reference to Shakespeare in her poetry, "Drama's Vitallest Expression is the Common Day," is not a song of devotion to him and is, accordingly, unlike many others written by her contemporaries, including Fanny Kemble and Herman Melville.[84] This 1863 poem contests a commonplace notion, that Shakespeare has, as Emerson was to put it in 1864, "taught us that the little world of the heart is vaster, deeper, and richer than the spaces of astronomy. What shocks of surprise and sympathetic power this battery, which he is, imparts to every fine mind that is born!"[85] In contrast to that expression—and to her own many later exuberant declarations of bardolatry—this poem asserts the existence of compelling, daily, internal dramas more potent and real than Shakespeare's plays. For the speaker, that which is most personal in the human experience is still unrecorded; although Shakespeare and his characters have examined the vast spaces of the heart, there remains something to be written about.[86] Although it is framed as an attack on the theatrical as opposed to the real, the poem in the process beards Shakespeare's unapproachable and unrivalled greatness and questions the authoritativeness of his presentations of characters and his insight into humanity. Here Dickinson employs language very similar to that of her skeptical male contemporaries. Like Emerson, the speaker asserts that Shakespeare's characters, to some extent, record the minds and hearts of the "common" people; but for both

Emerson and this speaker he has not gone far enough: the world still awaits a poet who will capture the intricacies of the most personal experiences. Her line "'Hamlet' to Himself were Hamlet - / Had not Shakespeare wrote -" echoes Melville's suggestion that Shakespeare is approached and that "hardly a mortal man, who, at some time or other, has not felt as great thoughts in him as any you will find in Hamlet. We must not inferentially malign mankind for the sake of any one man, whoever he may be."[87] Although Dickinson may not be specifically referring to Americans, she may like Melville be arguing that Shakespeare's representations were to an extent "muzzled," and that American writers are freer to record the powerful, even darker side, of humanity. Her opposition of Shakespeare's drama and the drama of "common" humanity is like Whitman's opposition of pro-aristocratic literature and a higher democratic art. This more "vital" and unrecorded drama equally corresponds with Whitman's suggestion that American writers must expand upon the "splendid personalizations of Shakspere" and make them suit an American subject matter.

But Dickinson qualifies what may be democratic and nationalistic skepticism. According to this poem the forceful and effective "Expression" of drama is not enacted by all, only by "the best," and "When the Audience is scattered / And the Boxes shut." There is, for her, an essential hierarchy of skill.[88] Moreover, the more vivid drama of everyday life is connected with a female-specific, domestic, and undisclosed sphere, beyond the realm of audiences. While Emerson, Melville, and Whitman continually address the problem of Shakespeare in their writings, Dickinson refers to him just once in her poetry, and appears to dismiss him with one line. Although she celebrates Shakespeare's genius in her letters, this effortless demotion suggests that she did not suffer the same kind of anxiety about his influence that her male contemporaries did.[89]

CHAPTER FIVE

"Pity me, however, I have finished Ramona. Would that like Shakespeare, it were just published!"

Shakespeare and Women Writers

IN A NOVEMBER 1871 letter to Higginson, alluding to Helen Hunt Jackson's recently published *Verses* (1870), Dickinson wrote, "Mrs. Hunt's Poems are stronger than any written by Women since Mrs - Browning, with the exception of Mrs. Lewes - but truth like Ancestor's Brocades can stand alone" (L368). Despite her praise for the achievement of these women poets, she concludes by noting, "While Shakespeare remains Literature is firm - An Insect cannot run away with Achilles' Head." It appears that compared with Shakespeare even her favorite women writers are no more than pathetic and ludicrous insects. This is strange considering the poet's admiration for Elizabeth Barrett Browning and George Eliot.[1] And Dickinson makes this remark to Higginson, a great supporter of women's writing, who regarded his protégée, Hunt, as "one of the most gifted poetesses in America" (Leyda II 131). Perhaps ambivalence, envy, and competitiveness accompanied her praise of and gratitude toward these women.[2]

Dickinson's relationship with Helen Hunt Jackson is particularly interesting: they shared a common mentor, exchanged letters, and met at least three times.[3] Jackson offered Dickinson much encouragement to publish, begging her to "sing aloud" (L444a) and pleading with her to "send a poem" for inclusion in the No Name series, *A Masque of Poets* (L573a); later, in 1884, Jackson even asked to be Dickinson's literary executor (L937a).[4] Jackson, however, herself had an ambiguous attitude toward the poet. In 1879, after receiving two of Dickinson's poems about birds, "One of the ones that Midas touched" (F1488) and "A Route of Evanescence" (F1489), she wrote, "We have blue birds here - I might have had the sense to write something about one myself, but never did: and now I never can. For which I am inclined to envy, and perhaps hate you" (L601a). In 1884, after having read Jackson's new novel, *Ramona*, Dickinson told her, "Pity me, however, I have finished Ramona. Would that like Shakespeare, it were just published!" (L976). *Ramona* was about the plight of Native American tribes in America, and Jackson sought political change by presenting the disgraceful way they were being treated by Americans and their government.[5] The meaning of Dickinson's remark surely baffled Jackson[6]; were *Ramona* like Shakespeare's works, could she then read it repeatedly and find it remained new and exciting? In 1895 Lavinia suggested that Emily "considered Mrs. Jackson's intellect very rare . . . [and] often spoke in praise of Ramona."[7] But perhaps, like Lowell, Dickinson felt that "the highest office of a great poet is to show us how much variety, freshness, and opportunity abides in the obvious and familiar," and believed that Shakespeare "invents nothing, but seems rather to *re*-discover the world about him, and his penetrating vision gives to things of daily encounter something of the strangeness of new creation."[8] She may have been harshly contrasting the continuing readability of Shakespeare, his infinite novelty, with Jackson's recently published but already "finished" novel. Perhaps, unlike the plight of the Native Americans, the suffering of Shakespeare's characters was unendingly alive for her.

Dickinson's contrasting of Shakespeare with women writers was timely, considering that women like Browning and Eliot were often, as a compliment, termed "female Shakespeares."[9] Like Shakespeare, they were specifically praised for their skills at characterization, their powers of sympathetic identification, their moral insight, and their representation of complex emotional states.[10] In 1850, unaware at the time that *Jane Eyre* had been written by Charlotte Brontë, an essayist in *The Indicator* praised "that Shakespeare of novelists, Currer Bell," for his (her) ability to faithfully represent "every-day life" and its real characters.[11] Women writers and critics throughout the centuries—even before his canonization in the mid-eighteenth century—regarded Shakespeare as a source of literary and intellectual support and identification.[12] Women readers found in the plays "personal" portraits of themselves; Shakespeare was not a threatening male who thwarted their creativity. In addition, the critical transformation of Shakespeare from literary rule breaker to literary rule maker by the Romantics was predicated on their celebration of his "feminine" qualities—his all-encompassing sympathy, his ego-less genius, and his altruism.[13] In fact, his elusiveness offered women writers a model of authorship consistent with the dominant view of proper femininity in the period. Thus, women writers, identified with and responded to Shakespeare, creatively appropriating his plays and his characters. This may be why Dickinson saw competitiveness between women writers and Shakespeare; their revisions involve a development and expansion of the hidden inner worlds of his characters, which by implication his plays had insufficiently explored. Their supplementation of Shakespeare's internal sphere is, to return to Dickinson's poem, more "Vital." Perhaps their more accurate representations of the internal drama of the heart, as the province of women's literature, affords the possibility that female "Insects," like Dickinson herself, could run away with "Achilles' head."

"Tenderness, patience, devotion, and constancy worthy of the gentlest womanhood are conspicuous in combination with a strength of passion and fervor of attachment belonging to manliest manhood"

In his article "On Reading Shakespeare" (1876) published in *The Galaxy*, Richard Grant White did not believe women had a special relationship with Shakespeare:

> On the whole I am inclined to think that Shakespeare is not a woman's poet. He deals too largely with life; he handles the very elements of human nature; he has a great fancy, but is not fanciful; his imagination moulds the essential and the central rather than the external; he is rarely sentimental, never except in his youngest work. Women, with the exception of a few who are not always the most loveable or the happiest of the sex, like something upon a lower plane, something that appeals more directly to them . . . they like the personal, the external; that which seems to be showing them either themselves of some other real person.[14]

But while White suggests that there is something "unfeminine" about Shakespeare, throughout Dickinson's era Shakespeare's works were, in fact, altered and expurgated, transforming him into a figure associated with women and children.[15] As Elizabeth Barrett Browning put it in *Aurora Leigh,* a poem Dickinson knew very well, "if Cervantes had been Shakespeare too / He had made his Don a Donna."[16] Two articles in the magazine *Shakespeariana,* "Shakespeare study for American Women" (1884) by William Taylor Thom and Mary Cowdan Clarke's "Shakespeare as the Girl's Friend" (1887), explain why the study and reading of Shakespeare was prescribed for women in this era.[17] Thom specifically attacks the "thoroughly Philistine view of women's education" that allows critics to believe that "very few women, even among the most intelligent, like and understand Shakespeare" (99, 98). Both Thom and Clarke present Shakespeare as the valuable friend and kind counselor of women, who offers moral guidance, intellectual stimulation, insight into human nature, and valuable resources for perfecting written and spoken language.[18] Also commended are Shakespeare's "pictures of noble womanhood," who are "creatures of angelic perfection" and "living breathing women, with faults and virtues and strengths and weaknesses."(100–101)[19] For Thom, women readers find examples of "such tenderness and truth of character as appear in Cordelia and Imogen" and "fatal weakness as ruined the life of Queen Gertrude of Denmark," adding that if "the women of our race would know and be what the men of our race love as their ideals, let them study Shakespeare." In contrast, Clarke asserts that the imitation of Shakespeare's female characters will make a girl "a worthy and admirable woman" (355–56), adding that Shakespeare offers her all possible female qualities, from modesty to magnanimity, as well as ideals of "moral introspection and self-culture." While Thom suggests that the study of Shakespeare's male characters furnishes "a standard of manhood" for women and offers displays of a natural male power, Clarke argues that his heroines demonstrate the superiority of women to men in matters of constancy, love, forgiveness, tolerance, truthfulness, and gentleness; he celebrates female wisdom, shrewdness, courage, fervor, ardor, and strength. For her, moreover, a special relationship exists between women and this "feminine" writer in whose sonnets "tenderness, patience, devotion, and constancy worthy of the gentlest womanhood are conspicuous in combination with a strength of passion and fervor of attachment belonging to manliest manhood." Clarke's assertion came at a time when many critics were wary of this sequence of poems, addressed to a Fair Youth and Dark Lady, which, when read as autobiography, associated the national poet of England with pederasty and adultery.[20] Clarke's comments, and the evidence of the much-used seventh volume of the Dickinsons' Shakespeare, containing the sonnets, suggest that these influenced Dickinson's love poems to male and female addressees, as well as to addressees whose gender is not specified.[21] In contrast, Thom underlines the cultural and national importance for American women of studying Shakespeare as a means of perpetuating connections between Anglo-Saxon Americans and the wider Anglo-Saxon race (102).[22] Consequently, Dickinson might have also understood Shakespeare and women as partners in preserving the culture and supremacy of her class in a disparate American society. In this context, Thom in fact praises the "brilliant and solid work of women" critics who "can be most worthily cited and compared with the best workers among the men" (99); one of the women he singles out for honor is Clarke, the other Anna Jameson.

"One Woman may justly speak of another—judging them not with sophisticated research nor oracular criticism, but simply, naturally, sympathetically"

Anna Jameson's *Characteristics of Women, Moral, Poetical, and Historical* (1832) was one of the most widely read pieces of nineteenth-century Shakespeare criticism, going through thirty editions in England and America by 1920.[23] Its popularity made the examination of Shakespeare's heroines integral to Shakespeare criticism and her work a reference point in all subsequent discussion.

It seems likely Dickinson knew of Jameson's criticism, which was frequently referred to by Knight and other critics.[24] Jameson created her own critical voice by defending Shakespeare's heroines against male critics who underestimated them, initiated a critical movement that liberated Shakespeare's heroines from his male-oriented plots, and addressed her female readers about their own femininity and their treatment in European society.[25] Her book is an alternative to a treatise on female education and morality, which argues for social change; she seeks to "illustrate the manner in which the affections would naturally display themselves in women—whether combined with high intellect, regulated by reflection, and elevated by imagination, or existing with perverted dispositions or purified by moral sentiments."[26] Such female characteristics "would naturally display themselves," but "the condition of women in society, as at present constituted, is false in itself, and injurious to them,— . . . the education of women, as at present conducted, is founded in mistaken principles, and tends to increase fearfully the sum of misery and error in both sexes."[27] Throughout Dickinson's life, women critics, on both sides of the Atlantic, followed Jameson's use of Shakespeare's cultural authority to speak on a range of social issues related to women and, in the process, interpreted his works as a means of empowering themselves.[28] On 23 October 1873 Dickinson might have read the *Springfield Republican,* in which, after hearing a lecture on "Shakespeare's Portia and the modern woman question," at a meeting of the Radical club, Thomas Wentworth Higginson discussed "the nature and position of women as certified by Shakespeare."[29] According to Higginson, the implication of the lecture was that Shakespeare recognized the insight and judicial faculty of women and with "prophet foresight" anticipated modern relations between the sexes, in which women are often the dominant and more intellectual in a marriage. "Shakespeare, if living now, would be a subscriber and probably a contributor to the Woman's Journal," he added.

Henrietta Lee Palmer's *The Stratford Gallery or the Shakspeare Sisterhood* (1859) was an early American emulation of Jameson's work. In her preface, Palmer distances herself from Shakespeare's "wise and faithful scholars and expounders" and disclaims "the intention of presumptuously identifying herself" with them. But she also asserts the right to speak about the "Shakspeare Sisterhood" to the extent that "one woman may justly speak of another—judging them, not with sophisticated research nor oracular criticism, but simply, naturally, sympathetically, as she may regard her fellow-women whom she meets from day to day."[30] This is very similar to Jameson's own apologetic introduction—"This little book was undertaken without a thought of fame or money: out of the fulness of my own heart and soul I have written it."[31] Both critics differentiate themselves from their male precursors by suggesting that they are not engaging in Shakespeare criticism but merely discussing women. Yet they implicitly replace male criticism with their own more knowledgeable insights into women. Dickinson may have read the favorable review of Palmer's book in the *Atlantic Monthly,* which stated, "It would not be strange, if womanly instinct were to prove oftentimes a truer guide in following the waywardness or the apparent contradictions of a woman's nature than the cold, logical processes of merely intellectual men."[32] Palmer offers a character study of forty-five of Shakespeare's female characters, along with plot summaries and an illustration of each heroine. Like Jameson, she individuates Shakespeare's heroines, develops their inner lives, and compares them to nineteenth-century women—to the extent, despite an acknowledgment of historical differences, that Shakespeare's characters become almost equivalent to nineteenth-century women.[33]

At various points Palmer differentiates her ideas from those of Jameson, and she widens the discussion to include many heroines Jameson excluded. In her first portrait, she discusses the character of Lady Macbeth, who has been treated with the "least unanimity" among critics (12–14). She notes that some believe this character to have "the rarest natural endowments—powerful intellect, marvellous force, and strong affections"; in fact, this was Jameson's view, which Palmer goes on to dispute.[34] For her, Lady Macbeth has little that is womanly in her character and "her affections are as profound as may coexist with a mind exclusively masculine, and a heart fully possessed of a very devil of ambition." In contrast to Jameson, Palmer denies that this character is interested only in her husband's advancement to the throne; Lady Macbeth is like many strong-minded contemporary women who are attached to men inferior in intellect and ability. The "individualization of Lady Macbeth is almost independent of her social relations, of her sex even; she is that hateful accident, a masculine heart, soul, and brain, clothed with a female humanity." The few reminders of her femininity in the play, which Jameson had carefully emphasized, are for Palmer "natural to any man not positively monstrous." Even Lady Macbeth's descent into madness and death are not signs of remorse, as Jameson would have it, but "the consequences of an organization physically inadequate to the demands of a too vigorous intellect." Palmer denies the femininity and humanity that Jameson ascribes to Lady Macbeth, instead re-creating her as a mannish woman superior to her husband. Dickinson, in letters, seems drawn to the details of Lady Macbeth's troubled mind, and may have been interested in Palmer's and Jameson's respective work. Perhaps like these contemporaries, she was fascinated with Lady Macbeth as a gender-blurring figure, combining power and ambition, on the one hand, and guilt and madness, on the other.[35] Lady Macbeth's call on the dark spirits to "unsex" her

(I v 40–54) is interestingly like the exclamation of one of Dickinson's speakers regarding a secret love troth, "Rearrange the 'Wife's' Affection! / When they dislocate my Brain! / Amputate my freckled Bosom! / Make me bearded like a man!" (F267).

Palmer goes on to dispute Jameson's interpretation of other heroines, including Beatrice, Portia, and Isabella.[36] But, her discussion of Juliet is the most revealing. She begins by quoting Jameson's assertion that such beautiful things have been said about Juliet that it is "impossible to say better—but it is possible to say something more," then adds, "Alas for our task! This latter clause was true only before Mrs. Jameson wrote: not a detail of the subject has been neglected by her sympathetic pen; at the best, we can hope but to repeat her" (19–25). Yet Palmer does say something more, by considering "a question which properly belongs to the province of legitimate criticism," namely textual scholarship: she argues in favor of the authenticity of the phrase "That run-away's eyes" from one of Juliet's speeches (III ii 6). To be Shakespeare's "scholar," she suggests, is a position "the humblest may with humility assume," and accordingly she makes "with all becoming diffidence, a suggestion, which can be valuable only because it is the fruit of long pondering with our heart." Her "long pondering" reveals that this phrase should not be changed to "rumour's eyes," as had been suggested by Richard Grant White, because "run-away's eyes" perfectly captures Juliet's passionate longing for Romeo and her abandonment of herself to "her newly found delight." Although she praises White's criticism, she disagrees with him, noting that it "should be glory enough for one woman; and without presuming to believe that the writer of this has succeeded where so abler have failed, she may still venture to hope that the promised honor may yet fall to her sex." Despite her disclaimer Palmer, following Jameson, has discovered in reading Shakespeare her critical voice, and justifies it by arguing for her more penetrating female understanding of the heroines because of "the quick, sympathetic understanding of a woman's heart, on a subject wherein her instincts are directly involved." While male criticism relies on learning and research, "the pure bridal mind of the Juliets of to-day" has a more "sympathetic understanding" of "the passionate outburst of their Shakspearian sister."[37] Palmer does feel it necessary, though, to underline Juliet's "rarest refinement and most delicate purity," as if to exonerate this heroine of her clear deviation from respectable femininity.[38]

These critics demonstrate the role Shakespeare played in the emergence of women's literary professionalism and of the female intellectual. Although Dickinson seems less than interested in his ideal heroines and more attracted by his more problematic, unorthodox ones, the work of Jameson and Palmer to an extent legitimizes her choice. Neither critic would recommend or approve of the actions of Queen Margaret, Lady Macbeth, or Cleopatra; yet they treat such as not simply debauched or wicked women but complex figures, with redeeming qualities and passions. Perhaps, like Palmer and Jameson, Dickinson felt as a woman (and in her case, as a poet) she had a greater understanding of these characters than her male counterparts. Her frequent, if brief, commentaries on an array of Shakespearean characters, as well as on issues like the Bacon-Shakespeare controversy, belong in line with the work of these critics. Additionally, the rivalry between Palmer and Jameson offers a parallel to the competitive nature of Dickinson and Helen Hunt Jackson's relationship. What seems to be at stake is the nature of literary professionalism. Like Palmer, Dickinson is creating a space for herself as a writer in opposition to a rival: she is the private poet and nonprofessional woman writer, Jackson the professional woman writer.[39] Jackson appreciates Dickinson as a "great," and perhaps even superior, poet (L444a). Similarly, although Dickinson may have found "great pleasure in reading" Jackson's poems, and despite her own refusal to publish, she may be envious of Jackson's literary status and cultural authority (L476c). Perhaps contrasting *Ramona* to Shakespeare's works suggests that although Jackson has been "published" and achieved fame, Dickinson seeks something else: the immortality of Shakespeare.

"My aim has been to direct his attention to very old truths, which, amid the multifarious productions of our day, are often overlooked"

Mary Preston's *Studies in Shakspeare* (1869) considers Shakespeare primarily from her position as an American, and its antidemocratic tone and aristocratic bias offer a particularly fascinating basis on which to discuss Dickinson's reading of Shakespeare.[40] Like her female contemporaries, Preston approaches Shakespeare with deference, suggesting in her preface that although she will not "say anything *very new* to the reader," yet, despite the achievement of other critics, his plays "remain an inexhaustible mine of wealth." Like other socially and politically conservative critics, Preston aims to direct her reader's "attention to *very old truths,* which, amid the multifarious productions of our day, are often overlooked"; she regards Shakespeare's plays as a reservoir of moral, political, and social values underestimated in her society. Unlike her female contemporaries, Preston throughout her book does not address her remarks specifically to female readers, except when she is didactically reminding them of some aspect of Christian and proper female behavior. Although Dickinson may not have been attracted to this moralizing, she must have concurred with Preston's attack on Puritanism and its attitude toward art and the imagination. Preston writes, "Perhaps if these refugees of fanaticism . . . had brought with them an edition of Shakspeare, and made it one of their household treasures, they would not have stained their colonial history with the blood of the innocent" (138). Throughout, like Jameson and Palmer, Preston personalizes her relationship with Shakespeare, making his characters her contemporaries, amplifying them to articulate her gravest concerns about gender, race, and class.

Preston continually opposes Shakespeare's morally enlightening "treasures" to the "worthless currency which is debasing modern taste and morals in literature," and she especially applauds Lady Macbeth, Portia, Cordelia, Rosalind, and Celia.[41] Unlike modern novelists, Shakespeare never "*idealized* in woman the material form, to the neglect of the immaterial mind" as if the intellectual were beyond a heroine's reach (72–73).[42] But Queen Katherine, from *Henry VIII,* is her paragon of femininity, and she praises Shakespeare's ability to "read accurately the feelings natural to a refined lady, to reflect the expressions which become the lips of women, *born* to command admiration, able to enforce respect" (77). Although Queen Katherine does not possess the youth, beauty, or charms of Shakespeare's other heroines, she appeals to readers, as does no other character, for her utmost dignity and her maintenance of her royal identity even when royal status is taken away. Shakespeare never allowed ignorance except in women of a lower class—housemaids or landladies of taverns (72). When Dickinson's speakers refer to themselves as queens, they probably evoke the sort of female majesty and regal dignity personified by Katherine.

Preston's discussion of *Coriolanus* offers some guidance as to how Dickinson may have read this play. In 1872, when she sent Sue the quotation "Doth forget that ever he heard the name of Death" (L484), the poet was probably summoning up what Preston describes as Coriolanus's "haughty and imperial will, born to command and which wisdom could not teach when to bow" (42). The line comes from a speech in which Menenius Agrippa attempts to explain that when proud Coriolanus is angry he "does forget that ever / He heard the name of death" (III i 258–59). Dickinson is suggesting that someone (not identified) has behaved as arrogantly and angrily as Coriolanus. Perhaps she also shares Preston's opinion that this play calls to mind "a truer philosophy" than "the rights of *all* men to have a voice in public affairs," or Jefferson's false notion that all men are created free and equal (37–38). For Preston, there are "*essential* differences" among "the Caucasian race," and despite the unpopularity of this idea, such diversity is part of the divine and natural law, and it is demeaning that disparate men should have the "*same* rights and privileges." Although Coriolanus's pride is responsible for his downfall, he gains sympathy because his ruin is the greater for having been caused by "the people, servitors, plebians" (46). His contempt for the people's attempt to influence the government is just, and his hate of their applause "natural." Yet his "coarseness of manner and address to his inferiors was the exhibition of a pride that was mean and cruel in a great man" (39). In Preston's hierarchical world, there is no mark of a gentleman or lady like their treatment of their inferiors. Charlotte Brontë's second novel, *Shirley* (1849), owned by Sue Dickinson, suggests another way in which Dickinson might have viewed the play.[43] In chapter 6, Brontë appropriates *Coriolanus* as a means of articulating political and social views that are opposed to those of Preston. Here, Dickinson might have read Caroline Helstone's sympathetic knowledge of class division and her warnings to the aristocratic and proud factory owner Robert Moore on the dangers of mistreating his workers.[44] In a brief 1878 letter to Mrs. Henry Hills, to sympathize with the family's recently failed hat-making business, the poet refers to Coriolanus's final words (III iii 135) as he begins his exile from Rome, "How near this suffering Summer are the divine words 'There is a world elsewhere'" (L557). Perhaps she is even indicating that the Hills family may be able to set up their trade somewhere else.[45] Perhaps the failure of the Hillses' long-established business is a sign of the economic threat that the mass-market, democratic politics and social mobility pose to time-honored social status.

Again, in her analysis of *Julius Caesar,* Preston advocates a traditionalist reading of this play, yet one complicated by her latent republicanism and her assertion of her right as an American to Shakespeare. Although clearly on Caesar's side, Preston quotes Cassius's lines, "The *fault,* dear Brutus, *is not in our stars,* / But in ourselves, *that we are underlings*" (I ii 140–41; Preston's emphasis), commenting:

> Who but our *Shakspeare,*—for England cannot claim *him;* he is the legacy of the whole civilized world,—who but our Shakspeare could have shown us that union of a Roman's pride with an honest and manly spirit, which is manifested in the Julius Caesar of the play. (105)

Preston is thus disputing England's claim to Shakespeare by identifying with Brutus and his fellow rebels, demanding the right to claim the bard in the face of the Caesarlike English. She goes on to argue that envy was the motivation for their assassination of Caesar. Brutus "lent some color of principle to the black enterprise of conspiracy," but he was "the greatest traitor that ever lived; a traitor to good government, a traitor to friendship; a traitor to his benefactor!" (109, 113). When Dickinson wrote to Sue in Antony's words, "For Brutus, as you know, was Caesar's Angel" (L448; III ii 181), she was referring, according to Martha Dickinson Bianchi, to "the betrayal of Austin by a friend in a matter of town politics."[46] Like Preston, Dickinson may have regarded Brutus as an archetype of ungratefulness and treachery, Caesar as his noble victim. In addition, Dickinson may have believed that Brutus's act reinvigorated Caesar's reputation and established his legend. On the other hand, the poet might have expected Sue to recognize that Antony is here attempting carefully to persuade his listeners that Brutus is no angel but a murderer. In this same essay, Preston praises the important lessons about reconciliation and the just treatment of traitors that Octavious teaches.[47] Preston's interpretation demonstrates the way Shakespeare's plays were frequently read as offering wise counsel on political dispute and conflict in post–Civil War America; this may also have influenced Dickinson's understanding of *Henry VI, part 1* (see chapter 2).

"Shakespeare,—that won't do; that's no book for Sunday; go put it away and take another"

While the American women critics discussed above engaged in Shakespeare criticism under the cover of modesty and hesitancy, research suggests that other nineteenth-century women alluded to and quoted from Shakespeare as a means of legitimizing themselves as writers, drawing attention to the importance of their work and displaying their intellectual credentials.[48] Dickinson's American female contemporaries transformed Shakespeare, reimagining his dramas in domestic and middle-class settings with women at the influential center, and read him consciously as Americans.[49] The role he played in the lives and writings of Margaret Fuller, Harriet Beecher Stowe, and Louisa May Alcott hints at certain shared features that further clarify Dickinson's Shakespeare. Like Dickinson, these women blended quotations from and references to Shakespeare into their letters and books, and were interested in current Shakespeare criticism.[50] In March 1839, Fuller attended a two-month series of lectures on Shakespeare by R. H. Dana, preferring them to Jones Very's.[51] Yet Fuller complained about Dana's lack of knowledge of more recent commentary and his regurgitation of Romantic criticism—although noting, like Sue Dickinson, that "the audience generally is very ignorant, there are only six or eight of us who are likely to be wearied at times."[52] Similarly, Alcott heard and delighted in readings of Shakespeare, like those by Fanny Kemble, and attended lectures by Henry Giles.[53]

Although Margaret Fuller was one of the first great American woman intellectuals, author of numerous books, editor of the Transcendentalist journal *The Dial,* and friend of Emerson, Thoreau, and Hawthorne, there is no evidence that Dickinson read her.[54] Fuller's "ever memorable" day she first read Shakespeare is strikingly similar to Dickinson's own early encounter: both are acts of defiance of authority, of antitheatrical prejudice and moral and religious wariness about Shakespeare.[55] At eight, Fuller read *Romeo and Juliet* on a Sunday, the only day when her father forbade her from reading novels and plays.

When he discovered her disobedience, he reprimanded her: "Shakespeare,—that won't do; that's no book for a Sunday; go put it away and take another." Although she obeyed him, the "unfinished story" and "the personages to whom [she] was but just introduced, thronged and burnt [her] brain. [She] could not bear it long; such a lure was impossible to resist. [She] went and brought the book again." Disobedient a second time, she was sent to her room, where, she records:

> Alone, in the dark I thought only of the scene placed by the poet before my eye, where the free flow of life, sudden and graceful dialogue, and forms, whether grotesque or fair, seen in the broad lustre of his imagination, gave just what I wanted, and brought home the life I seemed born to live. My fancies swarmed like bees, as I contrived the rest of the story;—what all would do, what say, where go. My confinement tortured me. I could not go forth from the prison to ask after these friends; I could not make my pillow of the dreams about them which yet I could not forbear to frame.

Here, Shakespeare's characters are friends whose fate concerns her. As in Dickinson's most famous poem about confinement, "They shut me up in Prose -" (F445), the internment of the imagination is impossible, and Shakespeare and his characters absorb her and stir her fancy, offering a glimpse of its potential and power. Fuller's description is echoed in Dickinson's "I think I was enchanted," in which the speaker records the powerful effect reading Elizabeth Barrett Browning's poetry had on her (F627). The way in which *Romeo and Juliet* captivates Fuller's young mind explains why so many commentators warned of the dangers of unmediated reading. Fuller recalled that from then on her "attention" was fixed on Shakespeare and she returned to him "at every hour [she] could command." Like Dickinson, she was particularly interested in his male heroes—men of action like Coriolanus and Julius Caesar as well as men of "deeper thought" like Hamlet.[56] These demonstrated that "the *natural history* of man, not what he should be, but what he is," was central to Shakespeare's art.

Unlike Dickinson, Fuller was very concerned with the challenge of Shakespeare's "Englishness" to an America self-consciously establishing its own literary and cultural identity. In her essay "American Literature" (1846) she suggests that books that "imitate and represent the thoughts and life of Europe do not constitute an American literature" but are useful for "people in a transition state; which lasts rather longer than is occupied in passing, bodily, the ocean which separates the new from the old world."[57] She contrasts America's great love for Continental literature with feelings about English literature, which has "the iron force of the Latins but not the frankness and expansion" and is "uncongenial and injurious" to "a mixed race, continually enriched with new blood from other stocks the most unlike that of our descent." What America needs is writers who have "enough to range in and leave every impulse free, and abundant opportunity to develop a genius, wide and full as our rivers, flowery, luxuriant and impassioned as our vast prairies, rooted in strength as the rocks on which the Puritan fathers landed." Fuller's Shakespeare epitomizes such a writer: he transcends his "insular" English character to become, like Lowell's, a spirit of the European "continent." Shakespeare is full of the "rich colouring, and more fluent life of the Catholic countries," and although other English poets "soar" skywards as he does, their works display the "reminiscence of walls and ceilings, a tendency to the arbitrary and conventional that repels a mind trained in admiration of the antique spirit." This is evocative of Dickinson's definition of poetry as an expansive "House of Possibility," with numerous windows, and "an everlasting Roof / The Gambrels of the Sky"; perhaps, like Fuller, Dickinson appreciated a Shakespeare of centrifugal range (F466). Certainly, Fuller had suggested to Emerson in 1839 that beneath Shakespeare's plays lay "a double meaning . . . so that while the obvious meaning covers but a point, a line may be drawn from it to the limit of the Universe."[58] Shakespeare is not a menace to the American writer, rather a model of a comprehensive author; his poetry is appropriate for an expanding and all-embracing America nation.[59]

Fuller's confirmation of Shakespeare's relevance was already apparent in her appropriation of his heroines in *Woman in the Nineteenth Century* (1845). Like other female critics, she here reinvents these characters as models of and for American women, using them to discuss various myths of femininity. Although she criticizes Anna Jameson as a sentimentalist, she praises "her refined perceptions of [Shakespearean] character."[60] The power of Shakespeare's representations of femininity is connected with "the fact of having a female sovereign on the throne [which] affected the course of a writer's thoughts" and "stimulated [his imagination] to the possibilities of Woman" (66–68). Shakespeare's Imogen, Desdemona, Rosalind, Portia, and Isabella display poetic power, rather than a heroic force or holy ideal, and the beauty of Cordelia "is neither male nor female; it is the beauty of virtue." Shakespeare makes these heroines both passionate and virtuous because he "too, saw that, in true love, as in fire, the utmost ardor is coincident with the utmost purity. It is a true lover that exclaims in the agony of Othello: 'If thou are false, O then Heaven mocks itself!'" Male readers and critics who praised the virtues of Shakespeare's heroines were forced to ignore, criticize, or justify their often unbecoming behavior and passions; Fuller highlights the complexity of these heroines. Many of Shakespeare's most ideal women behave in ways that might, to Victorians, seem insubordinate and inappropriate.[61] Like Palmer's analysis of Juliet's passion, Fuller's discussion suggests that Dickinson may have found in Shakespeare's most lauded female characters controversial ideas and actions, which unsettled her culture's admiration of them. Fuller explains her use of "Frailty thy name is Woman" as an epigraph to her book by suggesting that Hamlet's words express "deep melancholy when he finds his natural expectations disappointed." His mother, Gertrude, in her overly hasty marriage to Claudius, disappoints him because "She to whom he gave the name, disgraces from his heart's shrine all the sex." Hamlet has just cause for this condemnation, but Fuller argues that as a lover he "would not have so far mistaken, as to have finished with such a conviction. He would have felt the faith of Othello, and that faith could not, in his more dispassionate mind, have been disturbed into calumny." Hamlet's attack on women has a context, and reflects the character and circumstances of the man rather than revealing anything essential or universal about womanhood. The epigraph is suitable for Fuller's book, which aims to demonstrate the complexity of women and the prejudice of men.[62]

Fuller also enlarges on the individuality and inner life of *The Tempest's* heroine, Miranda, reimagining her as a model of female independence and self-assurance. Miranda symbolizes Fuller's own position as an American female artist and intellectual lacking models of female creativity and intellectuality.[63] Although Dickinson never mentions this heroine, Fuller identifies with her, noting in her journal, "I . . . proudly painted myself as Miranda."[64] Like Fuller's own father, Miranda's has a firm belief in the equality of the sexes; he makes her his "companion," addressing her "not as a plaything, but as a living mind" (38–39). This Prospero demands from his daughter traditionally male virtues, such as clear judgment, courage, honor, and fidelity, and she becomes self-reliant and self-assured, displaying originality of thought and character, qualities often "deprecated as a fault[s] in most women." Fuller's Miranda does not feel the social restraints on women, which are "insuperable only to those who think them so, or who noisily strive to break them," nor the bitterness that accompanies such subordination. Yet her Miranda acknowledges the prejudice that accompanies male praise of her intellect: men "never in an extreme of despair, wished to be women," and at any sign of weakness taunt each other with the prospect of being "like a woman." When men admire a woman, they suggest that she is "above her sex" or that she "deserved in some star to be a man" (41–42). For them, Miranda has "a masculine mind" and they cannot accept her belief in the importance of the feminine qualities when she asserts, "if either were better, it was better now to be a woman." Through Shakespeare, Fuller is examining her own denial of feminine traits within herself in order to be her father's intellectual companion.[65] Like Shakespeare's and her own Miranda, Fuller is caught despite advantages in the control of her cerebral father. However, Fuller's Miranda is more assertive, independent, and confident than Shakespeare's character, and is not finally trapped in marriage to a Ferdinandlike figure: "She had taken a course of her own, and no man stood in her way" (39).

Fuller similarly discusses Brutus and Portia, in *Julius Caesar,* as an example of a Roman marriage in which, "the stern and calm nobleness of the nation was common to both." She praises the way "Shakspeare has seized on the relation in its native lineaments, harmonizing the particular with the universal; and, while it is conjugal love, and no other, making it unlike the same relation as seen in Cymbeline, or Othello, even as one star differeth from another in glory" (52). As a means of explaining this, Fuller quotes the lines in which Portia demands to know what is troubling her husband, "I grant I am a woman; but withal, / A woman well reputed—Cato's daughter, / Think you I *am no stronger than my sex,* / Being so fathered and so husbanded?" [Fuller's emphasis] (II i 292–97). These lines demonstrate that Shakespeare was "not content to let Portia rest her plea for confidence on the essential nature of the marriage bond." The terms of Portia's demand to be told what is troubling her husband rest on her own individuality and strength, which is part of and yet beyond traditional womanhood. Dickinson also refers to this self-empowered character, in an 1860 poem:

> Great Caesar! Condescend
> The Daisy, to receive,
> Gathered by Cato's Daughter,
> With your majestic Leave!
> (F149)

Like many of Dickinson's other poems, this one, believed to have been sent to Austin, fashions vulnerability and innocence as an exaggerated and ultimately irreverent surrender to male ideals and ideas.[66] Cato's daughter is a sign of female strength; if Austin is "Caesar," then Dickinson is his female opponent, Cato's daughter. Although many critics tended to admire the submissive qualities of Shakespeare's heroines, Dickinson, like Fuller, is interested in the more self-asserting and self-affirming aspects of Portia. Along with Shakespeare's powerful queens, a figure like Portia offers her an ideal of authoritative femininity.

"That loving heart, that active fancy, that subtile, elastic power of appreciating and expressing all phases, all passions of humanity"

Like both Fuller's and Dickinson's, Harriet Beecher Stowe's reading of Shakespeare was affected by a lingering Puritan suspicion of his writings.[67] Dickinson may have read Sue's copy of Stowe's fictionalized autobiography, *The Pearl of Orr's Island* (1862), which offers insight into Stowe's reading of Shakespeare.[68] Stowe's central character, Mara, lives on Orr's Island with her fisherman grandfather; in the first chapter, there is a sense that she is shipwrecked, enclosed in a regimented "Puritan" life and within a world of curtailed and prescribed female roles. She notes that it will be a long time before "the beauties of Shakspeare, will be read in a stormy night on Orr's Island with the same sense of a Divine presence as the Psalms of David, or the prayer of Moses, the man of God."[69] When Mara discovers a copy of *The Tempest* "torn from an old Edition of Shakspeare," she becomes absorbed in its "delightful images of a lonely island, an old enchanter, a beautiful girl, and a spirit not quiet like those in the Bible, but a very probable one to her mode of thinking" (145). As for Fuller, and perhaps for Dickinson, Shakespeare represents poetic freedom and imagination beyond the limitations of a restricted female life. Mara imagines herself as Miranda, and her friend Moses as "the beautiful young Prince Ferdinand," and thinks how happy she would be to "pile up his wood for him"; in addition, the play inspires a "host of surmises and dreams" that she never reveals to anybody. When Mara tells the story of *The Tempest* to Captain Kittridge, he says he has seen the play performed in the theater, but asks Mara not to tell his wife about this; despite the obvious force of antitheatrical prejudice, Mara after hearing about that performance longs to see one herself (154). But when she tries to explain the play's significance to Moses, he is indifferent; this confronts her with the fact that her initiated imagination has no place in the real and practical world of the island.[70] Like Fuller's Miranda, Mara ultimately escapes Miranda's ending in marriage; Stowe chooses death as the only other option for her heroine. This reflects something frequently referred to in Dickinson's poems: that marriage for a nineteenth-century American woman was equivalent to social and cultural death. Stowe's Mara dies to offer her religiously skeptical beloved, Moses, salvation through the faith her death inspires. Both Fuller and Stowe associate reading Shakespeare with the initiation of female creativity and intellect; but while they use Miranda to articulate their position in nineteenth-century America, they reject the marriage-plot resolution that is a central motif in *The Tempest* and most of Shakespeare's romantic comedies.[71]

In a letter to Arthur Helps, dated 6 January 1853, Stowe, like Fuller, connects her bond with Shakespeare to her sense of herself as an American writer:

> Have not England and America one blood, one language, one literature, and a glorious literature it is! Are not Milton and Shakespeare, and all the wise and brave and good of old, common to us both, and should there be anything but cordiality between countries that have so glorious an inheritance in common?[72]

Not surprisingly, Stowe's visit to her "inheritance" at Stratford-upon-Avon is recorded in her travel book *Sunny Memories of Foreign Lands* (1854).[73] Like other pilgrims, Stowe discusses all the places connected with Shakespeare, while commenting on modernity, femininity, and religion. Like many of her contemporaries, Stowe opposes Shakespeare to the modern world of progress and change. Stratford is a place of "simple-hearted, kindly English people" and a vulnerable haven from the "bustle of modern progress" under whose "restless regenerating force" "old England" is disappearing (194–95). Modernity has destroyed all that inspired Shakespeare, and if he had been born in this century he would not have been able to build his "Gothic structures of the imagination." He might have been a shrewd observer of the "heat and dust of modern progress" but not a reformer, because perceiving injustice is not the same thing as having "the energy to reform it" (197–98). Despite his genius, he lacks Stowe's specifically female moral power as a champion of social change. Going further, Stowe connects aspects of Shakespeare's genius with his mother and the domestic setting of the birthplace. Like many of Stowe's own heroines, Shakespeare's mother, Mary Arden, is a "silent, deep-hearted, loving" mother and private woman with the sacred power to "quicken into life the struggling, slumbering elements of a sensitive nature" (203). Moreover, she is the model for his depictions of chaste and pure women, in a period "when coarseness was more common among women"; the dignity, patience, forgiveness, and enduring love of Desdemona reflect his mother's "household words and ways." Admiringly noting Jameson's *Women of Shakespeare,* Stowe suggests that other female family members (his belligerent grandmother and "rigorous grand-aunt") have a life-informing effect on Shakespeare's character, while his father is a more distant, thoughtful God-fearing man.[74] This underlines Stowe's central stress on the fundamental role the domestic sphere and the women within it have on the moral, literary, social, and public lives of others; it also supplements through reference to biography the fundamental link between women and Shakespeare.

Like other pilgrims, Stowe is intent on believing all things that "had a very plausible and probable sound," and her companions are surprised by her "unreasonable raptures" for "Shakspeare's house, when it wasn't his house," and her earnest attempt "to get sprigs from his mulberry, when it wasn't his mulberry" (214–16). Yet for Stowe the scarcity of facts demonstrates that the "very perfection of [Shakespeare's] dramatic talent has become an impenetrable veil." Throughout, but especially at Holy Trinity Church, her faith in the mysterious figure of Shakespeare is analogous to her religious belief. Although Shakespeare was not a religious writer, his plays testify to his struggle with faith and concern with "real religious principles." While at the church, she records a passing funeral train, and is overcome by "a thousand undefined emotions," wondering where is Shakespeare, "that loving heart, that active fancy, that subtile, elastic power of appreciating and expressing all phases, all passions of humanity" (222–23). Stowe's Christianity means that she envisions him as, like all the dead, "actively developing those habits of mind and modes of feeling" which he began on earth. Despite his suspect moral character, the beauty and worth of his works are admirable and lovable, and give readers a "glimpse and intimation" of God. Stowe advises her readers not to lose themselves "in admiration of worldly genius, but be led by it to a better understanding of what He is, of whom all the glories of poetry and art are but symbols and shadows." Dickinson may not have shared Stowe's religious faith, and when she deifies Shakespeare in remarks like "'Stratford on Avon' - accept us all," it is not an appeal to God's glory, rather to an alternate deity. She equates poetry with divinity, and in one verse her speaker evaluates poets as being "First" among all things, asserting that they prepare a beautiful heaven "For Those who worship Them" (F533).

"I know and love Shakespeare better than any of my other books, and can sing every song he wrote. How beautiful they are! See, I have worn out my dear book with much reading"

On 14 February 1884, Louisa May Alcott explained to her friend Maggie Lukens that authors like Shakespeare were a means of personal betterment and ultimately bring readers "nearer the source of all good."[75] On 18 December 1885, writing to Viola Price, she opposes her favorite author, Shakespeare, to "modern fiction," which "seems poor stuff when one can have the best of the old writers."[76] In Alcott's novel *Good Wives* (1869), Professor Bhaer is the "judicious friend" who guides Jo's reading of Shakespeare; he gives her a fine edition and tells her, "Read him well, and he will help you much; for the study of character in this book will help you to read it in the world and paint it with your pen."[77] Later Jo notes, "I never knew how much there was in Shakespeare before; but then I never had a Bhaer to explain it to me" (306). After reading Shakespeare, however, she is less than inspired as a writer: the narrator notes, it is unclear if "Shakespeare helped her to read character, or the natural instinct of a woman for what was honest, brave, and strong" (311). It is her own female insight and perception that facilitates her writing about character, rather than her reading Shakespeare.

Alcott had a great interest in theater and playwriting, central to it her reading of Shakespeare's plays.[78] In fact, she saw many of the most famous performers of the day, including Edwin Forrest, Edwin Booth, Henry Irving, and Ellen Terry.[79] In 1858, after seeing Booth play Hamlet, she announced "my ideal done at last"; but she criticized Forrest's performance of Macbeth, asserting, "I can make up a better Macbeth & Hamlet for myself than Forrest with his gasping & shouting can give me."[80] When she saw Charlotte Cushman, she had a "stage struck fit" and declared, "Perhaps it is acting, not writing, I'm meant for." She then worked off her "stage fever in writing a story."[81] Alcott's theatrical ambitions and her knowledge of how to stage Shakespeare's dramas derive from a childhood in which theatrical presentations were encouraged.[82] The sisters in her novel *Little Women* (1868) perform their own plays, and Beth calls Jo a "regular Shakespeare" because she writes and acts in them. During their private theatricals, the sisters domesticate and feminize Shakespeare: they perform *Romeo and Juliet* and would perform *Macbeth* except they have no trapdoor for Banquo; Jo wants her friend Laurie to teach her fencing so they can perform a scene in *Hamlet.*[83] Earlier, in June 1862, Alcott told Alfred Whitman her intention to combine her love of drama and Shakespeare with her need to write sensationalist fiction:

> I intend to illuminate the Ledger with a blood & thunder tale as they are easy to "compoze" & are better paid than moral & elaborate works of Shakespeare, so dont be shocked if I send you a paper containing a picture of Indians, pirates wolves, bears & distressed damsels in a grand tableau over a title like this "The Maniac Bride"; or "The Bath of Blood. A thrilling tale of passion."[84]

The once sensualist Shakespeare is now the writer of "moral" dramas; Alcott appropriates his plays in two of the stories she published anonymously in 1865 in *Frank Leslie's Chimney Corner:* "A Double Tragedy: An Actor's Story" and "Ariel, A Legend of the Lighthouse."[85] By incorporating Shakespeare into these financially remunerative tales, it is not clear if Alcott sought to elevate them, or merely to ensure their appeal to the widest possible audience.

In "A Double Tragedy: An Actor's Story" Paul Lamar recounts his passionate love affair with his co-star Clotilde Varian.[86] During rehearsals of *Romeo and Juliet,* their bliss ends when Clotilde's former husband, St. John, confronts the lovers. From then on, the distinction between Shakespeare's characters and Alcott's "star-crossed lovers" is moot. One of Lamar's fellow actors accuses him of playing "Romeo before the time"; later he is described as roaming "restlessly about the gloomy green room and stage" (260).[87] In Alcott's story, though, the assertive Clotilde murders her husband in an attempt to be free of him; but once Paul discovers this, he tells her he can never love her again. The story ends with a performance of *Romeo and Juliet* in which Clotilde is "all she had ever been" and Paul "enacted the lover with a power [he] had never known before, feeling the while that it might be for the last time." "The wildest of the poet's words were not too strong to embody [Paul's] own sorrow and despair," and he notes that the "the hapless Italian lovers never found better representatives than in us that night" (263–64). In the final scene of this supreme representation, Clotilde actually kills herself with the dagger. To clamorous applause, Paul takes her in his arms and forgives her; he spends the rest of his life alone, never acting again. In Alcott's story the boundaries between public performance and private experience dissolve; a sinister and shocking quality pervades the tale, perhaps building on what Melville identifies as the dark and black aspects of Shakespeare's plays.[88] Lamar's belief that *Romeo and Juliet* was never "better played" suggests that his and Clotilde's real passion exceeds and surpasses the limitations of Shakespeare's original. The inner drama of Paul and Clotilde is more potent than that which is presented on stage; although he will never again act upon the public stage, Paul's record of his "Juliet" is something he will "enact" indefinitely in the private theater of his heart.

In a similar manner, "Ariel: a Legend of the Lighthouse" re-creates *The Tempest.*[89] This story centers on Ariel and her father, Ralph March, who both live with the hunchback lighthousekeeper Stern. Ariel falls in love with Philip Southesk, a visitor to the island, and the resemblance of their story to Shakespeare's is obvious to the characters themselves:

> Here we all are! Prospero is not unlike my father, but Ferdinand is much plainer than you. Here's Ariel swinging in a vine, as I've often done, and Caliban watching her as Stern watches me. He is horrible here, however, and my Caliban has a fine face, if one can get a sight of it when he is in good humor. (277)

Philip is surprised by Ariel's insightful knowledge of the playwright, and she explains, "I know and love Shakespeare better than any of my other books, and can sing every song he wrote. How beautiful they are! See, I have worn out my dear book with much reading" (271). But mirroring the plot of *The Tempest,* her father, March, realizes that Philip is the son of his old enemy, Richard Marston; at once, he takes Ariel away from the island. When Philip follows them, March tells him that she is dead; on Philip's later return to the island, Stern traps him in a cave that is filling with water. In the same way her Shakespearean counterpart rescues Ferdinand, Alcott's Ariel rescues Philip from drowning. In the end, Ariel becomes Philip / Ferdinand's "happy wife." Alcott, in this story, both extends and complicates the Shakespeare characters she re-creates. Her courageous female is a combination of Shakespeare's Miranda and Ariel; her Ariel's initiative and daring draw attention to inadequacies in Shakespeare's submissive Miranda. She tells Philip that his poem is "better than Shakespeare," and maintains that Shakespeare's Ferdinand is "plainer than Philip." Like Fuller and Stowe, Alcott appropriates Shakespeare, but the act necessitates a re-fashioning of his works.

"She rose to His Requirement - dropt / The Playthings of Her Life"

Although a Shakespearean context may explicate some of Dickinson's "sceneless" poems, the trace of his influence, although often provocative, is generally indeterminable.[90] Shakespeare's plays are in her poems only insofar as his plays are already part of what Emerson called the text of modern life. The following poem, however, for which a specific Shakespearean source is suggested, can be seen as linked with the themes of Fuller, Stowe, and Alcott:

> She rose to His Requirement - dropt
> The Playthings of Her Life
> To take the honorable Work
> Of Woman, and of Wife -
>
> If ought She missed in Her new Day,
> Of Amplitude, or Awe -
> Or first Prospective - or the Gold
> In using, wear away,
>
> It lay unmentioned - as the Sea
> Develope Pearl, and Weed,
> But only to Himself - be known
> The Fathoms they abide
> (F857)

Paula Bennett argues that the immediate source of this poem is Ariel's song "Full fathom five thy father lies; / Of his bones are coral made; / Those are pearls that were his eyes" in *The Tempest* (I ii 397–99), adding "but unlike the transformation the lost father undergoes in Shakespeare's magic lyric, the 'sea change' which the wife (mother) experiences in Dickinson's poem is only ironically a form of rebirth."[91] Whereas Ariel tells Ferdinand that his drowned father has changed into "something rich and strange," Dickinson's wife does not drown but rises to her husband's requirements, dropping what is of greatest value in the process. Only the sea that she has ascended from knows, but will not mention, the great worth below the surface: the gold, the pearl, the amplitude and awe. The *Indicator* essay on "Desdemona" advises the imaginative woman to keep her powers secret until "he who has won that noble heart can draw forth its secret thoughts."[92] Her beloved will then find her "trembling to enter upon the voyage of life—fearful lest she fail to realize the high ideal she has formed of what the chosen of her love merits at her hands." For this student, the gifted woman will rise, revealing herself and her art to her chosen lover. Dickinson might be setting up an analogy between this "wife" and Shakespeare's heroines who "ideally" dwindle into wives; this Miranda-like figure drops the "Play" things of her life, drowning her powers in order to return to Naples as Ferdinand's wife. The poem associates the renunciation by this woman of her own riches and endowments with Prospero's giving up of his magic powers, "I'll break my staff, / Bury it certain fathoms in the earth, / And, deeper than did ever plummet sound / I'll drown my book" (V i 54–57).

Dickinson read Shakespeare in a community of American women who were given prescriptions on how to read his texts; yet as writers they transformed Shakespeare, developing his plots and characters to address issues important to them as women. They found in Shakespeare and his texts a means of self-empowerment and an outlet for their creativity and critical ingenuity. Despite acknowledgments of Shakespeare's "firm" and fixed genius, he remained "just published" because readers redeployed him, his plays becoming displaced by that which had more contemporary or personal relevance. This is very apparent in Dickinson's letters, in which she demonstrates the expected knowledge of Shakespeare's works by imaginatively transforming them.

CHAPTER SIX

"Shakespeare always and forever"

Dickinson's Circulation of the Bard

Regarding Dickinson's reading of Shakespeare, the poet's niece, Martha Dickinson Bianchi, wrote, "Shakespeare always and forever; Othello her chosen villain, with Macbeth familiar as the neighbors and Lear driven into exile as vivid as if occurring on the hills before her door."[1] In fact, in her letters, Dickinson through allusion transforms herself and her friends into Shakespeare's characters. This is hardly surprising considering that an expected acquisition of Shakespeare was promoted in her culture by its theaters, its magazines and journals, its Lyceums, its literary clubs, its scholarship, its publishing industry, its contemporary novels and poems, and, eventually, its schools and colleges. Quotations from Shakespeare played a major role in the newspapers Dickinson and her family read.[2] For instance, on the announcement pages of issues of the *Amherst Record* in September 1871 there is an advertisement for a clothes shop in Northampton: "TO BUY, OR NOT TO BUY, THAT'S THE QUESTION / But before you buy, be sure and examine the magnificent stock of goods just received by Draper & Ockington." Hamlet's musings have become incorporated into every consumer's dilemma. Shakespeare is a great writer, and this is a great place to buy clothes.[3] Earlier, on Wednesday, 26 July 1871, Shakespeare is front-page news in the *Record:* an article by George Clair presents him as the writer who triumphed over his own limited education, a scarcity of literary models, and the superstition and ignorance of his time to write "monuments of wonder," whose popularity and fascination remain.[4] Clair proceeds to praise the immensity of his genius, calling him "the moulder and embellisher of his native tongue," "the great exponent of nature," the "definer and interpreter of humanity":

> His *dramatis persona* are full of ill habits, frail by constitution, faulty and unequal, but they speak with human voices, and are actuated by human passions, as they pursue their affairs of life . . . we feel a deep interest in them, for they are the same nature as ourselves. Their precepts are an instruction, their fortunes an experience, their misfortunes a warning, and their testimony an authority.

Shakespeare and his characters are ubiquitous in the private and public lives of Dickinson and her contemporaries, teaching lessons on wisdom, courage, charity, love, man's blindness, and God's providence that "we may look for in vain in any other writer."

Such sentiments were responsible for a proliferation in the poet's lifetime of Shakespeareana—books and artifacts devoted to Shakespeare and his words.[5] Two examples in the Dickinson household incorporated Shakespeare quotations into daily life. The first was Mary F. P. Dunbar's *The Shakespeare Birthday Book* (1882), owned by the poet's niece. It offered quotations beside each day of the year, and thus for all birthdays in the Dickinson Homestead and the adjacent Evergreens. Beside her own birthday, on the tenth of December, Dickinson has written "Aunt Emily," and the quotations read "I hear, yet say not much, but think the more" (*Henry VI, part 3* IV i 83) and "Angels are bright still, though the brightest fell" (*Macbeth* IV iii 22).[6] Bianchi recalled bringing this book to her aunt and that the reticent poet "highly approved" of the quotations.[7] Bianchi also mentions the use of "a daily Shakespeare calendar" in both Dickinson households.[8] In fact, she refers to a note, in her mother Sue's handwriting, which reads, "March 7th 1883, Emily, speaking to Ned of someone who was a good scholar, but uninteresting, said 'She had the *facts* but not the *Phosphorescence* of books.'" Attached to the page are lines from a Shakespeare calendar that read, "When most I wink, then do my eyes best see / For all the day they view things unrespected Sonnet 43" and the words "Examples Loyola / Madame Beck / Emily."[9] Sue connects Dickinson's remark about a factual young scholar who fails to see the luminosity of her books with Shakespeare's sonnet in which the speaker rejects the facts of the daily world, where his lover is absent, in favor of a dream world, where his lover appears "darkly bright" and "shadow shadows doth make bright" (Sonnet 43). The sonnet ends, "All days are nights to see till I see thee, / And nights bright days when dreams do show thee me." The question is whether the link between Shakespeare's lines and Dickinson's words was the poet's or Sue's later addition. Dickinson appears to have had this particular sonnet in mind in 1865 when she wrote, "When I see not, I better see" (F869).[10] Although it is unclear if Sue knew this poem, written during the year of Dickinson's eye trouble, the similarity of theme and language is apparent when it is read alongside Shakespeare's sonnet:

> What I see not, I better see -
> Through Faith - my Hazel Eye
> Has periods of shutting -
> But, No lid has Memory -
>
> For frequent, all my sense obscured
> I equally behold
> As some one held a light unto

The Features so beloved -
And I arise - and in my Dream
Do Thee distinguish Grace -
Till jealous Daylight interrupt -
And mar thy perfectness -
(F869)
1 What] When
5 frequent] often
7 unto] opon

Perhaps this reflects Dickinson's tendency to capture the "condensed essences" of the poems of other writers (L503).[11] Both poems set up oppositions between not seeing and seeing, absence and presence, the dream world and reality; in Dickinson's, the speaker suggests that the "lidless" memory of not seeing is superior to the "Hazel Eye" of seeing. The senses can be "obscured," but the internal, dream vision is "As someone held a light unto / The Features so beloved -."[12] As in Shakespeare's sonnet, the absence of the beloved in the day world makes dreams of him or her even more intense; the jealous daylight is reprimanded for interrupting the "perfectness" of the dream.

Also among the papers of Sue Dickinson, at Harvard's Houghton Library, is a page from "a Shakespeare calendar," dated 1 July 1882, with a quotation from the last lines of the induction to *The Taming of the Shrew*, "Come, madam, wife, sit by my side and let the world slip, we shall ne'er be younger." Sue has written on this, "'Calendar for the 25' anniversary of our wedding."[13] The quoted line is spoken by Sly, a beggar who has been fooled into believing he is a lord, to his wife, a boy usurping "the grace, / Voice, gait, and action of a gentlewoman" (Induction i 131–32). Sue appears to have felt these lines appropriate for her marriage, although it is unclear if she is expressing her disillusionment and unhappiness, or merely amusement at this play's juxtaposition of marriage and duplicity. It is also not known whether a Shakespeare calendar was a yearly purchase for either the Dickinson Homestead or the Evergreens; but it seems likely that a Shakespeare quotation prefaced at least some days of Emily's life.

Such communication through Shakespeare was, of course, not unique to the Dickinson household. Kate Scott Anthon, an old friend of Sue's from Utica Female Seminary whom Dickinson met at the Evergreens, used her Shakespeare calendar similarly. Rebecca Patterson's examination of the Anthon books reveals that in 1861 she placed a page from her Shakespeare calendar—Tuesday, March 19, with the quotation "Repent what's past; avoid what is to come; / And do not spread the compost on the weeds, / To make them ranker" (*Hamlet* III iv 150–52)—in her copy of Longfellow's *Evangeline*.[14] Anthon placed two other calendar pages in *The Golden Legend*. One is from Saturday,

May 18 and reads, "Things without all remedy / Should be without regard: what's done is done" (*Macbeth* III ii 11–12); the other, dated Tuesday, October 22, contains the lines "Give sorrow words: the grief that does not speak / Whispers the o'erfraught heart, and bids it break" (*Macbeth* IV iii 209–10). Considering the sentiments on these preserved pages, it seems that Anthon had resolved to renounce something or someone. Patterson's suggestion that these enclosures reflect Anthon's necessary withdrawal of affection from Dickinson and a decision not to reply to the poet's passionate letters seems dubious. Nevertheless, Anthon's use of "a Shakespeare calendar" connects her with Sue and Dickinson and with their often complex and intricate use of his lines to represent, articulate, and reconfirm aspects of their lives. Anthon's habit of placing pages may even parallel Dickinson's own practice; in a letter dated May 1870, the poet tells her cousin Louise Norcross, "This little sheet of paper has lain for several years in my Shakespeare, and though it is blotted and antiquated is endeared by its resting place" (L340). Although the details are unclear, Dickinson appears to be revealing a habit of enclosing string, thread, paper, and cloth within Shakespeare's works.[15] These homemade bookmarks would transform the family's Shakespeare into the poet's secret shrine, and mark sites of personal significance in the plays.

"I can't help thinking every time I see this singular piece of humanity of Shakespeare's description of a tempest in a teapot"

Shakespearean allusion was a standard practice in nineteenth-century Anglo-American culture. Margaret Fuller suggested that once one has been acquainted with "admirable Shakespeare," his words "rise in the mind, on each day's intercourse with the world."[16] In 1864 Emerson recorded in his journal that the bard was America's "chosen closet companion," who astonishes his readers by his miraculous "mythologising [of] every fact of the common life."[17] Dickinson's writings circulate quotations from, references to, and paraphrases of his works to others who knew these texts as intimately as she did. His lines and characters are indicators of her thoughts and feelings, integrated into her own language on occasions both humorous and serious.[18] For these correspondents her Shakespearean shorthand was supposed to invoke a passage, a scene, a character, or an entire play, perhaps (Leyda I xxii). Shakespeare became part of intimate bonds of love, support, and passion, part of the enduring, loving friendships common among women of her class and time.[19]

When compared with the use of Shakespeare in the letters of her contemporaries, her praise for him is often more impassioned and her engagement with his works more imaginative. After the Bible, in fact, Shakespeare is the text that Dickinson refers to and quotes from most often. Jack Capps suggests that "Although she could be impudent with the deity, she displayed remarkable reverence for mortal Shakespeare."[20] (Recently, however, Marietta Messmer has complicated Capps's argument, demonstrating that although Dickinson often is in dispute with ideas in the Bible, she does not manipulate its language, preferring direct quotation.)[21] Yet while she shows deference to Shakespeare's thoughts, the poet modifies, fragments, and adds to his lines, converting his iambic pentameter into her own preferred hymnal meter. Messmer also draws attention to the fact that Dickinson could have quoted exactly if she needed to, so that her inaccuracies may be very significant. There are four ways in which the poet quotes from Shakespeare: she quotes exact lines, uses a mere phrase, adds words to transform a line, or puts his thoughts into her own words. For the most part, Dickinson places her (mis)quotations from, and her adaptations of, Shakespeare's lines within quotation marks, carefully distinguishing his thoughts from hers. Alternatively, she subordinates his texts to her message, demonstrating that, notwithstanding an author's quasi-divine status, reading involves creativity and ingenuity.

According to Newman's *A Practical System of Rhetoric,* allusions "give us pleasure" by "unexpected resemblances, or coincidences of thought and expression," and once a literary work gains celebrity "allusions may be made to such writings without incurring the charge of obscurity, and often with a favorable effect."[22] Allusions from such works also represent bonds between literary men, a language of fraternity, and a "common storehouse of imagery." Dickinson's first participation in this epistolary tradition, however, deviates from Newman's ideal. In a letter to her childhood friend Abiah Root, dated 7 May 1845, she describes a fellow student at Amherst Academy as follows:

> Then just imagine her as she is, and a huge string of gold beads encircling her neck, and don't she present a lively picture; and then she is so bustling, she is always whizzing about, and whenever I come in contact with her I really think I am in a hornet's nest. I can't help thinking every time I see this singular piece of humanity of Shakespeare's description of a tempest in a teapot. (L6)

What is most interesting about this first literary allusion is that Dickinson is so unspecific. Either Root is aware of the precise scene and play her friend refers to, or Dickinson is showing off, demonstrating a more esoteric knowledge of Shakespeare to impress her. Thomas Johnson, the editor of the poet's letters, suggests it is impossible to know what she is alluding to, and speculates that it is a section in *A Midsummer Night's Dream* where Puck remarks, "Lord, what fools these mortals be!" (III ii 115). Dickinson may be equating her fellow student with the confused heroines of this play, Hermia and

Helena, who experience a reversal of fortune and love in the forest. At the start of the play its romantic heroes, Demetrius and Lysander, are both in love with Hermia; now, however, because of the love potion Puck has placed on their eyes, both are enamored of the once unpopular Helena. She believes they are playing an elaborate and cruel joke on her, and both she and Hermia end up "bustling" and "whizzing" about in confusion. Referring to this scene, Mary Preston notes the bewilderment and discord Puck causes; for her, Shakespeare's nuanced presentation of Helena and Hermia as "maniacs," and this "laughable scene," demonstrate his understanding of the complexity of female behavior. Of course, Dickinson could as easily be alluding to perplexing circumstances in which heroines find themselves in one of Shakespeare's other comedies. For instance, Kate's behavior in *The Taming of the Shrew* is described as being like a hornet's nest: Tranio remarks, "That wench is stark mad or wonderful froward" (I i 69), and Kate later warns Petruccio "If I be waspish, best beware my sting" (II i 210).

In three 1853 letters to Austin, Dickinson's use of Shakespeare is more exact, even droll and witty. In two of these, she refers to Austin as "Oliver," equating his secret engagement to Sue with Oliver's sudden attachment to Celia in *As You Like It* (L110, 113). She writes, "Oh my dear 'Oliver,' how chipper you must be since any of us have seen you?" (L110). Like Shakespeare's Orlando, she is asking, "Is 't possible that on so little acquaintance you should like her? that but seeing, you should love her? and loving, woo?" (V ii 1–3). To this, Oliver in the play answers that his love for Celia was "my sudden wooing . . . her sudden consenting" (V ii 6–7). The poet may be expressing ambiguous feelings, to say the least, about Austin and Sue's future marriage. She ends the letter:

> Dear Austin, I am keen, but you are a good deal keener, I am *something* of a fox, but you are more of a hound! I guess we are very good friends tho', and I guess we both love Sue just as well as we can. (L110)

This sibling rivalry extends to poetry, as Dickinson goes on to assert, "Now Brother Pegasus, I'll tell you what it is - I've been in the habit *myself* of writing some few things, and it rather appears to me that you're getting away my patent, so you'd better be somewhat careful, or I'll call the police!" In these letters, she uses Shakespeare's play provocatively to emphasize her role as Austin's male adversary and equal (see L49). Paula Bennett suggests that much of this letter is about Austin's "encroachment on areas she felt rightfully belonged to her (Susan, poetry), the sobriquet had an appropriateness that would not have been lost on the poet even if, as some biographers believe, the nickname originated with Austin himself."[23] While overtly she is congratulating Austin as a successful suitor, she may also be alluding to Oliver's less attractive side;

at the start of the play, he is vicious and vindictive, jealous toward his younger brother, Orlando. Mary Preston begins her discussion of *As You Like It* with the stern moral observation, "Base envy snaps the ties of blood. Inflexible jealousy warps the best affections of the heart. Self-interest clamors down the voice of justice and of nature."[24] Dickinson is perhaps hinting at her understanding of the serious issues and familial tensions raised, and ultimately resolved, in Shakespeare's comedy.[25] Knight's edition of this play, although purchased by the Dickinsons later, contains an illustration of the fight between Oliver and Orlando above the line, "Wilt thou lay hands on me, villain?"[26]

On 20 December 1853, when Austin, who is away in Boston, has forgotten his slippers, Emily informs him that Lavinia has proposed they use congressional privilege and frank them, and thereby "sponge off Congress," adding, "I wish Vinnie could go as a member - She'd save something snug for us all, besides enriching herself, but Caesar is such 'an honorable man' that we may all go to the Poor House, for all the American Congress will lift a finger to help us -" (L145). Her politician father is both Caesar and Brutus, recalling Antony's refrain: "For Brutus is an honourable man" (*Julius Caesar* III ii 82). This equating of antagonists may not have been a mistake on Dickinson's part, for there is something suggestive in the way she combines them to present her father. Contemporary critics found it difficult to discover which of the two was the hero, which the villain; Antony's speech, of course, is a clever attempt to praise both men.[27] George Wilkes argued that even Brutus, in *Julius Caesar*, is merely another noble man protecting his own status and not interested in popular liberty.[28]

Inclusion of brief phrases from Shakespeare's plays is the predominant way in which Dickinson uses his works to clarify and extend her meaning; sometimes, in fact, her allusions underlie the tone of an entire letter. In an 1881 letter to Mrs. Holland, Dickinson incorporates a phrase from *Julius Caesar* (I ii 18) to indicate foreboding and describe recent terrible weather: "We have had two Hurricanes since the 'Ides of March,' and one of them came near enough to untie My Apron - a boldness please resent - " (L689). In an 1878 letter to Josiah Holland, she expresses joy at his "repaired health" and again refers to his literary reputation, noting that he has "reared Fames as rapidly as Houses" (L544). Mentioning the recent deaths of Samuel Bowles and her father, she says, "We hope that you are happy so far as Peace is possible, to Mortal and immortal Life - for those ways 'Madness lies.'" Peace of mind must be summoned up through the betrayed and outcast Lear, who laments:

When the mind's free
The body's delicate: the tempest in my mind

Doth from my senses take all feeling else,
Save what beats there.—Filial ingratitude!
Is it not as this mouth should tear this hand,
For lifting food to 't?—But I will punish home—
No, I will weep no more.—In such a night
To shut me out!—Pour on; I will endure:—
In such a night as this! O Regan, Goneril!—
Your old kind father, whose frank heart gave all,—
O, that way madness lies; let me shun that;
No more of that,—
(III iv 11–22)

Charles Knight provided Dickinson with two illustrations of a world-weary Lear; one, "After a Study by Sir Joshua Reynolds," and another, which shows him raging on the heath against the thunder and lightening.[29] Evoking similar images, Dickinson presents Holland as a Learlike figure whose "Soul's poor cottage [has been] battered and damaged"; subtly, she summons up the delicacy of Lear's body and mind to suggest that regret leads to "madness"; the best course of action is to be stoically resigned to one's fate.[30] This letter recalls Dickinson's "A little madness in the Spring" (F1356), written three years earlier, which summons up the King and Clown from *King Lear* as figures who ponder spring's "legacy of Green" as both a wholesome and "Tremendous" scene. She seems to be alluding to the fact that Lear's time spent amid the "madness" of the natural world, his homelessness in the terrible storm, restores his sanity, providing him with the kind of self-knowledge he had previously lacked. Similarly, in the above letter Dickinson offers the events depicted in *King Lear* as a "wholesome" means of transforming and easing the mind of her friend.

In another letter, dated March 1878, to Mrs. Edward Tuckerman, Dickinson includes a recipe, possibly for caramel, adding, "With it, I enclose Love's 'remainder biscuit,' somewhat scorched perhaps in baking, but 'Love's oven is warm.' Forgive the base proportions" (L545). This refers to Jacques's speech in *As You Like It* where he notes that the brain of a worthy fool "is as dry as the remainder biscuit / After a voyage,—he hath strange places cramm'd / With observation, the which he vents / In mangled forms" (II vii 39–42). Dickinson domesticates Jacques's satirical phrase to articulate her unalterable affection, and as if to reiterate, closes. "Again receive the love which comes without aspect, and without herald goes." Similarly, in an 1884 letter to Maria Whitney, Dickinson says, "The little packages of Ceylon arrived in fragrant safety, and Caliban's 'clust'ring filberds' were not so luscious nor so brown." (L889). She then reiterates her thanks in each subsequent sentence; the parallelism ends with Dickinson equating Whitney's gift with God's "fresher love" that "as the

Bible boyishly says, [is] 'New every morning and freshness every evening.'" Whitney's gift of (red seaweed) tea is equivalent to Caliban's "clust'ring filberds" that he offers to bring Trinculo and Stefano (*The Tempest,* II ii 171). With beautiful witty reversal, Dickinson equates her reclusive self with these sailors, the peripatetic Whitney with the island-bound Caliban. She does not appear to view Caliban as Miranda does when she calls him "Abhorred slave / Which any print of goodness wilt not take, / being capable of all ill!" (I ii 351–53). Her conception of Caliban may thus have been influenced by the illustrations in Knight's edition that show Caliban as a suffering monster.[31] She appears to concur with the 1876 essayist in the *Amherst Student* who defends Caliban and applauds his natural shrewdness and wisdom. Certainly, by comparing Caliban to Whitney and God, Dickinson summons up a loving figure who wants to share the secrets of his island with Trinculo and Stefano.[32]

The few Shakespearean phrases in Dickinson's poems usually have very specific connotations; thus, she refers to Puck in *A Midsummer Night's Dream* to symbolize the mischievous nature of the bobolink (F1348). Shylock, in *The Merchant of Venice,* is evoked in "What would I give to see his face?" (F266) to present love as an absurd bartering in which the speaker must utilize all her means to acquire her "Sovereign's face," from a stingy, silent, and self-hoarding beloved. Dickinson's rustic speaker, who has "'shares' in Primrose 'Banks' - / Daffodil Dowries - spicy 'stocks,'" makes a list of what she would give to see his face: her life, her biggest bobolink, June, "Roses" from Zenzibar, "Lily tubes," "Bees," and "Navies of Butterflies." These gifts are not jewels or rubies, rather natural and commonplace objects (apart from the Roses from Zenzibar). The poem concludes:

Now - have I bought it -
"Shylock"? Say!
Sign me the Bond!
"I vow to pay
To Her - who pledges *this* -
One hour - of her Sovereign's face"!
Extatic Contract!
Niggard Grace!
My Kingdom's worth of Bliss!
(F 266)

The speaker is not sure whether she has acquired the exchange or not; equating her mean lover with Shylock reminds him that it was because of Shylock's stubbornness that he lost everything. Clearly, Shylock symbolizes the danger of turning human contacts into economic "contracts"; the speaker herself is a type of Shylock trying to gain a pound of flesh in the form of her

Sovereign's face. Mary Loeffelholz argues that Dickinson's speaker is a "latter-day Portia" eloquently pleading with a silent Shylock, who may be a father figure, for this access.[33] Dickinson may have identified with Shakespeare's wittiest, cleverest cross-dressing heroine.[34] Anna Jameson presents Portia as the intellectual woman who, if placed in the nineteenth century, would "find society armed against her; and instead of being like Portia, a gracious, happy, beloved, and loving creature, would be a victim, immolated in fire to that multitudinous Moloch termed Opinion."[35] Perhaps Dickinson's speaker, like Portia, needs to assume a male disguise—legal and mercantile language—in order to win her lover. The poet's habitual use of such short phrases allows for many possible significations.

Among her contemporaries, Nathaniel Hawthorne shares Dickinson's practice of quoting Shakespeare. Like her, he often uses a short exact phrase to evoke a feeling or thought, and usually places the phrase in quotation marks. In June 1837, for example, he writes Sophia Peabody in anticipation of travel: "You, who have the dust of distant countries on your 'sandalshoon' cannot imagine how much enjoyment I shall have in this little excursion."[36] The word in quotation marks is from the distracted Ophelia's song in *Hamlet,* where she tells how she would know her lover from another "By his cockle hat and staff / And his sandal shoon" (IV v 26).[37] In contrast to Hawthorne and Dickinson, Herman Melville frequently places phrases—as from *Hamlet:* "flattering unction" (III iv 145); from *Henry IV, part 1:* "take my ease on mine mountain" (III iii 80); and from *As You Like It:* "mistress' eyebrow" (II vii 149)—within his letters without using quotation marks.[38] He thus seamlessly integrates Shakespeare's words into his message, leaving his recipients to recognize the hidden quotation. Similarly, Henry James often conceals allusions from Shakespeare within his own sentences. For instance, "the baseless fabric of this vision" from Prospero's speech in *The Tempest* (IV i 151) is combined with his own words in "I already feel as if Boston were the baseless fabric of a vision & shall have to depend upon letters to keep me convinced of its reality."[39] In Margaret Fuller's letters, she occasionally, places phrases from Shakespeare's plays in quotation marks; for instance, in an 1845 letter to James Nathan, she alters the phrase from *Henry V,* "babbled of green fields" (II iii 17), in describing the beauty of nature.[40] More often, like Melville and James, Fuller incorporates his lines into her letters without signaling that they are quotations. In a letter to Elizabeth Hoar on 30 May 1843 she alludes to Portia's famous speech on the quality of mercy (*Merchant of Venice* IV i 184–205): "The quality of Mercy is not strained not winnowed and double sifted like Charity for 'discovering objects.' But droppeth like the gentle dew from Heaven, alike on the careful and the careless, the forgetters and the rememberers of parasols."[41]

"Do you remember Peter, what the Physician said to Macbeth 'That sort must heal itself'"

Dickinson's early and continued fascination with *Macbeth* centers on her attraction to act V, scene five, which she refers to in seven letters. In fact, the first recognizable use occurs in a letter to Abiah Root, dated 25 September 1845, in which she remarks on her love of quoting from the Bible: "Excuse my quoting from the Scripture, dear Abiah, for it was so handy in this case I couldn't get along very well without it." She then adds, "Since I wrote you last, the summer is past and gone, and autumn with the sere and yellow leaf is already upon us" (L8). Obviously, Shakespeare is also "handy" as, without using quotation marks, she is making use of "my way of life / Is fallen into the sear, the yellow leaf" (V iii 22–23). Dickinson connects Macbeth's despair at the ruin of his life with her own downhearted feelings, which suggests that at fourteen she was already familiar with "wicked" Shakespeare. Later, in a letter of 6 February 1852 to Sue, she recounts a conversation with Lavinia about growing older: "Vinnie thinks *twenty* must be a fearful position for one to occupy," while she herself was indifferent (L73). Dickinson records that Vinnie "expresse[d] her sympathy at my 'sere and yellow leaf,'" adding, for clarification, "dear Susie, tell me how *you* feel - ar'nt there days in one's life when to be old dont seem a thing so sad - I do feel gray and grim, this morning, and I feel it would be a comfort to have a piping voice, and broken back, and scare little children." The Dickinson sisters refer to lines from *Macbeth:*

> My way of life
> Is fall'n into the sear, the yellow leaf:
> And that which should accompany old age,
> As honour, love, obedience, troops of friends,
> I must not look to have; but in their stead,
> Curses, not loud but deep, mouth-honour, breath
> Which the poor heart would fain deny and dare not.
> (V iii 22–28)

In this household Shakespeare's plays were clearly an encyclopedia of the human condition; Dickinson identifies her own melancholic feeling with that of the frustrated and doomed Macbeth, who wonders whether his actions were worth his present state. She may also be articulating her loneliness for the absent Sue. And considering Dana's lecture on Macbeth, (see chapter 1), she may have identified with this character as a poetlike figure overcome, in his ambition and doom, by the power of his imagination.

Like her female contemporaries, Dickinson was also interested in Lady Macbeth and in questions about this character's remorse, guilt, and madness;

she is particularly attracted to the moment when Macbeth's doctor informs him that his wife is "troubled with thick-coming fancies / That keep her from her rest" (V iii 38–39). When Macbeth demands that the doctor cure her, the physician replies "Therein the patient / Must minister to himself" (V iii 45–46). An 1854 article in *Harper's New Monthly,* "The Case of Lady Macbeth Medically Considered," by T. B. Thorpe, examines the doctor's assessment of her health.[42] Thorpe refers to a lecturer, Dr. Stubblefield, who argues that in this diagnosis, the doctor "was committing very treason against the profession" (397). According to Stubblefield, any modern doctor would have recognized that Lady Macbeth was suffering from a "congestion of the portal system," which causes sleepwalking, catalepsy, and sudden death, and tried to help her (396). In contrast, Lady Macbeth's doctor was unprofessionally concerned with "the dark revelations" of her mind, and failed to treat the congestion of her liver; his decision to do nothing "hastened her passage to the grave."[43] Dickinson, though, connects death, sadness, and actual physical pain. In an October 1869 letter to her cousin Perez Cowan, who had just been ordained a minister, she writes:

> It grieves me that you speak of Death with so much expectation . . . I suppose we are all thinking of Immortality, at times so stimulatedly that we cannot sleep. Secrets are interesting, but they are also solemn - and speculate with all our might, we cannot ascertain. I trust as Days go on your sister is more Peace than Pang . . . The subject hurts me so that I will put it down, because it hurts you. We bruise each other less in talking than in writing, for then a quiet accent helps words themselves too hard. Do your remember Peter, what the Physician said to Macbeth? "That sort must heal itself." (L332)

Lady Macbeth cannot sleep because she is troubled by death, or more specifically by her clandestine part in Duncan's murder; Dickinson connects this with the health of Cowan's sister, Cowan's own thoughts on death, and her own sense that "immortality" and its "secrecy" at times completely prevent sleep. She asks Cowan if he "remembers" this passage, then offers him her own, inaccurate remembrance of the quotation: "That sort must heal itself." She may have been offering her own version of Shakespeare's thought. Does Cowan actually remember "what the Physician said to Macbeth," or is he content to have it altered by Dickinson? Her version sounds so Shakespearean he perhaps believed it was authentic. Dickinson prefaces this allusion by distinguishing between a written and a spoken message; for her, how the Physician delivered these lines was obviously of utmost importance. The suggestion is that a voice, perhaps another "kind" one, can soften that which in writing may seem "too hard."

Dickinson repeats her own rather than Shakespeare's words in two later letters, seemingly revising him while preserving his oracular status. In an 1880 letter to one of her Norcross cousins, she writes:

> I forget no part of that sweet, smarting visit, nor even the nettle that stung my rose. When Macbeth asked the physician what could be done for his wife, he made the mighty answer, "That sort must heal itself;" but, sister, that was guilt, and love, you know, is God, who certainly "gave the love to reward the love," even were there no Browning. (L669)

Here she equates her feelings of loss after the departure of a visitor with Lady Macbeth's, but stresses that she suffers because of love, whereas Shakespeare's character is afflicted with guilt. Macbeth's doctor's prescription of self-healing is connected with a divine gift of love. God "gave the love to reward the love." Browning's line from "Evelyn Hope" and Shakespeare's words from *Macbeth* both offer truths about the human condition, which are true "even were there no Browning" (or, by implication, no Shakespeare). This reminds us of Dickinson's own lines, "'Hamlet' to Himself were Hamlet - / Had not Shakespeare wrote." In her own personal rendition from *Macbeth,* and in her poem, Shakespeare's and Browning's authority are undermined; they only articulate preexisting truths about the human condition. Dickinson is subverting Shakespeare, using his universality against him. Recalling Emerson's essay on Shakespeare, these eternal truths are not *his,* and can be articulated in better and new ways by others.

In an 1885 letter to Sue's brother, Thomas Gilbert, after the death of their brother Frank, Dickinson expresses her condolences, again using her misquotation:

> There is little to say, dear Mr. Gilbert, when the Heart is bruised. How hallowedly Macbeth said "that sort must heal itself," yet a grieved whisper from a friend might instruct it how - (L986)

It appears that Dickinson's personal translation of Shakespeare's words has now taken the place of the original, and she suggests also that Macbeth spoke them. Although Dickinson circulates Shakespeare's wisdom to her friends, she really is circulating her own. In this she is, like many of her contemporaries, reformulating Shakespeare to give his words new sense. Thus, Henry James misquotes a line from *The Merchant of Venice* (V i 91) by writing: "The news is a bright spot in a vulgar world."[44] But contemporaries like James are clearly altering Shakespeare's language and meaning; only Dickinson passes her lines off as if they were his, complete with quotation marks.

Dickinson had a particular fondness for the climactic moment where Macbeth realizes that the witches have given him a false sense of confidence, as their apparition's prophecy, which sounded so improbable—"Macbeth shall never vanquish'd be, until / Great Birnam wood to high Dunsinane hill / Shall come against him" (IV i 92–94)—actually comes true. In September 1870, after Higginson's first visit, Dickinson wrote, "After you went, I took Macbeth and turned to 'Birnam Wood.' Came twice 'to Dunsinane' - I thought and went about my work. I remember your coming as serious sweetness placed now with the Unreal" (L352). The scene reminded her of the fantastic and unexpected quality of Higginson's visit. Although she probably went to the scene where Macbeth realizes that "now a wood / Comes toward Dunsinane" (V v 44–45), she may also have turned to the illustrations of "Dunsinane Range" and "Birnam Wood" in Knight's edition.[45] Obviously she thought her comparison clever, for eight years later she used it again in a letter to Mrs. Holland, thanking her for a gift of some arbutus: "I thought that 'Birnam Wood' had 'come to Dunsinane.'" She also, however, connects this gift with the springtime visits of her recently deceased friend, Samuel Bowles, to Amherst (L551). In both letters there is a sense that Dickinson characterizes the visits of friends, from the perspective of her seclusion, as incredible, supernatural events. Of course, the allusion to *Macbeth* implies that such visits are actually possible and explicable.

The other part of *Macbeth* that seemed to particularly interest Dickinson is the first act. In an 1870 letter to the Norcross cousins, she refers to the death of an unidentified woman, noting, "She fledged her antique wings. 'Tis said that 'nothing in her life became her like the leaving it'." This draws on Malcolm's description of the Thane of Cawdor's death: "Nothing in his life / Became him like the leaving it" (I iv 7–8). Here we see Dickinson altering the gender of the line, but keeping all of Shakespeare's words. In an 1884 letter to Mrs. Holland, Dickinson invokes *Macbeth* through one phrase: "Upon the presumption that the 'Swallows homeward' flew, I address to their Nest, as formerly - I trust 'the Airs were delicate' the Day they made their flight, and that they still sing Life's portentous Music" (L950). This recalls Banquo's description of Macbeth's castle as a place of "delicate" air where "This guest of summer, / The temple-haunting marlet, does approve . . . Hath made his pendent bed and procreant cradle; / Where they most breed and haunt I have observ'd / The air is delicate" (I vi 3–4, 8–10). Holland's children had departed, leaving her to care for her grandchild, whom Dickinson seems eerily to be presenting as the "temple-haunting marlet," Holland's "guest of summer."

"The robb'd that smiles steals something from the thief"

Dickinson was fascinated with, and probably marked, the lines in *Othello* where Brabantio gives his daughter to Othello. In December 1879, she responded to

Higginson's gift of his *Short Studies of American Authors* by writing, "Brabantio's Gift was not more fair than your's, though I trust without his pathetic inscription - 'Which but thou hast already, with all my Heart I would keep from thee'" (L622). This compares Higginson's book to Desdemona, although Dickinson hopes he is no Brabantio. Of course she did, unlike Higginson, refuse to publish her "gift," and she may have identified with Brabantio on those occasions, when, as Sue put it, "some enthusiastic literary friends would turn love to larceny and cause a few verses surreptitiously obtained to be printed."[46] Emily herself described such publications as "robberies" (L316). Her letter to Higginson goes on to speak of Helen Hunt Jackson, whom he praises in his book: "Mrs. Jackson soars to your estimate lawfully as a Bird, but of Howells and James one hesitates - Your relentless Music dooms as it redeems - ." She appears to imply that Higginson's praise is undiscerning; he commends Jackson, who deserves it, but also Howells and James, about whom Dickinson is less certain. He thus "dooms" these authors as much as redeems them. Of course, if Dickinson was envious of Jackson, her allusion to this play about jealousy and her use of the word "dooms" are telling (see also L444).

Dickinson was also interested in the Duke's reply to Brabantio, "The robb'd that smiles steals something from the thief; / He robs himself that spends a bootless grief" (I iii 208–9), and uses it in two other letters. Like her repeated use of her own adaptation of a line from *Macbeth,* these lines from *Othello* appear on different occasions. Among the works of her contemporaries, Dickinson's repeated allusions to Shakespeare are unique. The first reference to the above scene occurs in an 1876 letter to Mrs. Joseph A. Sweetser, in which she apologizes for not writing sooner and offers condolences at the death of her correspondent's friend: "then seeing directly after, the death of your loved Dr. A—, I felt you might like to be alone - though Death is perhaps an intimate friend, not an enemy. Beloved Shakespeare says, 'He that is robbed and smiles, steals something from the thief'" (L478). Dickinson slightly adjusts the line to suit her purposes, and "Beloved" Shakespeare is again the oracle offering solace in the face of grief. Her other robbery of these lines is less straightforward, and more inventive. In an 1884 letter, the poet advises Helen Hunt Jackson, who has injured her foot, "He who is 'slain and smiles, steals something from the' Sword, but you have stolen the Sword itself, which is far better -" (L937). Here she alters Shakespeare's sense to praise Jackson not merely for smiling at grief, as Brabantio was advised to, but for stealing the thing that has "slain" her. In other words, Dickinson misappropriates Shakespeare to praise (and perhaps present her envy of) Jackson's more "active" orientation to life and established literary credentials. She adds, "I shall watch your passage from Crutch to Cane with jealous affection." As Messmer points out, Dickinson in this letter offers advice through quotations from the Bible, her own physician, Shakespeare, and her own poem "Upon his Saddle sprung a Bird" (F1663).[47] The last is not identified, but she coyly places herself on the same level of authority as Shakespeare and the Bible.

In one poem, dated around 1872, Dickinson alludes to the way Othello steals Desdemona's heart by telling her stories of his "hair-breadth 'scapes" (I iii 136):

> We like a Hairbreadth 'scape
> It tingles in the Mind
> Far after Act or Accident
> Like paragraphs of Wind
>
> If we had ventured less
> The Gale were not so fine
> That reaches to our utmost Hair
> It's Tentacles divine.
> (F 1247)

Like Othello, this speaker experiences "hair-breadth 'scapes i' the imminent deadly breach; / Of being taken by the insolent foe / And sold to slavery, of my redemption thence" (I iii 136–37). Dickinson's use of two words thus invokes an entire scene and mood, and, in the process, creates an Othellolike speaker. This allusion complements the gothic in her poem, evoking the exhilaration of a narrow escape from the frightening.[48]

"The mail from Tunis, probably, An easy Morning's Ride – "

What we know of Dickinson's response to Shakespeare in letters occurs mainly during the last twenty-one years of her life, and is concentrated in the final ten. There is a twelve-year gap, between 1853 and 1865, when she does not refer to Shakespeare or his texts. Thus, her recorded public engagement with Shakespeare, and much of her praise of him, comes after her eye trouble in the mid-1860s. It also follows the period when she wrote the majority of her poems, many of which she perhaps regarded as more powerful than Shakespeare's perishable dramas (F776). Moreover, she largely excluded references to Shakespeare—the man she called "Beloved" (L478) and "Laureate" (L1012)—from her poetry, to the extent that critics find her indebtedness to him insignificant or irrecoverable.[49] One of the most famous instances of her use of the bard, however, is in the imagistic creation she called "Hummingbird":

> A Route of Evanescence
> With a revolving Wheel
> A Resonance of Emerald

A Rush of Cochineal
And every Blossom on the Bush
Adjusts it's tumbled Head -
The mail from Tunis, probably,
An easy Morning's Ride -
(F1489B)

This is also Dickinson's most distributed poem, sent to six of her correspondents: Helen Hunt Jackson in 1879 (L602), Louise and Frances Norcross around 1879 (letter lost), Mrs. Sarah Tuckerman in 1880 (L627), Thomas Wentworth Higginson in 1880 (L675), Mabel Loomis Todd in 1882 (L770), and finally Thomas Niles in April 1883 (L814). With the exception of Niles, all frequently received her brief, elliptical Shakespearean references, sometimes merely phrases like this one, "The mail from Tunis." Dickinson appears to refer to *The Tempest,* in the scene where Prospero's brother Antonio and Sebastian, the brother of King Alonso of Naples, discuss the succession to the crown now that Ferdinand, Alonso's son, is feared drowned. The new heir would be Alonso's daughter Claribel, whom they had set out to see; as Antonio comments:

She that is queen of Tunis: She that dwells
Ten leagues beyond man's life; she that from Naples
Can have no note, unless the sun were post—
(The man i' the moon's too slow,)—till new-born chins
Be rough and razorable; she, from whom
We all were sea-swallow'd, though some cast again;
And by that destiny, to perform an act,
Whereof what's past is prologue; what to come,
In yours and my discharge.
(II i 246–54)

Antonio suggests that Claribel is so far that she will not discover treachery, for "How shall that Claribel / Measure us back in Naples?"—Keep in Tunis, / And let Sebastian wake" (258–60). He encourages Sebastian to kill his sleeping brother, Alonso, and thus himself become king. Dickinson seems to refer to this moment to suggest that her hummingbird is so quick that it could deliver the mail to and from Tunis in "an easy Morning's ride," and, thereby, as an emissary, prevent Sebastian and Antonio's plan. Her hummingbird is also like Ariel, who forestalls Sebastian and Antonio by singing in Gonzalo's ear: Gonzalo claims that "Upon mine honour, sir, I heard a humming, / And that a strange one too, which did wake me" (317–18). Ariel is thus also the "mail" Claribel would send from Tunis to protect her father from this conspiracy.

Charles R. Anderson suggests that Dickinson's allusion to *The Tempest* "brings to mind the figure of Prospero gazing in wonder at the elusive beauty of this green earth, and the even more shimmering beauty of the unseen world which the poet can create by invoking his muse Ariel."[50] Similarly, Linda J. Taylor equates Dickinson and Prospero, as they both "deal in the complex and ambiguous relation between nature and art and in the revelation of the wonder in nature through art."[51] Dickinson's poem invokes the central theme of *The Tempest*—the transformation of nature by human effort, perception, and art—and in the process a natural phenomenon becomes *her* hummingbird. Perhaps this poem succeeds where Antonio and Sebastian do not, in that, metaphorically, it overthrows her rival, Shakespeare: she appears to subordinate his text to hers by integrating it into *her* magical description. She describes a local and American bird; Shakespeare is merely one allusion among others demonstrating her hummingbird's power and beauty. Paula Bennett writes, "as the owner of a New England flower garden, Dickinson did not have to travel to 'Tunis'—or to Shakespeare's imaginary island—in order to experience this tiny creature's 'magical' mode of flight."[52] Dickinson's reference might be interpreted as slyly usurping Shakespeare by sending her hummingbird on "easy rides," journeys without "tempests."

"Though your Pages and Shakespeare's, like Ophir - remain - "

One of the recipients of Dickinson's hummingbird was Higginson, and other Shakespeare references play a role in their correspondence. In her first letter to him, dated April 1862, she asks "Are you too deeply occupied to say if my Verse is alive?" and encloses three poems and a Shakespearean allusion, "That you will not betray me - it is needless to ask - since Honor is it's own pawn - " (L260). This very Shakespearean phrase, found in at least three of his plays, reflects her education and cultivation: her acquisition of Shakespeare is as fundamental a part of her introduction to Higginson as the calling card she signs and encloses in her letter.[53] But in her next letter to him, when she answers his inquiry about her preferred books, she refers instead to authors he has praised in his article "Letter to A Young Contributor." Although there may have been many reasons for here excluding Shakespeare, it may be no small coincidence that Higginson in this essay understates Shakespeare's significance:

> Keats heads the catalogue of things real with "sun, moon and passages of Shakspeare" and Keats himself has left behind him winged wonders of expression which are not surpassed by Shakspeare, or by any one else who ever dared touch the English tongue.[54]

Probably following Higginson's suggestion, Dickinson here denies Shakespeare a place among her favorite poets, putting Keats above him.[55] In 1870, however, when Higginson visited her, she underlined, as if for clarification, Shakespeare's singular and essential importance to her: he was the only author she "needed" (L342a). During this interview, she also implied that Shakespeare wrote "real" books that presumably met her criterion that poetry made the "whole body so cold no fire ever" could warm it and caused her to feel as if the top of her "head were taken off." Reading Shakespeare (silently or aloud) is a violent sensuous experience. This corresponds to the way Shakespeare was then represented, as the unsurpassable, unrivaled genius who overawed American literary creativity. In contrast, Dickinson in her letters suggested he spurred creativity and inspired transformations.[56]

In subsequent letters, Dickinson associated Higginson with Shakespeare. In fact, in her 1871 letter to him, she follows her remark "While Shakespeare remains Literature is firm - An Insect cannot run away with Achilles' Head" by thanking him for "having written the 'Atlantic Essays'" (L368). Thus, although she calls these "a fine Joy," there is a level at which she puts Higginson among the other "insects" who try to take Shakespeare's crown. Later, in 1877, she combined a quotation from Higginson's "Letter to A Young Contributor" with one from *Antony and Cleopatra* to justify her own decision not to publish: "Often, when troubled by entreaty, that paragraph of your's has saved me - 'Such being the Majesty of the Art you presume to practice, you can at least take time before dishonoring it,' and Enobarbus said 'Leave that which leaves itself'" (L488). Here she is referring to a speech by Antony, not Enobarbus:

> Pray you, look not sad,
> Nor make replies of loathness: take the hint
> Which my despair proclaims; let that be left
> Which leaves itself
> (III xi 17–20)

As in her letter to Sanborn, she deploys Shakespeare in refusing to publish (L402); Higginson's caution to potential contributors, like Antony's loss of his honor and selfhood, reminds her that she should ignore encouragement.[57] She would lose her identity if she published; yet considering Antony's great love for Cleopatra, who causes his dishonor, Dickinson appears to be hinting at her own inconsistency.[58] Ironically, she reprimands Higginson in the same letter for not having published recently—"[I] wondered anew at your withdrawing Thought so sought by others"—reminding him that books importantly preserve the ephemeral, absent, and lost (L488). But she contrasts Shakespeare and Higginson, who write "thoughts so sought by others," with herself and her refusal to publish for fear of "dishonor."

In an 1879 letter, Dickinson actually compares the writings of Shakespeare and Higginson:

> I am sorry not to have seen your "Hawthorne," but have known little of Literature since my Father died - that and the passing of Mr Bowles, and Mother's hopeless illness, overwhelmed my Moments, though your Pages and Shakespeare's, like Ophir - remain - . (L593)

While this is typical of Dickinson's excessive deference toward Higginson, it is true that after those to the Bible and Shakespeare, most of Dickinson's allusions in letters are to the writings of this man who she claimed saved her life (L330).[59] But the comparison undermines, to an extent, her often equally hyperbolic praise of Shakespeare. Comparing the internationally celebrated bard with a nationally respected essay writer, she is demonstrating the vulnerability of Shakespeare's status. She has power as a reader to find significance in the work of both Shakespeare and Higginson, rejecting the literary and cultural hierarchy so important to Higginson. He, however, was not the only person Dickinson identified with Shakespeare.

"With the exception of Shakespeare, you have told me of more knowledge than any one living"

In 1882, Dickinson sent the following message to the woman she once called "sister of Ophir" (F1462): "Dear Sue - With the exception of Shakespeare, you have told me of more knowledge than any one living - To say that sincerely is strange praise" (L757). The question is, what kind of knowledge did Sue tell Dickinson about, and why does she qualify her praise with the word "strange"? George Frisbie Whicher writes, "The knowledge referred to can only be knowledge of the human heart, and if one reflects that Shakespeare had revealed to her the dark secrets of an Iago, a Lady Macbeth, a Goneril, and a Regan, then this is strange praise indeed."[60] Thomas Johnson suggests that the note illustrates Dickinson's sarcasm at a time of much animosity between the friends—when Sue was angry at, or perhaps jealous of, Dickinson's apparent attachment to Judge Otis Lord.[61] In fact, this late statement, from four years before the poet's death, acknowledges the central role Sue and Shakespeare had in Dickinson's acquisition of "knowledge": it presents both as lifelong, "living" emotional and intellectual influences. This is "strange," because when "sincerely" said it was probably Dickinson's supreme compliment; as George Clair's 1871 article on "Shakespeare" in the *Amherst Record* stated, "In knowledge, Shakespeare has dived as deep as ever sank the plummet of philosophy, and in fancy soared as high as the uninspired wing has ever ascended."[62] While comparing Higginson with Shakespeare sounds like sycophancy, comparing Sue with the bard is a fitting tribute to the woman with whom Dickinson had her most intense and passionate relationship. Sue was a well-read, highly cultivated, and creative individual with whom Dickinson shared her love of Shakespeare.[63]

Sue's daughter, Martha Dickinson Bianchi, suggests that there was a continual exchange of Shakespearean "quips" between Dickinson and Sue.[64] Between 1874 and 1876, there are three examples of the poet using a single line from Shakespeare as a note to her sister-in-law: "Egypt - thou knew'st" (L430) from *Antony and Cleopatra* (III xi 56–61); "For Brutus, as you know, was Caesar's Angel" (L 448) from *Julius Caesar* (III ii 181); and "Doth forget that ever he heard the name of Death" (L484) from *Coriolanus* (III i 258–59). Criticism of these notes has followed Johnson's suggestion that they derive from a "strain" between the Dickinson Homestead and the Evergreens. Martha Nell Smith, however, cautions that "readers can never be sure if these passages allude to real events or, if so, to what incidents or circumstances, public or private, she may have referred in these quotations, or if they are part of a literary game the two played, but Sue surely knew."[65] The notes may be a homemade version of the Shakespeare Calendar, or they may merely inform Sue of the plays Dickinson was reading at the time. Whatever their significance, they witness the women's shared domestic and ritualistic use of Shakespeare, a passion growing out of a lifetime reading and discussing his works. Dickinson implies that Shakespeare is, in some way, one of the "living," while Sue is just below him in her hierarchy. Not only is Shakespeare Dickinson's contemporary, whose works give the impression of being "just published," he is, like Higginson and Sue, an instructor, a literary friend.[66] Moreover, like Sue, he personally provides Dickinson with knowledge; this suggests that her relationship with him corresponded with that which Mary Cowden Clarke advocated for women readers. In fact, Clarke transforms Shakespeare into a girl's (female) friend by asserting that this "most manly thinker and most virile writer that ever put pen to paper, had likewise something essentially feminine in his nature, which enabled him to discern and sympathize with the innermost core of woman's heart."[67]

This comparison of Sue with Shakespeare is also evidence of the high affection, bordering on idolatry, that Dickinson felt for her sister-in-law. In 1868 she tells her, "Susan's Idolator keeps a shrine for Susan" (L325). In 1883, she writes, "To be Susan is Imagination. To have been Susan, a Dream" (L855). If Sue is imagination, why should she not be compared with the epitome of creativity, Shakespeare? Like Sue, he is an idol to be worshiped, and a highly ambiguous figure. In 1877, Dickinson sent Sue a variant on the final two stanzas of her poem on nature, "What mystery pervades a well!" (F1433):

> But Susan is a Stranger yet -
> The Ones who cite her most
> Have never scaled her Haunted House
> Nor compromised her Ghost -
>
> To pity those who know her not
> Is helped by the regret
> That those who know her know her less
> The nearer her they get -
> Emily (L530)

Sue embodies the mysterious spirit of nature, evoking Dickinson's 1876 definition: "Nature is a Haunted House - but Art - a House that tries to be haunted" (L 459a). There is also a case for arguing that this reference to Sue is applicable to Shakespeare, for critics of the day often regarded his texts as perfect representations of nature, and referred to him as "Nature humanized."[68]

At the time the poet sent Sue this comparison, their relationship was, to say the least, problematic. Emily had not visited Sue's house in fifteen years, and although Sue may have visited her, extant letters suggest that she was often refused an audience. Inside a Christmas gift to Dickinson, *Endymion* by Disraeli, Sue wrote, "Emily, whom not seeing I still love, Xmas 1880" (Leyda II 336). Sue is literally a "stranger" to the poet, although this does not detract from the passion of Emily's letters to her. By the 1860s, these become more elliptical and abstract: Dickinson has transformed Sue into the muse of her writings, while the real Sue is excluded from her life.[69] She guards against the influence of a flesh and blood Sue by creating her own controlled poetic version. The sense that she is trying to control Sue's power over her is further demonstrated in the one known occasion when she actually sought her sister-in-law's literary advice. When Dickinson sent the first version of the poem "Safe in their Alabaster Chambers," apparently in the summer of 1861, Sue appears to have objected to its second stanza, and when Dickinson sent a new one, it was also rejected. In reply, Dickinson sent another second stanza, this time a lighthearted one, saying "Your praise is good - to me - because I *know* it *knows* - and *suppose* - it *means*" (L238). Apparently she never asked Sue's advice again.

Instead, less than a year later, she wrote Higginson asking him for advice, and included the second version "Safe in their Alabaster Chambers." But although throughout their epistolary relationship Dickinson praised Higginson, telling him that he was her "safest friend" and "Master" and signing her letters

"Your Scholar" and "Your Pupil" (L268, 271, 381, 513), she never followed any of his advice, keeping him a bemused and perplexed onlooker (L330a). In fact, Dickinson cultivated distance in her life and art, preventing the establishment of relationships of influence. For her, Shakespeare may have been like Higginson and Sue—an idolized, intimate, influential—yet a friend whose relationship she needed to make safe through detachment. Such a distancing was an appropriate strategy for a writer in an American culture so full of contradictory impulses toward Shakespeare and of fear of his influence. But her numerous references to Shakespeare in her letters represent moments when Dickinson, cautiously, allows her intimacy with Shakespeare to manifest itself.

CHAPTER SEVEN

"Then I settled down to a willingness for all the rest to go but William Shakespear. Why need we Joseph read anything else but him"

Dickinson Reading *Antony and Cleopatra*

Of the fragile pages in the sixth volume of the Dickinsons' family Shakespeare, those containing the final three acts of *Antony and Cleopatra* are particularly loose, almost detachable. On page 490, there is also a faint, neat pencil mark along the right-hand side of the passage that begins with the line "Egypt, thou knew'st too well" and ends on the next page with "Thy beck might from the bidding of the gods / Command me" (III xi 56–61). Pages 516–17, which contain Antony's death scene (IV xv), have a piece of pink string carefully enclosed between them. The string begins between pages 384 and 385, in *Julius Caesar.* Possibly this connects the great hero of the earlier play with the now pitiable and ignoble man who fails to kill himself fully and dies in Cleopatra's monument, into which he has been, humiliatingly, raised by Cleopatra and her woman. In addition, throughout Antony's death scene, Cleopatra continually interrupts this once great orator. This bookmark is intriguing if we consider Dickinson's interest in Antony's rhetorical powers and her understanding of his tragedy as a warning about the dangers of personal dishonor. In addition, a triangular-shaped piece of brown material, clearly enclosed there for some time, has stained pages 528–29, which depict Cleopatra's preparations for her own death scene (V ii 174–241).[1] These homemade bookmarks probably indicate that these passages had a very special and personal importance for the poet. A letter to her friend Joseph Lyman, written sometime after 1865, may explain the fragile state of her edition of this play and its extraordinary significance for her. During her period of eye trouble her Boston doctor, Henry W. William, shut out "all her dearest ones of time, the strongest friends of the souls—BOOKS." She goes on to record the moment her "medical man" lifted the restriction and ended her "eight months of Siberia," which was "a woe, the only one that ever made [her] tremble":

> Well do I remember the music of the welcome home. It was at his office. He whistled up the fox hounds. He clapped and said 'Sesame.' How my blood

> bounded! Shakespear [sic] was the first; Antony & Cleopatra where Enobarbus laments the amorous lapse of his master. Here is the ring of it.
>
> "heart that in the scuffles of
> great fights hath burst the
> buck[l]e on his breast."
>
> then I thought why ~~touch~~ clasp any hand but this. Give me ever to drink of this wine. Going home I flew to the shelves and devoured the luscious passages. I thought I should tear the leaves out as I turned them. Then I settled down to a willingness for all the rest to go but William Shakespear. Why need we Joseph read anything else but him.[2]

Although this was a unique occurrence, intensified by enforced abstinence, it offers rich insights on how Dickinson read, and on the effects reading could have on her. Her choice of this play suggests that she sought a text she knew would offer her immediate stimulus and satisfaction. Shakespeare is the fox, Dickinson's eyes are bloodthirsty "fox hounds," and the hunt involves clasping, tearing, and devouring his pages. Even the expectation excites and stimulates, eroticizing the whole experience as she undergoes her own "amorous lapse." She appears to equate the loss of her beloved, and tormenting, books with Antony's loss of his Cleopatra. The last two lines propose that Shakespeare provides all she needs; she is like Antony, and the bard is her specific Cleopatra. Her "willingingness for all the rest to go" corresponds with Antony's declarations at the expense of Rome: "Let Rome in Tiber melt! and the wide arch / Of the rang'd empire fall! Here is my space" (I i 33–34), and "I will to Egypt . . . I' the east my pleasure lies" (II iii 39–41). This play is Dickinson's space; although passionate and violent, it satisfies her appetite.

Knight's remarks introductory to the play illuminate this sensual and unusually barbarous account of reading, and may explain why the recovering Dickinson chose this play first. Knight quotes Coleridge's recommendation that "Of all Shakespeare's historical plays, 'Antony and Cleopatra' is by far the most wonderful" and that it is "in all exhibitions of a giant power in its strength and vigour of maturity, a formidable rival of 'Macbeth,' 'Lear,' 'Hamlet' or 'Othello.'"[3] Reading it is an enormously physical experience because

> It is too vast, too gorgeous, to be approached without some prostration of the understanding. It pours such a flood of noonday splendour upon our senses, that we cannot gaze upon it steadily. We have to read it again and again; and the impression which it leaves again and again is that of wonder.

This "flood" of sensation and "wonder" corresponds to Dickinson's frantic and corporeal rereading, which confirms Knight's sense of the play as an irrational experience. Its vastness and "splendour upon our senses" means that "we have to read it again and again." In 1872, Henry Norman Hudson suggested that this is "the last of Shakespeare's plays that one grows to appreciate" because "it is marked beyond any other by a superabundance of external animation, as well as by a surpassing fineness of workmanship, such as needs oft-repeated and most careful perusal to bring out full upon the mind's eye."[4] This sense of abundance of sensation that the play offers further explains why Dickinson turned to it to provide her with "nourishment." Although Hudson criticizes the continual protean quality of the play, he qualifies this by noting, as Knight does, that a full appreciation comes only with time and rereading. The play's "sensuous" effect may initially divert one from its "subtleties of characterizations and delicacies of poetry," yet for Hudson there is

> none of Shakespeare's plays which, after many years of study, leaves a profounder impression of his greatness . . . The play abounds, more than any other, in those sharp instantaneous jets of poetic rapture, a kind of vital ecstasy, which keep the experienced reader's mind all aglow with animation and inward delight. (II 396)

Certainly, Dickinson's response indicates she was "experienced." But her description suggests that her reading of this play is extreme and destructive, and she seems to have physically damaged her edition. She quotes inaccurately from the opening speech—offering only the "ring" of it—and misapplies the lines spoken by Philo to Enobarbus. Her written account shows an almost blatant disregard for the play, her memory of Shakespeare's lines seeming to crowd out his actual lines. Her inability to remember the play recalls Hudson's remark about its "superabundance of external animation" as well as Georg Gervinus's 1863 observation that this is the one play of Shakespeare "so difficult to retain in the memory."[5] What is important is the poet's record of her response; her inaccuracy conveys actual rapture, as she devours and tears the "luscious passages," forgetting their lines. Her reading corresponds to her contemporaries' stress on its sensual effect, as well as her own bodily definition of poetry, given to Higginson around this time (L342a). Her engagement with this play reverses the deadening effect, whereby poetry makes her "whole body cold" and she feels as if the top of her head is "taken off"; for here, she presents herself as reader mutilating author—to adopt her own metaphor, as a foxhound would a fox.

Dickinson may have read Edwin Whipple's "The Growth, Limitations, and Toleration of Shakespeare's Genius" (1867), published in the *Atlantic Monthly*, which describes this play as full of "rapturous vision," exploring the "immeasurable opulence of the undiscovered and undiscerned regions of existence."[6] *Antony and Cleopatra* best indicates "The ecstatic action of [Shakespeare's] mind" as it "is alive in every part with that fiery sense of unlimited power which the mood of ecstasy gives." She may have understood her reading as a personal transference of ecstasy, from Shakespeare to her. Censorship is impossible: objectionable passages can be marked, but the danger lies in Shakespeare's highly poetic language. Of course, her account of reading the playwright would resonate with all those wary of Shakespeare's influence on the female mind, validating their warnings that his plays remove women readers from their roles as wives and mothers into "undiscovered regions of existence" and worlds of fantastic and sensual idleness. Dickinson's letter may have even astonished its recipient.

Lyman might also have been surprised that Dickinson chose a play regarded as morally suspect and centered on characters who had gone beyond self-restraint and decency. In 1875, the influential Edward Dowden argued that they "insinuate themselves through the senses, trouble the blood, ensnare the imagination, invade our whole being like colour or like music . . . the figures dilate to proportion greater than human, and are seen through a golden haze of sensuous splendour."[7] Antony is "careless of his own moral being, incapable of self-control," and Cleopatra is a "Dalila" against whom Shakespeare utters an invective.[8] Gervinus regarded the play as representing a "debased period" in the lives of its central characters, when moral nobleness is wanting in them; he criticizes Shakespeare for his choice of subject and for making Antony a too "attractive personage."[9] Tellingly, Hudson avoided reference to this morally suspect play in his 1848 *Lectures*. In his later criticism, he described the protagonists as gods who transcend "all relative measure and know no centre or source of law outside of their own personality: their own wills are the ultimate reason . . . the moral gravitation of the world having, as it were, no hold upon them, no right to control them" (II 397). The play offers readers "a glad holiday in a strange country where the laws of duty undergo a willing suspension, and conscience temporarily abdicates her throne" (II 399). But "the laws of duty are all the sweeter to us after such a brief escape from them." In other words, the very extravagance of these characters, for Hudson, makes them "strictly exceptional," and, accordingly, this conservative critic justifies and praises this play because it ultimately reaffirms ordinary standards of morality. The modern view that Dickinson and her sister-in-law Sue identified with these two immoral characters and used the sensual language of this play to articulate aspects of their passionate relationship would have shocked all these critics, especially Hudson.

"Susan's calls are like Antony's Supper - 'And pays with his Heart for what his Eyes eat, only'"

Dickinson's passionate and sensual response to *Antony and Cleopatra* may be linked to the sensual nature of its language and shifting scenes, rather than primarily to her identification with its central characters. But most critics in their discussion of this play focus on its role in Dickinson and Sue's relationship.[10] Paula Bennett links Dickinson's use of oriental imagery to this play, arguing that Sue was the poet's Cleopatra to the end of her life and that Antony symbolized her own quest for love and poetry, as he "came closest to having the 'Cleopatra' that both love and poetry were."[11] Cleopatra is not simply Sue but Dickinson's emblem for a desired world of luxury, exotic coloring, and erotic splendor, in stark contrast to the restricted puritanical world she occupied. Judith Farr argues that Dickinson's poetry, like this play, oscillates between poles of abstinence and abundance and that *Antony and Cleopatra* offered the poet a sensual language that reflected her passionate, troubled, and frustrated interaction with her surroundings. At its center, the play is an "emblem for the domination of one person by another"[12]: Sue is the Cleopatralike party lover and mistress of ceremonies, whose house, the Evergreens, stands in the metaphoric East. Dickinson is Antony, caught between a Roman sense of duty and self-restraint and a passion for this fascinatingly attractive yet deceitful woman.[13] Both critics—although Bennett to a lesser extent—remythologize a negative interpretation of Sue's role in the poet's life, using Dickinson's references to this play to reconfirm a particular reading—although these references are highly ambiguous, and if anything imply that either woman may at times have been identified either Cleopatra or Antony.

Dickinson's letter to Lyman, noting "the amorous lapse of" Antony, whose heart "in the scuffles of great fights hath burst the buckle on his breast," suggests that she, like most critics of her day, was concerned chiefly with Antony's relationship with Cleopatra.[14] Dickinson might have specifically identified with Antony, but her inaccurate quotation is from the very beginning of the play, and is not necessarily her summary of it; it may merely represent a rapturous record of her actually reading this first scene. These lines demonstrate only that Shakespeare's text, from the beginning, emphasizes Antony's emotional struggle. The other evidence that suggests Dickinson's identification with Antony is a single note, sent to Sue in 1874, that reads "Egypt - thou knew'st" (L430). The passage the phrase comes from is marked in both Sue's and Dickinson's editions of Shakespeare:[15]

> Egypt, thou knew'st too well
> My heart was to thy rudder tied by the strings,
> And thou shouldst tow me after. O'er my spirit
> Thy full supremacy thou knew'st; and that
> Thy beck might from the bidding of the gods
> Command me.
> (III xi 56–61)

Dickinson may have sent this note to remind Sue of her continued affection, to reproach her for some unreported behavior, or to clarify the immense power and influence she had over the poet. It may even derive from a sense of Sue's betrayal, neglect, or indifference; it has been read as demonstrating Sue's selfish and cruel, as well as charming and fascinating, disposition.[16] It evokes other notes sent to Sue that reveal the lifetime passion between these women: one, dated April 1852, reads, "Loved One, thou knowest!" (L88); another, dated 1885, declares, "The tie between us is very fine, but a Hair never dissolves" (L1024). But there is no reason to assume that Dickinson saw herself as Antony tied to Sue's "rudder" "by the strings"; it is not clear that Sue is the Cleopatra figure addressed by this message.[17] Was Sue aware that Dickinson identified her as Cleopatra, and might she have interpreted this as these critics suggest? In her own poem "Minstrel of the passing days," Sue depicts "strangling vines" clasping "their Cleopatras / Closer than Antony's embrace": her Cleopatra is not the voluptuous seductress, rather a woman "strangled" by her lover's grasp.[18] Moreover, Dickinson's other Shakespearean lines sent as notes to Sue have not inspired critics to suggest, for instance, that the poet is Caesar and Sue is Brutus, or that either of them is Coriolanus (L448, L484).[19]

The supposition that Dickinson identified herself with Antony and Sue with Cleopatra lends certain biographical readings of their relationship the support of the most predominant nineteenth-century reading of this play. In 1898 George Brandes asserted that "just as Antony's ruin results from his connection with Cleopatra, so does the fall of the Roman Republic result from the contact of the simple hardihood of the West with the luxury of the East. Antony is Rome, Cleopatra is the Orient."[20] Antony and Cleopatra are part of a larger set of oppositions that they come to represent: Rome and Egypt, West and East, Man and Woman, and, in Dickinson criticism, Emily and Sue. Dickinson's contemporaries, however, frequently saw the idea that this play was about the ruin of an honorable Western man through his connection with a luxurious Eastern woman[21] as too simple; they argued that the protagonists were not opposites, rather figures similarly ambiguous, deceitful, full of contradictions. In 1871 the *Amherst Record* characterized the play as about the "voluptuous Anthony [sic] and Egypt's sensual Queen."[22] Knight also refers to the hero's "voluptuousness" as well as to his "Asiastic manner of speaking" and his bringing of "the revelry of Egypt to Rome"; he describes Antony's subsequent return to Egypt as "the voluptuary [having] put on his Eastern magnificence"—leaving his wife, Octavia, and Caesar.[23] Gervinus calls Antony an "attractive personage" made up of contradictory features, "accustomed by turns to luxury and privation, to excess and want, to effeminacy and endurance, to epicurean extravagance and stoic forbearance"; Antony is "ivy leaning on ivy" (728–31). Antony and Cleopatra's passion is magnificent and godlike, for "never was a pair of human beings more wonderfully formed for each other than these." Gervinus also extends a remark about Cleopatra ("everything becomes her") to Antony: Cleopatra discovers that "the violence of sadness and mirth, and the mingling of both become him as 'no man else;' and [Antony] 'that to chide, to laugh to weep,—everything becomes her'." Hudson contrasts Antony, "the Nile god," with the "cold-blooded and astute Octavius," thereby presenting Antony in the language with which he himself described Cleopatra: "my serpent of old Nile" (II 394). In their 1889 introduction to the play, Oscar Fay Adams and Arthur Symons call it a very "public" drama, "a lover's tragic comedy played out in the sight of the world, on an eminence and with the fate of nations depending upon it."[24] They suggest that if Cleopatra has the "instinct of posing," there is in Antony "almost always something showy—an element of somewhat theatrical sentiment." Although critics blamed Cleopatra's conquest of Antony for his decline, they were also aware that he too is deceptive and ambiguous. For Dickinson, Antony and Cleopatra may not have been so much alternatives with which to identify as figures that were noticeably similar.

The poet's attraction to *Antony and Cleopatra* may in fact have been a result of the fact that its characters complicate the oppositions they seem on another level to confirm (West/East male/female, abstinence/pleasure).[25] Gervinus argues that Cleopatra's influence on Antony transforms him into a figure not unlike herself: Antony loses himself as "triple pillar of the world," and "with the woman he becomes a woman." Octavius comments on Antony's emasculation and transformation into a feminine figure who is "not more manlike / Than Cleopatra; nor the queen of Ptolemy / More womanly than he" (I iv 5–7). Later, Cleopatra describes a cross-dressing scene after one of their nightly "revels":

> That time!—O times!—
> I laugh'd him out of patience; and that night
> I laugh'd him into patience, and next morn,
> Ere the ninth hour, I drunk him to his bed;
> Then put my tires and mantles on him, whilst
> I wore his sword Philippan.
> (II v 18–23)

Cleopatra desires to be on the battlefield and to "Appear there for a man" (III vii 18). Later, Antony's soldiers declare: "So our leader's led / And we are women's men" (III vii 69–70). Surely, Dickinson, whose writing is laden with disruption of gender roles, would have found this aspect of the play especially provocative.[26] In addition, the Romans in the play, from Enobarbus to Octavius, regard Antony as a contradictory figure who betrays Cleopatra by marrying Octavia and then deceives both Octavius and Octavia when he returns to Cleopatra. His duplicity is comparable to Cleopatra's betrayals of Antony at Actium (III xi) and later at sea (IV xii). As Philo remarks, "when he is not Antony / He comes too short of that great property / Which still should go with Antony" (I i 57–59). It is Antony's indeterminacy, the sense that his behavior is inexplicable to those around him, especially the Romans, that requires Cleopatra's seductiveness as its explanation.

Just as both Antony and Cleopatra are misleading and intriguing, capable of betrayal and inconsistency, Dickinson and Sue were proficient in rejection, betrayal, and great love. The poet's niece, Martha Dickinson Bianchi, suggests that when Dickinson sent "Egypt thou knew'st" as a note to Sue, it represented a reassurance after Sue had "seen through [Dickinson's] social earthworks—using Egypt as a synonym for guile."[27] In 1883, in her second note to Sue that refers to this play, Dickinson's fortifications are again on display, along with her Egyptian "guile":

> Will my great Sister accept the minutae of Devotion, with timidity that it is no more? Susan's Calls are like Antony's Supper - "And pays his Heart for what his Eyes eat, only - " (L854).

This letter refers to Enobarbus's lines:

> And, for his ordinary, pays his heart,
> For what his eyes eat only.
> (II ii 225–26)

But here role assignment by critics is confounded: it is unclear who is Antony and who is Cleopatra.[28] The message might indicate that "Susan's Call" is like "Antony's Supper": Sue's presence costs Dickinson's heart but satisfies only her eyes. This note, however, comes at a time when Dickinson refuses to see anyone outside her family and may not have seen Sue for some time. It must be viewed along with many others to Sue that offer devotion as a means of avoiding a face-to-face encounter.[29] These refusals are elaborate compliments, explaining denial by stressing that Sue's presence is "too momentous" (L581). Dickinson's quotation aptly indicates that Sue did not have a monopoly on frustration and allure, that Antony and Cleopatra were roles both women could embody. In fact, in both of her references to this play, Dickinson may have regarded herself as the Cleopatra figure refusing to see Sue, her unsatisfied Antony. Emily and Sue evidently did not occupy stable roles in their relationship, and the play may have attracted the poet because the central characters were also a "mutual pair," their relationship, like hers and Sue's, varying and reciprocal (I i 37).[30] While Dickinson expressed her passionate and erotically charged relationship with Sue through reference to this play, however, in other references to it she may have straightforwardly identified with Cleopatra.[31]

"Ready now for their admission, she lets the eager public in; but what they were most intent to find still eludes them"

In Dickinson's era, Cleopatra was understood in four interrelated ways:—as a seductress, as the epitome of female enigma, as Shakespeare's ultratheatrical heroine, and as an adulteress—all of which suggest how the poet may have related to this character.[32] For August Wilhelm von Schlegel, Antony becomes unworthy of himself through "the seductive arts of Cleopatra" that are in "no respect veiled over; she is an ambiguous being made up of royal pride, female vanity, luxury, inconstancy and true attachment."[33] Edward Dowden sees Cleopatra as the ideal of sensual attractiveness who weaves "her snares with endless variety, or Antony will escape"—"beneath each fold or layer of sincerity lies one of insincerity, and we cannot tell which is the last and innermost."[34] George Brandes calls Cleopatra the "great coquette"—"What she says and does is for only the outcome of the coquette's desire and power to captivate by incalculable caprices."[35] Henry N. Hudson calls Cleopatra "Shakespeare's masterpiece in female characterization" and "an inexhaustible magazine of coquetry," linking her "ever changing physiognomy" to the play itself, which is always turning into "something new each instant, before you can catch it in any one form it has passed into another" (396, 407–8). According to Oscar Fay Adams and Arthur Symons, it is Cleopatra's "spirit of change" that fascinates; she is the "queen whom everything becomes," with an "instinct of posing."[36] She knows how to interest Antony and "To be to him everything he would have, to change with or before every mood of his as it changes." The interest of all these critics in Cleopatra is part of her seduction, and as Adams and Symons note, "Before the thought of Cleopatra every man is an Antony."[37] The assumption is that only a male reader will become, like Antony, seduced by Cleopatra. But what about a woman reader, like Dickinson?

One woman who was not at all "seduced" by Cleopatra was Lucy Snowe, Charlotte Brontë's heroine in *Villette* (1853).[38] This novel, owned by Sue, records Snowe's encounter in an art gallery with a giant picture of Rubens's Cleopatra, which "seemed to consider itself the queen of the collection."[39] Snowe regards Cleopatra as an indolent, "extremely well fed," gypsy queen who lounges "half-reclined on a couch" in "broad daylight" without wearing "decent garments." Cleopatra represents all that Brontë's heroine regards as distasteful: she is an overweight temptress, passively and listlessly waiting to gratify the tempted. Professor M. Paul Emanuel is disturbed and worried by Snowe "looking upon that picture" and escorts her away from it, leading her to images of respectable femininity—the young girl, the wife, the mother, and the widow. These Lucy regards to be as "insincere, ill-humoured, bloodless, brainless, nonentities" and just as bad as Cleopatra. What is important is not only Lucy's rejection of the voluptuous sensuality and affluence of Cleopatra but also the male responses to this seductive heroine. Professor Emanuel reprimands Snowe's gazing upon the painting as "astounding insular audacity," inquiring "How dare you, a young person, sit coolly down, with the self-possession of a garçon, and look at *that* picture?"; he calls Cleopatra "Une femme Superbe." To stare at such a picture is to be "male," and seduced, and he must remove Lucy from this moral danger. Professor Emanuel appears himself to be seduced by Cleopatra's image, as are Colonel de Hamal, who gazes at her in admiration and awe, and the French fops, who regard Cleopatra as "le voluptueux." When a crowd of women stands before the picture, though, their gazes are permitted because they are "des dames" and not, like Lucy, a "demoiselle."

This section of the novel reemphasizes the seductiveness of Cleopatra for men and the danger her example might have for a young woman. Brontë's Snowe, however, rejects this seventeenth-century Cleopatra as a wicked, weak, and royal object of the male gaze, as well as other images of respectable, obedient, and subservient women. Her dismissal of all these images of femininity suggests the lack of models available to her, and clears her way to search for an alternative. Although it is uncertain if Dickinson knew Rubens's painting, it is unlikely that she shared Snowe's disapproval of Cleopatra. Obviously, Snowe is reacting to a painting and not to the Shakespeare protagonist. Although Shakespeare's play and its critics associated Cleopatra with indolence and indulgence, other women readers saw her as more complex, alluring, and ultimately elusive. Anna Jameson regarded her as one of Shakespeare's most miraculous works of art, different from his other heroines; "Cleopatra is a brilliant antithesis, a compound of contradictions of all that we most hate, with what we most admire" (304–5). She compares the queen to one of "her country's hieroglyphics," noting that there is some "deep meaning and wondrous skill in the apparent enigma, when we come to analyze and decipher it. But how are we to arrive at the solution of this glorious riddle, whose dazzling complexity continually mocks and eludes us?" Cleopatra is "consistent inconsistency," and it is the "absence of unity and simplicity which strikes us; the impression is that of perpetual and irreconcilable contrast." She "dazzles our faculties, perplexes our judgment, bewilders and bewitches our fancy; from the beginning to the end of the drama, we are conscious of a kind of fascination against which our moral sense rebels, but from which there is no escape" (306). Thus, the female reader shares Antony's "fascination": "an engrossing feeling" created by Cleopatra who has "subjected him to every species of female enchantment" (324). The American critic Henrietta Palmer follows Jameson in noting that Cleopatra's rare intellect, royal elegance, and grace are accompanied by her voluptuousness, her debasing pleasures, her insolence and "vixenish temper" (165–66). Cleopatra's seduction is "eternal and unfading"; "this 'serpent of old Nile' shall unwind her coils from about the hearts of men, only when Time shall cease to be." Palmer goes on to tell her (female) readers that the charms of Cleopatra's "imperial coquetry" "bewilder one's moral sense, overwhelm[ing] it with kaleidoscopic brilliancies, tinge its grave conclusions with the spirit of their maddest intoxication, till, like Mark Antony, we find ourselves wondering, applauding, paying participating tribute, where we had thought to sit in austere judgment." Although neither critic could possibly recommend Cleopatra as a model of femininity, both praise and defend Cleopatra as a complex female figure and, to an extent, are as intrigued as their male contemporaries by her charms.[40]

For Dickinson, Cleopatra may thus have been a model for her own elusiveness and perplexity. This would seem to be supported by Julia Ward Howe's 1861 article on "George Sand," printed in the *Atlantic Monthly,* which discusses *Historie de ma Vie,* Sand's autobiography. Dickinson read this piece, for she refers to it in one of her 1861 letters to her Norcross cousins (L234). Howe begins her discussion of Sand's disclosures about her life by comparing these revelations to the death scene of Cleopatra. She suggests that both Sand and Cleopatra retain their dignity by maintaining mystery, even through disclosure. Like Cleopatra, Sand capitulates to the world but does not allow it "the ignoble triumph of plundering the secrets of her life." Howe suggests: "They have long clamored at its gates, long shouted at its windows, in defamation and in glorification. Ready now for their admission, she lets the eager public in; but what they were most intent to find still eludes them."[41]

According to Lucy Hughes-Hallett, Cleopatra was at the time regarded as a profoundly mysterious spectacle, an "object of wonder."[42] This contemporary comparison of Cleopatra with Sand might easily be extended to Dickinson; in 1869, Higginson commented that the poet enshrouded herself in "fiery mist" and he could not reach her (L330a). In the same letter, he told her, "I have the greatest desire to see you," adding, "& know that you are real." But when he asked her to visit him in Boston, she refused, suggesting instead, "Could it please your convenience to come so far as Amherst" (L330). With reference to this, Bianchi compares her to one of Shakespeare's modest and virtuous heroines, Imogen (from *Cymbeline*), although it seems more likely the poet would have associated this maneuver with his Egyptian queen.[43] In an article published in the *Atlantic Monthly* in October 1891, Higginson calls her "enigmatical," and referring to her poem "The nearest Dream recedes - unrealized - " (F304B), he writes, "The bee himself did not evade the schoolboy more than she evaded me; and even at this day I still stand somewhat bewildered like the boy."[44] In 1870, when he finally met Dickinson, she had presented him with two daylilies as her "introduction"; these signify, in the language of flowers, coquetry—something Dickinson would expect Higginson to know.[45] Obviously she was presenting herself as someone he could not "solve in an hour's interview"; some months later, very aware of the success of her Cleopatralike evasive performance, she sent him the following poem:

> The Riddle that we guess
> We speedily despise -
> Not anything is stale so long
> As Yesterday's Surprise -
> (L353)

Higginson also recalls that when he offered her criticism she "evaded" it with "a naïve skill such as the most experienced and worldly coquette might envy" (445). He notes her "naïve adroitness," her "affectation," and her need to maintain an "overstrained relation" with him, which was far from "simple truth and every-day comradeship"; he refers to her letters to him as showing "her mainly on her *exaltée* side" (448, 452–53). The poet's brother Austin told Mabel Loomis Todd about Dickinson's flair for such dramatics:

> As to the letters . . . Those to Mr Higginson are not of a private nature, and as to the "innocent and confiding" nature of them, Austin smiles. He says Emily definitely posed in those letters, he knows her thoroughly through and through, as no one else ever did.[46]

Of course, later Dickinson critics have underlined the poet's talent for self-dramatization and her posing, her calculated presentations of herself in person and in letters, and her poetic creations as a concatenation of alternative roles or personae.[47] If Shakespeare's texts provided her with a reservoir of the dramatic, Dickinson's preference for this play may derive from its heroine's preeminent ability to represent every conceivable aspect of femininity.[48] Judith Pascoe argues that "Dickinson fashioned herself after Shakespeare's most theatrical heroine, naming herself 'Amherst' in imitation of Antony's 'Egypt.'"[49] One of the reasons *Antony and Cleopatra* was not frequently performed on the stage, on either side of the Atlantic, was because of the difficulty of finding an actress willing to play one of Shakespeare's most intricate and mutable characters, who was also an adulteress.[50] According to a contemporary, "The representation of Cleopatra herself has been reckoned one of the impossibilities of the histrionic art."[51] He goes on to praise the most famous Cleopatra in Dickinson's day, Isabella Glyn; she first performed the role in Samuel Phelps's production in London on 22 October 1849, and went on to play and give readings of the part for the next twenty years. This critic praises Glyn's beauty, dignity, power, and ability: "she aimed at the infinite variety of the heroine's character, and impersonated it in some respects to a marvel." Although others criticized the wickedness and extravagance she brought to this role, Glyn created a Cleopatra acceptable to the Victorian stage.[52] The Norcross cousins may have heard Fanny Kemble read *Antony and Cleopatra* in Boston on 16 December 1859, and there is the enticing prospect that later they read this play for the eye-troubled Dickinson, while she stayed with them in Cambridge.[53] Perhaps this is why she chose this play first after the restriction on reading was removed.

The prize-winning essay "The Cleopatra of History and of Fiction," in the *Amherst Student* on 10 September 1870, praises Shakespeare's character as a majestic and powerful queen whose passion is full of dignity and poetry.[54] Yet it also underlines another important aspect of Cleopatra: she was "herself, bitterly conscious that [her passion] lacked purity. The humiliating conviction that she is not Antony's wife, haunts her throughout the play." Dickinson's "Master" letters and many of her poems examine a similar plight, and she may have had no moral scruples about Cleopatra's position as a mistress and adulteress.[55] To "Master," she writes, "If it had been God's will that I might breathe where you breathed - and find the place - myself - at night - if I (can) never forget that I am not with you - and that sorrow and frost are nearer than I - if I wish with a might I cannot repress - that mine were the Queen's place - the love of the Plantagenet is my only apology" (L233). In later poems, she calls herself "The Wife - without the Sign" (F194) and declares, "Seven years of troth have taught thee / More than Wifehood ever may!" (F267). In these writings, Dickinson creates female speakers who become royalty through the denial of their "beloved": they call themselves queens, and at least one of them refers to herself as "Empress."[56] Two spurious allegations questioned the poet's ethical principles. Sue allegedly warned Mabel Loomis Todd not to let her husband go to the Dickinson Homestead, because the women there had no "idea of morality," and she had once "found Emily reclining in the arms of a man."[57] And after the poet's death, Abbie Farley described Dickinson as a "Little hussy" with "Loose morals" who was "crazy about men."[58]

Dickinson, though, may also have regarded Cleopatra as a model of female power. Cleopatra is a combination of what Mary Hamer calls "a woman's body and the notion of authority together" that generates fantasy, myth, and identification.[59] For Hamer, this comes especially into focus because in Dickinson's era definitions of femininity were changing and being changed by women entering the public sphere who were demanding political, social, and educational reform.[60] The *Amherst Student* essay presents Cleopatra as "a stately Queen, conquering, ruling and disposing" and a "true woman, powerful and grand in her fascination, yet neglecting none of those lesser arts, by which women enhance their attractiveness."[61] In an 1878 article on "New England Women" in the *Atlantic Monthly,* one man asks if a New England woman would become "a political Cleopatra, an antislavery Delilah, and use some wiles unworthy of the Mayflower standard to advance the cause she advocates and believes in,—some high-toned flatteries, some eloquent arguments."[62] The unambiguous (and perhaps overly hopeful) response to his question is "Never!" because New England women do not possess "the instincts of Cleopatra or Delilah." Thus, Cleopatra offers Dickinson an authoritative and potent figure of femininity unconnected with domesticity and marriage—a character who may appeal to her awareness of her own secret, regal powers as a poet.[63]

Nineteenth-century critics connected Cleopatra's power with that of other great seductresses, like Delilah and Lilith; this, of course, is especially provocative when we consider Dickinson's own identification with figures of deception and allure like Satan and Eve.[64] In one 1846 letter she tells Abiah Root, "I have lately come to the conclusion that I am Eve, alias Mrs. Adam" (L9); and in others she presents herself as Eve, seduced by the serpent, and as a satanic serpent tempting her female addressee (L 30, 31). Like Eve, Cleopatra is one of the founding myths of Western civilization. Margaret Homans points out that Dickinson's identification with Eve and Satan are part of her need to construct a poetics that is deceptive, that disrupts, figuratively and obliquely, the male poetic tradition and language.[65] Brandes says that "Cleopatra poisons slowly, half-involuntarily, and in wholly feminine fashion . . . [she is] woman of women, quintessentially Eve or rather Eve and the serpent in one" (462). Recently, Robert McClure Smith has argued that many of Dickinson's poems are actually about scenes of seduction, and relate to the hyperbolic interest in the details of seduction in newspaper articles and popular novels.[66] He argues that Dickinson's texts seduce, and were structured to seduce, deceive, and enchant their readers, endlessly deferring satisfaction and signification.[67] He demonstrates, in addition, that Dickinson's critical reception is a story of the seduction of both male and female readers by this most elusive and fascinating writer. This associates the poet's rhetorical and existential strategies with her favorite play, one of the most famous stories of seduction, whose central characters seduce each other, other characters, and their readers. Hudson's association of this play's frequent changes of scene and mood with the seductive nature of Cleopatra's "ever changing physiognomy" invites a parallel comparison of Dickinson's own poetics of seduction with this unpredictable and mutable play.

Most of Dickinson's references to *Antony and Cleopatra* derive from Enobarbus's description of the first meeting of the lovers and of Cleopatra's initial seduction of Antony, where at supper with Cleopatra he "pays his heart for what his eyes eat only."[68] In 1885, Dickinson uses the same lines in a note to her nephew Ned:

> What an Embassy -
> What an Ambassador!
> "And pays his Heart for what his Eyes eat only!"
> Excuse the bearded Pronoun -
> Ever, Aunt Emily -
> (L1026)[69]

Apologizing for not seeing Ned, perhaps because of illness, and identifying herself as Antony—hence the "bearded Pronoun"—Dickinson may yet be presenting herself as a Cleopatra figure who will not satisfy the "beard-less" Ned, an "Embassy" and "Ambassador"; in the play, Enobarbus describes Antony's arrival in Egypt as an ambassador. These lines had significance for the poet, perhaps encapsulating her own strategies of rejection: her writings became a substitute for face-to-face encounters. Other allusions to this play transport us to scenes of seduction, where Dickinson responds to a friend's request for a meeting with both refusal and longing.

After Mabel Loomis Todd and her husband came to Amherst, Mabel began to record her interest in Dickinson. In her November 1881 letters to her parents, she describes Emily as "the *Myth*" who has not been outside her house in fifteen years but "writes finely," adding, "no one knows the cause of her isolation, but of course dozens of reasons are assigned" (Leyda II 357). Todd also mentions Lavinia's invitation to sing at the Dickinson Homestead, noting, "The *myth* will hear every note—she will be near, but unseen. . . . Isn't that like a book? So interesting." In September 1882, Todd sings for the Dickinsons, while the "rare, mysterious Emily listened in the quiet darkness outside," and is rewarded with a glass of rich sherry and the poem "Elysium is as far as to / The very nearest Room" (Leyda II 376; F1590). Dickinson now became one of Todd's preoccupations, and they entered into a correspondence that lasted the remaining five years of Dickinson's life. In the first of these messages, Dickinson wrote, "The parting of those that never met, shall it be delusion, or rather, an unfolding snare whose fruitage is later?" (L736). Dickinson seems aware of the enthrallment Todd felt; and Todd's entrapment did provide "fruitage," in the 1890s, when she edited Dickinson's poems and letters. Before this, Todd began an affair with Austin Dickinson. In a March 1885 letter to Todd, Dickinson writes:

> Dear Friend -
> Nature forgot - the Circus reminded her -
> Thanks for the Ethiopian Face.
> The Orient is in the West.
> "You knew, Oh Egypt" said the entangled Antony -
> (L978)

This letter appears to be a thank-you note on receiving a jug of shaded yellow with red trumpet vine blossoms from Todd. The exotic jug summons up the Orient for the poet, and Cleopatra's Egypt. Yet there is a sense also that Dickinson connects her brother and Todd's adultery with Antony and Cleopatra's, and she seems intrigued by her brother's "entanglement." On 4 August 1885, in fact, Austin compared his love for Todd with "the famous loves of history," finding no "parallel" to theirs.[70] He referred to other lovers as fools: "Antony. Madly in love with Cleopatra—but with the opportunity before him marrying Octavia instead, for political policy. I love you darling—all I am I am yours—for time—and for Eternity. Are you not equally mine!" Of course, Emily in her letter may also be saying that Todd herself was an "entangled Antony" caught up in her fascination with the Dickinson myth. In September 1882, Todd wrote in her journal, "She wanted me to come & sing to her, but she would not see me . . . I know I shall yet see her. No one *has* seen her in all those years except her family" (Leyda II 377). In December of the same year, after receiving a letter from Dickinson, Todd recorded in her journal that "This letter made me happier than almost any other I have ever received. It fairly thrilled me" (Leyda II 379). However, despite her affair with Austin and despite their correspondence, Todd was never permitted to see the poet.

Similar self-protective ploys and theatrical manipulation are apparent in Dickinson's relationship with Judge Otis Lord, again evoking the specter of Cleopatra. Lord was a close friend of Dickinson's father, with whom Emily grew especially intimate after Lord's wife died in 1877; their relationship continued until his death in 1884. Millicent Todd Bingham suggested that Dickinson had a love affair with and intended to marry Lord in the last years of her life; this claim, however, rests on rough drafts and scissored fair copies of the letters she sent to Lord.[71] Martha Dickinson Bianchi described their epistolary friendship as "shared scraps of current nonsense" that flew between "the grim Court-house in Salem and the little desk by her conservatory window, where

Emily oftenest sat."[72] Bianchi also emphasized their shared love of the bard, noting, "Her approach was sure on the high themes of Shakespeare, his favorite author re-read and known by heart by them both, but their enjoyment of the comedy of everyday was also broadly akin." Moreover, Sue indicated within Dickinson's copy of *The Complete Concordance to Shakspere* by Mrs. Cowden Clarke (Boston, 1877) that it was a Christmas present given to her by Lord in 1880 (Leyda II 336). Dickinson and Lord's relationship appears to have begun in 1880. It is not surprising that in the course of this highly literary and playful affair, the poet not only referred to her favorite heroine, she called Lord her "lovely Salem" and became his "Amherst."[73] In a letter dated 8 May 1882, to Lord's niece Abbie C. Farley, Dickinson asks, "Is he able to speak or hear voices or to say 'Come in,' when his Amherst knocks?" (L751). Earlier, in 1880, Dickinson had rejected Lord's love, telling him, "Don't you know you are happiest while I withhold and not confer - dont you know that 'No' is the wildest word we consign to Language?" (L562). Throughout the play, Cleopatra never meets others' desires, especially Antony's. We are reminded of the exchange between the queen and Charmian, where Cleopatra tells Alexas: "If you find him sad, / Say I am dancing; if in mirth, report / That I am sudden sick" (I iii 3–5). Charmian advises that the way to "hold" Antony is to "in each thing give him way; cross him in nothing." Cleopatra replies, "Thou teachest like a fool: the way to lose him" (I iii 10). The following lines precede Dickinson's favored passage describing Antony paying with his heart for what his eyes eat only:

> Our Courteous Antony,
> Whom ne'er the word of "No" woman heard speak,
> Being barber'd ten times o'er, goes to the feast;
> (II ii 222–24)

Like Cleopatra, Dickinson is telling her lover "No"; by withholding she makes him happiest, because refusal inspires further request. In the same year, she told Lord, "I have a strong surmise that moments we have *not* known are tenderest to you" (L750). In an 1882 letter, she refers explicitly to Cleopatra's most deadly deception, in which she pretends to have killed herself and Antony emulates her "noble" deed. Dickinson here compares Antony's declaration that he shall be with Cleopatra again with Christ's promise to the thief that he shall see paradise, commenting, "The Propounder of Paradise must indeed possess it - Antony's remark to a friend, 'since Cleopatra died' is said to be the saddest ever lain in Language - That engulfing '*Since*' - " (L791). The actual lines she refers to are, "Since Cleopatra died, / I have liv'd in such dishonour, that the gods / Detest my baseness. I, that with my sword / Quarter'd the world, and o'er green Neptune's back / With ships made cities, condemn myself to lack /

The courage of a woman" (IV xiv 55–60). The poet is reiterating the opinion of Higginson, who, in an 1867 *Atlantic Monthly* article titled "Sunshine and Petrarch," suggests that Petrarch's Sonnet 251 may have inspired Shakespeare's passage. Higginson writes that "Shakespeare might have taken from them his 'Since Cleopatra died,'—the only passage in literature which has in it the same wide spaces of emotion."[74] This saddest "Since" "ever lain in Language" implies that Antony's loss of Cleopatra immerses and engulfs all else, until the only answer is death: Cleopatra's absence floods the present, until he is willing to kill himself to be with her. At this moment in the play, however, Cleopatra is not dead but in her monument, protecting herself from Antony's anger. Antony's beautiful rhetoric is therefore premised on a lie. The allusion perfectly captures Dickinson's lifetime of Cleopatralike self-defensive maneuvers. Like Cleopatra, she offers Lord absence rather than presence, postponing satisfaction by prolonging her diversions. Yet in 1876, she told Higginson that "Judge Lord was with us a few days since - and told me the Joy we most revere - we profane in taking" (L477); perhaps her "Salem" had already taught her the "extatic limit / Of unobtained Delight" (F1239A).

Dickinson's appropriation of this play in her letters suggests that its importance derived from its reiteration of a sentiment she expressed repeatedly in her writings—for desire to remain desire it must be unattainable.[75] As she told Mrs. Edward Tuckerman in 1878, "To see is perhaps never quite the sorcery that it is to surmise, though the obligation to enchantment is always binding -" (L565); around the same time, she informed Sue that "In a Life that stopped guessing, you and I should not feel at home - " (L 586). In poems, she described "How Human Nature dotes / On what it cant detect" (F1440) and how "Wonder - is not precisely knowing / And not precisely knowing not - " (F1347). One of her many eloquent poems on this subject employs Cleopatra as a sign of the infinite attraction of that which is unknowable and unknown in nature.[76]

"The Tint I cannot take - is best - / The Color too remote"

The Tint I cannot take - is best -
The Color too remote
That I could show it in Bazaar -
A Guinea at a sight -

The fine - impalpable Array -
That swaggers on the eye
Like Cleopatra's Company -
Repeated - in the sky -

The Moments of Dominion
That happen on the Soul
And leave it with a Discontent
Too exquisite - to tell -

The eager look - on Landscapes -
As if they just repressed
Some secret - that was pushing
Like Chariots - in the Vest -

The Pleading of the Summer -
That other Prank - of Snow -
That Cushions Mystery with Tulle,
For fear the Squirrels - know.

Their Graspless manners - mock us -
Until the Cheated Eye
Shuts arrogantly - in the Grave -
Another way - to see -

16 Chariots - in the Vest] Columns - in the Breast -
19 Cushions Mystery with Tulle,] Covers Mystery with Blonde -
(F696)

As in her other poems about the natural world, Dickinson's speaker here attempts to articulate a sense of loneliness and alienation amid nature.[77] Its "otherness" and sublimity, its mystery and secrecy, are far beyond the comprehension of humanity.[78] The "too remote" color or "Tint" is "best" because it is a sign of all that cannot be easily appropriated with "certainty" into human knowledge or language: it is that which inspires human desire, causing both "Moments of Dominion" and "Discontent" as nature represses "some Secret" "that was pushing / Like Chariots - in the Vest." This surreptitious knowledge is "Cushioned" by "Snow" and known by "Squirrels," but hidden from the speaker until death offers the "Cheated Eye" "Another way - to see." The ambiguous ending may refer to the loss of actual sight, or to a new revelation, at the moment of death. The poem's use of "Cleopatra's company" is insightful, as the Egyptian queen becomes a human embodiment of this "Tint." She is Antony's "rare" Egyptian whose "tawny front" like "The Color too remote" swaggers on the eye (I i 6). Her "Company," whether it means herself alone, or her Egyptian company, is enigmatic, beyond comprehension. Similarly, this queen inspires a powerful longing ("Moments of Dominion") and loss as her "pranks" and "Graspless manners - mock" those who desire her.

The suggestion that this "Tint" could earn the speaker money at a bazaar is reminiscent of Octavius's remark that Cleopatra's "life in Rome / Would be eternal in our triumph" (V i 65–66). Of course, Cleopatra's specific worry is that "they [will] hoist [her] up / And show [her] to the shouting varlotry / Of censuring Rome" (V ii 55–57); a piece of brown material in the Dickinson's Shakespeare has stained the scene where Cleopatra expresses her fears about being "taken" and turned into an "Egyptian puppet." She is horrified by the idea that "Mechanic slaves / With greasy aprons, rules, and hammers, shall / Uplift us to the view; in their thick breaths, / Rank of gross diet, shall we be enclouded, / And forc'd to drink their vapour" (V ii 209–13). For a reclusive poet, not to mention one who regarded "Publication" as an "Auction" of the "Mind of Man," Cleopatra's class-inflected concerns about self-exposure and self-display are clearly evocative (F788). The queen's suggestion of the commercial exploitation of her "rarity" is echoed in Dickinson's: "But reduce no Human Spirit / To Disgrace of Price -":

> Saucy lictors
> Will catch at us like strumpets; and scald rhymers
> Ballad us out o' tune: the quick comedians
> Extemporally will stage us, and present
> Our Alexandrian revels: Antony
> Shall be brought drunken forth, and I shall see
> Some squeaking Cleopatra boy my greatness
> I' the posture of a whore
> (V ii 214–21)

Also on this page, however, is Cleopatra's declaration that she will "conquer / Their most absurd intents" through suicide (V ii 225–26). Dickinson's speaker is similarly unable to "take" the "Tint" to the Bazaar. In both cases, it is the unusualness and unpredictable nature of the "Tint," and of Cleopatra, which causes its fascination and excites a need to dominate or control it. But at her death, Cleopatra has "Cheated" the Romans' eyes and remains as seductive as she was in life. Octavius acknowledges that in death "she looks like sleep, / As she would catch another Antony / In her strong toil of grace" (V ii 346–48), adding that "No grave upon the earth shall clip in it" the elusive Cleopatra (V ii 359–60).

To an extent, Dickinson's poem supports Paula Bennett's suggestion that Cleopatra represents "otherness" and mystery, which is typical of the meaning of the Orient in Dickinson's culture.[79] It also implies, however, that Cleopatra and the Orient point to an otherness found in all forms of knowledge, particularly about nature and death—in uncanny moments that refuse all requests for explanation. Dickinson's use of *Antony and Cleopatra* is not primarily an evocation of contrast between opposites, rather part of the poet's complication of this; its significance lay not simply in identification with Antony; probably, she identified with both protagonists. Her reading of this play and its echoes of her own personal and literary concerns can be traced among her own writings. The play represents the ambiguity of a seduction in which the seduced and seducer are already confused, calling to mind her poetry's examination of the relationship between yearning and refutation and her protective strategies of refusal. Certainly the poet was attracted to the play's highly charged and evocative language, yet her references to it center on instances where a desiring Antony, whether "he" be Sue, Mabel Loomis Todd, Ned, Otis Lord, Higginson, or the modern reader, is denied a Cleopatra. Dickinson, in her art and life like Cleopatra, sought to be the enigmatic "Tint" that is "best" because it cannot be taken.

CHAPTER EIGHT

"Heard Othello at Museum"

Junius Brutus Booth, Tommaso Salvini, and the Performance of Race

Dickinson and her sister Lavinia stayed in Boston with their aunt Lavinia Norcross between the sixth and twenty-second of September 1851; on September 9, Lavinia recorded in her diary, "Heard Othello at Museum."[1] The antitheatrical prejudice of the day is implicit in Lavinia's reference to hearing *Othello,* when in fact she saw it performed, at the Boston Museum, a theater on Tremont Street.[2] In 1841, Moses Kimball had established the hall, calling it the Boston Museum to deflect attention from the fact it was a theater and avoid the deep-rooted objections Boston had to dramatic entertainment. Kimball's museum was more than a theater: it had educational value, offering visitors the opportunity to view displays of rare artifacts, paintings, and engravings; collections of stuffed animals and birds; and wax statues of anthropological interest.[3] Advertisements for the plays presented them as of moral and educational benefit, and socially instructive; performances promised not merely to entertain an audience but to morally enlighten it.[4] Moreover, as the *Boston Evening Transcript* underlined on 2 September 1843, all performances at the Museum were strictly censored, and the respectable could attend this theater without being shocked or morally outraged:

> Gentlemen of high literary attainments are retained to translate some of the most chaste and elegant productions of French, Italian, and German drama. It is respectfully submitted that in all Pieces produced at this Establishment, all profane expletives and indecent allusions will be totally expurged. The aim being to offer an Evening's Entertainment of innocent mirth and rational amusement. It is almost needless to add, that the same order and decorum that have prevailed will still be preserved through the Establishment.[5]

This commitment made the Museum a financial success: it induced those who would not have otherwise set foot in a theater to visit without fear of impropriety.[6] It is at this respectable and morally upright theater that Lavinia heard *Othello.*

The Museum was clearly on the agenda for the Dickinsons' visit to Boston —part of what the poet called Austin's "many plans for our pleasure and happiness" (L51). This reflects the level of respectability it had gained. In an earlier letter to her brother, dated 6 July 1851, the poet seems uninterested in visiting:

"About our coming to Boston - we think we shall probably *come* - we want to see our friends - yourself and Aunt L's family - we don't care a fig for the *museum,* the stillness, or Jennie Lind" (L46). A few lines later, referring to friends offering them "kind invitations," the poet remarks, "tell them we are coming not to see *sights* but *them,* and therefore all the stillness will not incommode us." Perhaps the poet is not against going to the Museum, merely emphasizing that she is going to Boston to see her friends; in addition, her rejection should be read skeptically because in the same letter she expresses her wonder and great joy at actually seeing Lind in Northampton the previous Friday evening.[7] But reflecting later on her time in Boston, she does not mention the Museum, and suggests she and Lavinia were "rich in disdain for Bostonians and Boston, and a coffer of *scorn, pity,* and *commiseration,* a miser hardly had" (L54). In a letter to Sue, dated 25 September 1851, Austin reveals that while his sisters were there they "had some capital times together—Vinnie enjoyed herself, as she always does among strangers—Emily became confirmed in her opinion of the hollowness & awfulness of the *world*" (Leyda I 213). It seems likely that Austin suggested they visit the Museum because "hearing" Shakespeare might appeal to his sisters as fellow members of the Shakespeare Club. Perhaps, when she mentioned in her letter to Louise Norcross that she had heard many "bad readers," Emily included "hearing" *Othello* in her assessment. But there is no evidence that Dickinson attended the performance.[8] Nevertheless, it is unlikely that Lavinia attended even this most respectable theater alone. Austin, whose idea it probably was and who "devoted every spare moment to them" while they were in Boston, must have accompanied her (Leyda I 211). If we cannot determine that Dickinson went to her first, and only, theatrical performance in Boston in 1851, she must have heard about it from her brother and sister. More important, the details of the performance offer an essential context for Dickinson's later remarks about *Othello,* as well as the markings in the Dickinsons' edition of this play.

The Museum added to its reputation by including Shakespeare's plays at a time when his popularity was at its highest in America. *Richard III, Romeo and Juliet, Hamlet, As You Like It, The Merchant of Venice,* and *Othello* were the plays most frequently performed; usually, such performances occurred when the Museum was playing host to a visiting star, with the theater's stock company providing support.[9] Shakespeare was rarely staged without a star, suggesting the integral connection between them and the nineteenth-century cult of celebrity.[10] Austin appears to have planned it so that his sister could see one of the most eminent actors of this period, Junius Brutus Booth.[11] Whitman called Booth "the grandest histrion of modern times" and praised his "unswervingly perfect vocalization without trenching at all on mere melody, the province of music."[12] Booth had been the visiting star at the Boston Museum since August 12, and had been praised by the *Boston Evening Transcript,* the "official opinion of Boston élite upon every sort of aesthetic matter," for his central role in productions of *King Lear, Hamlet, The Merchant of Venice,* and *Richard III.*[13] On September 8, according to the *Boston Post,* "the public must therefore make the most of the few opportunities left [to see Mr. Booth] and judging from the attendances of last week, it will not be at all slow in doing so."[14] On September 9, the *Boston Daily Transcript* called Booth's performance of Othello "a master piece of elocution," noting that "the display of dramatic feeling in the latter part of the play has seldom been exceeded in power and pathos."[15] This publicity is not surprising when we consider Booth's status; and the Dickinsons saw him play one of his most celebrated roles, Iago.[16] His Iago was particularly famous; on 20 February 1817, when he performed the part at London's Drury Lane with Edmund Kean as Othello, one theater critic, William Oxberry, had remarked that "Kean on this occasion, outdid all his former outdoings, and Booth, though *Iago* is not a part for applause, elicited it in every scene save the drinking one."[17] This was high admiration, as Kean was considered the greatest actor of the nineteenth century.[18] Later critics commented on the "devilish unconcern" of Booth's Iago, who looks up to heaven at one point with a "defiant forehead and gesture, and with a cold and mocking smile."[19] Although small in stature, Booth delivered his dialogue with "a strong, metallic voice" and his Iago "was subtle, saturninely humorous, serpent-like and devilish, without any apparent conscience or a single moral inspiration."[20]

The Dickinsons saw Mrs. Wulf Fries play Desdemona and Mrs. Emanuel Judah play Emilia. Both were popular and talented actresses: Fries was admired for her "unaffected and correct deportment in private life" as well as her "histrionic excellence," Judah for her strong, almost masculine, features combined with a "womanly sympathy [that] softened the lines of her face."[21] That night the manager of the Museum, William H. Smith, played Othello, having played Iago the previous night to Booth's Othello.[22] Like most Shakespeare plays performed at the time, Othello on 9 September 1851 was accompanied by and integrated into popular forms of entertainment.[23] There was singing by Miss Gaszinski, dancing by Miss Arvila and Masters Adrian and Phillips, and a short afterpiece, a farce titled *Grimshaw, Bagshaw and Bradshaw,* performed by Mr. William Warren, the chief comic actor at the Museum, and Mrs. Thomas.[24] Presumably Smith's Othello resembled Booth's, and Booth's, in turn, was a compromise between Kean's overly passionate, physically expressive, and sexually charged Othello and William Macready's controlled, self-conscious, introverted, intellectual, and quietly dignified hero.[25] Booth played Othello as a Christian soldier who becomes a barbaric prince led astray by Iago's lies; this honorable, noble, and clever man allows his passions to erupt and commits desperate acts.[26] Booth stresses Othello's virtues and magnanimity; the character never loses the audience's respect, and continues to move their sympathies. Following Booth's example, Smith's performance on September 9 would underline the Museum's commitment to rational entertainment and avoid extreme or sensationalist spectacle.[27]

"Kean regarded it as a gross error to make Othello either a negro or a black, and accordingly altered the conventional black to the light brown which distinguishes the Moors by virtue of their descent from the Caucasian race"

Othello's race was a central issue for all performers of this role, and it was fundamental to Dickinson's understanding of the play. In this era, Shakespeare's indicators of Othello's race, such as Roderigo's reference to Othello's "Thick-lips" (I i 66), were scrutinized to determine the meaning of the play and the appropriate response to Shakespeare's character. From Shakespeare's time a white man with a blackened face had played the role, but in 1814 Edmund Kean became the first actor to introduce a "tawny" Othello to the stage.[28] According to his biographer F. W. Hawkins,

> Kean regarded it as a gross error to make Othello either a negro or a black, and accordingly altered the conventional black to the light brown which distinguishes the Moors by virtue of their descent from the Caucasian race. Although in the tragedy Othello is described with a minuteness which leaves no doubt that Shakespeare intended him to be black, there is no reason to suppose that the Moors were darker than the generality of Spaniards, who, indeed, are half Moors, and compared with the Venetians he would even then be black.[29]

Coleridge famously justified Kean's innovation, asking "Can we imagine [Shakespeare] so utterly ignorant as to make a barbarous negro plead royal birth,—at a time, too, when negroes were not known except as slaves?—As for Iago's language to Brabantio, it implies merely that Othello was a Moor, that is, black. Though I think the rivalry of Roderigo sufficient to account for his wilful confusion of Moor and Negro."[30] Coleridge suggested that for an English audience, there was "something monstrous to conceive this beautiful Venetian girl falling in love with a veritable negro." For an American audience, the idea of a black Othello transformed the play into an object of national anxiety and fear. In fact, the play could not have been more controversial, dealing as it does with an interracial marriage, a white woman's attraction to a black man, black male sexuality, and the murder of a white woman by a black man. Kean's presentation of Othello as "tawny" and Macready's need to intellectualize him are clear attempts to separate the "refined" Moor from contemporary blacks by rigorously eliminating characteristics prejudicially associated with them, such as the tendency to be overly passionate, irrational, or sensual. Nineteenth-century ethnology, eugenics, and phrenology, which claimed to demonstrate the intellectual and moral inferiority and criminal tendencies of the black race, endorsed racist views like those of Coleridge and Kean[31]; the idea of a black Othello who was a tragic hero or intellectual was thus an aberration. In the 1840s the American actor Edwin Forrest altered his early characterization of Othello, which was too "barbaric" and full of "illimitable rage," because the savagery came "so close to popular fears about animallike free blacks"; he was also forced to delete "lines dealing with racial amalgamation."[32] Such modifications transformed Othello's murder of Desdemona from an act of "black" savagery to a poetic sacrifice.

Dickinson, who was interested in the word "Domingo," may have read a March 1863 article by John Weiss in the *Atlantic Monthly* called "The Horrors of San Domingo," which discusses the most famous African-American actor in Dickinson's day, Ira Aldridge.[33] Amid Weiss's remarks on the history of slavery in San Domingo (now Haiti) and the bloody slave revolts in the early nineteenth century, he distinguishes between the black races; at one point, he refers to contemporary studies of ethnology to explain Aldridge's talent. Aldridge's abilities are said to derive from the fact that in him "the Felatah was mixed with Moorish or Kabylic blood to make the Foulah," and "when the good qualities of the Negro are crossed with a more advanced race, the product will be marked with intelligence, mobility, spiritual traits, and an organizing capacity." Weiss notes that Hermann Burmeister, the author of *The Comparative Anatomy and Physiology of the African Negro,* "saw nothing negro about [Aldridge], except the length of his arm, the shrillness of his voice in excitement, the terrible animality of the murder-scenes, and his tendency to exaggerate." Burmeister also mentions that Aldridge's "bright-colored nails" and his "whole physiognomy, in spite of his beard was completely negro-like." Weiss points out, however, that this exaggerated and hyperbolic acting style was not "African" in origin; if it were, then "some of our distinguished actors, who are presumptively white before the foot-lights" would need to take out their "free-papers" at once. In fact, Aldridge played Othello and other theatrical parts successfully in England, Germany, and Russia; he aimed to intellectualize Othello and thus demonstrate that a cerebral black hero was not a contradiction in terms.[34] Théophile Gautier commended his successful differentiation of his Othello from the idea of the savage African:

> We looked forward to an energetic manner, troubled, impetuous, a little barbaric and savage in the manner of Kean; but . . . doubtless to appear as civilized as a white, he has a quiet acting style, regulated, classic, majestic, recalling Macready . . . he smothers Desdemona with taste, and he roars properly . . . he seemed to us to have more talent than genius, more science than inspiration.[35]

Despite Aldridge's attempt to defy stereotypes about blackness, the color of his skin remained a significant factor for many theatergoers. In an 1865 *Atlantic Monthly* article, "Between Europe and Asia," by Bayard Taylor, Aldridge's performance of a "mulatto Macbeth" in Russia is praised.[36] Taylor admires the success and talent of a man of Aldridge's "blood and antecedents," acclaiming his deep and powerful voice and very fine acting; still, although his performance equaled Edwin Forrest's, and he "deserves an honorable place among tragedians of the second rank," "his complexion continually suggested Othello." Aldridge was either judged as a typically passionate, irrational, or sensual Othello despite all his best efforts to intellectualize the role, or praised as having superior "blood" that explained his more refined and cerebral Moor. Smith would have wanted to avoid any traces of traits that might be associated with African-Americans; he was socially and politically conservative, and a loyal supporter of Daniel Webster's antiabolitionist arguments and compromise over the recently passed Fugitive Slave Law of 1850.[37] Like Booth's, Smith's Othello allowed "an Oriental temperament to show itself, slowly prevailing over the adopted customs of the Christian."[38] Interestingly, Moses Kimball, the founder of the Museum, was a staunch abolitionist, and the Dickinsons may also have seen a seven-figure display he constructed in 1850, representing the "Horrors of Slavery," in the main hall of the Museum.[39]

Although Kean's "tawny" innovation became popular, and eclipsed the "blackened" Othello, controversy still surrounded the play, and actors and directors needed to carefully consider their presentation of the relationship between Othello and Desdemona.[40] Most theaters, especially a respectable establishment like the Museum, would have cut far more from Shakespeare's plays than had any expurgated editions, or even the most zealous of Amherst College tutors.[41] The Dickinsons thus would have seen a performance that toned down the violence, and Othello's murder of Desdemona would have taken place off stage, so the audience merely heard her cries.[42] Similarly, this production would have heavily censored the sexual and bawdy in Shakespeare's most erotic play. Offensive words like "whore" would have been eliminated or changed to "strumpet" or "wench," and it is unlikely that the Dickinsons would have heard Iago tell Brabantio an "old black ram / Is tupping your white ewe," that his daughter was "covered with a Barbary horse," or that she and Othello were "making the beast with two backs" (I i 88–89, 111, 115–16). For whether Othello was black or not, the play still dealt with an interracial marriage, and, its presentation in American theaters in this era avoided lines dealing with Othello and Desdemona's sexual relationship, and scenes depicting Desdemona's openly passionate behavior.[43]

"Dey say dat in the dark all cullers am de same"

Although the Dickinsons, like other American theatergoers, expected to see a "tawny" Othello when the play was properly produced, the visual and pictorial distinction between "tawny" Moor and black African was minimal.[44] Moreover, they may have been aware of popular burlesques, travesties, and parodies in which his blackness was exaggerated. Versions of Othello and Desdemona on the popular stage caricatured their depiction on the main stage, complicating its presentation of an innocent, nonsexual Desdemona and a whitened or Oriental Othello. In the later printed editions of these burlesques and travesties, such as *Othello: An Ethiopian Burlesque* (1870), *Desdemonum: An Ethiopian Burlesque* (1874), *Othello and Dars De Money: A Negro Burlesque* (1880), and *O-Thello and Dars-de-money* (1905), Othello's "blackness" and the interracial relationship are clearly a source of humor and amusement.[45] Such plays belittled the African-American community, making its members absurd and inept failures in the "white man's world."[46] Their central characters lacked knowledge and understanding of Shakespeare and his eminent plays, suggesting the African-American's inability to appreciate or recognize high art. Burlesques made the cultural, social, and economic mobility of African-Americans in (both antebellum and post–Civil War) America less threatening by presenting audiences with black characters who embody stereotypical traits such as laziness, ignorance, joviality, and gullibility. The relationship between Othello and Desdemona is made laughable: Othello is socially inept and sexually incompetent, and Desdemona's voracious sexuality is presented as ludicrous; her deviations from proper femininity and patriarchal norms, although condemned, are essentially comic.[47] Typically, Desdemona is a commodity, referred to in one play as "Dersde-Money," through which Othello can succeed in society. This is evident from the beginning of *Othello: a Burlesque* (1870), performed by Christy's Minstrels, which begins with Iago lamenting that his Desdemona has left him and is "now with a nasty, dirty fellar, / As black as mud—a white-washer—a nager called Othello."[48] Yet sometimes these plays suggested more complexity: there was a minstrel sung version that condemns Othello for stealing Desdemona, then sympathizes with him because he is deceived by Iago.[49] In one Southern parody, Othello and Desdemona were allowed to sing together, "Dey say dat in the dark all cullers am de same."[50] One of the plays, *Desdemonum,* actually ends with all the characters dancing on stage and holding hands, including the now risen-from-the-dead "Oteller and Desdemonum."[51] These burlesques suggest that despite attempts to control its interpretation, *Othello* was in Dickinson's era understood equivocally.[52]

"Shakspeare was too correct a delineator of human nature to have colored Othello black"

Critical uncertainty also abounded regarding Othello's race. Former U.S. president John Quincy Adams totally disagreed with the whitewashing of Othello and the purifying of the text, especially of Desdemona's passion; for him, such underplaying of the interracial relationship undermined the central moral message of the play. He makes this case in an article published an 1835 in the *New England Magazine,* titled "Misconceptions of Shakspeare upon the Stage"; here he explains that mixed marriages cause tragedy because they are a violation of the laws of nature, and "Nature will vindicate her laws."[53] In Adams's reading, Desdemona is "little less than a wanton" who "violates her duties to her father, her family, her sex, and her country," and "makes the first advances" on Othello, an "unbleached African soldier." This tragedy does not emanate from jealousy, although Othello's jealousy is well founded in the licentious character of Desdemona, but from her disrespect for her father and for ideals of female purity and delicacy. Adams finds her fondling of Othello on stage "disgusting," yet a necessary way of teaching an audience the play's central moral. He asks, "Who, in real life, would have her for his sister, daughter, or wife?" In the following year, Adams published "The Character of Desdemona" in the *American Monthly Magazine,* expanding on his ideas.[54] He examines all of Shakespeare's lines that indicate Othello's race, although he refuses to quote some of these because of their indecency. Although Adams spent his entire political career battling against slavery, for him Othello is "a thick-lipped wool-headed Moor," who referred to himself as a "cursed, cursed slave" (V ii 276) and is called a "Bond-slave" by Brabantio (I ii 99). Accordingly, Desdemona is not "the perfection of female virtue," and brings about her own destruction by becoming involved with him.

Throughout his essay, Adams is aware that his attack on Desdemona might be construed as unreasonably severe.[55] In reaction, Richard Grant White in *Shakespeare's Scholar* (1854) notes that "the ex-President seems to reason with less than his usual acumen."[56] White blames Adams's error on Shakespeare's own lack of knowledge about the race of Moors:

> He had doubtless never seen either a Moor or a Negro, and might very naturally confuse their physiological traits; but a man of his knowledge and penetration could not fail to know the difference between the position and character of the nation which built the Alhambra, and that which furnished their stock in trade to the Englishmen, who, when he wrote *Othello,* were supplying the plantations in the West Indies with slaves, and, soon after his death, introduced Negro slavery into Virginia.[57]

Othello's race is further confirmed by the fact that the Venetians had little to do with the "Negroes" and had a lot to do with the Moors; Shakespeare confuses the two when he has Roderigo refer to Othello's "thick-lips." For White, Desdemona was not a wanton, but a girl of vivid imagination, quiet self-reliance, tenderness, and unbounded devotion to her husband.[58] Similarly, Knight offers his readers a note on the above phrase that acknowledges the cultural confusion about the Moors, who were actually descendants of the proud Arabs. Despite the "practice of the stage, even in Shakspeare's time,—and it is by no means improbable that Othello was represented as a Negro,—the whole context of the play is against the notion."[59] Shakespeare's character was "one of the most noble and accomplished of the proud children of the *Ommiades* and the *Abbasides.*"

Mary Preston goes even further, arguing "Othello *was* a *white man*!"[60] She begins her essay by praising Shakespeare's ability to present "the passions that agitate man's heart," and more particularly, to show how jealousy "often lodges in a fair temple, and accounts for many speeches and many actions in those from whom we hoped better things."[61] However, Shakespeare's ability to represent humanity is qualified by and dependent on Othello being white:

> I have always *imagined* its hero a *white* man. It is true the dramatist paints him black, but this shade does not suit the man. It is a stage decoration, which *my taste* discards,—a fault of color, from an artistic point of view . . . Shakspeare was too correct a delineator of human nature to have colored Othello *black,* if he had personally acquainted himself with the idiosyncrasies of the African race. (71)

The "daub of black" on Othello is an "*ebullition* of fancy, a *freak* of imagination,—the visionary conception of an ideal figure,—one of the few erroneous strokes of the great master's brush, the *single* blemish on a faultless work." Here Preston's prejudice complicates her appreciation of Shakespeare's genius, undermining her suggestion that his characters have universal scope, for Othello can only speak about and to the essential passions of all humanity if he is white.[62] Similarly, an 1858 essay on "Othello" in the *Ichnolite: Amherst Collegiate Magazine* examines the question of Othello's blackness, stating that because most of the indicators of his race come from his disparaging rivals, Iago and Roderigo, they are not to be trusted.[63] Accordingly, Othello is tawny and refers to his own skin as black only at moments when his pride is wounded or he experiences despair. The essayist concludes that each reader is offered a choice with regard to Othello's race:

> We must either suppose Desdemona "fitly mated" to a comely man; or with an unimaginative rendering of the passage, we must believed that she does literally see "Othello's visage in his mind," and thus necessarily behold this fair and lovely woman allied to a *brusque* Negro! There is something too revolting in the bare idea.

How might Dickinson have regarded this character?

"We have a new Black Man and are looking for a Philanthropist to direct him"

Whether read, performed properly, or burlesqued *Othello* summoned up ideas of race and eroticism, despite critical and theatrical attempts to prevent this. It is impossible to approach Dickinson's understanding of *Othello* in isolation from these issues, and from her own attitudes towards race. Betsy Erkkila, Domhnall Mitchell, and Paula Bennett have examined the racist overtones in Dickinson's writings, as well as the status- and class-inflected meanings of her use of white imagery in her poetry, her choice to dress in white, and her interest in Anglo-Saxon and northern European culture.[64] Acknowledging this scholarship, Vivian Pollak suggests that the poet was ambivalent about her own whiteness; in much of her writing she used imagery referring to Asia, South America, and Africa, to express aspects of herself that deviated from ideals of white feminity such as self-denial, self-sacrifice, purity, and reticence. The poet's "representations of whiteness emerge out of a culture in flux: traditional definitions of both racial and gender subordination were hotly contested, as they are in such now classic texts as *Moby-Dick* and *Leaves of Grass*."[65] Similarly Daneen Wardrop argues that Dickinson uses the language of race, slavery, and abolition to describe states of oppressed consciousness, agonies of parting, violations of the human spirit, smoldering and hidden anger, violence, and rebellion. In other words, when she addressed issues of individualism and identity from her position as a woman, she evoked the African-American slave.[66]

One Dickinson poem that deals explicitly with race seems to reimagine the white American anxieties and fears about blacks that informed *Othello's* reception in this culture:

The Malay - took the Pearl -
Not - I - the Earl -
I - feared the Sea - too much
Unsanctified - to touch -

Praying that I might be
Worthy - the Destiny -
The Swarthy fellow swam -
And bore my Jewel - Home -

Home to the Hut! What lot
Had I - the Jewel - got -
Borne on a Dusky Breast -
I had not deemed a Vest
Of Amber - fit -

The Negro never knew
I - wooed it - too -
To gain, or be undone -
Alike to Him - One -
(F451)

Dickinson's Malay gains the Pearl through his fearless skill, in contrast with the speaker-Earl, who is afraid of the "unsanctified" sea and yet calls the Pearl "my Jewel." While the Earl "prays" to be worthy of such a destiny and contemplates the sort of resting place he "deemed" fit for such a Pearl, the less self-conscious Malay takes the Pearl and places it in his "Hut," borne upon his "Dusky Breast." The worthy Earl, who is overly conscious of the Pearl's value, is shocked that the Pearl is now in the Malay's home, and angry that he should lose it to the undeserving Malay, who is unaware of its significance and value. In the last stanza, the Malay ("swarthy fellow" with a "Dusky breast") becomes a "Negro." If Dickinson had consulted Webster's dictionary, she would have found "Negro" defined as "a native or descendant of the black race of men in Africa. The word is never applied to the tawny or olive-colored inhabitants of the northern coast of Africa, but to the more southern race of men who are quite black." Dickinson's dictionary did not have a definition of "Malay," but a later one might have informed her that the Malay was "One of a race of a brown or copper complexion in the Malay Peninsula and the western islands of the Indian Archipelago."[67] While the Earl's antagonist remains dark-skinned, "Negro" was the lowest term on the scale of the ethnography of the day, and it is as if the speaker's anger manifests itself in this downward shift of racial terms. The poem may record Dickinson's undifferentiated fear of the black "other." In an 1881 letter to Mrs. Holland, the poet makes her fear explicit:

> The Pilgrim's Empire seems to stoop - I hope it will not fall - We have a new Black Man and are looking for a Philanthropist to direct him, because every time he presents himself, I run, and when the Head of the Nation shies, it confuses the Foot - When you read in the "Massachusetts items" that he has eaten us up, a memorial merriment will invest these preliminaries (L721).

Here Dickinson blends her disdain for philanthropy, the suggestion of cannibalism, and a clear sense of her own superiority as the "Head of the Nation." The quirky fear and humorous tone of this recluse does not hide the racial attitudes also evident in another poem, "Removed from Accidents of Loss" (F417), where the speaker compares herself to "the Brown Malay" who is unconscious of the "Pearls in Eastern Waters." This Malay lacks awareness and the ability to even dream of a "fraction" of the treasures that might have been his. Like much of Dickinson's writing that employs allusions to otherness, these Malay poems—and the above letter—tend to embrace racial ideas.[68] In "The Malay - took the Pearl" the Earl is intellectual, meditative, and aware of the Pearl's value, the Malay/Negro more bodily and less reflective; it is his physical ability and daring, not his mentality, that allows him to win the Pearl. This invokes the rising egalitarian America in which a lower-class "swarthy fellow" might gain the Pearl, a sign of economic and social status, instead of the more deserving Earl.[69] In effect, this poem describes white American anxiety about other races, and perhaps reflects the poet's own worries about her family's economic and social position in a time of civil war. The sexual imagery is also unsettling, especially if we assume the Pearl represents a white woman lying upon the Malay's/Negro's chest[70]; the poem becomes even more erotic when we consider that an upper-class white woman wrote it, imagining an aristocratic male voyeuristically watching a black male steal and manhandle his Pearl.

In the same year (1862), the *Atlantic Monthly* published "Plays and Play-Acting," reminding her of Othello's "swarthy skin" by criticizing the use of a mirror by the contemporary French actor Charles Albert Fechter when playing this role.[71] The article asserts that "Othello had been too reproached with his swarthy skin and likened to the Devil by Desdemona's father to need any such commonplace reminder of his defects, in his agony of doubt." The confusion about the specificity of Othello's race is mirrored in Dickinson's "black" character, who moves from "Malay" to "Negro." When her "Malay" places the Pearl upon his "Dusky Breast," it echoes Brabantio's incredulity that his daughter could "Run from her guardage to the sooty bosom / Of such a thing as thou"

(I ii 70–71). Earlier in the same scene, we learn that, as Dickinson's Malay will, Othello has wooed Desdemona through (an account of) his brave endeavors. The poem also summons up the main impetus behind Iago and Roderigo's hatred of Othello: their belief that he has undermined their position. Not only has Othello promoted Cassio instead of Iago, but Iago tells the audience, "it is thought abroad that 'twixt my sheets / He has done my office. I know not if 't be true; / But I, for mere suspicion in that kind, / Will do as if for surety" (I iii 387–90). Jealousy is also clear in Roderigo, a man of wealth and status in Venice, who watches Othello steal "his" Pearl, Desdemona. The lines of Dickinson's poem, "The Negro never knew / I - wooed it - too - " take on an aura of threat in this context. In the play, many in Venice, including Roderigo and Iago, have desired Desdemona, and this is exactly Othello's fear: that she has been secretly "wooed" by another, namely Cassio. Dickinson's text almost hints at the power of a contemplative Iagolike Earl to destroy the less self-conscious Malay through sexual jealousy.

This poem reiterates Dickinson's association of theft and robbery with *Othello*. In the Dickinsons' edition of Shakespeare the lines, "For your sake, jewel, / I am glad at soul I have no other child" (I iii 195–96) are marked; also notched are Iago's words, "Poor and content, is rich, and rich enough; / But riches, fineless, is as poor as winter, / To him that ever fears he shall be poor: / Good heaven, the souls of all my tribe defend / From jealousy!" (III iii 172–76). The play's themes of emotional and economic gain and loss are further emphasized in Othello's final speech, in which he compares himself to "one whose hand / Like the base Indian, threw a pearl away / Richer than all his tribe" (V ii 346–48). Although Dickinson's poem examines the moment her "Malay"—"swarthy fellow" and "Negro"—gains the Pearl, rather than the moment he throws it away, neither her Malay/Negro nor Othello recognize the great worth of their respective pearls. This may suggest that Dickinson regarded Othello as threateningly "other," and the play as depicting his acquisition of something precious he does not deserve, which is equivalent to theft. This would explain why, according to Martha Dickinson Bianchi, Othello was the poet's "chosen villain."[72] However, considering her interest in that loss of something of unrecognized worth, or as she put it "the Pearl - / That slipped [her] simple fingers through - / While just a Girl at School" (F418C), she may also have sympathized with his plight. One of the markings in the family's copy of this play suggests that this character provided the poet with lines that easily encapsulated her familiar refrain to people closest to her:

> I will deny thee nothing:
> Whereon, I do beseech thee, grant me this,

To leave me but a little to myself.
(III iii 83–85)

In fact, her conception of this play and its central character appears to have been (or become) more complicated; in her later letters, she actually identified with Othello as the personification of extreme possessiveness and jealousy, despite, and perhaps because of, the racial and sexual controversy that surrounded the play.

"We think of others possessing you with the throes of Othello"

On 20 June 1877, Dickinson wrote to Mrs. Jonathan L. Jenkins, the wife of the former pastor of the First Church in Amherst, who had left with their family for Pittsfield the previous May. She tells Jenkins, humorously, of a family excursion (Austin taking his son Gilbert for a horse ride) and local events (the Amherst Agricultural College commencement and a circus), and then describes how the Dickinson family miss their friends: "I hope you are each safe. It is homeless without you, and we think of others possessing you with the throes of Othello" (L506).[73] There is a sense in which Mrs. Jenkins and her family are "safe" because they are far away from the poet's fit of possessiveness. Although Dickinson's remark is comic, it is also a provocative and unusual way for one white woman to address another; it is also controversial, considering the theatrical and critical history of this play. It might summon up predominent conceptions of Othello: the "thick-lipped" black man Adams condemns Desdemona for marrying; the tawny, safe stage Othello; the black-faced burlesque Othello; and Preston's necessarily "white" Othello. Dickinson places Mrs. Jenkins, the wife of a pastor, in the position of a flattered but baffled interpreter. This letter is in stark contrast with Dickinson's fashioning in art and life of her role as the woman "white - to be" (F307). Despite dressing exclusively in white—to symbolize virtue, purity, heavenly election, worldly renunciation, racial superiority, or simply class and cultural difference—she here uses Othello to articulate her jealousy.[74] Her "exaggerated" jealousy is represented not only by a man, but a black man, since she wants to place herself far beyond such ideals of femininity as passivity, sexual reticence, and innate morality and altruism.[75] Whereas other women frequently identified with Shakespeare's tragic heroes, particularly Hamlet, none of Dickinson's female contemporaries identified with Othello.[76] Obviously she is using this extreme symbol of otherness to speak of that which should not be found in herself and that may hint at aspects of herself she regarded as unorthodox.

In an 1884 letter to Elizabeth Holland that congratulates her on the birth of her grandchild, Dickinson again identifies with Othello, claiming that this "little Engrosser" will take Mrs. Holland's love and attention away from her (L882). She suggests that she "will try to bear it as divinely as Othello did, who had he had Love's sweetest slice, would not have charmed the World -"; she signs the letter "With longings for the sweet Health and Seraphic Peace of my little Sister, Her lover Emily." Holland's jealous *lover* is humorously implying that if she is offered only a paltry portion of Holland's love she will react, like Othello and God, with anger. Yet Dickinson is also suggesting that it is Othello's denial of his "sweetest slice," Desdemona, which makes him such a fascinating character. In an 1885 letter to Mabel Loomis Todd, who was in the midst of her affair with Austin, the poet writes, "Why should we censure Othello, when the Criterion Lover says, 'Thou shalt have no other Gods before Me'?" (L1016). In both of these letters, Dickinson justifies Othello's actions, and presumably her own jealousy. Perhaps Austin's affair with Todd clarifies Emily's interest in *Othello* at this time, and in this letter to Todd, perhaps the poet is justifying Sue's understandable jealousy.

In an autumn 1884 letter to Maria Whitney, who was away in the Adirondacks, Dickinson had referred to Othello to express her own jealousy:

> Has the journey ceased, or is it still progressing, and has Nature won you away from us, as we feared she would? Othello is uneasy, but then Othellos always are, they hold such mighty stakes. Austin brought me the picture of Salvini when he was last in Boston. The brow is that of Deity - the eyes, those of the lost, but the power lies in the *throat* - pleading, sovereign, savage - the panther and the dove! Each, how innocent!" (L948)

As in her letter to the new "Grandma," Dickinson is a covetous Othello. This time the "Engrosser" is "Nature" and Dickinson, like the Moor, holds "such mighty stakes." Again, she presents Othello as "divine" and lost. Dickinson's understanding of the character was complex. While actors and critics disputed whether he was black or a Moor, Othello had become both: he is sovereign and savage, panther and dove—the intellectual Othello, the sensual Othello, the black Othello, the Moorish Othello, and the white Othello.

"Austin heard Salvini before his Idol died, and the size of that manifestation even the Grave has not foreclosed"

All of Dickinson's allusions to *Othello* occur after Austin's attendance at one of Tommaso Salvini's performances in America in 1873–74.[77] In her 1884 letter to Elizabeth Holland, she says, "Austin heard Salvini before his Idol died, and the size of that manifestation even the Grave has not foreclosed - " (L882). Salvini's wife, "his Idol," died in 1878, and the allusion suggests that Dickinson wonders if his wife's death has altered Salvini's performance in the role of a wife-killer. Dickinson's letter to Whitney seems to describe an actual picture of Salvini, which Austin probably gave her after he saw Salvini again in 1883. Despite all indications that Dickinson would find theater and performance in nineteenth-century America abhorrent, Salvini's performances in the early 1880s may have caused her to reevaluate Othello; and perhaps they made it possible for her to identify with this character. That Austin brought Dickinson a picture of Salvini is not surprising in a time when pictures and souvenirs of stars elevated their celebrity.[78] In his biography of Salvini, Celso Salvini notes the immense publicity campaign that accompanied the first American visit:

> Everywhere there were photographic pictures; lithographs by the thousands, in a hundred different poses, distributed to every part of the city; his name in block capitals on every wall, in every public place . . . [along with] thousands of biographies everywhere, in the hotels, in the theatres, in all public places, scattered along the thoroughfares by huge coaches—biographies each one different from the next, containing the most arbitrary and fantastic things, and truthful in nothing except Salvini's name."[79]

This campaign was obviously very successful; Salvini played to packed theaters eager to see his unique interpretation of Othello. It is not clear if Austin gave Dickinson a photograph or an illustration of the actor. The poet was interested in photography as a means of preserving people's faces, yet wary of this new medium (L268).[80] Any disparity she may have identified between the fixed image and the living subject seems moot: the picture captures the essence of his performance of Othello and spurred Dickinson's own written portrait.[81]

Dickinson's description of Salvini suggests definite familiarity with his performance in this role. She may have been informed by conversations with Austin, but her poetic appraisal reflects two contemporary reviews in the November 1881 edition of the literary magazine *The Century,* "Tommaso Salvini" by Emma Lazarus and "Impressions of Some Shakspearean Characters" by Salvini himself.[82] The first two pages of Lazarus's article, one of which includes an illustration of Salvini, are scissored out of the volume of *The Century* among the Dickinsons' books at Harvard's Houghton Library. Perhaps even before receiving Austin's gift Dickinson had been sufficiently interested in Salvini's appearance to perform this excision. On one of the missing pages Lazarus offers imagery and language for the poet's own later assessment of this actor's face, voice, and sovereignty:

> No man could be more perfectly equipped by nature for the tragic stage than Tommaso Salvini. His physical gifts are a frame of massive and harmonious proportions, uniting an incomparable majesty of bearing with the utmost grace

> of movement, a handsome and singularly mobile face, and, most memorable of all, a voice of such depth and volume of tone, and such exquisite and infinitely varied modulations, that having been once heard, it haunts the sense like noble music. (111)

As Dickinson would later, Lazarus refers to what she calls Salvini's "superb picture of oriental grace and majesty" (114). Both women also mention his face and eyes; Lazarus suggests that his eyes and lips are entrusted with "the task of forcing conviction" upon his listeners and that "it is these features which finish and complete the work of his words." Like Lazarus, Dickinson is most interested in Salvini's throat; according to Lazarus, it is the voice of this actor that casts a "magnetic spell" upon the audience, adding to "expressiveness of gesture" his "thrilling and unanswerable eloquence." Salvini enthralls his hearers with "his sudden electric transitions through every phase of emotion" (113). This underlines Dickinson's belief in the importance of owning the ear, "Enamored - impotent - content - " (F348), especially when it came to Shakespeare's plays, and it recalls the fact that Desdemona becomes enamored of Othello because of how he spoke to her about his adventures.

Also on the missing page, Lazarus describes how Salvini met his "Idol," a young English lady, during his stay in London in 1875, and how after three years of "domestic happiness" she died. Lazarus records Salvini's anguish: "With her the largest part of my inspiration has vanished, and I fear that I must now always remain as I am, without hope of improving in my art" (111). But she reassures an inquisitive reader that he has not lost his power as an artist, confirming that although a "grotesquely bad" English-speaking company is supporting him, his genius is transcendent.[83] She argues that when compared with Shakespeare's text, Salvini's Othello is true to "the spirit of Shakspere," and she dismisses those who think it is "brutal, coarse and *un-Shaksperean*" (113). In fact, readers are reminded that Salvini softens the play to suit modern refine tastes, leaving out "Shakspere's own words and explicit directions," although he does include the moment Othello strikes Desdemona before the Venetian ambassadors. For Lazarus:

> Salvini represents to us, at the outset of this play, a loyal, fiery nature, reveals the fierce conflict of insane pride, jealousy, and vengeance, in which the noble qualities seem for a time completely extinguished and ends by showing us "him that *was Othello*," broken by remorse, shattered with grief, but substantially the very same as at the beginning of the tragedy!

But the "frenzy of his awakened wrath in the last three acts" overshadows the audience's memory of this smiling and happy Othello, and suggests Dickinson's own description of a divided Othello (114).[84] For Lazarus, however,

Salvini's final speech "connects the *Othello* of *Desdemona's* love with the *Othello* who assassinated her." He rises with the "old majesty of carriage and commanding trumpet-tones," ceasing to be the man "whose whole frame" had just been "quivering with affliction" (113). Salvini's Othello is a complex figure, not "an embodiment of a single furious passion but a rounded, many-sided human being, who anon compels our love, our admiration, our pity, our horror, and in the end our aching sympathy." An audience is left having experienced "a colossal power" as Salvini's Othello "sweeps the whole gamut of passion, from frankest loyalty and simplicity of affection, through doubt, anguish, livid wrath, insensate jealousy, and blood-thirsty revenge to a sublime despair." In Dickinson's words, he is sovereign and savage, panther and dove.

Salvini in his article, as Dickinson does, refers to Othello as "sovereign," stating that "Othello was descended from a royal race, of whose honor, however, he never boasted" (122). Emphasizing Othello's innocence, as Dickinson does, Salvini calls him "too credulous," arguing that "without experience in evil himself, he had no idea of dissimulation in others" (123). He is naïve in the face of Iago, who is "the personification of all deception," "the crucible in which all deceptions are fused together," and "the very ideal of perfidy and treachery."[85] Desdemona admires Othello's "noble qualities, sees beneath his dark complexion the whiteness of his soul and declares her love," but Othello is prevented from expressing his love because of "the impediments of difference in race and in position." This corresponds with Dickinson's color-inflected description of Salvini/Othello as both a panther and a dove. Salvini attempts to underplay Othello's race, arguing that he is "no more jealous than any other man in the same circumstances would be." Yet he also notes how Iago bids Othello to "remember the difference of color and of customs between" Desdemona and himself.[86] Salvini argues that his murder of Desdemona was not barbaric and passionate, as some critics claimed; for him, "her death is a sacrifice which he owes to society; he has the right to inflict this punishment and has no thought of concealment" (124). In accomplishing this "act of justice," Othello sacrifices himself as well as Desdemona. Salvini specifically cites Othello's race to justify his own unorthodox performance of Othello's suicide, in which he cuts his throat rather than stabbing himself:

> this manner [of death] is more in accordance with the customs of the people of Africa, who usually execute their criminals and enemies in this way; then the arms used by these people are of a curved form, and, as such, are more adapted to this mode than to any other. . . . This form of suicide may indeed be opposed to tradition, but while I respect this authority, I cannot submit to it. I must, therefore, insist upon dying in my own way.

He justifies this by referring to Shakespeare's line, "I took by the throat the circumcised dog, / And smote him—thus" (V ii 355–56).[87]

The month before Austin attended Salvini's 1883 performance in Boston, Henry James published the article "Tommaso Salvini" in the *Atlantic Monthly*.[88] James refers to the devotion and sympathy Salvini inspires in his audience and says that "no other artist today begins to be capable of giving us such an exhibition of tragic power" (378). Austin's diary entry on April 11 reports, "Evng went to the Museum to hear Salvini and Clara Morris as Othello and Desdemona, a revelation to me of human power" (Leyda II 396).[89] That Salvini spoke in Italian and his company replied in English is condemned by James as "grotesque, unpardonable, abominable" and the production's only flaw. Yet this did not prevent great numbers of Bostonians from coming to hear a language they did not understand—such was Salvini's "art of inspiring sympathy" and his "inexhaustible energy." Despite the presence of the "ugly, repulsive and bestial," James, like Dickinson, finds depths of nobility and passion in the visual and audible aspects of Salvini's performance:

> His powerful, active, manly frame, his noble, serious, vividly expressive face, his splendid smile, his Italian eye, his superb, voluminous voice, his carriage, his tone, his ease, the assurance he instantly gives that he holds the whole part in his hands and can make of it exactly what he chooses,—all this descends upon the spectator's mind with a richness which immediately converts attention into faith, and expectation into sympathy. He is a magnificent creature, and you are already on his side. (379)

For James, Othello has heroic qualities, and his "noble intention" lies behind every one of Salvini's actions on stage; the writer also praises Salvini's exclusion of Othello's "manly melancholy," his "deep reflections." But unlike Lazarus and Salvini, James underlines Othello's race. He argues that Salvini did not read Shakespeare in the Anglo-Saxon way, rather with "the Italian imagination." Moreover, "No more complete picture of passion can have been given to the stage in our day,—passion beginning in noble repose and spending itself in black insanity" (380). This performance is a portrait of "an African by an Italian": Salvini's Othello displays the rage of a "wounded animal," which never turns to excess, and "the rage of an African, but of a nature that remains generous to the end." The performance is "intensely human," and "in spite of the tiger-paces and tiger-springs, there is through it all, to my sense at least, the tremor of a moral element" (381). Even Salvini's tigerlike spring across the room to catch Iago James regards as "the high-water mark of dramatic experience"; after wounding the villain, Othello falls into a chair and lies there for some moments, "prostrate, panting, helpless, annihilated, convulsed with long, inarticulate moans."[90] Although some critics regarded Salvini's performance as coarse, and were sickened by its "bestial fury," Dickinson's own references to his animality suggest she shared James's praise for the way this actor thrilled his audience. Like James, she appears to have believed he was offering the American public Shakespeare's authentic Othello, combining passion and violence, innocence and pain.

Salvini's became the definitive Othello of the era; as James asserted, "Some of his tones, movements, attitudes, are ineffaceable; they have passed into the stock of common reference" (380). Appropriately, Dickinson's description of the actor's picture is the concentrated substance of these shared ideas; it reflects Salvini's central role in her conception of *Othello* and its central character. Yet her identification with Othello's jealousy, particularly in letters to her female friends, while explained through reference to the Italian actor, remains problematic because of the connections with what James regards as "black insanity" and African passion, and even with Salvini's racially inflected representation of Othello felt by many critics to be vulgar and unnecessarily violent, transforming the noble hero into an animal.[91] Some suggested that the violence and eroticism that pleased and attracted a sensation-loving audience stripped away the façade of sentimentality of a genteel age.[92] Perhaps Dickinson's own championing of Salvini and her fascination with Othello suggest she believed that human passion was more complex than morality and decorum allowed.

CHAPTER NINE

"Hamlet wavered for all of us"

Dickinson and Shakespearean Tragedy

IN THE SUMMER of 1877, Dickinson sent a cape jasmine to Thomas Wentworth Higginson's wife, with the following message: "I send you a flower from my garden - Though it die in reaching you, you will know it lived, when it left my hand - Hamlet wavered for all of us - " (L512). Her message makes the simple gift of a flower a transaction equivalent to a Shakespearean tragedy. It also underlines the way Dickinson ascribed human feelings and characteristics to her flowers, here elevating the death of a jasmine through reference to English theater's greatest tragic hero.[1] This flower has been sacrificed for Mrs. Higginson; it was taken from the poet's garden as a sign of her love; alive when it left her hand, it is dead on arrival, a tragic hero that is predestined to die and "touch" its audience. While Mrs. Higginson will only witness the final moment of Dickinson's flower, Emily's reference to Hamlet's wavering hints at its "unseen" tragic story. "Wavering" invokes a flower quivering in the wind, but also Hamlet's struggle with mortality. All human beings share in this struggle, and Dickinson, through reference to a flower, is making Hamlet a representative figure. Shakespearean tragedy is the representation, before an audience, of the intensity of a lived life; the audience can identify with the lives and, particularly, the deaths of its characters. Hamlet's life of wavering and his death are essential: perhaps, like Dickinson's flower, he must die to have his story endlessly retold.

In "The American Scholar" (1837), Emerson calls his time an "age of Introversion" infected by "Hamlet's unhappiness," in which every thought is overanalyzed.[2] Hamlet becomes an emblem for an age of procrastination, introspection, melancholy, misanthropy, irresolution, and inaction. Later, in his essay on Shakespeare, he suggests that this play attracts readers because the nineteenth century's speculative genius is "a sort of living Hamlet."[3] Dickinson's use of the word "wavers" perfectly encapsulates Hamlet's constant vacillation between alternatives of mood, action, and thought. A February 1851 article in *The Indicator* describes Hamlet as "a man of many theories, great moral thoughts, and the keenest sensibility; and he joined to these characteristics a will, which, though it sometimes wavered, was ultimately invincible."[4] On 24 April 1875, two years before Dickinson sent her note, an essayist in the *Amherst*

Student argued that Hamlet's irresolution, incongruity of action, and misanthropy were a result not of madness but of a diseased morality.[5] This led to his inability to distinguish between right and wrong, his heightened emotions and imagination, and his "deep brooding gloom." Consequently, "the restraining power of his life has been destroyed, and he is incapable of self-restraint. He wavers between the good and evil—hilarity and despair." Perhaps Dickinson's note to Mrs. Higginson ascribes such complexity to her flower; certainly the poet shared the views of the prize-winning composition on Hamlet in the 1872 *Amherst Student,* which stressed Hamlet's universality—his life "finds an echo ever in [our] own"; "to this strange mysterious existence you feel yourself linked by the bond of a common humanity"; "he is of ourselves, our flesh and blood."[6] Without using the word "wavers," the writer suggests that in Hamlet "we see simply the wrestling of a strong human mind, with the great problems of human life and destiny. He but exhibits the mental conflict which must come to each one of us in some degree." The essay declares that "If truest heroism lies in self-sacrifice, in devotion to another, then the life and death of Hamlet is grandly heroic. Far out of sight he placed self and sought solely principle." Dickinson's reference to Hamlet attributes this self-sacrifice, "devotion to another," heroism, and selflessness to her flower.

The dead cape jasmine in Mrs. Higginson's hand, and Hamlet's dead body at the end of the play, evoke the silence and mystery of death, a topic Dickinson addresses in much of her writing.[7] Her use of *Hamlet* in this letter reflects her "life long preoccupation" with exploring death from "every possible angle," making it "the most important single factor in shaping the contours of her poetry."[8] The last ten years of Dickinson's life were particularly crowded with the deaths of her closest friends: her letters become a string of condolences, her poems epitaphs and elegies. As she told Higginson in 1879, however, although she had known "little of Literature," his pages "and Shakespeare's, like Ophir - remain" (L593). Dickinson's allusions to Shakespeare now focused on the death scenes of his protagonists and on how they died; she was particularly interested in the moment of death, and sought descriptions as a means of determining the fate of the dying person's immortal soul.[9] As her dead friends have for her, Shakespeare's characters have overcome death, becoming mysterious celebrities: "Brave names of Men - / And Celestial Women - / Passed out - of Record / Into - Renown!" (F323). Her many allusions to Lady Macbeth's death scene and her reading of Talbot's parting with his son, like her letter to Mrs. Higginson, demonstrate that the bard's dead and dying characters are "exhilirants" who become "Lures - Keepers of that great Romance still to us foreclosed -" (*Letters* Prose Fragment 50). They are also instructive figures who add to life's mystery and splendor, as well as signs warning of the danger of human passion and error. In the last ten years of her life, Dickinson's references to Shakespeare's tragedies frequently occur in newly established epistolary relationships, with Otis Lord, Maria Whitney, Samuel Bowles the younger, and Abbie C. Farley. As she began writing to the friends and relatives of her recently deceased family and friends, Shakespeare played an important role in her life-affirming strategy in the face of death and sorrow.[10]

"Oh, my too beloved, save me from the idolatry which would crush us both"

Dickinson shared her great love of Shakespeare with Judge Otis Lord. In Lord's Memorial Address, delivered at the Essex Institute in Salem on 5 September 1871, he had praised Shakespeare:

> The great poet of nature wrote songs and sonnets, which would have given high place to another; but how insignificant they are in comparison with his magnificent exhibitions of human action![11]

For Lord, Shakespeare's power resides not merely in his language but in his characterizations, and certainly Dickinson found Shakespeare's "exhibitions of human action" awe-inspiring. On 14 May 1882, she thought that Judge Lord was dying, but later she discovered he was making a full recovery. Her first letter to him after this scare presents him as a figure who has come back from what Hamlet calls "The undiscovered country, from whose bourn / No traveller returns" (III i 78–79). She writes, "To remind you of my own rapture at your return, and of the loved steps, retraced almost from the 'Undiscovered Country,' I enclose the Note I was fast writing, when the fear that your Life has ceased, came, fresh, yet dim, like the horrid Monsters fled from in a Dream" (L752). Dickinson's reference to Hamlet's most famous speech—"To be, or not to be" (III i 55–89)—suggests that she had been morbidly musing, as Hamlet does, about Lord's possible demise, and was all the more overjoyed at his triumph over death. Among the extant letters to Lord there are references to others among Shakespeare's heroes. In one of these, written when their relationship was at its most passionate, probably in late 1880 or early 1881, Dickinson begins with an account of a humorous dialogue between herself and her nephew, Ned, over Lord's religion and his brilliance as a judge.[12] She records that she had never "tried any case" before Lord except her own, then presents a sudden, exaggerated declaration of fervent passion:

> Don't you know you have taken my will away and I "know not where" you "have laid" it? Should I have curbed you sooner? "Spare the 'Nay' and spoil the child"?

> Oh, my too beloved, save me from the idolatry which would crush us both - "And very Sea - Mark of my utmost Sail -" (L560).

Dickinson here employs a phrase from the climactic final scene from *Othello* to enhance her performance (V ii 268). Considering that Lord probably knew Shakespeare's plays as well as she did, she would have expected him to find and read the passages surrounding her short quotation. This final scene is marked in the Dickinsons' copy of Shakespeare from "It is the cause, it is the cause, my soul" to "Put out the light, and then—put out the light" (V ii 1–7); also marked are the lines "Thou cunning'st pattern of excelling nature / I know not where is that Promethean heat" (V ii 11–12); "It is a sword of Spain, the ice-brook's temper; / O, here it is:—Uncle, I must come forth," just above Dickinson's allusion (V ii 253–54); and Othello's final declaration, "I kiss'd thee, ere I kill'd thee;—No way but this, / Killing myself, to die upon a kiss" (V ii 358–59). These markings suggest that Dickinson, or someone in the household, scrupulously studied this final scene, with a particular interest in how Desdemona and Othello died. Dickinson's quotation reflects Othello's belief that "'t is happiness to die" (V ii 290) now that he has discovered that Iago has tricked him into murdering the faithful and beloved Desdemona. It is intriguing to consider how Lord might have interpreted this. He may have reread the passage where Othello tells Desdemona's uncle, Gratiano, who is guarding him,

> Be not afraid though you do see me weapon'd;
> Here is my journey's end, here is my butt,
> And very sea-mark of my utmost sail.
> Do you go back dismay'd? 'Tis is a lost fear;
> Man but a rush against Othello's breast,
> And he retires;—Where should Othello go?
> (V ii 266–71)

Through reference to the suicidal and defeated Othello, Dickinson might be warning Lord that their passion must end; they must love "wisely" and not "too well," otherwise, their idolatrous love will crush them both, as Othello's crushed him. But given an epistolary relationship that had been self-consciously literary and playful, Lord may have wondered if the poet was being provocative. Certainly it is unclear which of the lovers is the idolatrous Othello. Perhaps Dickinson, considering her identification with Othello in other letters, has transcended both gender and race to shock and, probably, amuse the elderly Judge. Alternatively, she could be evoking the savagery of the play's final scene to characterize the extremity of Lord's passion for her. Their relationship appears to have continued, whatever the case.

In an 1882 letter to Lord, Dickinson referred to the moment Antony decides to kill himself. She began by apologizing: "I know you [are] acutely weary, yet cannot refrain from taxing you" (L791), then revealed that she was taxing him "with an added smile - and a pang in it" before launching into her elaborate and painful humor:

> Was it to him the Thief cried "Lord remember me when thou comest into thy Kingdom" and is it to us that he replies, "This Day thou shalt be with me in Paradise"? The Propounder of Paradise must indeed possess it - Antony's remark to a friend, "since Cleopatra died" is said to be the saddest ever lain in Language - That engulfing "*Since*" -

Equating the self-protective ploys of Cleopatra with Dickinson's own, this can be read, like her allusion to Othello, as merely part of her hyperbolic style. She puns on Lord's name by summoning up the thief's request, and appears to be asking him to defer their union in this world—to be a "propounder" of a future paradise rather than the possessor of a present one. Her letter may also refer to an earlier passage from the same scene, where Antony imagines his heaven with Cleopatra:

> I will o'ertake thee, Cleopatra, and
> Weep for my pardon. So it must be, for now
> All length is torture:—Since the torch is out,
> Lie down, and stray no farther: Now all labour
> Mars what it does; yea, very force entangles
> Itself with strength. Seal then, and all is done.—
> Eros!—I come, my queen:—Eros!—Stay for me:
> Where souls do couch on flowers, we'll hand in hand,
> And with our sprightly port make the ghosts gaze.
> (IV xiv 44–52).

The propounding of paradise by Antony, like Christ's promise to the thief, anticipates one of the central themes of Dickinson's poetry: the reunion in paradise of lovers separated on earth.[13] In fact, both letters to Lord explore this idea, evoking the scenes in which Othello and Antony lay out their reasons for suicide. Antony has lived in dishonor since Cleopatra's "death," and Othello has reached his "journey's end" now that he is without Desdemona. Unlike Antony, Othello does not imagine a meeting with his beloved in paradise; instead he will encounter the woman he has killed "at compt [the final accounting or Last Judgment]," and her look "will hurl [his] soul from heaven, / And fiends will snatch at it" (V ii 272–75). Dickinson might be suggesting that Shakespeare's plays offer her and Lord two alternative paths. Either their idolatrous love will crush them both, as it did Desdemona and Othello, and they will be separated in the next life, or their renunciation of each other in this world will allow them to be reunited in paradise, like Antony and Cleopatra. Perhaps, after carefully studying and marking the final scene of *Othello,* she symbolized her choice by placing bookmarks in the death scenes of *Antony and Cleopatra.* Habegger notes that in 1871 Dickinson had written "Somewhere opon the general Earth" (F1226), her last datable poem on such "heavenly reunion."[14] These late letters may indicate exactly why these two plays were her favorites, and that her reading of Shakespeare was an imaginative resource, and later even a symbolic substitute, reiterating the central themes of her poetry.

"An envious sliver broke' was a passage your Uncle peculiarly loved in the drowning Ophelia"

Although Dickinson's extant letters never refer to Cleopatra's death scene, her edition of the play has a piece of brown material enclosed in the pages that depict Cleopatra's preparation for her suicide. The importance of this scene to the poet may also have been tied to the fact that Cleopatra also imagines a future paradise with her beloved. The enclosure marks Cleopatra's goal:

> Show me, my women, like a queen:—Go fetch
> My best attires;—I am again for Cydnus,
> To meet Mark Antony :—Sirrah, Iras, go.—
> Now, noble Charmian, we'll despatch indeed:
> And, when thou hast done this chare [chore], I'll give thee leave
> To play till doomsday.—Bring our crown and all.
> (V ii 227–32)

Also on this page is Cleopatra's presentation of her own transcendence: death brings her "liberty / My resolution's plac'd, and I have nothing / Of woman in me: Now from head to foot / I am marble-constant: now the fleeting moon / No planet is of mine." Obviously Dickinson admired this scene, and it was perhaps, a catalyst for her own representations of the way beloved figures undergo a form of apotheosis at death.[15] The 1870 essay on Cleopatra in the *Amherst Student* suggests there is a sublimity in this death scene, at which our "sympathy is lost in admiration" because Shakespeare "exhibits all the nobility and grandeur of this heroic soul."[16] For this essayist, it is in this scene that Cleopatra demonstrates her real love for Antony: "he is almost the last word upon her lips" and "she claims a right to the coveted name [of wife] by virtue of her courage." The leading actress in the part in Dickinson's day, Isabella Glyn, presented the scene as a joyous event, smiling to emphasize that she was about to be reunited with her lover Antony.[17] Westland Marston complimented Glyn's imperial dignity and smile as she abandoned herself to death with "eager majesty that converted it into a triumph."[18] An 1868 article titled "Mrs. Frances Anne Kemble," published in *The Galaxy,* recognizes Kemble's ability as a reader to become each character in this play, particularly Cleopatra;[19] it praises the splendor of Kemble's delivery of the whole play, but particularly of the death scene, which is "singularity suited to her powers"—"She is the real Cleopatra, 'keeping her queen-like state in the last disgrace, and her sense of the pleasurable in the last moments of her life'." While Shakespeare's other tragic heroes and heroines kill themselves impetuously, or are killed in the course of the tragedy, Cleopatra organizes and plans her own death, showing her need to control her own ending and her lasting reputation. She does not want to live a sign of Roman victory and triumph, preferring to die dignified, the queen of Egypt. This surely appealed to a poet who spent her life attempting to control her own representation and who left very clear instructions about her funeral arrangements—that she be brought to the cemetery by her Irish servants and "out the back door" "through the fields, full of buttercups" (Leyda II 475, 474).

Dickinson alludes explicitly to the death scenes of Ophelia and Desdemona. Her interest was not unusual in an era when pictorial representations of Shakespeare's heroines, particularly of their death scenes, were very popular.[20] Ophelia, for insance, was rendered by contemporary artists such as Delacroix, John Everett Millais, and Arthur Hughes as a deranged woman drowning or half-submerged in water.[21] In fact, Dickinson's Shakespeare contained an illustration of Ophelia sinking in the brook, gripping her hair and with a crazed expression on her face, above the line "There is a willow grows aslant a brook."[22] Likewise, the representation of Desdemona's murder in art and on stage determined how Othello's character was judged.[23] Fanny Kemble suggested that the audience "cannot be expected to sit by and see Desdemona smothered: the curtains of the alcove in which the bed is are therefore lowered during that operation, but it is very desirable, if not absolutely necessary, that she should be both heard and seen when she gasps out her dying exculpation of her husband."[24] Such fascination was intensified by the popularity of poems and artworks that depicted the deaths of beautiful women—an obsession perhaps reaching its apex in Edgar Allan Poe's "The Philosophy of Composition" (1846), which declares that "the death, then, of a beautiful woman, is unquestionably the most poetical topic in the world—and equally is it beyond doubt that the lips best suited for such topic are those of a bereaved lover."[25] Dickinson's own poetry complicates this tradition by examining in detail the deaths of both male and female lovers, and especially by creating women who speak beyond the grave, preventing their male lovers from expressing their sorrow.[26] In her references to the deaths of Shakespeare's heroines, she makes them less spectacular or aesthetic objects than occasions to discuss suicide, religion, and female heroism.

In an 1880 letter, Dickinson mentions Gertrude's description of Ophelia's watery death (IV vii 166–83) to Mrs. Holland, who at the time was nursing her sick husband: "I trust the 'Hand' has 'ceased from troubling' - it has saved too many to be assailed by an 'envious sliver -' Had we known the Doctor was falling, we had been much alarmed, though Grace - perhaps - is the only hight from which falling is fatal -" (L678). Two years earlier, Dickinson had characterized him as Lear; now Holland is Ophelia, death the "envious sliver." This famous phrase loses its associations with the madness and suicide of a woman, suggesting that death does not discriminate but, to an extent, feminizes all. In other letters, however, Ophelia's death relates directly to the deaths of women. In an August 1885 letter to Abbie C. Farley, written a little more than a year after her uncle, Judge Lord, had died, the poet sympathizes with Farley over the drowning of her cousin Mary Farley in Walden Pond:

> What a reception for you! Did she wait for your approbation? Her deferring to die until you came seemed to me so confiding - as if nothing should be presumed. It can probably never be real to you. The Vail that helps us, falls so mercifully over it. "An envious Sliver broke" was a passage your Uncle peculiarly loved in the drowning Ophelia. Was it a premonition? To him to whom Events and Omens are at last the same? (L1006).

In this period Ophelia represented the suspected female death, and Dickinson appears to be hinting that Mary Farley, like Ophelia, has committed suicide. Obviously, the poet and Lord had spoken about *Hamlet,* because Dickinson knew that he "peculiarly" loved the passage "An envious Sliver broke"—perhaps indicating his preference for the idea that Ophelia's death was accidental, not suicide. Dickinson seems to be expressing the sentiments of the essayist on "Hamlet" in *The Indicator,* who calls Ophelia "a pure spirit from a better world, sent to breathe a blessing on us."[27] Farley's cousin is like "The beautiful, the pure, the holy Ophelia—far too pure, far too holy for earth—was never made to breathe the cold air of a heartless world" (222). Unlike the *Indicator* writer, Dickinson seems less interested in Shakespeare's heroine as a paragon of virtue, and instead offers Ophelia's death as a way of making sense of an event that "can probably never be real to [Abbie]." Mystery mercifully shrouds this suicide, as it does Ophelia's. As a means of further comforting Farley she emphasizes Lord's interpretation of Ophelia, giving it an otherworldly authority where "Events" have become equivalent to premonitions and omens: Lord can see under the "Vail." But Dickinson's final reflections are very appropriate: she reminds Abbie of the hazardous and frightening nature of concealed "Anguish," and demonstrates her awareness of the religious and social stigma attached to suicide—hence, she adds her "holy wish" that the cousins are not separated in the next world.

Earlier in the same year Dickinson had referred to Ophelia's death in a letter to Mrs. Holland, thanking her for reviews of a recently published biography, believed to be that of George Eliot by her widower, John Cross.[28] Perhaps some of these reviews had condemned the novelist's earlier relationship with a married man, George Henry Lewes, her religious skepticism, and her late marriage to the much younger Cross.[29] Dickinson begins, "To 'gain the whole World' in the Evening Mail, without the baleful forfeit hinted in the Scripture, was indeed achievement" (L979). Yet she goes on to defend this very worldly author through reference to the gravediggers' discussion of Ophelia:

> Thank you tenderly - I was breathlessly interested. Contention "loves a shining Mark." Only *fight* about me, said the dying King, and my Crown is sure - It is only the Moss upon my Throne that impairs my Dying. None of us know her enough to judge her, so her Maker must be her "Crowner's Quest" - Saul criticized his Savior till he became enamored of him - then he was less loquacious - (L979)

Here the publicity-shy poet is arguing that this controversy about Eliot only affirms her status, importance, and power (her Kingship), and is preferable to "Moss upon [the] throne." The debate about Eliot is like the discussion of the clowns/gravediggers of Ophelia's death. According to them, Ophelia is given a Christian burial only because she was a "gentlewoman": the "Crowner's Quest" was prejudiced (V i 1–55).[30] Dickinson's reference to Ophelia, however, implies that only God can really judge Eliot's life, and this view was certainly shared by others. In the same year, Henry James argued that Eliot was "one of the noblest, most beautiful minds of our time," and Edwin P. Whipple suggested, "Christ himself in the largeness of his wisdom and life may include George Eliot among those who yet are not against him."[31] Dickinson might, ironically, be summoning up the widely reported fact that in 1881 Cross, in a fit of dementia, had thrown himself into the Grand Canal in Venice, while on honeymoon with Eliot.[32] Unlike Ophelia, he was rescued; Eliot died shortly after their return to England. By associating Ophelia with the heroic figures of Eliot and Saul, Dickinson makes Shakespeare's heroine less submissive, less ethereal, more complex. Ophelia's decision to die becomes an act equivalent to Eliot's defiance of convention and tradition.

Between Dickinson's two references to Ophelia's death, she refers to Desdemona, in a mysterious letter, dated Christmas 1884, to her neighbor Mrs. Henry Hills. She writes, "When the 'Children' for whom the Cakes were founded are 'Merchants of Venice' and 'Desdemonas,' Santa Claus must tell me. I should never guess" (L958). Dickinson appears to be asking if the Hills children deserve the cakes she has sent them. The implication is that she wants to be informed if they are bad or good—depending on whom she means by the Merchant of Venice, Antonio or Shylock—and how she perceives Desdemona—as a rebellious daughter or dutiful wife? Her frequent references to Brabantio suggest her interest in Desdemona's defying her father. Moreover, the Dickinsons' edition has a mark beside Desdemona's erotically charged demand to accompany Othello to Cyprus:

> And to his honours, and his valiant parts
> Did I my soul and fortunes consecrate.
> So that, dear lords, if I be left behind,
> A moth of peace, and he go to the war,
> The rites for which I love him are bereft me
> (I iii 253–57)

Dickinson was perhaps interested in the rebellious and erotic aspects of Desdemona's character, but in this obscure note is also referring to Shylock, and wants to be told when children are naughty and undeserving of her presents. But it seems more likely she is asking if they have warranted their rewards; her Desdemona is in fact Othello's virtuous and submissive wife, and accordingly, the Merchant of Venice is the virtuous Antonio.[33] Othello's assessment of Desdemona's high merit, interestingly, is also marked in the Dickinson family Shakespeare—"If she be false, O, then heaven mocks itself!—/ I'll not believe 't." (III iii 278–79). The ambiguity of Dickinson's note, and of the markings in the play, again draws attention to contradictions in this character that problematize her status as an ideal heroine.

In another equally confusing letter, Dickinson focuses on Desdemona's death scene and compares it to the giving of a "little flower" sent to Sara Colton by the poet's niece, Martha, in the summer of 1885: "Mattie will hide this little flower in her friend's Hand. Should she ask who sent it, tell her as Desdemona did when they asked who slew her, 'Nobody - I myself'" (L1010). Salvini argues that this line demonstrates that "Shakspere, even at the peril of admitting an improbable prolongation of life in *Desdemona,* wished to express her touching generosity by causing her to accuse herself of suicide, rather than permit her cruel yet beloved husband to suffer the imputation of having murdered her."[34] Emma Lazarus says that "one of the gentlest of women" she knew remarked, "I do not wonder that *Desdemona* forgave his killing her, when she had his perfect love for a little while."[35] Dickinson is clearly fascinated with this moment when Desdemona absolves Othello despite his cruelty to her. The transformation of

Desdemona's death into a suicide acquits Dickinson, the Othellolike flower-plucker, of the responsibility of having killed this Desdemona-flower.

"That you have answered the Prince Question to your own delight, is joy to us all"

Dickinson's childhood friend Joseph Lyman was also deeply interested in Shakespeare: in his letters he uses Hamlet, Romeo, and Ferdinand (from *The Tempest*) to describe himself, and refers to Shakespeare's heroines (Desdemona, Juliet, and Imogen) in discussing femininity, women, and love.[36] In an 1857 letter, reflecting on his thwarted romance with Lavinia Dickinson, he characterizes himself as a "more curious riddle" to her "than Lord Hamlet was to Ophelia." For him, Ophelia is neither suicidal nor insane, rather someone who misunderstood Hamlet. In a later letter, he maintains that "Vinnie might have done something with me if she had not done just as Laertes and Polonius told Ophelia *not* to do." Thus Lavinia lacked conviction and understanding and was too easily influenced by others. He adds that "Portia or even Miranda (certainly Lady Macbeth) could have done Lord Hamlet an unspeakable good. Lady Macbeth would have made a Julius Caezar [sic] of him."[37] Like Ophelia, though, Lavinia was happy to "*drink*" the "*honey music,*"

> but when the trump of war blew in her ears she was frightened & the waves covered her. Hamlet had "thought of all that" & knew Ophelia by heart & it seemed he was right for as soon as the plot darkened Hamlet playing crazy—she couldn't see through it—& her pa got killed—the first bloody step in Hamlet's "flint path"—She went real crazy & was drowned.

Although Lyman does not equate Dickinson with any of Shakespeare's heroines, his reminiscences of her suggest that he found her a fascinating, perceptive, unique, and intellectual woman, probably similar to Miranda or Portia rather than Ophelia. But although it is unclear if Dickinson knew about Lyman's equating Lavinia with Ophelia, the poet identifies with this character in a late-1860s letter to him:

> We used to think, Joseph, when I was an unsifted girl and you so scholarly that words were cheap & weak. Now I don't know of anything so mighty. There are [those] to which I lift my hat when I see them sitting princelike among their peers on the page. Sometimes I write one, and look at his outlines till he glows as no sapphire.[38]

This refers to Polonius's accusing his daughter of speaking "like a green girl / Unsifted in such perilous circumstance" (I iii 101–2). When Dickinson was an Ophelialike figure and Joseph the "so scholarly" Hamlet, both were unaware of how "mighty" words were. Now, she lifts her hat to these princelike (perhaps an allusion to Hamlet) entities. Possibly she is telling Lyman about her rediscovery of Shakespeare following her period of eye trouble. Along with the "luscious" passages of *Antony and Cleopatra* and sorrowful partings from the *Henry VI* plays, Dickinson was now reading *Hamlet* and aware just how powerful literature could be.

Dickinson alludes to this play frequently in later letters, transforming its imagery and language of despair and treachery to speak of friendship. In an 1878 letter to Mrs. Holland, she paraphrases the "whips and scorns of time," from Hamlet's "To be, or not to be" speech, to thank her for her letter and friendship: "Your little Note protected, as it always does, and the 'Whips of Time' felt a long way off" (L547). Similarly, in 1881, she reassures Mary Bowles of their friendship through reference to Hamlet's resignation to this fate—"there is a special providence in the fall of a sparrow" (V ii 219–20)—writing, "The timid mistake about being 'forgotten,' shall I caress or reprove? Mr. Samuel's 'sparrow' does not 'fall' without the fervent 'notice'" (L724). Here Hamlet's most troubled soliloquy and later resignation to his fate offer hope, comfort, and support, his words altered to ease the anxieties and confusions of life. In an 1885 letter to Samuel Bowles the younger, Dickinson offers her own shortened version of Claudius's articulation of his desire to know more about Hamlet's eccentric behavior—"Oh speak of that; that I do long to hear" (II ii 50)—mischievously appropriating this villain's line to offer assistance to the son of her dead friend: "If ever of any act of mine you should be in need, let me reply with the Laureate, 'Speak that I live to hear!'" (L1012).

Dickinson also refers to *Hamlet* in an 1883 letter to an unidentified recipient, thought to be Samuel Bowles the younger, on his marriage:

> To ask of each that gathered Life, Oh, where did it grow, is intuitive. That you have answered this Prince Question to your own delight, is joy to us all.
> Lad of Athens, faithful be
> To Thyself,
> And Mystery -
> All the rest is Perjury - (L865).

Dickinson links the "Prince Question," as to where life grows, to *Hamlet,* and, in particular, to Polonius's advice to Laertes, "to thine own self be true; / And it must follow, as the night the day, / Thou canst not then be false to any man" (I iii 78–80). Yet she complicates Polonius's advice by suggesting that at the heart of human life is "mystery"; the "Lad of Athens" should be faithful to this as well. Hamlet's question in his "To be, or not to be" speech is related to the obscurity at the heart of the human condition, to the difficulty of being "faithful" or "true" to a self ultimately unknowable. In 1864, Dickinson sent a poem, "'Soto' - Explore Tyself - ," to her brother Austin; it expresses a similar idea in cognate language, transforming Hamlet's "undiscovered country," death, into the "Undiscovered Continent" of the human mind (F814). Knight's introduction to *Hamlet* also addresses this theme, arguing that "the comprehension of this tragedy is the history of man's own mind": its scenes and characters, found in schoolbooks and popularized on stage, have become part of the lives of most readers.[39] As the years progress they grow to appreciate the mysterious and representative nature of Shakespeare's, rather than the stage's, Hamlet:

> There is something altogether indefinable and mysterious in the poet's delineation of this character;—something wild and irregular in the circumstances with which the character is associated . . . Perhaps some of the very charm of the play to the adult mind is its mysteriousness. It awakes not only thoughts of the grand and the beautiful, but of the incomprehensible. Its obscurity constitutes a portion of its sublimity."[40]

In a similar manner, "Drama's Vitallest Expression is the Common Day" (F776) concerns the "mysterious" nature of the inner drama of each human being, symbolized by the character of Hamlet.[41] According to this poem, the difference between Shakespeare's plays and the inner drama lies in the questions of duration and intensity. If "'Hamlet' to Himself were Hamlet / Had not Shakespeare wrote," then Hamlet merely represents on stage a part of what all humans experience in private. Hudson writes,

> [Hamlet's] history is the very extraction and efficacy of the thoughts and feelings and inward experiences of us all; his life is a picture of blighted hopes and crushed affections, from which we may solve the darkest enigmas of our existence, and over which our aching hearts may bleed themselves into repose.[42]

It may be that Hamlet's hidden and mysterious internal drama, although hinted at in his soliloquies and actions upon the stage, is unrecorded—something only Hamlet himself can experience. This returns us to Dickinson's use of Hamlet's "wavering"—he "wavers for all of us," not only between life and death, but because his struggles evoke those private experiences that are inexpressible and ungraspable. These, of course, were central subjects of Dickinson's poetry.

Dickinson may already have been particularly interested in Hamlet in the early 1850s, when Dana's lecture presented him as an idealistic poet estranged from the real world around him. The 1851 article in the *Indicator* says, "there are many Hamlets living now; but they are unpopular men": impractical, unmanly, and isolated individuals who are removed from the ordinary "busy scenes of every-day life" because they have "too much honesty, joined to a love of seclusion, to be eminently popular, or successful now-a-days."[43] The writer goes on to note that his noble sentiments, his filial devotion, and his high ideas of love are converted into gloomy misanthropy by the duplicity he finds around him. Particularly in the early 1850s, Dickinson's own letters often reflect feelings of distance and isolation from others. In one, she tells Austin that "since the 'world is hollow, and Dollie is stuffed with sawdust,' I really do not think we had better expose our feelings" (L42); in another, this time to Sue, she writes, "I am lonely too, and this is a lonely world, in the cheerfullest aspects of it" (L63). Like many contemporary articles on Hamlet, the *Indicator* piece goes on to consider whether the prince's madness was feigned or real. Of the love letter he wrote to Ophelia, which she shows to Polonius, the essayist says, "whether the portfolio of many a New England maiden could not afford us professions as strong and glowing—and that, too, perhaps from some who will read this; and still we are not all mad! If his madness was real, it was reasonable; if feigned, it was faultless" (225). Polonius was incorrect to divine madness in such a declaration of love; many female readers had received, perhaps even fashioned themselves, such declarations. Dickinson's own interest in solitude and stigma is especially evident in a poem like "Much Madness is divinest Sense / To the discerning Eye -," which suggests that if you assent you are "sane," but if you demur you are "handled with a Chain" (F620).[44] A strip of lined paper is found between pages 188 and 189 in the family edition of Shakespeare; here Gertrude describes how Hamlet being "Mad as the seas, and wind, when both contend / Which is the mightier: In his lawless fit," killed Polonius (IV i 7–8). Also in these pages, Claudius, aware of the danger Hamlet poses to all, says that this "mad young man" should be "restrain'd" and sent to England.[45] In one of her final messages to Sue, dated 1886, Emily clearly identifies with Hamlet, asking her beloved sister-in-law, "Do you remember what whispered to "Horatio"?" (L1028). There are two answers to Dickinson's question: the dying Hamlet, who whispered, and the words he whispered, "report me and my cause aright / To the unsatisfied . . . If thou didst ever hold me in thy heart, / Absent thee from felicity awhile, / And in this harsh world draw thy breath in pain / To tell my story" (V ii 339–340, 346–49). Emily apparently is giving Sue the responsibility of telling her "story," which Sue did when she wrote her obituary for the *Springfield Republican* on 18 May 1886; in it Sue mentions that the poet sifted "libraries to Shakespeare."[46]

"She frequently rose to the level of the Shaksperean Mind"

Connected with Dickinson's use of *Hamlet* in her letters is the play's American stage history. The greatest actors of Hamlet in Dickinson's day, Charles Albert

Fechter and Edwin Booth, emphasized his innate nobility, grace, and dignity, but also his sensitivity and feminine traits. In an 1870 article in the *Atlantic Monthly* on Fechter, Kate Field defends his portrayal against those who argued that he made the prince soft and whining, unmanly, sentimental, and pensive. She argues that Fechter is "thoroughly manly" and "robust without being unpleasantly so, he is graceful, he is supple as an athlete, he is courtly, he is wonderfully picturesque."[47] Similarly, E. C. Stedman argued that the genius of Booth's Hamlet derived from a "feminine quality" in his acting which made him the "*princeliest* Hamlet that ever trod the stage."[48] Clearly, Booth's Hamlet suited a culture that Ann Douglas has described as "feminized," in which sentimentality, gentleness, and depths of feeling were celebrated and praised; in 1882 Booth told William Winter, "I doubt if ever a robust and masculine treatment of the character [of Hamlet] will be accepted so generally as the more womanly and refined interpretation."[49] Not surprisingly, considering Hamlet's femininity, actresses frequently played him, including Sarah Siddons in 1776, Anna Dickinson in 1882, and Sarah Bernhardt in 1899; women writers, like George Eliot, also identified with the Danish prince.[50] Charlotte Cushman, the most famous American actress of Dickinson's day, also played Hamlet; she first performed the role in New York in 1851, and went on to play it again in 1861 in Boston. According to Lisa Merrill, unlike actresses who "played up the possibility of titillating the predominantly male audience by displaying shapely bodies and legs," Cushman aimed at verisimilitude and became the male characters she played. At the time, Edwin Booth wrote, "She is down on me as an actor; says I don't know anything at all about 'Hamlet,' so she is going to play here in Feb."[51] Emma Stebbins comments on Cushman's "matchless delivery of the immortal language" and that her "commanding well-made figure appeared to advantage in the dress of the princely Dane."[52] Contemporary reviewers were surprised and astonished by her subtle attention to detail, frequently praising her Hamlet as the true and definitive version; one noted, "She appreciates the influence of the supernatural upon his mind, and does not therefore, fall into the error of representing him as one who is merely playing a part, while throughout she enters into his melancholy, his poetic philosophy, his resolution and his impulsiveness."[53] Another spectator, Lawrence Barrett, recorded that "she gave a novel color to that complex character," confirming her talent and intellect.[54]

Although she never mentions Cushman, Dickinson must have been aware of an actress who inspired national worship.[55] This devotion is apparent in an 1876 memorial on the actress in *Scribner's Monthly*, which the poet may have read.[56] This begins by lamenting that although she was seen by millions during her forty years on the stage, her most famous roles "so far as they lived in her, they are gone forever" (262). It praises her female roles such as Lady Macbeth and as Emilia in *Othello,* referring to her as the greatest exponent of Shakespeare in her day: "She rendered an inestimable service to her sex by demonstrating the most brilliant methods, and, with conclusive force, the extent of its intellectual capacity" (263). Through her combination of beautiful elocution, stately figure, reserved power, and unrivaled imagination,

> She frequently rose to the level of the Shaksperean mind, was kindled with the Shaksperean fire, so that in her inspired moments she realized the character. It was not always thus, for the greatest of actors can only effect by supreme effort that which Shakspere did with apparently unconscious ease. But it is enough glory for an actress when she can cause her auditors to forget, even if only for a moment, the difference between the Lady Macbeth of the stage and the Lady Macbeth of the book.

This offers the prospect that Dickinson may have regarded Cushman as a contemporary woman who, despite the questions about her profession, gained fame and authority through an intellectual and passionate engagement with Shakespeare's plays. The article places Cushman among a "sisterhood of artists" and female intellectuals, including Charlotte Brontë, George Eliot, Mrs. Browning, and George Sand. Although they are great, however, the writer reminds readers that their works are inferior to those of their male contemporaries, whereas Cushman "was not surpassed by the tragedians of this generation, and was, in fact, equaled by very few" (265). Indeed, she had "no superior on the modern stage, and, therefore, was excelled by none of the women of her time, no matter in what profession they labored" (266). She had the ability to play two of the central parts in *Henry VIII:* "Only an actress of great imagination and commensurate powers of execution could play Queen Katherine on one night and Cardinal Wolsey on the other, and make them seem like two utterly distinct beings." As to the most famous of Cushman's "breeches parts," Romeo, she had the unique ability to fill the stage with passion, especially when she stretched "upon the ground, taking 'the measure of an unmade grave'."

Cushman first played Romeo in Albany in 1837, and went on to perform the role successfully throughout her career. Nineteenth-century male actors found this a difficult part to play, believing it required a boy and not a man: they saw the behavior of Romeo as overly romantic and embarrassingly womanish, while others thought it too erotic a role for a male actor.[57] On 16 November 1860 a reviewer for the *New York Times* wrote that "there is in the delicacy and gentleness of *Romeo's* character something which requires a woman to represent it, and unfits almost every man for its personation. The luscious language which draws its rich, lascivious color from the fiery blood of Young Italy, sounds ridiculous alongside of the rather *blazé* sensible style of love-making of Young New-York, and here seems strange on the lips of a man."[58] As a result at least thirteen different women had performed the part before Cushman did, and between 1837 and 1845 she played the role at least 240 times.[59] Critics praised her above male contemporaries for her convincing presentation of a boy in love, and some spectators found it hard to believe she was a woman. In 1845, in London's Haymarket, she famously played Romeo to her sister Susan's Juliet, in doing so becoming an icon of American cultural achievement.[60] Although she had been criticized before her performance for refusing to use Garricks's 1774 adaptation, she was praised afterward for restoring Shakespeare's version to the stage, minus its bawdier aspects.[61] Cushman presented audiences with a Romeo who was an impulsive and emotional adolescent, making his passion the central focus of play. James Sheridan Knowles acclaimed the "real, palpably real" passions Cushman depicted and the "genuine heart-storm" from which Romeo seems to die.[62] Nineteenth-century audiences were comfortable watching a performance of passionate and ardent scenes between two women that, for most Victorians, could not be anything other than platonic. As one contemporary critic remarked, "To give an adequate embodiment of the true feeling of this play, would certainly outrage the sense of a modern audience, were the performers of *opposite* sex."[63]

Lisa Merrill argues that Cushman's expressions of passion for Juliet onstage, and her habit of dressing in male attire and her close female friendships offstage, were for most onlookers merely unsettling, if anything, but excited no public prurience.[64] For those who could decode it her behavior was indecorous and dangerously attractive to female spectators: it became a partially seen sign of women's sexual desire for one another. Cushman's performances offered her a way of expressing her same-sex passion; their popularity suggested emerging sexual possibilities. How might Dickinson, given her passionate relationship with Sue and her possible same-sex orientation, have interpreted Cushman?[65] On the 13th and 14th of May, 1861, the *Springfield Republican* announced Cushman's final performance as Romeo, speaking of her "celebrated male assumptions" and that she is "acknowledged the *greatest* Romeo."[66] It also reports the general desire to see her and the pleasure she gave her audience, which was "the largest house of the season." On May 15 Dickinson's and Sue's friend Samuel Bowles told Austin that he saw "Mrs Cushman's Romeo at Music Hall," adding, "She is wonderfully dear, but real tragedies are so plenty in life that the stage ones, however well done, do not impress my soul."[67] This echoes Dickinson's sense of the inadequacies of the stage, expressed in "Drama's Vitallest Expression is the Common Day." She chose to include Hamlet and Romeo in her poem, instead of Othello or Antony, perhaps because of Cushman's celebrated performances. These are Shakespeare's most representative heroes, with whom both men and women can identify, and this was obviously important for a poem about the universal internal drama. Suzanne Juhasz and Cristanne Miller point out that "the quotation marks around 'Hamlet' and 'Romeo' might signal the *lack* of (gender) congruence between" the (possibly) female speaker of the poem and Shakespeare's two heroes.[68] On the other hand, Dickinson's poem may be subverting the stress on the universality of Shakespeare's characters, making available the idea that a woman, like herself, could identify with Shakespeare's heroes rather than his heroines. A piece of black thread remains in place in the Dickinsons' edition between pages 34 and 35, where Romeo reveals his fervent love for Juliet to the astounded Friar, "When, and where, and how, / We met, we woo'd, and made exchange of vow, / I'll tell thee as we pass; but this I pray, / That thou consent to marry us today" (II iii 61–64).[69] This bookmark hints that Dickinson may have identified with the passionate Romeo.[70] The gender confusion introduced by the poem's use of quotation marks is the more provocative when read with the poet's possible same-sex orientation in mind. What if the more vital, and unnamed, counterparts of the Shakespearean characters, those whose internal dramas do not end and whose theaters do not close, were females? These introspective Hamlets and impassioned Romeos enact in private a drama of hidden feelings and unsettling desires superior to that permitted in the public eye. Dickinson's unknown female performers are analogous to Cushman's coded stage representations of same-sex passion, as well as her more private enactments of such passion. Her female counterparts to Shakespeare's heroes may suggest that his predominantly male-centered plays provided women like Dickinson and Cushman with a means of articulating cross-gender identification and same-sex attraction.[71]

"But perhaps Shakespeare has been 'up street' oftener than I have"

In the last five years of her life, Romeo played a provocative part in Dickinson's thoughts. In November 1881, Romeo became part of one of her most imaginative uses of Shakespeare. In a letter thanking her cousin Fanny Norcross for a recipe for graham bread, she writes, "The bread resulted charmingly, and such pretty little proportions, quaint as a druggist's formula - 'I do remember an apothecary.' Mother and Vinnie think it the nicest they have ever known, and Maggie so extols it" (L737). Here receiving Fanny's recipe is like Romeo gaining the apothecary's potion, which he describes as "cordial and not poison" because it will reunite him in death with his beloved Juliet, believed to be dead

(V i 85). Dickinson is again concerned with the moment a Shakespearean hero plans to commit suicide and with death as a way of reuniting separated lovers. In a Christian context, of course, the bread of Christ brings life after death. Nancy Johnson argues that the poet's "praise identifies her friend as a creator: a criminal or performer of outrageous acts, the originator of new species or theories, and the distributor of alms to the needy."[72] Fanny's is an indulgence equated with the Apothecary's tragic dose—illegal like the apothecary's drug and yet pleasurable for those fortunate Romeos allowed to consume.

Dickinson's ingenious use of this play is seen also in a letter from January 1882 to her aunt, Mrs. Joseph A. Sweetser, who is transported to a scene where Romeo's father, Montague, worries about his son's mysterious behavior and sadness, which is "So far from sounding and discovery, / As is the bud bit with an envious worm / Ere he can spread his sweet leaves to the air, / Or dedicate his beauty to the sun" (I i 150–53). Dickinson makes these lines describe actual plants, *her* plants: "One might possibly come up, having sown itself - if it should, you shall share - it is an Eastern Creature and does not like this Soil. I think it's first Exuberance was purely accidental - Last was a fatal season - An "Envious Worm" attacked them - then in early Autumn we had Midwinter Frost - 'When God is with us, who shall be against us,' but when he is against us, other allies are useless - " (L746). Her plants are "Eastern" Romeos, out of place in the world, melancholic figures cut down by a mysterious "Envious Worm." As in her letters in which Hamlet and Desdemona are blooms that travel in the mail, her Romeos are doomed flowers, fated to die by the uncaring whim of an all-powerful God. Dickinson frequently transforms children, other women, and herself into flowers, yet although she often associates a man with a particular flower, she does not usually compare men generally to flowers.[73] Desdemona as a flower seems almost expected in a culture that presented Shakespeare's heroines as ideals of femininity. The *Indicator* essay on Hamlet refers to Ophelia as "the tender flower" crushed by sorrow and woe until she becomes insane (222–23). Similarly, Henrietta Palmer writes, "we shrink from the task of dissecting the sensitive beauties of Ophelia's character, as we should from the necessity of tearing apart the blushing bosom of a rose to count its stamens."[74] Dickinson's presentation of Shakespeare's tragic heroes as flowers is thus unusual and highlights her identification of these characters as feminine men.

Romeo plays a role in one of the last letters Dickinson wrote, dated 17 April 1886, in which she tells her sick aunt Elizabeth Currier,

> "I do remember an Apothecary," said that sweeter Robin than Shakespeare, was a loved paragraph which has lain on my Pillow all Winter, but perhaps Shakespeare has been 'up street' oftener than I have, this Winter. Would Father's

> youngest Sister believe that in the "Shire Town," where he and Blackstone went to school, a man was hung in Northampton yesterday for the murder of a man by the name of Dickinson, and that Miss Harriet Merrill was poisoned by a strolling Juggler, and to be tried in the Supreme Court next week? Dont you think Fumigation ceased when Father died? Poor, romantic Miss Merrill! But perhaps a Police Gazette was better for you than an Essay - (L1041)

The suggestion is that Dickinson was reading Shakespeare in her final month, or had this play by her "Pillow all Winter." John E. Walsh argues that this letter reflects a morbid outlook in the poet's last months, in which she turned to this most famous of suicides to articulate her own longing for death and for reunion with a dead lover.[75] Failing health may have made her preoccupied with Romeo's description of a dram by drinking which "the life-weary taker may fall dead" (V i 62). But Dickinson had been interested for many years in Shakespeare's death scenes. Here, as in other letters, her application of them is complex; their protagonists are cleverly transformed into the poet's contemporaries. Dickinson particularly connects the violent dispute, troubled love, poisoning, family conflict, and death in *Romeo and Juliet* with two incidents in Amherst. The first involved a man named Allen J. Adams, who was executed on May 16 for the murder of Moses Billings Dickinson. The other involved "Poor, romantic Miss Merrill," who became infatuated with a younger man, Dr. De Vore, and left him all her money; as a result, her family believed, Vore poisoned her.[76] Dickinson may be referring Currier to the previous lines in this speech, in which Romeo declares, "O mischief! thou art swift / To enter in the thoughts of desperate men!" (V i 35–36), as a fitting summary of these local events. In her last days she was still turning to Shakespeare's pages; she regarded him as locally relevant, and more "up street," than herself. And at this moment when, as she notes, "I hav'nt felt quite as well as usual since the Chestnuts were ripe," the poet's wit and good humor remain a feature of her epistolary style.

"With all the modern improvements, We reproduced from Shak-es-peare"

Dickinson's many allusions to Shakespeare's tragic characters imply that they offered wisdom, caution, and consolation; she chose them as a way to express her feelings and thoughts in the last years of her life. As in the above letter, though, many of her allusions are humorous. This is not surprising considering that at the time Shakespeare's plays were being turned into burlesques, travesties, and parodies, themselves a central aspect of American popular entertainment.[77] Suspicion and prejudice toward the stage was rife in Dickinson's

Amherst, but attitudes were changing. In "The Theater and Morality" in the *Amherst Student* on 13 January 1877, the essayist had argued that if the plays on the stage and the theater establishment itself were kept within the bounds of decency and morality through the influence of Christian men, then drama could have a beneficial and ennobling effect.[78] On 23 March 1882, Mabel Loomis Todd recorded in her journal on how "jolly" Amherst was, and that she was "happy as a lark," counting each hour only by pleasures; she mentions the existence of "the Alpha Delta private theatricals, the Senior masquerade, the Glee Club concert" (Leyda II 361).[79] Like Austin Dickinson, Todd had a real love of drama, and in November 1883 she starred in a local production of *A Fair Barbarian* by Frances Hodgson Burnett.[80] Before this, however, Amherst College students had sought to rectify Shakespeare's absence from the stage by putting on two travesties: *Romeo and Juliet, A Travesty* and *The Travesty of Hamlet.*[81] Such productions make fun of "everything in the standard drama which was serious and ought to have been respected," and Shakespeare's most read and staged plays were obvious targets.[82] An examination of these local efforts illustrates how this culture's familiarity with Shakespeare was employed to amuse audiences by inaccurately, profanely, and surprisingly disorganizing and reorganizing that which they knew best, and offers insights into how Dickinson's culture perceived Shakespeare's plays.[83]

The Amherst College Senior Dramatic Company put on *Romeo and Juliet, A Travesty* on 13th and 15th of June 1881 in the College Hall, with the Amherst College Glee Club as the chorus; it was a great success.[84] Romeo here is not a great romantic hero but a greedy materialist, interested in Juliet only because she is an heiress. She, in turn, is not a fourteen-year-old maiden but a middle-aged spinster who is also fundamentally concerned with money; she is especially delighted to hear of Tybalt's death because she will inherit his fortune. The Apothecary, discontented with his minor role, enters the play in act I; he does everything he can to upstage Romeo, even pursuing his own love interest, Juliet's nurse. Each of Shakespeare's most famous scenes, including the balcony scene and the tomb scene, is misrepresented. No one dies, and even Tybalt and Mercutio come back at the end of the play, Mercutio lamenting, "I should have said - my - tardy memory rouses - / When I was killed, a plague o' both your houses." The play ends happily, as Juliet asks the audience to unite "in our motto—to laugh while we may." Throughout, there are specific references to aspects of American life: the Italian feud, for instance, becomes a political dispute between two congressional candidates, Michael Montague and Carl Capulet. The contemporary social issue of Irish immigration is addressed: at one point, Romeo disguises himself in red whiskers and green goggles, and Juliet's nurse mistakes him for "an odious red-haired Irishman." In addition to its attack on materialism, the play hints at corruption in the legal, political, clerical, and medical professions.[85] As is typical of travesties, this play makes fun of the pretensions of "proper" Shakespeare productions and idiosyncratic acting styles.[86] For instance, when the nurse arrives at the tomb, revealing that Juliet is not dead, Capulet demands a full explanation, declaring, "Tell me what you mean eh! / Or I will strangle you—à la Salvini." The prologue examines the question of Shakespeare's unrivaled genius and, assuming its audience's awareness of this controversy, acknowledges "That critics wink and say they think / Lord Bacon wrote, anonymously, / The works of William Shak-es-peare." In addition, it suggests the need to alter his play, declaring that although he was "very bright / for one who wrote, so long ago" now "His dramas no great shakes appear," so "With all the modern improvements, / We reproduced from Shak-es-peare."

As was also usual in travesties, characters sing their lines to the tune of famous airs such as "Little Brown Jug" and "Massa's in de Cold Ground." Similarly, *The Travesty of Hamlet,* presented by the Amherst College Glee Club in Amherst College Hall on Saturday, 23 June 1883, used popular airs like "Pop goes the Weasel."[87] This play examines student life, female tyranny, and domesticity, and makes fun of the concern with suicide and madness in *Hamlet.* It contains more verbal allusions to the play it is mocking than the *Romeo and Julie* travesty, as well as recognizable lines from other plays including *King Lear* and *Macbeth.*[88] References are made to the pretensions of Shakespearean acting; at the beginning, Hamlet is most worried about whether he should dress, and presumably act, "like Fechter or like Edwin Booth."[89] Here, Hamlet is a student at "Wittenburg University" when his mother Gertrude, Queen of Denmark, arrives and demands he return there, ordering his hard-drinking, leisurely student friends to accompany him so that they can replace her servants in the palace (who have gone to fight Fortinbras). Throughout, Gertrude is the dominant character. This despotic and tyrannical queen forces the protesting male students to sweep and clean her house and serve tea to her and her ladies in waiting. Although less driven by social and cultural comment than the *Romeo* production, this one certainly raises the question of changing gender roles. Like its predecessor, it deforms the most famous aspects of Shakespeare's play: Hamlet's father is not a ghost, only disguised as one. Claudius is a minor character who is eventually banished to Chicago for his attempted murder of Old Hamlet. Hamlet is not melancholic but, as Ophelia asserts, a "masculine flirt"; and it is Polonius's infatuation with Gertrude that causes Ophelia madness. Hamlet's own madness derives from his imitation of Ophelia's, and even Horatio joins his friends, declaring he "too, must go stark idiotic." The queen's fury, however, becomes an antidote to their insanity, and she promises to flay them alive and boil them to the bone if they descend into madness again. In addition, in act V, as Hamlet is about to deliver Shakespeare's most famous speech, he is interrupted by Horatio, who says that their friendship forbids him from letting Hamlet "soliloquize alone." The speech is then further trivialized as the Chorus sing "To be, or not to be" to the air of "Three Blind Mice." The play ends with Gertrude and Old Hamlet reunited, and Hamlet and Ophelia together. Finally, the queen tells all the students that they have graduated, and the Ghost laments that "Denmark will ne'er forget the day / You swept her floor and washed her dishes!"

We do not know if the details of these presentations reached the reclusive poet. But even if they did not, such travesties and burlesques were already an aspect of Shakespeare's afterlife in Dickinson's day,[90] amusing an audience in proportion to its familiarity with Shakespeare's works. Dickinson's often amusing use of Shakespeare in her letters is analogous. In her 1884 letter to Mrs. Holland, for instance, in the space of a few lines, she alludes to three of Shakespeare's plays:

> The contemplation of you as "Grandma" is a touching novelty to which the Mind adjusts itself by reverent degrees. That nothing in her Life became her like it's last event, it is probable - So the little Engrosser has done her work, and Love's "remainder Biscuit" is henceforth for us - We will try to bear it as divinely as Othello did, who had he had Love's sweetest slice, would not have charmed the World - Austin heard Salvini before his Idol died, and the size of that manifestation even the Grave has not foreclosed - (L882).

The rapid, breathless movement from *As You Like It* to *Macbeth* to *Othello* demonstrates her impressive familiarity with Shakespeare and ability to appropriate him. In addition, Dickinson blurs genre boundaries, moving from tragedy to comedy, and from a close reading of Shakespeare's text to details of a specific performance; here she chooses to reuse quotations employed in previous letters (L545, L339). Malcolm's remark about the death of a traitor becomes a celebration of new life (*Macbeth* I iv 7–8). Dickinson jokes that this birth will take Mrs. Holland's love and attention away from her, leaving the poet with "Love's 'remainder Biscuit,'" which according to Jacques is dry "after a voyage" (*As You Like It* II vii 39–40). Yet Dickinson wryly maintains that she will bear this like the murderous Othello, who charmed the world because he was denied his Desdemona. The poet ends by connecting her loss of her addressee with Salvini's loss of his wife, and assuring Holland that like Salvini she will not be stifled, as an artist, by this loss. Like one assembling a Shakespeare travesty or burlesque, Dickinson combines improbable lines and characters from different plays, bombarding her audience with multiple references.

As Laurence Hutton would suggest in 1890, to burlesque meant to joke, banter, play: it was language used with the "intention to excite laughter."[91] On comparison with the letters of her contemporaries, Dickinson is more playful and witty than Hawthorne, Alcott, Fuller, James, or Melville.

In many other letters as well, Dickinson uses her correspondents' acquaintance with Shakespeare as a catalyst for wit and humor. While some of her references to Shakespeare demonstrate self-enlargement through identification with Shakespeare's tragic protagonists, many are simply part of the hyperbolic theatrics of her writing style.[92] Her humorous employment of Shakespeare is analogous to a major cultural use of the bard, epitomized by these local travesties. As in these plays, Dickinson in her letters elevates "a daily occurrence . . . into a situation of classic dignity," or invests "subjects or events of 'great pith and moment' in the costume and dialect of vulgar life."[93] At the same moment that she makes her own life or the lives of her friends important through reference to Shakespeare, she on some level belittles the pretensions of his grand tragedies. This is evident in her comparison of herself to Othello, in her identification of the lovers in *Antony and Cleopatra* with herself and Sue or with herself and Otis Lord, and in her projection of the tragic characteristics of Hamlet, Romeo, and Desdemona onto her flowers. She comically transforms lines by placing them in new contexts, surprising her recipient with unexpected associations—Higginson's book with Desdemona, Fanny Norcross's recipe with the Apothecary's poison, local children with Desdemona and Antonio. She refuses a visitor entry through reference to Cleopatra's first refusal of Antony, or compares the coming of a visitor to the moving of Birnam Wood to Dunsinane. In her last known reference to Shakespeare, she transforms Harriet Merrill into an "older" Juliet and Dr. De Vore into a poisoning Romeo, as well as turning Moses Billing Dickinson and Allen J. Adams into feuding Montagues and Capulets. For her, Shakespeare himself has been "up [the] street" causing trouble. Like the writers of travesties, Dickinson in her letters offers a "knowing" audience the amusement of unlikely and imaginative connections with Shakespeare and his plays; she misrepresents his plot, lines, and characters, even pokes fun at the atmosphere of sacredness that accompanied Shakespeare's American reception at the time.[94]

On one level, Dickinson's use of Shakespeare suggests that she engaged with erudite and highbrow texts in order to examine weighty contemporary philosophical, literary, social, and personal issues. Her reading of his tragedies was part of her own pervasive concern with death, love, and immortality, which grew in her final years. She refers to heroes' famous deaths as a means of performing her final act upon the epistolary stage, perhaps with the hope that her death, like theirs, may be immortalized. Her death, like the dead jasmine in

Mrs. Higginson's hand, may record the fact that she herself once lived and, like Hamlet and Romeo, wavered for all of us. On another level, however, much of her use of Shakespeare in letters reflects his reception in contemporary burlesques and travesties. The poet probably never saw any of these productions, and may have been appalled by such "uncultured" use of Shakespeare, yet viewed in their context her letters are also burlesquing Shakespeare.

CONCLUSION

"Touch Shakespeare for me"

When Emily Dickinson's many hyperbolic statements of praise for Shakespeare, and her abundant references to his works, are examined within the historical context from which they emanated, they are rarely found to be straightforward. Provocative and timely, they reflect the fact that Dickinson read Shakespeare as a member of a culture in which he was a problematic actor who figured in its dialogue on a range of social and cultural issues. Her response to and conception of Shakespeare developed at a time when he was treated with reverence—in effect, as the greatest "American author." In her letters she presents him as the "future" and "firm" foundation of literature. He is also like her influential best (female) friend, Sue, and should not be confused with Francis Bacon; he is her "Beloved" writer, who is not wicked and always seems "just published." Her letters promote Shakespeare's supremacy in a culture in which literary and social values were changing. Its prescription that she read (and worship) Shakespeare offered her the opportunity to engage in inspired and original ways with overly familiar materials. They become for her a field of possibility, imagination, fantasy; she appropriated them to either validate or undermine traditional attitudes on a number of issues. Shakespeare, though, was also disdained by many in Dickinson's culture as an "English" author, whose mythic greatness suppressed the appreciation of American literature. Her virtual exclusion of direct references to his works in her poetry, and her poem "Drama's Vitallest Expression is the Common Day," demonstrate that her understanding of him was entangled in her sense of identity as an American writer. One of her most provocative letters, which has received little critical attention, addresses the issue of devotion to Shakespeare and Dickinson's sense of her Americanness.

In the summer of 1885, a year before she died, Dickinson wrote to Mabel Loomis Todd, who was traveling in Europe. The poet begins her most patriotic letter by reminding Todd of an American anthem, "Sweet Land of Liberty," which seems "superfluous" until it "concerns ourselves" (L1004). Following the dictates of American cultural nationalism, she invokes distinctive cultural aspects of her country and its natural landscape, offering Todd a substitute for what she is missing and ending by telling Todd "Touch Shakespeare for me," signing her letter, Cleopatralike, "America." Dickinson/America is not begging acceptance by "Stratford on Avon"; rather, her/its emissary Todd should, with a secure and authoritative sense of nationality, both cultural and political, pay Dickinson's/America's respects to Shakespeare:

> Brother and Sister's Friend -
>
> "Sweet Land of Liberty" is a superfluous Carol till it concerns ourselves - then it outrealms the Birds. I saw the American Flag last Night in the shutting West, and I felt for every Exile. I trust you are homesick. That is the sweetest courtesy we pay an absent friend. The Honey you went so far to seek, I trust too you obtain. Though was there not an "Humbler" Bee?" "I will sail by thee alone, thou animated Torrid Zone." Your Hollyhocks endow the House, making Art's inner Summer, never Treason to Nature's. Nature will be just closing her Picnic, when you return to America, but you will ride Home by Sunset, which is far better. I am glad you cherish the Sea, We correspond, though I never met him. I write in the midst of Sweet-Peas and by the side of Orioles, and could put my Hand on a Butterfly, only he withdraws. Touch Shakespeare for me. The Savior's only signature to the Letter he wrote to all mankind, was, A Stranger and ye took me in.
>
> America.

NOTES

Introduction

1. Charles Knight, ed., *The Comedies, Histories, Tragedies and Poems of William Shakspere; with a Biography and Studies of his Works by Charles Knight: The Pictorial and National Edition,* 8 vols. (Boston: Little, Brown, 1853). All subsequent references are to this edition. As Knight's edition does not provide line references, *The Riverside Shakespeare,* ed. G. Blakemore Evans (Boston: Houghton Mifflin, 1997), is used, where possible, to indicate line numbers.

2. See Julian Markels, "Melville's Markings in Shakespeare's Plays," *American Literature* 49, no. 1 (1977): 34–48; and Jonathan Bate, *Shakespeare and the English Romantic Imagination* (Oxford: Clarendon Press, 1986), 168–70. *The Tempest, Love's Labour's Lost, The Merchant of Venice, Richard III,* and *Hamlet* are marked in Susan Dickinson's edition of Shakespeare, also at the Houghton: *The Complete Works of William Shakspeare: with Dr. Johnson's Preface; A Glossary, and an account of each play; a Memoir of the author by Rev. William Harris* (New York: Geo. F. Cooledge & Brother, 1847), 41, 168, 205, 522, 847.

3. See Knight, *Shakspere,* V 261, 262, 283, 292, 293, 295, 298, 300, 316, 322, 333, 334, 341, 343.

4. Emily Dickinson, *The Poems of Emily Dickinson, Variorum Edition,* ed. R. W. Franklin, 3 vols. (Cambridge, Mass.: Belknap Press of Harvard University Press, 1998). All subsequent references are to this edition, cited as F followed by the poem number.

5. See Roger E. Stoddard, "Note to the Catalogue of the Emily Dickinson Room," dated 9 October 1997.

6. See Alfred Habegger, *My Wars Are Laid Away in Books: The Life of Emily Dickinson* (New York: Random House, 2001), 116, 182–83, 223, 250–51, 386–87, 712. Richard B. Sewall is more cautious, suggesting that while the thin pencil marks in the Dickinsons' books are probably hers, "other people in the Dickinson circle had pencils too, and followed the same practice." See *The Life of Emily Dickinson* (1974; Cambridge, Mass.: Harvard University Press, 1994), 678. See also Jack L. Capps, *Emily Dickinson's Reading, 1836–1886* (Cambridge, Mass.: Harvard University Press, 1966), 61–62, 67, 168–69.

7. Of course, someone in the Dickinson household may have marked this edition after the poet's death to indicate lines she referred to in letters or lines they believed had special significance for her. See Judith Farr, *The Passion of Emily Dickinson* (Cambridge, Mass.: Harvard University Press, 1992), 115.

8. Emily Dickinson, *The Letters of Emily Dickinson,* ed. Thomas Johnson and Theodora Ward (1958; Cambridge, Mass.: Belknap Press of Harvard University Press,

1986). All subsequent references are to this edition, cited as L followed by the letter number.

9. See Richard Wilbur, "Sumptuous Destitution," in *Emily Dickinson: A Collection of Critical Essays,* ed. Richard B. Sewall (Englewood Cliffs, N.J.: Prentice-Hall, 1963), 127–36; Joan Burbick, "Emily Dickinson and the Economics of Desire," *American Literature* 58, no. 3 (1986): 361–78; and Vivian R. Pollak, "Thirst and Starvation in Emily Dickinson's Poetry," *American Literature* 51, no. 1 (1979): 33–49.

10. Jay Leyda, *The Years and Hours of Emily Dickinson,* 2 vols. (New Haven: Yale University Press, 1960), I: 352. Subsequent quotations are referred to within the text as Leyda followed by the volume and page number (e.g., Leyda I 352).

11. See Budick, "Emily," 366–67; Habegger, *My Wars,* 613.

12. See Rebecca Patterson, *Emily Dickinson's Imagery,* ed. Margaret H. Freeman (Amherst: University of Massachusetts Press, 1979), 28–29.

13. See Richard Sewall, *The Lyman Letters: New Light on Emily Dickinson and Her Family* (Amherst: University of Massachusetts Press, 1965), 76. See also L304 and L342a.

14. Sewall, *Life,* 701; George Frisbie Whicher, *This Was a Poet: A Critical Biography of Emily Dickinson* (1938; Amherst: Amherst College Press, 1992), 209–10, 223–24; Capps, *Emily,* 62–66, 182–84; Helen McNeil, *Emily Dickinson* (London: Virago, 1986), 27–29; Elizabeth Phillips, *Emily Dickinson: Personae and Performance* (University Park: Pennsylvania State University Press, 1988), 127–30; Robert F. Fleissner, "If Dickinson did not see a Moor, she at least Read of The Moor," *College Language Association Journal* 37, no. 1 (1993): 55–63; Benjamin Lease, *Emily Dickinson's Readings of Men and Books* (London: Macmillan 1990), 35–45; Linda J. Taylor, "Shakespeare and Circumference: Dickinson's Hummingbird and *The Tempest,*" *ESQ: A Journal of the American Renaissance* 23 (1977): 252–61; Eleanor Heginbotham, "Dickinson's 'What If I Say I Shall Not Wait!'" *Explicator* 54, no. 3 (1996): 154–60; Paula Bennett, "'The Orient Is in the West': Emily Dickinson's Reading of *Antony and Cleopatra,*" in *Women's Re-Visions of Shakespeare,* ed. Marianne Novy (Urbana: University of Illinois, Press, 1990): 108–22; Michael West, "Shakespeare Allusions in Emily Dickinson," *American Notes and Queries* 10 (1971): 51; Jane F. Crosthwaite, "Dickinson's 'What I see not, I better see,'" *Explicator* 36, no. 3 (1978): 10–12; Adrian Richwell, "Poetic Immortality: Dickinson's 'Flood-Subject' Reconsidered," *Dickinson Studies* 69 (1989): 1–31; John R. Byers, "The Possible Background of Three Dickinson Poems," *Dickinson Studies* 57 (1986): 35–38; Kristin M. Comment, "Dickinson's Bawdy: Shakespeare and Sexual Symbolism in Emily Dickinson's Writing to Susan Dickinson," *Legacy* 18, no. 2 (2001): 167–81; Judith Farr, "Emily Dickinson's Engulfing Play: *Antony and Cleopatra,*" *Tulsa Studies in Women's Literature* 9, no. 2 (1990): 231–50.

15. Although George Bernard Shaw coined this term in 1901, it aptly clarifies the indiscriminate eulogizing of Shakespeare in nineteenth-century Anglo-American culture. See Edwin Wilson, ed., *Shaw on Shakespeare* (New York: E. P. Dutton, 1961), 217; Howard Felperin, "Bardolatry Then and Now," in *The Appropriation of Shakespeare:*

Post-Renaissance Reconstructions of the Works and the Myth, ed. Jean I. Marsden (New York: St. Martin's, 1991), 129–44.

16. See Robert Darnton, "What Is the History of Books?" *Daedalus* 111, no. 3 (1982): 65–83; Robert Darnton, "First Steps Towards a History of Reading," *Australian Journal of French Studies* 23, no. 1 (1986): 5–30; Guglielmo Cavallo and Roger Chartier, eds., *The History of Reading in the West* (Cambridge, U.K.: Polity, 1999); David Finkelstein and Alister McCleery, eds., *History of the Book Reader* (London: Routledge, 2001); and James L. Machor and Philip Goldstein, eds., *Reception Study from Literary Theory to Cultural Studies* (London: Routledge, 2001).

17. See Ashley Thorndike, "Shakespeare in America," *Aspects of Shakespeare* (Oxford: Clarendon Press, 1933), 108–27; Esther Cloudman Dunn, *Shakespeare in America* (New York: Macmillan, 1939); Alfred Van Rensselaer Westfall, *American Shakespearean Criticism 1607–1865* (New York: H. W. Wilson, 1939); Louis Marder, *His Exits and His Entrances: The Story of Shakespeare's Reputation* (London: John Murray, 1964); James McManaway, "Shakespeare in the United States," *PMLA* 79, no. 5 (1964): 513–18; Nancy Webb and Jean Francis Webb, *Will Shakespeare and His America* (New York: Viking, 1964); Robert Falk, "Shakespeare in America: A Survey to 1900," *Shakespeare Survey* 18 (1965): 102–18; Raoul Granqvist, "Some Traits of Cultural Nationalism in the Reception of Shakespeare in the Nineteenth Century U.S.A," *Orbis Litterarum* 43 (1988): 32–57; Gary Taylor, *Reinventing Shakespeare: A Cultural History from the Restoration to the Present* (London: Hogarth Press, 1989); Stephen Brown, "The Uses of Shakespeare in America: A Study in Class Domination," in *Shakespeare: Pattern of Excelling Nature, Shakespeare Criticism in Honor of America's Bicentennial,* ed. David Bevington and Jay L. Halio (Newark: University of Delaware Press, 1978), 230–38; Charles H. Shattuck, *Shakespeare on the American Stage,* vol. I, *From the Hallams to Edwin Booth,* and vol. II, *From Booth and Barrett to Sothern and Marlowe* (Washington, D.C.: Folger Shakespeare Library, 1976 and 1987); Michael Bristol, *Shakespeare's America, America's Shakespeare* (London: Routledge, 1990); Sanford E. Marovitz, "America vs. Shakespeare: From the Monroe Doctrine to the Civil War," *Zeitschrift für Anglistik und Amerikanistik* 34, no. 1 (1986): 33–46; Helene Wickham Koon, *How Shakespeare Won the West: Players and Performances in America's Gold Rush, 1849–1865* (Jefferson, N.C.: McFarland, 1989); Alan Sinfield, *Faultlines: Cultural Materialism and the Politics of Dissent Reading* (Oxford: Oxford University Press, 1992), 254–304; Thomas Cartelli, *Repositioning Shakespeare: National Formations, Postcolonial Appropriations* (London: Routledge, 1999); Peter Rawlings, ed., *Americans on Shakespeare 1776–1914* (Aldershot, U.K.: Ashgate, 1999); Hilary Rowland, "Shakespeare and the Public Sphere in Nineteenth Century America" (Ph.D. diss., McGill University, 1998; Ann Arbor, Mich.: UMI, 2002); Henry Simon, *The Reading of Shakespeare in American Schools and Colleges: An Historical Survey* (New York: Simon and Schuster, 1932); and John Hampton Lauck, "The Reception and Teaching of Shakespeare in Nineteenth and Early Twentieth Century America" (Ph.D. diss., University of Illinois–Champaign-Urbana, 1991; Ann Arbor, Mich.: UMI, 1998).

18. See Roger Chartier, "Labourers and Voyagers: From the Text to the Reader," *Diacritics* 22, no. 2 (1992): 49–61 (59); and Darnton, "What," 79.

19. See Hans Robert Jauss, *Towards an Aesthetics of Reception,* trans. Timothy Bahti (Minneapolis: University of Minnesota Press, 1982), 22.

20. See Chartier, "Labourers," 50–51; Darnton, "First," 22–23.

21. See S. Schoenbaum, *Shakespeare's Lives* (Oxford: Clarendon Press, 1991), 274; Jonathan Bate, "Pictorial Shakespeare: Text, Stage, Illustration," in *Book Illustrated: Text, Image, and Culture 1770–1930* (New Castle, Del.: Oak Knoll Press, 2000), 31–59.

22. Darnton, "First," 16–17.

23. See Roger Chartier, "The Practical Impact of Writing," in *History of the Book Reader,* ed. Finkelstein and McCleery, 127–29.

24. Bristol, *Shakespeare,* 25–28.

25. Chartier, "Labourers," 50; and Chartier, "Practical," 125–38.

26. Darnton, "First," 20–21.

27. Thorndike, "Shakespeare," 114–15; and Falk, "Shakespeare," 105–7.

28. Chartier, "Labourers," 51.

29. See Toni Morrison, *Playing in the Dark: Whiteness and the Literary Imagination* (Cambridge: Harvard University Press, 1992); Ronald J. Zboray and Mary Saracino Zboray, "'Have You Read . . . ?': Real Readers and Their Responses in Antebellum Boston and Its Region," *Nineteenth-Century Literature* 52, no. 2 (1997): 139–70; Ronald J. Zboray and Mary Saracino Zboray, "Books, Reading and the World of Goods in Antebellum New England," *American Quarterly* 48, no. 4 (1996): 587–622; Patrocinio P. Schweickart, "Reading Ourselves: Toward a Feminist Theory of Reading," in *Gender and Reading: Essays on Readers, Texts, and Contexts,* ed. Elizabeth A Flynn and Patrocinio P. Schweickart (Baltimore: Johns Hopkins University Press, 1986), 31–62; Barbara Sicherman, "Sense and Sensibility: A Case Study of Women's Reading in Late-Victorian America," in *Reading in America: Literature and Social History,* ed. Cathy N. Davidson (Baltimore: Johns Hopkins University Press, 1989), 201–25; Barbara Sicherman, "Reading and Ambition: M. Carey Thomas and Female Heroism," *American Quarterly* 45, no. 1 (1993): 73–103; and Paula Bennett, "Gender as Performance: Shakespearean Ambiguity and the Lesbian Reader," in *Sexual Practice, Textual Theory: Lesbian Cultural Criticism,* ed. Susan J. Wolfe and Julia Penelope (Oxford: Blackwells, 1993), 94–109.

30. See Novy ed., *Women's;* Marianne Novy, ed., *Cross-Cultural Performances: Differences in Women's Re-Visions of Shakespeare* (Urbana: University of Illinois Press, 1993); Marianne Novy, *Engaging with Shakespeare: Responses of George Eliot and Other Novelists* (Athens: University of Georgia Press, 1994); and Ann Thompson and Sasha Roberts, eds., *Women's Reading of Shakespeare, 1660–1900* (Manchester, U.K.: Manchester University Press, 1997).

31. See Christy Desmet and Robert Sawyer, eds., *Shakespeare and Appropriation* (London: Routledge, 1999), 6–10.

32. Theodora Van Wagenen Ward, ed., *Emily Dickinson's Letters to Dr. and Mrs. Josiah Gilbert Holland* (Cambridge, Mass.: Harvard University Press, 1951), 212.

33. See H. M. Plunkett, *Josiah Gilbert Holland* (New York: Scribner's, 1894). After Holland's death, Rev. P. W. Lyman declared, "It is no small accomplishment to put eighteen different volumes of good literature upon the world's book-shelves; books, too, of such intrinsic merit, and such pertinence to the wants of men, that every one of them was a business success, and that upward of five-hundred thousand volumes, all told, have already been paid for by the public. In this respect certainly his success has been unequalled among Americans" (180).

34. J. G. Holland, *Every-Day Topics; a Book of Briefs* (New York: Scribner, Armstrong, 1876), 7–8.

35. Holland, *Every-Day,* 40.

36. See Thomas Carlyle, *On Heroes, Hero-Worship, and the Heroic in History* (New York: D. Appleton, 1842), 126–42; Tricia Lootens, *Lost Saints: Silence, Gender, and Victorian Literary Canonization* (Charlotteville: University Press of Virginia, 1996), 15–44.

37. Thorndike, "Shakespeare," 122.

38. Ralph Waldo Emerson, "The American Scholar," *The Collected Works of Ralph Waldo Emerson,* 5 vols., ed. Alfred R. Ferguson et al. (Cambridge, Mass.: Harvard University Press, 1971–94), I: 69. Subsequently cited by parenthetical page references in the text.

39. Stephanie A. Tingley, "'My Business is to Sing': Emily Dickinson's Letters to Elizabeth Holland," in *Dickinson and Audience,* ed. Martin Orzeck and Robert Weisbuch (Ann Arbor: University of Michigan Press, 1996), 181–99; Marietta Messmer, *A Vice for Voices: Reading Emily Dickinson's Correspondence* (Amherst: University of Massachusetts Press, 2001), 97–103; and Sewall, *Life,* 609–25.

40. In 1862, she told Higginson when he suggested that she should delay to publish, "If fame belonged to me, I could not escape her - if she did not, the longest day would pass me on the chase" (L265). She asked her sister-in-law, Susan Dickinson, "Could I make you and Austin - proud - sometime - a great way off - 'twould give me taller feet - " (L238).

41. Habegger, *My Wars,* 383. See also Cynthia Griffin Wolff, *Emily Dickinson* (New York: Alfred A. Knopf, 1986), 244–45.

42. See Cristanne Miller, *Emily Dickinson: A Poet's Grammar* (Cambridge, Mass.: Harvard University Press, 1987), 118–22.

43. Peter Rawlings, "Henry James, Delia Bacon, and American Uses of Shakespeare," *Symbiosis: A Journal of Anglo-American Literary Relations* 5, no. 2 (2001): 151; Thorndike, "Shakespeare," 125; and George Churchill, "Shakespeare in America," in *Americans on Shakespeare,* ed. Rawlings, 433.

44. Richard Grant White, "A Visit to Stratford-On-Avon," *The Galaxy* 24, no. 2 (1877): 250.

45. See Knight, *Shakspere,* VII, 16–159.

46. James G. Wilson, "Stratford-Upon-Avon," *Harper's New Monthly* 23, no. 136 (1861): 433–46; and William Winter, "Stratford-Upon-Avon," *Harper's New Monthly* 58, no. 348 (1879): 864–86. Subsequently both are cited by parenthetical page references in the text.

47. Wilson also prints the following verse, which reads, "Ah, Shakspeare, when we read the votive scrawls / With which well-meaning folks deface these walls; / And while we seek in vain some lucky hit, / Amidst the lines whose nonsense nonsense smothers, / We find, unlike thy Falstaff in his wit, / Thou art not here the cause of wit in others" (437).

48. See Peter Rawlings, "Introduction," in *Americans on Shakespeare,* ed. Rawlings, 15–18.

49. Washington Irving, *The Sketch-Book* (Oxford: Oxford University Press, 1996), 251–70. In one letter, Dickinson refers to reading "Rip Van Winkle," which is included in *The Sketch-Book* (L412).

50. Wilson, "Stratford," 446; Winter, "Stratford," 879–80.

51. Winter, "Stratford, 879, 880. See Irving, *Sketch,* 269–70.

52. Irving, *Sketch,* 226.

53. Wilson offers a half crown to an "aged mendicant who claimed alms from us as being a descendant or in some way related to Shakspeare," without "very closely investigating the correctness of his claims," believing he had encountered "a person related, however distantly, to the great dramatist" (444).

54. Dickinson told Higginson, "Hawthorne appalls, entices - " (L622). See Karl Keller, *The Only Kangaroo among the Beauty: Emily Dickinson and America* (Baltimore: Johns Hopkins University Press, 1979), 125–47; Capps, *Emily,* 123; and Nathaniel Hawthorne, "Recollections of a Gifted Woman," *Atlantic Monthly* 11, no. 63 (1863): 43–58. Subsequently cited by parenthetical page references in the text.

55. Mabel Loomis Todd, ed., *Letters of Emily Dickinson* (Boston: Roberts Brothers, 1894), 130. See also Christopher E. G. Benfey, *Emily Dickinson and the Problem of Others* (Amherst: University of Massachusetts Press, 1984).

56. Martha Dickinson Bianchi, *Emily Dickinson: Face to Face* (Boston: Houghton Mifflin, 1932), 49.

57. Barbara Hodgdon, *The Shakespeare Trade: Performances and Appropriations* (Philadelphia: University of Pennsylvania Press, 1998), 191–240; Graham Holderness, "Bardolatry: or, The Cultural Materialist's Guide to Stratford-upon-Avon," in *The Shakespeare Myth,* ed. Graham Holderness (Manchester: Manchester University Press, 1988), 2–15.

58. See White, "Stratford," 255, 259.

59. Robert McClure Smith, "Dickinson and the Masochistic Aesthetic," *Emily Dickinson Journal* 7, no. 2 (1998): 15.

60. See Farr, *Passion,* 314–33; Paula Bernat Bennett, "Emily Dickinson and her American Women Poet Peers," in *The Cambridge Companion to Emily Dickinson,* ed. Wendy Martin (Cambridge: Cambridge University Press, 2002), 215–35; Domhnall Mitchell, *Emily Dickinson: Monarch of Perception* (Amherst: University of Massachusetts Press, 2000), 99–105.

61. Richwell, "Poetic," 22–31.

62. Henry James, "The Birthplace," in *The Jolly Corner and Other Tales* (Har-

mondsworth, U.K.: Penguin, 1990), 108–60. Subsequently cited by parenthetical page references in the text.

63. See Rawlings, "Henry," 151, 155. See also William T. Stafford, "James Examines Shakespeare: Notes on the Nature of Genius," *PMLA* 73, no. 1 (1958): 123–28.

64. Henry James, "Introduction to *The Tempest,*" in *Americans on Shakespeare,* ed. Rawlings, 462. See also Henry James, "In Warwickshire," *The Galaxy* 24, no. 5 (1877): 672, 676.

65. Henry James, *The American Scene* (London: Chapman and Hall, 1907), 263.

66. James, *American,* 261.

67. Joanne Dobson, *Dickinson and the Strategies of Reticence: The Woman Writer in Nineteenth-Century America* (Bloomington: Indiana University Press, 1989).

Chapter One

1. All references are to Lavinia Dickinson's 1851 diary, now at the Houghton Library, Harvard. bMS Am 1118.95, box 8. By permission of the Houghton Library, Harvard University. See Leyda I 195–208; Habegger, *My Wars,* 254–55.

2. See Capps, *Emily,* 19–20; See Leyda I 197.

3. Todd ed., *Letters,* I 129–30.

4. Leyda I 201–2.

5. Sewall, *Life,* 91, 96, 104–6, 111; Habegger, *My Wars,* 182–83, 336–37.

6. Capps, *Emily,* 63. Capps also misrepresents the situation by suggesting that the tutors came from the Amherst Academy rather than Amherst College.

7. See Eric Partridge, *Shakespeare's Bawdy: A Literary and Psychological Essay and a Comprehensive Glossary* (London: Routledge, 1947).

8. See Kate Flint, *The Woman Reader 1837–1914* (Oxford: Clarendon Press, 1993), 209–18.

9. See Catherine J. Golden, *Images of the Woman Reader in Victorian British and American Fiction* (Gainesville: University of Florida Press, 2003), 17–47.

10. See Barbara Sicherman, "Reading and Middle-Class Identity in Victorian America," in *Reading Acts: U.S Readers' Interactions with Literature, 1800–1950,* ed. Barbara Ryan and Amy M. Thomas (Knoxville: University of Tennessee Press, 2002), 137–60; Elizabeth Long, *Book Clubs: Women and the Uses of Reading in Everyday Life* (Chicago: University of Chicago Press, 2003), 1–58; Flint, *Woman;* Nina Baym, *Novels, Readers and Reviewers: Responses to Fiction in Antebellum America* (Ithaca: Cornell University Press, 1984); James L. Machor, "Historical Hermeneutics and Antebellum Fiction, Gender, Response Theory, and Interpretative Contexts," in *Readers in History: Nineteenth-Century American Literature and the Contexts of Response* ed. James L. Machor (Baltimore: Johns Hopkins University Press, 1993), 54–84; Sicherman, "Sense," 201–25; and Sicherman, "Reading," 73–103.

11. The Houghton Library has Rev. John Bennett, *Letters to a Young Lady on Useful and Interesting Subjects,* 2 vols. (New York: G. Long, 1824), which is inscribed on

the cover "E. Norcross." All further references are to Rev. John Bennett, *Letters to a Young Lady on Useful and Interesting Subjects*, 4th edition, 2 vols. (London: T. Cadell and W. Davies, 1812). Subsequently cited by parenthetical page references in the text. Edward Dickinson bought William B. Sprague, D.D., *Letters on Practical Subjects to a Daughter* (Albany, N.Y.: E. H Pease, 1851), inscribing it "Emily from her father April 18, 1852"; his poor handwriting makes it possible the book was given to her in 1852 or 1862; see Habegger, *My Wars*, 46. All references are to an earlier edition: William B. Sprague, D.D., *Letters on Practical Subjects to a Daughter* (New York: John P. Haven, 1831). Subsequently cited by parenthetical page references in the text. The third advice manual in the Dickinson library makes only a few references to reading practice; see Dr. Gregory, *A Father's Legacy to His Daughter* (New York: J. P. Peaslee, 1834) 12, 39, 43–44.

12. Sprague, *Letters*, 13–14. See also *A Young Lady's Own Book: A Manual of Intellectual Improvement and Moral Deportment, by the Author of the Young Man's Own Book* (Philadelphia: John Locken, 1841), 98–105; *The Young Lady's Friend (by a Lady)* (Boston: American Stationer's Company, 1837), 425–27; and *Ladies Vase or Polite Manual for Young Ladies by An American Lady* (Lowell, Mass.: N. L. Dayton/Boston: Lewis & Sampson, 1843), 113–16, 140–45.

13. See Bennett, *Letters*, II 93; Sprague, *Letters*, 13–14.

14. See Bennett, *Letters*, I 36, II 69–71; Sprague, *Letters*, 54–55, 61–62.

15. See Bennett, *Letters*, I 73; Young Lady's Friend, 425.

16. See Habegger, *My Wars*, 103.

17. Rev. E. Thomson, "Hints to Youthful Readers, Part II," *The Ladies Repository* 4, no. 11 (1844): 326.

18. E. W. Gray, "Books and Reading," *The Ladies Repository* 7, no. 6 (1847): 179.

19. Rev. A. Stevens, "The Domestic Library," *The Ladies Repository* 6, no. 12 (1847): 372; Rev. A. Stevens, "The Family Library," *The Ladies Repository* 7, no. 3 (1847): 69.

20. Rev. W. C. Hoyt, "Shakespeare," *The Ladies Repository* 6, no. 2 (1846): 53.

21. See Henrietta Bowdler, ed., *The Family Shakespeare*, 4 vols. (London: J. Hatchard, 1807), v–vii. See Taylor, *Reinventing*, 207.

22. Charles and Mary Lamb, *Tales From Shakespeare* (London: J. M. Dent and Sons, 1906), 2.

23. John W. S. Hows, ed., *The Shakspearian Reader: A Collection of the Most Approved Plays of Shakspeare; prepared expressly for the use of Classes, and the Family Circle* (New York: D. Appleton, 1857), ix–x. See Noel Perrin, *Dr. Bowdler's Legacy: A History of Expurgated Books in England and America* (London: Macmillan, 1969), 101–5.

24. See also Thomas Bulfinch and Rev. S. G. Bulfinch, eds., *Shakespeare: Adapted for Reading Classes, and for the Family Circle* (Boston: J. E. Tilton, 1865); and Rev. Henry N. Hudson, ed., *William Shakespeare, Plays of Shakespeare, selected and prepared for use in Schools, Clubs, Classes, and Families* (Boston: Ginn Brothers, 1872).

25. See Bennett, *Letters*, I 161, II 78; Sprague, *Letters*, 59.

26. The poet's sister-in-law, Susan Dickinson, owned *The most excellent historie of the merchant of Venice* (New York: D. Appleton, 1860), which excluded "a few lines, which, in the present age, might be thought objectionable."

27. Vivian R. Pollak, ed., *A Poet's Parents: The Courtship Letters of Emily Norcross Dickinson and Edward Dickinson* (Chapel Hill: University of North Carolina Press, 1988), 51.

28. Pollak ed., *A Poet's Parents,* 14.

29. See Harvey C. Minnich, ed., *Old Favorites from the McGuffey Readers* (New York: American Book Company, 1936), 252; John A. Nietz, *Old Textbooks* (Pittsburgh: University of Pittsburgh Press, 1961), 70–74; Hall, *The Literary Reader for Academies and High Schools* (Boston: John P. Jewett, 1851); and John Pierpont, *The American First Class Book or exercises in Reading and recitation selected principally from Modern authors of Great Britain and America* (Boston: Charles Bowen, 1836) 418–21, 431–33, 441–42, 442–44, 450–53, 453–54, 457–60. See also Lauck, "Reception," 20–23; and Simon, *Reading,* 8–10.

30. See Dunn, *Shakespeare,* 226–36; Simon, *Reading,* 45–59; Lauck, "Reception," 9–35.

31. See Sewall, *Life,* 358–62; Wolff, *Emily,* 99–104; and Habegger, *My Wars,* 200–212.

32. See Isaac Watts, *Improvement of the Mind, with corrections, questions and supplement by Joseph Emerson* (Boston: James Loving, 1832). Emily Dickinson used the 1833 edition published by Jenks, Palmer & Co. Subsequently cited by parenthetical page references in the text. See Carlton Lowenberg, *Emily Dickinson's Textbooks,* ed. Territa A. Lowenberg and Carla L. Brown (Lafayette, Calif.: Carlton Lowenberg, 1986), 100–101; and Capps, *Emily,* 189–91.

33. See also Watts, *Improvement,* 60–70, 73, 76.

34. See Sewall, *Life,* 670–75; Harold Bloom, *A Map of Misreading* (New York: Oxford University Press, 1975), 53, 178; Margaret Homans, *Women Writers and Poetic Identity: Dorothy Wordsworth, Emily Brontë, and Emily Dickinson* (Princeton: Princeton University Press, 1980); and Mary Loeffelholz, *Dickinson and the Boundaries of Feminist Theory* (Urbana: University of Illinois Press, 1991).

35. See Joseph Emerson, "Editor's Introduction," *Improvement,* viii.

36. See Ebenezer Porter, The *Rhetorical Reader* (New York: Mark H. Newman, 1835), v; and Samuel Phillips Newman, *A Practical System of Rhetoric* (New York: Gould and Newman, 1839), 13. Subsequently both are cited by parenthetical page references in the text. Dickinson used an 1841 edition of Porter published in New York by Dayton & Saxton at Amherst Academy, and an 1839 edition of Newman published in Andover by Gould and Newman at both Amherst Academy and Mount Holyoke. See Lowenberg, *Emily,* 78–80; 88–89. See also Albert R. Kitzhaber, *Rhetoric in American Colleges 1830–1900* (Dallas: Southern Methodist University Press, 1990), 49–73.

37. Newman, *Practical,* v, ix.

38. See W. H. Wells, *Elementary Grammar of the English Language* (Andover, Mass.: Allen, Morrill and Wadswell, 1847), 82, 116, 136, 138. This text was used at both Amherst Academy and Mount Holyoke and explains specific grammatical rules with reference to Shakespeare's *Julius Caesar* and *The Merchant of Venice.* See Lowenberg, *Emily,* 106–7.

39. Noah Webster, *An American Dictionary of the English Language,* 2 vols. (Springfield, Mass.: George & Charles Merriam, 1848). All references are to this edition. Subsequently cited by parenthetical page references in the text. See Lowenberg, *Emily,* 105–6.

40. Sewall, *Lyman,* 78.

41. See also Daniel Dana, D.D., *Address delivered to the Ipswich Female Seminary, January 15th, 1834,* (Newburyport, Mass.: Published by the Committee, printed at the Essex-North Register Office, 1834), 9.

42. Leyda I 252; Sewall, *Life,* 33–43, 52–55, 115–16, 344–57; Wolff, *Emily,* 499–500; and Habegger, *My Wars,* 88, 222, 236–38, 319–21, 559–60.

43. Heman Humphrey, *Discourses and Reviews* (Amherst: J. S. & C Adams, 1834), 411–12. Subsequently cited by parenthetical page references in the text.

44. Heman Humphrey, *Domestic Education* (Amherst: J. S. & C Adams, 1840), 93. See also Daniel Lombardo, *Tales of Amherst: A Look Back* (Amherst, Mass.: Jones Library, 1986), 45.

45. Rev. Edward Hitchcock, *The Highest Use of Learning: An Address delivered at his Inauguration to the Presidency of Amherst College* (Amherst: J. S. & C Adams, Printers, 1845), 6–8. See Sewall, *Life,* 340–50.

46. Hitchcock, *Highest,* 10, 11–12.

47. Cristanne Miller, *Emily Dickinson: A Poet's Grammar* (Cambridge, Mass.: Harvard University Press, 1987), 131–32, 143–49.

48. During his 1870 visit to Amherst, Higginson talked with Stearns about Dickinson (L342a, 342b), and Stearns's wife was one of Dickinson's correspondents in the mid-1870s (see L424, 434, 435).

49. Rev. Dr. Stearns, "Reading," *The Hampshire and Franklin Express* 11 January 1856.

50. Dunn, *Shakespeare,* 228. See *The Young Lady's Own Book,* 78, 97.

51. See David Reynolds, *Beneath the American Renaissance* (Cambridge, Mass.: Harvard University Press, 1988), 429–37. See also Flint, *Woman,* 274–93.

52. See Comment, "Dickinson's," 169–71. See also Ellen Louise Hart, "The Encoding of Erotic Desire: Emily Dickinson's Letters and Poems to Susan Dickinson 1850–1886," *Tulsa Studies in Women's Literature* 9, no. 2 (1990): 251–72.

53. Dobson, *Dickinson,* xi–xiii.

54. See Mitchell, *Emily,* 89–90.

55. Bristol, *Shakespeare,* 25–26.

56. See Bate, *Shakespeare,* 1–21; Taylor, *Reinventing,* 100–61; and Jonathan Bate, ed., *Romantics on Shakespeare* (Harmondsworth, U.K.: Penguin, 1992). See C. P. Wakefield, "Shakspeare's Characters," *Horae Collegianae* 2 (1839): 209, 211–12.

57. See Bate ed., *Romantics,* 130–32.

58. William Gardiner Hammond, *Remembrance of Amherst: An Undergraduate's Diary 1846–1848,* ed. George F. Whicher (New York: Columbia University Press, 1946), 17. Subsequently cited by parenthetical page references in the text. This text was consulted at the Archives and Special Collections, Amherst College Library.

59. See Sewall, *Life,* 419–21, 413; Habegger, *My Wars,* 222–26, 236–38, 317–19. Hammond's roommate, William J. Rolfe, contributed essays to the *Indicator;* he would go on to become a very important American Shakespeare critic and editor (see *Remembrance* 252–53, 259, 296). He was also a friend of the Dickinson family; in 1897, Lavinia asked Rolfe's help to publish Dickinson's poems; see Ralph Franklin, "Introduction," *Poems,* 3–4.

60. "Prolegomena," *The Indicator: A Literary Periodical conducted by Students of Amherst College* 1, no. 1 (1848): 2–3. The *Indicator* was consulted at the Archives and Special Collections, Amherst College Library. See Barton Levi St. Armand, "Emily Dickinson and *The Indicator:* A Transcendental Frolic," *Emily Dickinson Journal* 2, no. 2 (1993): 78–96.

61. "Thoughts on Novel Reading," *The Indicator: A Literary Periodical conducted by Students of Amherst College* 1, no. 6 (1850): 161–64 (163).

62. "Desdemona," *The Indicator: A Literary Periodical conducted by Students of Amherst College* 1, no. 6 (January 1850): 175–83 (179). Subsequently cited by parenthetical page references in the text. See also "Hermione," *The Indicator: A Literary Periodical conducted by Students of Amherst College* 3, no. 4 (1850): 115–19; "Hamlet," *The Indicator: A Literary Periodical conducted by Students of Amherst College* 3, no. 7 (1851): 216–26; "Catherine of Aragon," *The Indicator: A Literary Periodical conducted by Students of Amherst College* 3, no. 2 (1850): 59–67; and S. P. Tuck, "Imogen," *The Ichnolite, The Amherst Collegiate Magazine* 5 (1858): 379–84. The *Ichnolite* was consulted at the Archives and Special Collections, Amherst College Library.

63. See Genevieve Taggard, *The Life and Mind of Emily Dickinson* (New York: Alfred. A. Knopf, 1930), 360–71. Taggard italicizes certain words in the above essay to confirm her argument that Dickinson's "*indignant father,*" like Brabantio, refused George Gould permission to marry his daughter.

64. See Philips, *Dickinson,* 100–108; Farr, *Passion,* 194–224.

65. See "Jane Eyre," *The Indicator: A Literary Periodical conducted by Students of Amherst College* 1, no. 1 (1848): 27–31. See Barbara Welter, *Dimity Convictions: The American Woman in the Nineteenth Century* (Athens: Ohio University Press, 1976); Russell Jackson, "'Perfect Types of Womanhood': Rosalind, Beatrice and Viola in Victorian Criticism and Performance," *Shakespeare Survey* 32 (1979), 15–26; Taylor, *Reinventing,* 210.

66. Habegger, *My Wars,* 46–50, 53.

67. See Dobson, *Dickinson,* 128–30; Karen Dandurand, "Dickinson and the Public," in *Dickinson and Audience,* ed. Martin Orzeck and Robert Weisbuch (Ann Arbor: University of Michigan Press, 1996), 255–77; Mitchell, *Emily,* 154–77; Habegger, *My Wars,* 23–24, 49–50, 389–91. See also Martha Nell Smith, *Rowing in Eden: Rereading Emily Dickinson* (Austin: University of Texas Press, 1992).

68. "Valentine Eve," *The Indicator: A Literary Periodical conducted by Students of Amherst College* 2, no. 7 (1850): 233–34.

69. "Shakespeare's Women," *The Indicator: A Literary Periodical conducted by Students of Amherst College* 2, no. 7 (1850): 209–13 (209). Subsequently cited by parenthetical page references in the text.

70. Sewall, *Life*, 419–21; St. Armand, "Emily," 79–82; Habegger, *My Wars*, 234–36.

71. In an 1854 letter to Emmons, she alluded to his article entitled "The Words of Rock Rimmon" from the July 1854 edition of the magazine (L171). See Sewall, *Life*, 411–15; Habegger, *My Wars*, 315–21.

72. For example, see James C. Parson, "Macbeth," *Amherst Collegiate Magazine* 3 (1855–56): 117–25. The *Amherst Collegiate Magazine* was consulted at the Archives and Special Collections, Amherst College Library.

73. E. D. Gardner, "Jack Falstaff," *The Ichnolite, The Amherst Collegiate Magazine* 5 (1858): 180, 181.

74. Lawrence Buell, *New England Literary Culture: From Revolution Through Renaissance* (Cambridge, U.K.: Cambridge University Press, 1986), 167.

75. See *The Olio 1871* (Pittsfield, Mass.: Chickering & Axtell, Steam Printers, 1869): 52. *The Olio 1874* (Springfield, Mass.: Clark W. Bryan and Company, Printers, 1872): 69. See also "Shakspearianisms," *The Olio 1870* (Springfield, Mass.: Samuel Bowles & Co., Printers, 1868): 52. Between 1868 and 1878 *The Amherst Student* contained articles on Lady Macbeth, Hamlet, Queen Catherine, Brutus, Cleopatra, Portia, Othello, Macbeth, Caliban, and Iago. *The Olio* and the *Amherst Student* were consulted at the Archives and Special Collections, Amherst College Library.

76. See also "Richard Henry Dana," *Springfield Republican* 2 February 1849.

77. "Lectures on Shakspeare," *Hampshire and Franklin Express* 20 September 1850.

78. See also Julius H. Ward, "Richard Henry Dana," *Atlantic Monthly* 43, no. 258 (1879): 518–24; R. H. Stoddard, "Richard Henry Dana" *Harper's New Monthly* 58, no. 347 (1879): 769–76.

79. See Doreen M. Hunter, *Richard Henry Dana, Sr.* (Boston: Twayne Publishers, 1987), 105–15; John Stafford, *The Literary Criticism of "Young America": A Study in the Relationship of Politics and Literature 1837–1850* (Berkeley: University of California Press, 1952), 34, 50; John Stafford, "Henry Norman Hudson and the Whig Use of Shakespeare," *PMLA* 66, no. 5 (1951): 649–61; Richard Henry Dana, *Collected Prose and Poems*, 2 vols. (New York: Baker & Scribner, 1930), II 39, 84, 95. An 1850 edition of Dana's works is in the Dickinson Reading Room at Harvard, and Austin Dickinson appears to have been reading Dana in 1851 (Leyda I 218).

80. See Erkkila, "Emily Dickinson and Class', *American Literary History* 4, no. 1 (1992): 1–27; Mitchell, *Emily*, 12–13.

81. Dana, *Collected*, II 40.

82. During the 1850s, Dickinson often attended Lyceum lectures and commented on them (see L52, 76).

83. Millicent Todd Bingham, *Emily Dickinson's Home: Letters of Edward Dickinson and His Family* (New York: Harper & Brothers Publishers, 1955), 109.

84. H bMS Am 1118.95, Box 9. By Permission of the Houghton Library, Harvard. See "Writings of Susan Dickinson," Dickinson Electronic Archives, <http://www.emilydickinson.org/susan/socdex.html>.

85. Dana Papers Box 37, Massachusetts Historical Society. Typed Transcript of Richard Henry Dana Sr.'s Lectures on Shakespeare. Lectures on Shakespeare. By

permission of the Massachusetts Historical Society, Boston. Richard Henry Dana, "Introductory Lecture," 9, 6.

86. Dana, "Introductory," 10.

87. Jane Donahue Eberwein, *Dickinson: Strategies of Limitation* (Amherst: University of Massachusetts Press), 16.

88. Dana Papers Box 37; Massachusetts Historical Society. Richard Henry Dana, "The Condition of Society in its Influence on the Poet, and the Converse," 1839–1840, Dana Family Papers, Massachusetts Historical Society, 22.

89. Dana, "Condition," 7, 11.

90. Dana, "Condition," 22, 26, 28–29.

91. Dana, "Condition," 21.

92. Dana, "Condition," 17.

93. Dana Papers Box 37, Massachusetts Historical Society. Richard Henry Dana, "Shakspeare in the Supernatural," 1839–1840, Dana Family Papers, Massachusetts Historical Society, 24–25.

94. Dana, "Supernatural," 24.

95. See also L 166, 177, 244. See Peter Stonely, "'I - Pay - in Satin Cash -': Commerce, Gender and Display in Emily Dickinson's Poetry," *American Literature* 72, no. 3 (2000): 575–94.

96. "Mr. Dana's Lectures," *Hampshire and Franklin Express,* 27 September 1850.

97. "Amherst—Lecture on Woman," *Hampshire and Franklin Express,* 4 October 1850.

98. "Amherst—Lecture on Woman," *Hampshire and Franklin Express,* 4 October 1850.

99. "Amherst—Lecture on Woman," *Hampshire and Franklin Express,* 4 October 1850.

100. Dana Papers Box 37, Massachusetts Historical Society. Richard Henry Dana, "Woman," 1839–40, Dana Family Papers, Massachusetts Historical Society, 16, 20–21, 28–30, 33.

101. See Eberwein, *Dickinson,* 100–103.

102. Dana Papers Box 37, Massachusetts Historical Society. Richard Henry Dana, "Woman, as in the Old Dramatists—Desdemona," 1839–1840, Dana Family Papers, Massachusetts Historical Society, 8–16.

103. Dana, "Desdemona," 16–17.

104. Dana, "Desdemona," 20.

105. Dana, "Desdemona," 19.

106. Dana, "Desdemona," 32, 35, 34.

107. Dana Papers Box 37, Massachusetts Historical Society. Richard Henry Dana, "Representation of Violent Deaths on the English Stage," 1839–1840, Dana Family Papers, Massachusetts Historical Society, 10, 11–12.

108. Bingham, *Emily,* 109.

109. See Ward, "Richard," 522.

110. Dana Papers Box 37, Massachusetts Historical Society. Richard Henry Dana,

"Macbeth," 1839–1840, Dana Family Papers, Massachusetts Historical Society, 11. See also Hunter, *Dana,* 120.

111. Dana, "Macbeth," 11–12.

112. Dana, "Macbeth," 32; see also Lauch, "Reception," 52.

113. Dana, "Macbeth," 18.

114. See Taylor, *Reinventing,* 157–58; Bate ed., *Romantics,* 160–61, 325–26.

115. Dana Papers Box 37, Massachusetts Historical Society. Richard Henry Dana, "Hamlet," 1839–1840, Dana Family Papers, Massachusetts Historical Society, 2.

116. Dana, "Hamlet," 15.

117. Dana, "Hamlet," 18.

118. Brown, "Uses," 233–35; Thorndike, "Shakespeare," 119.

119. Mitchell, *Emily,* 88–111.

120. Sinfield, *Faultlines,* 41–42.

Chapter Two

1. See Habegger, *My Wars,* 490–91.

2. Martha Ackmann, "Biographical Studies of Dickinson," in *The Emily Dickinson Handbook,* ed. Gundrun Grabher, Roland Hagenbüchle, and Cristanne Miller (Amherst: University of Massachusetts Press, 1998), 19–20.

3. Information about the garret was made available to me on a private tour of the homestead kindly given to me by Cindy Dickinson in April 2002. See also Jean McClure Mudge, *Emily Dickinson and the Image of Home* (Amherst: University of Massachusetts Press, 1975), 3, 88–89, 144, 244 n. 38; and Diana Fuss, "Interior Chambers: The Emily Dickinson Homestead," *Differences* 10, no. 3 (1998): 1–46.

4. See Sandra Gilbert and Susan Gubar, *Madwoman in the Attic: The Woman Writer and the Nineteenth-Century Literary Imagination* (New Haven: Yale University Press, 1979); Maryanne M. Garbowsky, *The House without the Door: A Study of Emily Dickinson and the Illness of Agoraphobia* (London: Associated University Press, 1989); and John Cody, *After Great Pain: The Inner Life of Emily Dickinson* (Cambridge, Mass.: Harvard University Press, 1971).

5. See Taylor, *Reinventing,* 212. See Bate ed., *Romantics,* 368–69; Ralph Waldo Emerson, *Works* IV 112.

6. See Michael Hattaway, "Introduction," *The First Part of King Henry VI,* ed. Michael Hattaway (Cambridge, U.K.: Cambridge University Press, 1990), 43–44.

7. Richard Grant White, "An Essay on the Authorship of the Three Parts of King Henry the Sixth," in *The Works of William Shakespeare,* ed. Richard Grant White, 12 vols. (Boston: Little, Brown, 1861–71), VII 401–68; Richard Grant White, "On Reading Shakespeare," *The Galaxy* 23, no. 1 (1877): 71; Henry Norman Hudson, *Shakespeare: His Art and Life,* 2 vols. (1872; Boston: Ginn, 1891), I 33.

8. Knight, *Shakspere,* IV 3.

9. See Hattaway, "Introduction," 21–22.

10. See Edward Burns, "Introduction," *King Henry VI, Part 1,* ed. Edward Burns (London: Arden Shakespeare, 2000), 83.

11. Knight, *Shakspere,* VIII 187.

12. Knight, *Shakspere,* IV 90.

13. See Phyllis Rackin, *Stages of History: Shakespeare's English Chronicles* (Ithaca: Cornell University Press, 1990), 155.

14. Knight, *Shakspere,* IV 60.

15. When Frazer Stearns was killed at New Bern, N.C., in 1862, Dickinson wrote three letters about her own sadness and that of the Dickinson family (L255, 256, 257). For Dickinson's attitude toward the war, see Shira Wolosky, *Emily Dickinson: A Voice of War* (New Haven: Yale University Press, 1984).

16. Knight, *Shakspere,* IV 98, VIII 192–93.

17. Knight, *Shakspere,* VIII 195.

18. For another defense of Queen Margaret, see Henry Reed, *Lectures on English History and Tragic Poetry as Illustrated by Shakespeare* (Philadelphia: Parry and Mcmillan, 1856), 190, 292–94.

19. Anna Jameson, *Characteristics of Women: Moral, Poetical, and Historical* (Boston: Houghton, Mifflin, 1887), 396–400. Subsequently cited by parenthetical page references in the text. In 1753, Charlotte Lennox's *Shakespear Illustrated; or the Novels and Histories of Shakespear* defended Margaret: "With this more than fiendlike Cruelty, has *Shakespear* represented a Queen, whose Motives for taking Arms were far from being unjust, the Recovery of her Husband's Liberty and Crown, and the Restoring of her Son to the Rights and Privileges of his Birth. And for the Sake of this shocking Absurdity in the Manner of a Female Character in so high a Rank he contradicts a known Fact in History." See Brian Vickers, ed., *Shakespeare: The Critical Heritage,* 6 vols. (London: Routledge, 1976), IV 138.

20. See Bate, ed., *Romantics,* 367. See also "Parting Lovers," *Shakspeare Gems by the author of "the book of familiar quotations"* (New York: Lee & Shepard, 1872), 291–92.

21. Henrietta Lee Palmer, *The Stratford Gallery or the Shakspeare Sisterhood* (New York: Appleton, 1859), 258–59. Subsequently cited by parenthetical page references in the text.

22. See Barton Levi St. Armand, *Emily Dickinson and Her Culture: The Soul's Society* (Cambridge, U.K.: Cambridge University Press, 1984), 137–51; and Vivian R. Pollak, *Dickinson: The Anxiety of Gender* (Ithaca: Cornell University Press, 1984), 157–89.

23. Farr, *Passion,* 96–97; Camille Paglia, *Sexual Personae: Art and Decadence from Nefertiti to Emily Dickinson* (New Haven: Yale University Pres, 1990), 660–65.

24. In 1592, Robert Greene famously attacked Shakespeare by linking him to the adulterous queen in *Greenes Groats-Worth of Wit:* "There is an upstart Crow, beautified with our feathers, that with his Tygers heart wrapt in a Players hide, supposes he is as well able to bombast out a blanke verse as the best of you."

25. Knight offers his readers illustrations of both Joan of Arc and Margaret; see Knight, *Shakspere,* IV 83, 190.

26. See Caroline Field Levander, *Voices of the Nation: Women and Public Speech in Nineteenth-Century American Literature and Culture* (Cambridge, U.K.: Cambridge University Press, 1998); and James Perrin Warren, *Culture of Eloquence: Oratory and Reform in Antebellum America* (University Park: Pennsylvania State University Press, 1999).

27. Porter, *Rhetorical,* 2. See Kitzhaber, *Rhetoric,* 49–73; Nan Johnson, *Nineteenth-Century Rhetoric in North America* (Carbondale: Southern Illinois University Press, 1991).

28. See also *Young Lady's Own Book,* 46–47.

29. See Edith Wylder, *The Last Face: Emily Dickinson's Manuscripts* (Albuquerque: University of New Mexico Press, 1971), 12–28. Wylder argues that Dickinson's falling and rising dashes are modeled on Porter's notational system, and represent Dickinson's attempt to convey the tone of her written message, giving the "*impression* of voice." The central problem with this theory is that Dickinson placed her dashes after the words, whereas in Porter's text accents are above the specific words.

30. See Levine, *Highbrow,* 36–37; and Dunn, *Shakespeare,* 225–36.

31. Porter, *Rhetorical,* 94.

32. The edition in the Dickinson library was Richard Whately, *Elements of Rhetoric, Comprising the substance of the Article in the Encycloaedia Metropolitana,* 4th ed. (Cambridge, Mass.: James Munroe, 1834). All references are to Richard Whately, *Elements of Rhetoric, Comprising the substance of the Article in the Encyclopaedia Metropolitana,* 3rd ed. (Oxford: John Murray, 1830). Subsequently cited by parenthetical page references in the text. See Lowenberg, *Emily,* 107.

33. See Henry James, *The Bostonians* (1886; Harmondsworth, U.K.: Penguin, 2000). In this novel, Verena Tarrant is the woman who can inspire and move an audience through the power of her speech. At the end, however, she leaves the public stage and begins a private life of silence with Basil Ransom.

34. See Bryan C. Short, "Emily Dickinson and the Scottish New Rhetoric," *Emily Dickinson Journal* 5, no. 2 (1996): 261–66; Christine Ross, "Logic, Rhetoric, and Discourse in the Literary Texts of Nineteenth-Century Women," *Rhetoric Society Quarterly* 32, no. 2 (2002): 93–99. See also Suzanne Juhasz, Cristanne Miller, and Martha Nell Smith, *The Comic Power of Emily Dickinson* (Austin: University of Texas Press, 1993), 1–25, 40.

35. See Philip Collins, *Reading Aloud: A Victorian Métier* (Lincoln, U.K.: The Tennyson Society, 1972). See also Hammond, *Remembrance,* 43. Dickinson attended many such public readings, and mentions being entertained by the oratorical feats of young gentlemen (L50) on one occasion and "by the rhetoric of the gentlemen and the milder form of the girls" on another (L91). In 1851, Lavinia sends Austin a short note in which she apologizes, "I would write *too,* if it were not for my recitations, but I cant stop now." See Bingham, *Emily,* 199.

36. Quoted in Habegger, *My Wars,* 398.

37. Austin also read for the family; Mabel Loomis Todd recorded in her diary on 9 December 1884 that "In the evening Mr. Dickinson came in like a brilliant

north west breeze & read us a sparkling little story in the current *Century*" (Leyda II 438).

38. In an 1850 letter to Jane Humphrey, Dickinson offers to read from Ralph Waldo Emerson's *Poems* (1847), which she had recently received as a gift from Ben Newman, and from Newman's letter that accompanied the gift (L30). Dickinson also read Austin's letters with Sue and Sue's letters with her sister, Martha (L115, 57). She read frequently for Lavinia and later for her invalid mother (L133, 666, 667, 721, 727).

39. See "Housework Defended," *Woman's Journal* 26 March 1904, 98; Gary Scharnhorst, "A Glimpse of Dickinson at Work," *American Literature* 57, no. 3 (1985): 483–85; and Martha Ackmann, "'I'm Glad I finally Surfaced': A Norcross Descendant Remembers Emily Dickinson," *Emily Dickinson Journal* 5, no. 2 (1996): 120–26.

40. See L470, Leyda II 361 and Millicent Todd Bingham, *Ancestor's Brocades: The Literary Debut of Emily Dickinson* (New York: Harper & Brothers, 1945), 142. Fuss, "Interior," 23–26; Loeffelholz, *Dickinson,* 122–31. This complicates a dominant trend among Dickinson critics to emphasize the provocative and suggestive lettering, lineation, punctuation, and capitalization, subordinating the aural aspects of her poetry to the visual. See Domhnall Mitchell, "Grammar of Ornament: Emily Dickinson's Manuscripts and Their Meaning," *Nineteenth-Century Literature* 55, no. 4 (2001): 479–514; Cristanne Miller, "The Sounds of Shifting Paradigms, or Hearing Dickinson in the Twenty-first Century," in *A Historical Guide to Emily Dickinson,* ed. Vivian R. Pollak (Oxford: Oxford University Press, 2004), 201–34.

41. Joseph Emerson, *The Poetic Reader, containing Selections from the most approved authors, designed for Exercises in Reading, Singing, Parsing, Hermeneutics, Rhetoric and Punctuation. To which are prefixed Directions for Reading* (Wethersfield, Conn.: Wethersfield, 1832), 19.

42. "San Francisco Shakespeare Class," *Shakespeariana* 3 (1886): 522.

43. See "The Tempest," *The American Shakespeare Magazine* 3 (October 1897): 311–315; *Shakespeariana* 4 (1887): 514. See also Theodora Penny Martin, *Sound of Our Own Voices: Women's Study Clubs 1860–1910* (Boston: Beacon, 1987), 106–7. See also Westfall, *American,* 185–91, 192–200.

44. J.V.L., "Shakespeare Societies of America: Their Method and Work," *Shakespeariana* 2 (1885): 482. See also A.R.D. K.L.G., "A Club of Two," *Shakespeariana* 4 (1887): 407 and "Shakespeare Societies," *Shakespeariana* 4 (1887): 175–79, 375–77.

45. "The Shakespeare Society of Seneca Falls," *Shakespeariana* 4 (1887): 179.

46. See John S. Gentile, *Cast of One: One-Person Shows from Chautauqua Platform to the Broadway Stage* (Urbana and Chicago: University of Illinois Press, 1989).

47. "An Evening with Shakspeare," *Hampshire and Franklin Express* 18 June 1852.

48. "Shaksperian Reading," *Hampshire and Franklin Express* 18 June 1852.

49. Kemble did not include the *Henry VI* plays in her repertoire; she read from *King Lear, Macbeth, Cymbeline, King John, Richard II,* the two parts of *King Henry IV, Richard III, Coriolanus, Julius Caesar, Antony and Cleopatra, Hamlet, Othello, Romeo and Juliet, The Merchant of Venice, The Winter's Tale, Measure for Measure, Much Ado about Nothing, As You Like It, A Midsummer Night's Dream, The Merry Wives of Windsor,* and

The Tempest. See Frances Anne Kemble, *Records of Later Life* 3 vols. (London: Richard Bentley and Son, 1882), III 372.

50. See Catherine Clinton, *Fanny Kemble's Civil Wars* (New York: Simon and Schuster, 2000).

51. See Elizabeth Reitz Mullenix, "'*So* Unfemininely Masculine': Discourse, True / False Womanhood, and the American Career of Fanny Kemble," *Theatre Survey* 40, no. 2 (1999): 27–42.

52. Herman Melville, *The Correspondence, The Writings of Herman Melville,* vol. 14 (Chicago: Northwestern Press and Newberry Library, 1993), 119–20. Subsequently cited by parenthetical page references in the text.

53. Mullenix, "*So* Unfemininely," 29. In 1849, Longfellow's sonnet, "On Mrs. Kemble's Readings from Shakespeare," celebrated Kemble's power to bring Shakespeare alive. See Henry Wadsworth Longfellow, "Sonnet on Mrs. Kemble's Readings from Shakespeare," *The Complete Poetical Works of Henry Wadsworth Longfellow* (Boston and New York: Houghton Mifflin, Riverside Press, 1893), 112. See Habegger, *My Wars,* 388.

54. See "Mrs Butler Coming to Springfield," *Springfield Republican* 16 February 1849. See also "Mrs Butler," *Springfield Republican* 22 February 1849; "Mrs Butler," *Springfield Republican* 26 February 1849; "Fanny Kemble Butler," *Springfield Republican* 16 March 1849; "Fanny Kemble Butler," *Springfield Republican* 3 April 1849.

55. "Amusements in Boston," *Springfield Republican* 6 February 1849.

56. "Shakspeare," *Springfield Republican* 1 June 1849.

57. "Amusements in Boston," *Springfield Republican* 6 February 1849.

58. "Fanny Kemble," *Springfield Republican* 16 January 1850.

59. See "Advertisement," *Boston Evening Transcript* 5 December 1859. Kemble read Monday, Wednesday, and Friday evenings and Saturday afternoons from 5 December 1859 to 7 January 1860.

60. For example, see "King Lear," *Boston Evening Transcript* 13 December 1859; "Mrs. Kemble's Readings," *Boston Evening Transcript* 15 December 1859; "King John," *Boston Evening Transcript* 20 December 1859; "Macbeth," *Boston Evening Transcript* 22 December 1859.

61. "Letters From New York," *Springfield Republican* 15 January 1859.

62. See Habegger, *My Wars,* 388–89.

63. "Amusements in Boston," *Springfield Republican* 6 February 1849.

64. See Richard H. Brodhead, *Cultures of Letters: Scenes of Reading and Writing in Nineteenth-Century America* (Chicago and London: University of Chicago Press), 48–68; Judith Pascoe, "'The House Encore Me So': Emily Dickinson and Jenny Lind," *Emily Dickinson Journal* 1, no. 1 (1992): 17–18 (17).

65. Henry James, "Frances Kemble," *Temple Bar* 97 (1893): 508.

66. See Pascoe, "House," 11–12, 16.

67. See "More Readings of Shakspeare," *Springfield Republican* 27 February 1849; "Readers of Shakspeare," *Springfield Republican* 20 April 1849. The first of these articles declares that despite the proliferation of Shakespeare readers, "none of them, however, can expect to rival Mrs. B[utler]., whose Readings seem to us to be beyond the skill,

taste and power of any person living. Few or none have her natural gifts for excellence in this department and where is the person who has her education for it."

68. "Mrs. Scott-Siddons," *Amherst Record* 15 March 1871. There is an advertisement for this event at The Jones Public Library in the collection, Amherst theater.

69. "Mrs. Scott-Siddons," *Amherst Record* 22 March 1871.

70. In 1873, Mrs. Scott-Siddons read in Springfield; see "Mrs Siddons and Master Walker," *Springfield Republican* 20 November 1873.

71. "Shakspeare" *Springfield Republican* 1 June 1849.

72. See also John Anthony Scott, *Fanny Kemble's America* (New York: Thomas Y. Crowell, 1973), 115.

73. "Amusements in Boston," *Springfield Republican* 6 February 1849.

74. "Springfield and Vicinity," *Springfield Republican* 21 March 1871.

75. Catherine Clinton, ed., *Fanny Kemble's Journals* (Cambridge, Mass.: Harvard University Press, 2000), 28.

76. Clinton ed., *Fanny,* 56.

77. Frances Anne Kemble, "On the Stage," *Harper's New Monthly* 28, no. 165 (1864): 364–67. Gerald Kahan, "Fanny Kemble Reads," *Theatre Survey* 24 (1983): 77–98.

78. See Charles Lamb, "On the Tragedies of Shakspeare," in *Romantics on Shakespeare,* ed. Bate, 111–27. John Quincy Adams, "Misconceptions of Shakspeare upon the Stage," *New England Magazine* 9, no. 12 (1835): 438.

79. A. Dexter, "Plays and Play-Acting," *Atlantic Monthly* 10, no. 59 (1862): 288.

80. See Dramatic Activities Collection, Archive and Special Collection, Amherst College Library. Professor Ralph Cleland McGoun spent ten years putting together a collection of records of all dramatic activities that took place in Amherst College and Amherst from 1815 to the present day.

81. Edward Carpenter and Charles Morehouse, *A History of The Town of Amherst, Massachusetts* (Amherst: Carpenter & Morehouse, 1896), 455.

82. Sewall, *Life,* 93–96.

83. See also Claudia D. Johnson, *American Actress: Perspective on the Nineteenth Century* (Chicago: Nelson Hall, 1984), 14–16, 30–31.

84. "Mrs Butler in Springfield," *Springfield Republican* 29 May 1849. See Kemble, *Records,* III 371–72.

85. See "Dana's Lectures," *Evening Post* 8 December 1849.

86. Clinton, *Fanny Kemble,* 145–46.

87. "Mrs Fanny Kemble Butler," *Springfield Republican* 16 April 1849.

88. Quoted in Kahan, "Fanny," 93.

89. See also Scott, *Fanny Kemble,* 114.

90. Mabel Loomis Todd, ed., *Letters of Emily Dickinson: New and Enlarged Edition* (New York: Harper & Brothers, 1931), 132. This description of Dickinson is not in Todd's earlier 1894 edition of the letters. Also added is reference to Dickinson's desire for "distinction" and "renown."

91. Herman Melville, "Hawthorne and his Mosses," in *The Literary World* 17 August 1850.

92. Walt Whitman, "The Old Bowery," in *Prose Works 1892, The Collected Writings of Walt Whitman,* 2 vols., ed. Floyd Stovall (New York: New York University Press, 1964), II 595.

93. "The Riot in New York," *Springfield Republican* 12 May 1849. See Taylor, *Reinventing,* 219–20; and Dunn, *Shakespeare,* 138–74.

94. "Row at the Opera House," *Springfield Republican* 9 May 1849. See Levine, *Highbrow,* 63.

95. "Terrible Riot in New York," *Springfield Republican* 12 May 1849. See also *Hampshire and Franklin Express* Friday, 18 May 1849.

96. See Mader, *His Exits,* 311.

97. Richard Moody, *The Astor Place Riot* (Bloomington: Indiana University Press, 1958), 154.

98. Quoted in Levine, *Highbrow,* 65. Moody, *Astor,* 190.

99. Mader, *His Exits,* 310; and Sinfield, *Faultlines,* 264

100. Levine, *Highbrow,* 68.

101. A. A. Lipcomb, "Uses of Shakespeare off the Stage," *Harper's New Monthly* 65, no. 387 (1882): 431–38 (438).

Chapter Three

1. See James C. Parson, "Macbeth," *Amherst Collegiate Magazine* 3 (1856): 117.

2. See M. D. Conway, "Mr. William Shakspeare, At Home," *Harper's New Monthly* 29, no. 171 (1864): 336–46; Winter, "Stratford," 884.

3. In the above letter Dickinson told Mrs. Holland, "When I looked in the Morning Paper to see how the President is, I know you are looking too, and for once in the Day I am sure where you are, which is very friendly" (L721). In March 1878, she writes, "We learn of you in the Papers and of your new House, of which, it is said there will be a Portrait" (L547). Dickinson's knowledge of Holland's usual reading habits and concern with the president's health offer the reclusive poet a means of entering into the private life of her friend, of establishing closeness. In two other letters to Mrs. Holland, she refers to the popularity of *Scribner's* articles among her neighbors (L502, 689). In the 1881 letter, she refers to Dr. Holland's poem "My Dog Blanco," published in *Scribner's* that August; she asks Mrs. Holland, "Doctor's betrothal to "Blanco" I trust you bear unmurmuringly. Mother and Vinnie wept" (L721). Similarly, in a letter to Sue, she demonstrates her awareness of the unusual nature of publication in *Scribner's* of a story by William D. Howells, then editor of the *Atlantic Monthly* (L714).

4. E. O. Vaile, "The Shakespeare-Bacon Controversy," *Scribner's Monthly* 9, no. 6 (1875): 743–54. Subsequently cited by parenthetical page references in the text.

5. See also Nathaniel Holmes, *The Authorship of Shakespeare* (New York: Riverside, 1867).

6. According to Vaile there is no manuscript of any kind in Shakespeare's handwriting; there is no evidence he had a library or was very well read; he seems to have

had no interest in the future of his art or his reputation; and none of the plays bore his name. There is no evidence he traveled beyond England, and contemporaries like Robert Greene suggested he stole the plays attributed to him (747–48). On the other hand, Bacon "combined all those powers and attainments which the writer of these plays possessed, but in which the real William Shakespeare was certainly deficient, if the evidence of his life is only admitted" (748).

7. Richard Grant White, "The Bacon-Shakespeare Craze," *Atlantic Monthly* 51, no. 306 (1883): 507–21 (521, 508).

8. See Sewall, *Life*, 619–20. Perhaps Dickinson was an "old fashioned" reader affronted by the idea Bacon wrote Shakespeare's plays (L395).

9. See Nina Baym, "Delia Bacon, History's Odd Woman Out," *New England Quarterly* 69, no. 2 (1996): 223–49.

10. Hawthorne, "Recollections," 43–58.

11. Arnold Goldman, "Hawthorne's Old Home" in *Nathaniel Hawthorne: New Critical Essays*, ed. A. R. Lee (London: Vision, 1982), 160. For a discussion of Twain's reaction to the controversy, see Antony J. Berret, *Mark Twain and Shakespeare* (Lanham, Md.: University Press of America, 1993), 31–41.

12. See Rawlings, "Henry," 143–44.

13. It seems very likely that Higginson read Hawthorne's article. In fact, two of his articles on Hawthorne appeared in the years following his meeting with Dickinson: "An Evening with Mrs. Hawthorne," *Atlantic Monthly* 28, no. 168 (1871): 432–33; and "Hawthorne's Last Bequest," *Scribner's Monthly* 5, no. 1 (1972): 100–105.

14. Thomas Wentworth Higginson, "Emily Dickinson's Letters," *Atlantic Monthly* 68, no 408 (1891) : 453.

15. See Nathaniel Hawthorne, "Preface," *Philosophy of the Plays of Shakspere Unfolded* (London: Groomsbridge and Sons, 1857), xv. Hawthorne declares that if Bacon's book is a failure, it "will be more honorable than most people's triumphs; since it must fling upon the old tombstone, at Stratford-on-Avon, the noblest tributary wreath that has ever lain there."

16. Delia Bacon, "William Shakspeare and his Plays; an Enquiry Concerning Them," *Putnam's Monthly* 7, no. 37 (1856): 1–19. (3). Subsequently cited by parenthetical page references in the text.

17. See also White, "Bacon," 508.

18. James, "The Birthplace," 138.

19. Delia Bacon, *The Philosophy of the Plays of Shakspere Unfolded* (London: Groombridge and Sons, 1857), xix, xlix, lxxxvi, xli. Subsequently cited by parenthetical page references in the text.

20. See Erkkila, "Emily," 15.

21. Taylor, *Reinventing*, 210–23.

22. For a discussion of Anti-Stratfordians, see Schoenbaum, *Shakespeare's*, 385–408; Marjorie Garber, *Shakespeare's Ghost Writers* (London: Methuen, 1987), 1–27; and Louise Budd, "The Baconians Madness Through Method," *South Atlantic Quarterly* 54 (1955): 365.

23. Vivian C. Hopkins, *Prodigal Puritan: A Life of Delia Bacon* (Cambridge, Mass.: Belknap Press of Harvard University Press, 1959), 194.

24. Hopkins, *Prodigal,* 190.

25. Hopkins, *Prodigal,* 201.

26. Harold Bloom, *The Western Canon* (New York: Harcourt Brace, 1994), 291.

27. Ellery Sedgwick, *The Atlantic Monthly 1857–1909: Yankee Humanism at High Tide and Ebb* (Amherst: University of Massachusetts Press, 1994), 2–3, 10, 41–51.

28. See Edward E. Chielens, ed., *American Literary Magazines: The Eighteenth and Nineteenth Centuries* (New York: Greenwood, 1987), xii, 50–57, 164–69, 166–71. See also Capps, *Emily,* 128–34. Dickinson frequently alludes to reading Higginson's writings in the *Atlantic Monthly* and *Scribner's* (L280, 323, 353, 692, 728, 413, 449). Although Lavinia referred to *Harper's* as "my usual magazine" (Leyda I 191, 196, 199), evidence suggests its early and continued importance to Dickinson herself (see Leyda II 148, L456).

29. See "William Shakespeare, Attorney and Solicitor," *Atlantic Monthly* 4, no. 21 (1859): 84–106; E. P. Whipple, "Shakespeare, The Man and the Dramatist," *Atlantic Monthly* 19, no. 116 (1867): 715–23; E. P. Whipple, "Growth, Limitations, and Toleration of Shakespeare's Genius," *Atlantic Monthly* 20, no. 118 (1867): 178–88; E. P. Whipple, "Characteristics of Elizabethan Literature," *Atlantic Monthly* 20, no. 112 (1867): 144–55; E. P. Whipple, "Minor Elizabethan Dramatists," *Atlantic Monthly* 20, no. 122 (1867): 692–704; Abby Sage, "The Hamlets of the Stage I," *Atlantic Monthly* 23, no. 140 (1869): 665–76; Abby Sage, "The Hamlets of the Stage II," *Atlantic Monthly* 24, no. 142 (1869): 188–99; Charles Dudley Warner, "The People for whom Shakespeare wrote," *Atlantic Monthly* 43, no. 260 (1879): 729–41; Charles Dudley Warner, "The People for whom Shakespeare wrote," *Atlantic Monthly* 44, no. 261 (1879): 44–56. See also Duncan Pell, "Shakespeare And Hollingshed," *Harper's New Monthly* 23, no. 136 (1861): 486–91; John S. Hart, "The Shakespeare Death-Mask," *Scribner's Monthly Magazine* 8, no. 3 (1874): 304–17; and William Page, "A Study of Shakespeare's Portraits," *Scribner's Monthly Magazine* 10, no. 5 (1875): 558–74.

30. See Willis J. Buckingham, "Emily Dickinson and the Reading Life" in *Dickinson and Audience,* ed. Orzeck and Weisbuch, 233–54. See Dickinson's eagerness to acquire the biographies of her favorite female authors: Emily Brontë (L822), Charlotte Brontë (L471), and George Eliot (L814, 962). See also Capps, *Emily,* 92–95.

31. According to the advertisement preceding Knight's biography, "This 'Biography' is only so far more conjectural than any other, as regards the form which it assumes, by which it has been endeavoured to associate Shakspere with the circumstances around him, in a manner which may fix them in the mind of the reader by exciting his interest." Knight's biography "surround[s] the known facts with the local and temporary circumstances, and with the social relations amidst which one of so defined a position must have moved."

32. See Richard Grant White, "King Lear," *Atlantic Monthly* 45, no. 272 (1880): 111–21; Richard Grant White, "On the Acting of Iago," *Atlantic Monthly* 48, no. 286 (1881): 203–13; Richard Grant White, "Stage Rosalinds," *Atlantic Monthly* 51, no. 304 (1883): 248–59; Richard Grant White, "The Two Hamlets," *Atlantic Monthly* 48, no. 288

(1883): 467–79; and T. B. Thorpe, "The Case Of Lady Macbeth Medically Considered," *Harper's New Monthly* 8, no. 45 (1854): 391–98.

33. See "The Collier-folio Shakespeare," *Atlantic Monthly* 4, no. 24 (1859): 512–19; and two articles, "Some Notes on Shakspeare," *Atlantic Monthly* 6, no. 35 (1860): 288–94; and "The Shakespeare Mystery," *Atlantic Monthly* 8, no. 47 (1861): 257–80.

34. Westfall, *American*, 167.

35. "Collier-folio," 512.

36. "Shakespeare Mystery," 263, 257; "Some Notes," 289.

37. See "Shakespeare Mystery," 260, 263; "Collier-folio," 515.

38. "Shakespeare Mystery," 260.

39. See Avon Y. Stavisky, *Shakespeare and the Victorians* (Norman: University of Oklahoma Press, 1969); Taylor, *Reinventing*, 162–230; and S. Schoenbaum, *Shakespeare's*, 273–382.

40. Conway, "William," 336–46. Subsequently cited by parenthetical page references in the text.

41. See J. M. Rogers, "Shakespeare," *Atlantic Monthly* 38, no. 226 (1876): 142; and Minnie Irving, "Shakspere," *Scribner's Monthly* 21, no. 2 (1880): 310–11.

42. O.W. Holmes, "Shakspeare," *Atlantic Monthly* 13, no. 80 (1864): 762–63.

43. A copy of James Russell Lowell's *Among My Books*, 1st ser. (Boston: Fields, Osgood, 1870), signed S. H. Dickinson, is in the Dickinson collection at the Houghton Library, Harvard. Subsequently cited by parenthetical page references in the text. See Capps, *Emily*, 180.

44. Thomas Wentworth Higginson, "An Open Portfolio," *The Christian Union* 42, no. 13 (1890): 393; Higginson, "Emily," 451. See also David Porter, *Dickinson: The Modern Idiom* (Cambridge, Mass.: Harvard University Press, 1981); Miller, *Emily*, 20–112.

45. Sewall, *Life*, 708; and Charles Anderson, *Emily Dickinson's Poetry: Stairway of Surprise* (1960; New York: Anchor, 1966), 35.

46. Brita Lindberg-Seyersted, *The Voice of the Poet: Aspects of Style in the Poetry of Emily Dickinson* (Cambridge, Mass.: Harvard University Press, 1968), 115, 164, 221–3.

47. See Miller, *Emily*, 40–43.

48. Taylor, *Reinventing*, 206.

49. Jones Very, *Essays and Poems* (Boston: Charles C. Little and James Brown, 1839), 40. For Very, "Shakspeare is not to be esteemed so much a man, as a natural phenomenon. We cannot say of him that he conformed to God's will; but that the Divine Will in its ordinary operations moved his mind as it does the material world. He was natural from an unconscious obedience to the will of God" (76).

50. See Dobson, *Dickinson*, 9–10.

51. W. C. Wilkinson, "Mr. Lowell's Prose," *Scribner's Monthly* 4, no. 2 (1872): 229.

52. Wilkinson, "Mr. Lowell's," 227.

53. Knight, *Shakspere*, VI 231; Lowell, *Among*, 152; Bacon, "William," 15.

54. Charles T. Congdon, "The Statesmanship of Shakspeare," *Harper's New Monthly* 27, no. 160 (1863): 492–95 (493). See also Cartelli, *Repositioning*, 27–45.

55. Knight calls Cade's rebellion "a movement of the most brutal ignorance, instigated by a coarse ruffian." See Knight, *Shakspere,* IV 99, VIII 190. See Cartelli, *Repositioning,* 35–41.

56. George Wilkes, *Shakespeare, From an American Point of View* (London: Sampson Low, Marston, Searle & Rivington, 1877), 7. Subsequently cited by parenthetical page references in the text. See also Stafford, "Henry," 650; Lauck, "Reception," 141–42.

57. With regard to the Bacon-Shakespeare controversy, Wilkes asserts that Americans have a particular interest in which of the British men wrote the plays (4). He suggests the benefit to aristocracy of accepting Shakespeare as a lower-class playwright who validates aristocracy and legitimizes an order that keeps the lower class—*his* class—in its place. For Wilkes, the attempts by members of the British aristocracy to claim Shakespeare's plays as the work of Bacon—one of their own—is mere greediness (225–26).

58. "Recent Literature," *Atlantic Monthly* 40, no. 202 (1877): 247–48.

59. See Erkkila, "Emily," 9. See also Eberwein, *Dickinson,* 99–102.

60. Lease, *Emily,* 37. For a discussion of Dickinson's use of Christology, see Sewall, *Life,* 460–61, 690–92; and Loeffelholz, *Dickinson,* 49–80, 99–101.

61. See Knight, *Shakspere,* III 192, 413; IV 2, 199.

62. He published *Shakspeare's Scholar* (1854); one of the first American editions of *The Works of William Shakespeare* (1858); an account of Shakespeare's life, *Memoirs of the Life of William Shakespeare* (1865); his Riverside edition of *Shakespeare's Works* (1883); and his collection of essays, *Studies in Shakespeare* (1885).

63. See James Russell Lowell, "White's Shakspeare," *Atlantic Monthly* 3, no. 15 (1859): 120–21. Lowell's essay "Shakespeare Once More" began as a review of White's edition of Shakespeare.

64. Richard Grant White, *Memoirs of the Life of William Shakespeare* (Boston: Little Brown, 1865), x–xi.

65. See Westfall, *American,* 163–64; Taylor, *Reinventing,* 199–200.

66. Richard Grant White, *Studies in Shakespeare* (London: Sampson Low, Marston, Searle & Rivington, 1885), 209.

67. Richard Grant White, "The Anatomizing of William Shakespeare I," *Atlantic Monthly* 53, no. 319 (1884): 595–613; Richard Grant White, "The Anatomizing of William Shakespeare II," *Atlantic Monthly* 53, no. 320 (1884): 815–35. Richard Grant White, "The Anatomizing of William Shakespeare III," *Atlantic Monthly* 54, no. 322 (1884): 257–67; Richard Grant White, "The Anatomizing of William Shakespeare IV," *Atlantic Monthly* 54: no. 323 (1884): 313–26.

68. White, "Anatomizing," II 833–34.

69. White, "Anatomizing," III 260.

70. White, "Anatomizing," I 597.

71. White, "Anatomizing," III 262; Wilkes, *Shakespeare,* 11.

72. White, "Anatomizing," III 263.

73. White, "Anatomizing," IV 314.

74. White, "Anatomizing," III 260.

75. Schoenbaum, *Shakespeare's*, 279.
76. Knight, *Shakspere*, VII 138.
77. White, "Anatomizing," III 260, I 595.
78. White, "Anatomizing," I 597.
79. White, "Anatomizing," I 598.
80. White, "Anatomizing," IV 315–17.
81. Richard Grant White, "On Reading Shakespeare," *The Galaxy* 22, no. 4 (1876): 519.

Chapter Four

1. Sanborn was the Boston correspondent for the *Springfield Republican* from 1856; in 1868, Samuel Bowles asked him to be the resident editor; he continued in this post until 1872.
2. See Tom Foran Clark, "The Significance of Being Frank: The Life and Times of Franklin Benjamin Sanborn," chaps. 18 and 19, at <http://www.ameribilia.com/sanborn/.>
3. Clark, "Significance," chap. 19. Although no longer the editor of the *Republican* Sanborn still received inquiries from writers eager to have their work published in the newspaper. Clark quotes two 1872 letters in which Amos Bronson Alcott, the father of Louisa May Alcott, writes to Mrs. Perry in Keokuk, Iowa, assuring her that Sanborn is acquainted with her daughter's genius and will print her letters. See Dickinson, *Poems*, ed. Franklin, III 1531–32.
4. F. B. Sanborn, *Recollections of Seventy Years* 2 vols. (Boston: Richard G. Badger, 1909), II 256.
5. Sanborn, *Recollections*, I ix.
6. Sanborn, *Recollections*, II 308.
7. Sanborn, *Recollections*, II 309.
8. Clark, "Significance," chapter 5.
9. See Clark, "Significance," chapter 19.
10. On 15 July 1879, Sanborn was one of the founding members, and was later treasurer, of the Concord School of Philosophy. The school included Emerson, William James, Julia Ward Howe, Elizabeth Peabody, and Thomas Wentworth Higginson. In early August 1884, in a letter to her Norcross cousins, Dickinson refers again to Sanborn, specifically to a lecture he had just given to this school, which she assumed her cousins had attended (L907).
11. See Benjamin T. Spencer, *The Quest For Nationality* (Syracuse: Syracuse University Press, 1957), ix, 75–76. See also Larzer Ziff, *Literary Democracy: The Declaration of Cultural Independence in America* (New York: Viking, 1981). Ziff excludes Dickinson from his discussion.
12. Robert Weisbuch, *Atlantic Double-Cross: American Literature and British Influence in the Age of Emerson* (Chicago: University of Chicago Press, 1986). See Bloom, *Map*, 53; Harold Bloom, *The Anxiety of Influence* (New York: Oxford University Press, 1973).

13. Weisbuch, *Atlantic,* 32–34.

14. See W. H., "Peculiarities, National and Literary," *Amherst Collegiate Magazine* 3 (1855–56): 246; T. Herrick, "Prospects of American Literature," *Amherst Collegiate Magazine* 3 (1855–56): 238.

15. See Eugene Exman, *The House of Harper: One Hundred and Fifty Years of Publishing* (New York: Harper & Row, 1967), 67–79. See also Capps, *Emily,* 128–29. *Harper's New Monthly* became very popular in America by publishing the new English fiction of writers like Dickens and George Eliot. By the 1860s however, after receiving severe criticism for this practice, it published less foreign writing and began to stress its own commitment to American literature. From its inception, the *Atlantic Monthly* defined itself as a journal specifically committed to American literature.

16. Evert A. Duyckinck and George L. Duyckinck, eds., *Cyclopaedia of American Literature: Embracing Personal and Critical Notices of Authors,* 2 vols. (New York: Charles Scribners, 1856), I v; other examples include Rufus Griswold, *The Poets and Poetry of America* (1842), *The Prose Writers of America* (1847), and *The Female Poet of America* (1849).

17. L38, L342b, L619.

18. Henry Wadsworth Longfellow, *The Works of Henry Wadsworth Longfellow,* 14 vols. (Boston and New York: Houghton, Mifflin, 1886), VIII 365–66. Subsequently cited by parenthetical page references in the text.

19. See Mitchell, *Emily,* 88–92.

20. Thomas Wentworth Higginson, "Letter to a Young Contributor," *Atlantic Monthly* 9, no. 54 (1862): 401–11. Subsequently cited by parenthetical page references in the text.

21. Sewall, *Life,* 543–44.

22. Levine, *Highbrow,* 213. Thomas Wentworth Higginson, "A Plea for Culture," *Atlantic Monthly* 19, no. 111 (1867): 29–38. Subsequently cited by parenthetical page references in the text.

23. Higginson also published a *Short Studies of American Authors* (1879), with sketches on Hawthorne, Poe, James, and Howells. Dickinson remarked on this book, "Remorse for the brevity of a Book is a rare emotion" (L622).

24. Mitchell, *Emily,* 88–100.

25. Gary Lee Stonum, *The Dickinson Sublime* (Madison: University of Wisconsin Press, 1990), 33–34. See Tingley, "My Business," 192.

26. Higginson, "Plea," 37.

27. See Weisbuch, *Atlantic,* 16–21.

28. James Fenimore Cooper, *Notions of the Americans,* 2 vols. (New York: Frederick Ungar, 1963), II 100.

29. Wilkinson, "Mr Lowell," 233.

30. Cartelli, *Repositioning,* 29.

31. *Edgar Allan Poe: Essays and Reviews,* ed. G. R. Thompson (New York: Viking, 1984), 1392–93.

32. See Burton R. Pollin, "Shakespeare in the Works of Edgar Allan Poe," *Studies in the American Renaissance* 9 (1985): 157–86.

33. Stafford, "Hudson," 650.

34. Henry Norman Hudson, *Lectures on Shakspeare,* 2 vols. (New York: Baker & Scribner, 1848), I 1. Subsequently cited by parenthetical page references in the text.

35. Henry Norman Hudson, *Shakespeare: His Life, Art and Characters,* 2 vols. (Boston: Ginn, 1872), I 244–45. Subsequently cited by parenthetical page references in the text.

36. Stafford, "Hudson," 654.

37. Emerson, *Works,* I 57.

38. See also Ralph Waldo Emerson, *The Journals and Miscellaneous Notebooks of Ralph Waldo Emerson,* 16 vols., ed. W. H. Gilman et al. (Cambridge, Mass.: Belknap Press of Harvard University Press, 1978), XVI 127, XV 156, 379. See Ralph Waldo Emerson, *The Letters of Ralph Waldo Emerson,* ed. Ralph L. Rusk (New York: Columbia University Press, 1939), III 267.

39. See Emerson, *Journals,* VII 141.

40. Emerson, *Journals,* XIV 256.

41. See Emerson, *Journals,* XV 44–51. At this time, his journal records many thoughts on Shakespeare and a series of quotations from ten different texts—*Measure for Measure, Macbeth, The Merchant of Venice, A Midsummer Night's Dream, Henry V, Hamlet, Love's Labour's Lost, Coriolanus, The Winter's Tale,* and *The Sonnets* (46–47).

42. Quoted in Dunn, *Shakespeare,* 253.

43. Ralph Waldo Emerson, "Shakespeare," *Atlantic Monthly* 94, no. 563 (1904): 365–66. According to James Elliot Cabot's memory of the event, Emerson never actually gave this speech. Having got up to give it, he looked around the room and could think of nothing to say. In the actual manuscript of the speech he notes, "We can hardly think of an occasion where so little need be said," adding "[Shakespeare's] fame is settled on the foundations of the moral and intellectual world. Wherever there are men, and in the degree in which they are civil, have power of mind, sensibility to beauty, music, the secrets of passion, and the liquid expression of thought, he has risen to his place as the first poet of the world" (365).

44. See Emerson, *Journal,* XIV 135, XV 46–47.

45. See Emerson, *Journal,* XV 51, XVI 296. See Robert P. Falk, "Emerson and Shakespeare," *PMLA* 56, no. 2 (1941): 539–40; Dunn, *Shakespeare,* 250–51; Sanford E. Marovitz, "Emerson's Shakespeare: From Scorn to Apotheosis," *Emerson Centenary Essays,* ed. Joel Myerson (Carbondale: Southern Illinois University Press, 1982), 122–55. See also Emerson, *Journals,* XIII 30, XIII 229.

46. See Capps, *Emily,* 113–19; Keller, *Only,*148–83. Emerson's lecture is believed to have initiated Henry Clay Folger's interest in Shakespeare, when he heard it at Amherst College in 1879; see Bristol, *America's,* 70–71, 72–78.

47. See Stonum, *Dickinson,* 13–14; Bate ed., *Romantics,* 246–56.

48. Todd, *Ancestors,* 128–30.

49. See Stonum, *Dickinson,* 34–50; and Robert McClure Smith, *The Seductions of Emily Dickinson* (Tuscaloosa: University of Alabama Press, 1996), 8–10.

50. See Emerson, *Journals,* XV 52.

51. See Emerson, *Journals,* XIV 262.

52. Bristol, *Shakespeare's,* 123–30.

53. See Julian Markels, *Melville and the Politics of Identity: From King Lear to Moby Dick* (Urbana: University of Illinois Press, 1993), 41–42, 45–47. See also Cartelli, *Repositioning,* 33–35.

54. Ziff, *Literary,* 62–66.

55. For Melville's interest in Shakespeare, see Jay Leyda, *The Melville Log: A Documentary Life of Herman Melville,* 2 vols. (New York: Gordian Press, 1969), I 208–9, 278, 282–83.

56. Melville, *The Correspondents,* 119–20.

57. See Markels, "Melville's,'" 34–48. See also Leyda, *Melville Log,* I 297, II 654, II 718.

58. "Hawthorne and His Mosses," *The Literary World* 17 August 1850, 125–27. "Hawthorne and His Mosses," *The Literary World* 24 August 1850, 145–47. See Markels, *Melville,* 35–56.

59. "Hawthorne," *Literary,* 126.

60. "Hawthorne," *Literary,* 146, 126.

61. See Leyda, *Melville Log,* I 363.

62. "Hawthorne," *Literary,* 126, 145.

63. "Hawthorne," *Literary,* 126, 145.

64. Elizabeth Peabody told her daughter, Sophia Hawthorne, that their Aunt Rawlins had agreed with most of the review but commented that she thought "he had injured the subject by saying too much. "No man of common-sense," she said "would seriously name Mr. Hawthorne, deserving as he is of respect and admiration, in the same day with Shakespeare! . . . to compare anyone to Shakespeare argues weakness and ignorance, and only injures the friend he is attempting to serve." Quoted in Leyda, *Melville Log,* I 392.

65. "Hawthorne," *Literary,* 126.

66. Bingham, *Emily,* 413.

67. Paula Bennett, *Emily Dickinson: Woman Poet* (Iowa City: University of Iowa Press, 1990), 34, 135–38; and Daneen Wardrop, *Emily Dickinson's Gothic: Goblin with a Gauge* (Iowa City: University of Iowa Press, 1996).

68. Quoted in Sewall, *Life* 153.

69. Melville supported Macready during Astor Place Riot (Leyda, *Melville Log* I 302–3, 333–34). Later, on 3 May 1857, Melville traveled to Stratford on Avon, see Leyda, *Melville Log* II 576.

70. See Leyda, *Melville Log,* I 461, II 581.

71. Charles Olson, *Call me Ishmael* (London: Jonathan Cape, 1967), 68.

72. F. O. Matthiessen, *American Renaissance: Art and Expression in the Age of Emerson and Whitman* (New York: Oxford University Press, 1941), 435.

73. On 22 November 1851, as part of his review of *Moby Dick* for *The Literary World,* Evert Duyckinck wrote, "The intense Captain Ahab is too long drawn out . . . If we had as much of Hamlet or Macbeth as Mr. Melville gives us of Ahab, we should be tired even of their sublime company." See Leyda, *Melville Log,* I 437.

74. See Ziff, *Literary,* 287–92; and Markels, *Melville,* 17–34.

75. See Sandra M Gilbert, "The American Sexual Poetics of Walt Whitman and Emily Dickinson," in *Reconstructing American Literary History,* ed. Sacvan Bercovitch (Cambridge, Mass.: Harvard University Press, 1986), 123–54. See also Keller, *Only,* 151–93.

76. Walt Whitman, *Prose Works 1892,* 2 vols., ed. Floyd Stovall (New York: New York University Press, 1963), II 675. Subsequently cited by parenthetical page references in the text.

77. Richard Clarence Harrison, "Walt Whitman and Shakespeare," *PMLA* 44 (1929): 1203; Alwin Thaler, *Shakespeare and Democracy* (Knoxville: University of Tennessee Press, 1941).

78. Reynolds, *Beneath,* 157.

79. Harrison, "Walt Whitman," 1205–7; Dunn, *Shakespeare,* 267.

80. Harrison, "Walt Whitman," 1220–38.

81. Jonathan Trumbull, "Walt Whitman's View of Shakespeare," *Poet-Lore* 2 (1890): 368–71.

82. Jonathan Trumbull, "The Whitman-Question," *Poet-Lore* 3 (1891): 626–29.

83. Trumbull, "The Whitman," 628.

84. Compare Dickinson's skepticism with the more devotional celebrations of Shakespeare: Herman Melville, "The Coming Storm," in *Battle-Pieces and Aspects of the War* (New York: Da Capo Press, 1995), 143; Fanny Kemble, "To Shakespeare," *The Praise of Shakespeare: An English Anthology,* ed. Cecil Eldred Hughes (London: Methuen, 1904), 183. See also Rogers, "Shakespeare"; and Irving, "Shakspere."

85. Emerson, "Shakespeare," 365–66.

86. Vivian Pollak, "Emily Dickinson's Literary Allusions," *Essays in Literature* 1 (1974): 65.

87. "Hawthorne," *Literary,* 126.

88. Mitchell, *Emily,* 13; Erkkila, "Emily," 14.

89. See Bloom, *Map,* 178; Gilbert and Gubar, *Madwoman,* 48–53; Joanne Feit Diehl, *Dickinson and the Romantic Imagination* (Princeton: Princeton University Press, 1981); McNeil, *Emily;* and Loeffelholz, *Dickinson.*

Chapter Five

1. See Capps, *Emily,* 83–87, 92–94; Keller, *Only,* 327–34; Habegger, *My Wars,* 317–20, 385–87, and 604–6. See L234 and "I think I was enchanted" (F627). In spring 1862, she wrote to Samuel Bowles, "Should anybody where you go, talk of Mrs. Browning, you must hear for us -and if you touch her Grave, put one hand on the Head, for me - her unmentioned Mourner -" (L266). She also wrote two elegies for Browning, "Her - 'last

Poems'" (F600) and "I went to thank Her" (F637). By 1871, Dickinson had read *Adam Bede* and *Mill on the Floss;* in 1873 she declared, "'What do I think of *Middlemarch?*' What do I think of glory - except that in a few instances this 'mortal has already put on immortality'" (L389). After reading *Daniel Deronda* in 1876 she declared, "She is the Lane to the Indes, Columbus was looking for" (L456), and upon hearing of Eliot's death she wrote, "Her Losses make our Gains ashamed" (F1602).

2. See Betsy Erkkila, *Wicked Sisters: Women Poets, Literary History, and Discord* (New York: Oxford University Press, 1992), 55–98; and Vivian Pollak "American Women Poets Reading: The Example of Helen Hunt Jackson," in *Emily Dickinson Handbook,* ed. Grabher et al., 323–41. See also Stonum, *Dickinson,* 34–46; Smith, *Seductions,* 129–33; and Habegger, *My Wars,* 317–20, 385–87.

3. Richard B. Sewall, "Emily Dickinson's Perfect Audience: Helen Hunt Jackson," in *Dickinson and Audience,* ed. Orzeck and Weisbuch, 201–13. See also see Elizabeth A. Petrino, *Emily Dickinson and Her Contemporaries: Women's Verse in America 1820–1885* (Hanover, N.H.: University Press of New England, 1998), 161–200. See also Georgiana Strickland, "'In Praise of Ramona': Emily Dickinson and Helen Hunt Jackson's Indian Novel," *Emily Dickinson Journal* 9, no. 2 (2000): 120–33. See also Erkkila, *Wicked,* 86–98; Pollak, "American," 330.

4. In October 1875, Jackson wrote, "You are a great poet,—and it is wrong to the day you live in that you will not sing aloud. When you are what men call dead you will be sorry you were so stingy" (L444a). Later, in September 1884, she tells Dickinson, "It is a cruel wrong to your 'day & generation' that you will not give them light" (L937a).

5. See Strickland, "In Praise," 122.

6. In October 1875, when Jackson was about to marry William S. Jackson, Dickinson sent her the following curious note: "Have I a word but Joy? / E. Dickinson / Who fleeing from the Spring / The Spring avenging fling / To Dooms of Balms" (L444). Jackson asked Dickinson what she meant, but the poet never replied (444a).

7. Bingham, *Ancestors,* 320.

8. Lowell, *Among My Books,* 203.

9. See Novy, *Engaging,* 23–25, 44; Stonum, *Dickinson,* 36; Erkkila, *Wicked,* 84; and Lootens, *Lost,* 112–13. See also "Elizabeth Barrett Browning," *The Editor* 4, no. 2 (1866): 247.

10. Novy, *Engaging,* 12–25.

11. "Desdemona," *The Indicator,* 181.

12. Novy ed., *Women's,* 1–15; Novy, *Engaging,* 1–21; and Thompson and Roberts eds., *Women Reading Shakespeare.*

13. See Margaret Cavendish, "Letter CXXIII," in *Women Reading Shakespeare,* ed. Thompson and Roberts, 12, 13; and Elizabeth Montagu, *An Essay on the Writings and Genius of Shakespeare* (Dublin: J. Potts, 1778), 31.

14. Richard Grant White, "On Reading Shakespeare," *The Galaxy* 22, no. 4 (1876): 518.

15. See Susan J. Wolfson, "Explaining to His Sisters: Mary Lamb's Tales from Shakespeare," in *Women's Re-Visions of Shakespeare,* ed. Novy, 16–40. Taylor, *Reinventing,* 207.

16. Elizabeth Barrett Browning, *Aurora Leigh,* (London: Woman's Press, 1978), 285.

17. W. T. Thom, "Shakespeare Study for American Women," *Shakespeariana* 1 (1884): 97–102. Mary Cowden Clarke, "Shakespeare as the Girl's Friend," *Shakespeariana* 4 (1887): 355–69. Subsequently both are cited by parenthetical page references in the text. See also George C. Gross, "'The Girlhood of Shakespeare's Heroines,' and the Sex Education of Victorian Women," *Victorian Studies* 16 (1972): 37–58.

18. See Thom, 97–98, 99, 100. See Clarke, 355–56.

19. Thom, "Shakespeare," 100.

20. See Margreta De Grazia, "The Scandal of Shakespeare's Sonnets," *Shakespeare Survey* 46 (1993): 37–49; See also Marjorie Garber, *Vice Versa* (Harmondsworth, U.K.: Penguin, 1995), 507–10; Peter Stallybrass, "Editing as Cultural Formation: The Sexing of Shakespeare's Sonnets," *Modern Literary Quarterly,* 54, no. 1 (1993): 91–103.

21. See Patterson, *Riddle,* 89; Farr, *Passion,* 132, 167, 182–83; Sylvia Henneberg, "Neither Lesbian nor Straight: Multiple Eroticism in Emily Dickinson's Love Poetry," *Emily Dickinson Journal* 4, no. 2 (1995): 1–19.

22. See Linda Rozmovits, *Shakespeare and the Politics of Culture in Late Victorian England* (Baltimore: Johns Hopkins University Press, 1998), 34–35.

23. Christy Desmet, "'Intercepting the Dew Drop': Female Readers and Readings in Anna Jameson's Shakespearean Criticism," in *Women's Re-Visions of Shakespeare,* ed. Novy, 41–57.

24. Knight, *Shakspere,* VIII 239, 347, 361, 420. See Jennifer Johnson, "Writing Romeo Out: Rereading Shakespeare's Women," in *Anna Jameson: Victorian, Feminist, Woman of Letters* (Aldershot, U.K.: Scolar Press, 1997), 74–76.

25. See Nina Auerbach, *Woman and Demon: The Life of a Victorian Myth* (Cambridge, Mass.: Harvard University Press, 1982), 207–15.

26. Quoted in Thompson and Roberts eds., *Women Reading Shakespeare,* 67.

27. Jameson, *Characteristics,* 13–14.

28. See Mary Cowden Clarke, *The Girlhood of Shakespeare's Heroines* 5 vols. (London: W. H. Smith and Sons, 1850–52), and Helena Faucit, *On Some of Shakespeare's Female Characters* (Edinburgh: Blackwood and Sons, 1885). See also Thompson and Roberts eds., *Women Reading Shakespeare,* 165–72, 173–83.

29. "From Boston," *Springfield Republican* 23 October 1873.

30. Palmer, *Stratford,* "Preface."

31. Jameson, *Characteristics,* 11.

32. "Reviews and Literary Notices," *Atlantic Monthly* 3, no. 15 (1859): 135.

33. See Jameson, *Characteristics,* 29–30; Palmer, *Stratford,* 25, 75, 195.

34. See Jameson, *Characteristics,* 437–67.

35. See Georgianna Ziegler, "Accommodating the Virago: Nineteenth-Century

Representations of Lady Macbeth," in *Shakespeare and Appropriation,* ed. Desmet and Sawyer, 119–41.

36. See Palmer, *Stratford,* 75–78, 119–21, 157–59.

37. See Palmer, *Stratford,* 75. See Jameson, *Characteristics,* 100, 101.

38. Philip Davis, "Nineteenth-Century Juliet," *Shakespeare Survey* 49 (1996): 131–40.

39. See Palmer, *Stratford,* 119–20, 158.

40. Mary Preston, *Studies in Shakspeare: A Book of Essays* (Philadelphia: Claxton, Remsen and Haffelfinger, 1869). Subsequently cited by parenthetical page references in the text.

41. Preston argues that *Macbeth* is a warning to contemporary ambitious men, who sacrifice honor to circumstance, and to their devout wives, who out of love place their husbands before their own ideas of virtue (23–24).

42. See Preston, *Studies,* 16–24, 25–32, 54–62, 154–55.

43. See the Houghton's inventory of books removed from the Dickinson household. Sue owned an 1849 edition of this novel; Samuel Bowles gave it to her. Charlotte Brontë, *Shirley* (Oxford: Oxford University Press, 1998), 89–93.

44. See Margaret Arnold, "Coriolanus Transformed: Charlotte Brontë's Use of Shakespeare in *Shirley,*" in *Women's Re-Visions of Shakespeare,* ed. Novy, 76–88.

45. West, "Shakespeare," 51.

46. Bianchi, *Emily,* 245.

47. See also Preston, *Studies,* 131–32, 164. Preston compares the "famously infamous Gen. Ben. Butler" to Richard III and Puck from *A Midsummer Night's Dream* to Gen. Ulysses S. Grant. Similarly, in her essay on *Macbeth,* she equates the dauntless courage of "the Confederate generals on the bloody field of Manassas," with Shakespeare's character, declaring that even a "*bad* man" should "win a certain degree of respect for his valor" (13).

48. Novy, *Engaging,* 2–4, 20–21.

49. See Novy, *Engaging,* 61–66, 94–116, 119–31.

50. Fuller alluded to *The Tempest,* paraphrased *Hamlet,* and quoted from *Henry IV part 1, Othello, The Merchant of Venice, Henry V, As You Like It,* and *A Midsummer Night's Dream;* see *The Letters of Margaret Fuller,* ed. Robert N. Hudspeth, 6 vols. (Ithaca: Cornell University Press, 1983), I 186, I 325, II 42, II 124, III 126 IV 97, VI 145, VI 267. See Harriet Beecher Stowe, *Uncle Tom's Cabin,* ed. Elizabeth Ammons (New York: W. W. Norton, 1994). 82, 155, 366. See also Edward Wagenknecht, *Harriet Beecher Stowe: The Known and the Unknown* (New York: Oxford University Press, 1965), 140–41.

51. See Fuller, *Letters,* II 53.

52. Charles Capper, *Margaret Fuller: An American Romantic Life* (New York: Oxford University Press, 1992), 248–49.

53. See Louisa May Alcott, *The Journals of Louisa May Alcott,* ed. Joel Myerson and Daniel Shealy (Boston, Little Brown, 1989), 84; Louisa May Alcott, *The Selected Letters of Louisa May Alcott,* ed. Joel Myerson and Daniel Shealy (Boston: Little, Brown, 1987), 29.

54. See Karl Keller's discussion of Dickinson and Fuller, *Only,* 235–39.

55. Bell Gale Chevigny, ed., *The Woman and the Myth: Margaret Fuller's Life and Writings* (Boston: Northeastern University Press, 1994), 43–44.

56. Chevigny ed., *Woman,* 44.

57. Chevigny ed., *Woman,* 185–86.

58. Fuller, *Letters,* II 116.

59. See Maurice Morgann, *Shakespearian Criticism,* ed. Daniel A Fineman (Oxford: Clarendon Press, 1972), 170.

60. Margaret Fuller, *Woman in the Nineteenth Century* (New York: W. W. Norton, 1971), 131. Subsequently cited by parenthetical page references in the text.

61. Russell Jackson, "'Perfect Types of Womanhood': Rosalind, Beatrice and Viola in Victorian Criticism and Performance," *Shakespeare Survey* 32 (1979): 16.

62. At the beginning of Fuller's book she alters the quotation from *Hamlet* so that it reads "Frailty, thy name is MAN" (15). See Novy, *Engaging,* 69–97.

63. See Elaine Showalter, *Sister's Choice: Tradition and Change in American Women's Writing* (Oxford: Oxford University Press, 1991), 29–31; and Phyllis McBride, "In Her Father's Library: Margaret Fuller and The Making of The American Miranda," *Shakespeare Survey* 53 (2000): 127–36.

64. Fuller, *Letters,* III 199 n.4.

65. Chevigny ed., *Woman,* 39. See Thomas Wentworth Higginson, *Margaret Fuller Ossoli* (Boston: Houghton Mifflin, 1884), 18. See Showalter, *Sister's,* 30.

66. Marianne Noble, "The Revenge of Cato's Daughter: Dickinson's Masochism," *Emily Dickinson Journal* 8, no. 2 (1998): 22–47; Petrino, *Emily,* 156.

67. Showalter, *Sister's,* 33. For a discussion of Dickinson and Stowe, see Keller, *Only,* 97–124.

68. See Joan D. Hedrick, *Harriet Beecher Stowe: A Life* (New York: Oxford University Press, 1994), 296–99. See the inventory of the Dickinson Collection at the Houghton Library, Harvard.

69. Harriet Beecher Stowe, *The Pearl of Orr's Island: A Story of the Coast of Maine* (Boston: Ticknor & Fields, 1866), 46. Subsequently cited by parenthetical page references in the text.

70. See Showalter, *Sister's,* 34.

71. See Novy, *Engaging,* 64–65. Showalter, *Sister's,* 34–35.

72. Charles Edward Stowe, *The Life of Harriet Beecher Stowe: Compiled from Her Letters and Journals* (Boston: Houghton, Mifflin, 1890), 177.

73. Harriet Beecher Stowe, *Sunny Memories of Foreign Lands,* 2 vols. (Boston: Philips, Sampson, 1854), I 191–223. Subsequently cited by parenthetical page references in the text.

74. Again Stowe mentions Shakespeare's daughter Mistress Hall, who was the wit of the Shakespeare family and her father's favorite (211). She also mentions the little love between Ann Hathaway and Shakespeare, and the fact that Shakespeare's lineage died out (212).

75. Alcott, *Letters,* 279–80.

76. Alcott, *Letters,* 296.

77. Louisa May Alcott, *Little Women and Good Wives* (London: Everyman Library, 1992), 305–6. Subsequently cited by parenthetical page references in the text.

78. Louisa May Alcott, *Comic Tragedies written by "Jo" and "Meg": and acted by The "Little Women"* (Boston: Roberts Brothers, 1893), 7.

79. Alcott, *Journals,* 74, 81, 85, 245.

80. Alcott, *Journals,* 91; and Alcott, *Letters,* 14.

81. Alcott, *Journals,* 90.

82. See Alan L. Ackerman Jr., *The Portable Theater: American Literature and the Nineteenth-Century Stage* (Baltimore: Johns Hopkins University Press, 1999), 155–80.

83. Alcott, *Little Women,* 7, 227, 8, 133. In 1840, on reading her first poem "The Robin," her mother commented "You will grow up a Shakspeare!" See Ednah D. Cheney, *Louisa May Alcott, Her Life, Letters, and Journals* (London: Sampson Low, Marston, Searle & Rivington, 1889), 20. Alcott, *Letters,* 115.

84. Alcott, *Letters,* 79.

85. See Alcott, *Journals,* 140. Two other stories also allude to Shakespeare's plays: "A Pair of Eyes; or Modern Magic" focuses on a painter attempting to paint a picture of Lady Macbeth, and "Taming a Tartar" examines the rivalry between the sexes with reference to *The Taming of the Shrew.* See Madeleine B. Stern, "Introduction," *A Double Life: Newly Discovered Thrillers of Louisa May Alcott,* ed. Madeleine B. Stern (Boston: G. K Hall, 1984), 11–13.

86. Louisa May Alcott, "A Double Tragedy: An Actor's Story," in *Louisa May Alcott Unmasked: Collected Thrillers,* ed. and intro. Madeleine Stern (Boston: Northeastern University Press, 1995), 251–64. Subsequently cited by parenthetical page references in the text.

87. John Gavin, "Caught in the Act: Or, the Prosing of Juliet," in *The Appropriation of Shakespeare,* ed. Marsden, 101.

88. See Novy, *Engaging,* 13–15.

89. Alcott, "Ariel: A Legend of the Lighthouse," in *Louisa May Alcott Unmasked,* ed. Stern, 265–93.

90. Robert Weisbuch, *Emily Dickinson's Poetry* (Chicago: University of Chicago Press, 1975), 23–24. See Henry Wells, *Introduction to Emily Dickinson* (1947; New York: Hendricks House, 1959), 127; Rebecca Patterson *The Riddle of Emily Dickinson* (1951; New York: Cooper Square Publishers, 1973), 260–61; Philips, *Emily,* 127–30; and Lease, *Emily,* 41–42.

91. Paula Bennett, *Emily Dickinson: A Woman Poet* (New York: Harvester Wheatsheaf, 1990), 11–12.

92. "Desdemona," *The Indicator,* 180.

Chapter Six

1. Martha Dickinson Bianchi, *Life and Letters of Emily Dickinson* (Boston: Houghton Mifflin, 1924), 80.

2. See the following discussions of Shakespeare: "Taking it in Earnest," *Springfield Republican* 16 January 1850; "A Lesson for Young Ladies," *Springfield Republican* 26

January 1850; "Scraps from the Last Knickerbocker Magazine," *Springfield Republican* 10 April 1852.

3. Bristol, *America's,* 15–16.

4. George Clair, "Shakespeare," *Amherst Record* 26 July 1871.

5. William Dodd's *The Beauties of Shakespear* (1752) went through thirty-nine editions between 1752 and 1893, and inspired many other books, especially in the nineteenth century, that aimed to familiarize readers with the beauties of Shakespeare's lines. In Dickinson's era, there was *A Shakespearean Dictionary* (1832), *The Shakespeare Calendar* (1850), *Cupid's Birthday Book: One thousand Love-Darts from Shakespeare, gathered for every day in the year* (1875), and *Sweet Silvery Sayings of Shakespeare on the Softer Sex* (1877). See Marder, *His Exits,* 26; and Michael Wheeler, *Art of Allusion in Victorian Fiction* (London: Macmillan, 1979), 14–15.

6. Mary F. P. Dunbar, *The Shakespeare Birthday Book* (New York: Thomas Whittaler, 1882), 262–63. This book is contained within the collection of Dickinson's Books at the Houghton Library, Harvard.

7. Bianchi, *Emily,* 66.

8. Bianchi, *Emily,* 29.

9. bMS Am 1118.95, box 9. By permission of the Houghton Library, Harvard.

10. Wells, *Introduction,* 126–27

11. Todd, *Ancestors,* 130.

12. Dickinson offers "When" as a variant to "What," demonstrating that her need to distance herself from Shakespeare's poem was as great as her need to respond to it in some way.

13. bMS Am 1118.95, box 9. By permission of the Houghton Library, Harvard. See "Writings of Susan Dickinson," Dickinson Electronic Archives, <http://www.emilydickinson.org/susan/calendar.html>.

14. Patterson, *Riddle,* 190, 191, 206.

15. There are enclosures in the following plays: *Love's Labour's Lost, Henry V, Henry VI part 1, Romeo and Juliet, King Lear, Julius Caesar,* and *Antony and Cleopatra.* See Knight, *Shakspere,* I 206–7; III 507-7; IV 54–55; V 34–35, 188–89, 524–25, 542–43; VI 384–85, 516–17, 528–29.

16. Fuller, *Letters,* II 116. Emerson, *Works,* IV 121.

17. Emerson, *Journals,* XV 51.

18. Sewall, *Life,* 702–3.

19. See Carroll Smith-Rosenberg, *Disorderly Conduct: Visions of Gender in Victorian America* (Oxford: Oxford University Press, 1985), 53–75.

20. Capps, *Emily,* 65.

21. Messmer, *Vice,* 148–52, 166–72.

22. Newman, *Practical,* 93, 98. See also *The Fashionable American Letter Writer, or The Art of Polite Correspondence* (Newark, N. J.: Benjamin Olds), xxviii; and *The Young Lady's Own Book,* 127.

23. Paula Bennett, *My Life, a Loaded Gun: Female Creativity and Feminist Poetics* (Boston: Beacon, 1986), 34.

24. Preston, *Studies,* 143.
25. Messmer, *Vice,* 107–14.
26. Knight, *Shakspere,* II 173.
27. See Hudson, *Shakespeare,* II 228–48.
28. Wilkes, *Shakespeare,* 358.
29. Knight, *Shakspere,* V 434, 481.
30. See E. G. Cobb, "King Lear as Character," *Amherst Collegiate Magazine* 4 (1856–57): 55–59.
31. Although these lines are Prospero's in Knight's edition, in modern editions they are Miranda's. See also Knight, *Shakspere,* II 545, 563.
32. "Caliban," *Amherst Student* 10, no. 5 (1876): 52. William Gardiner Hammond likes Caliban, despite his treachery, "because he is a *character,*" whereas he is bored by Prospero, a "rather a prosy matter-of-fact old gentleman." See Hammond, *Diary,* 194.
33. See Loeffelholz, *Dickinson,* 30–34.
34. Julie Hankey, "Victorian Portias: Shakespeare's Borderline Heroine," *Shakespeare Quarterly* 45, no. 4 (1994): 426–48.
35. Jameson, *Characteristics,* 76.
36. Thomas Woodson, L. Neal Smith, and Norman Holmes Pearson, eds., *The Letters,* vols. XV–XX of *The Centenary Edition of the Works of Nathaniel Hawthorne* (Ohio State University Press, 1985–88), XV 253.
37. *Letters,* ed. Woodson et al., XV 185, XVI 158, XVI 407.
38. Melville, *Correspondence,* 133, 171, 378.
39. Philip Horne ed., *Henry James: A Life in Letters* (Harmondsworth, U.K.: Penguin, 1999), 23.
40. Fuller, *Letters,* IV 97.
41. Fuller, *Letters,* III 126. See also *Letters,* I 325; II 42, 124; VI 145, 267.
42. T. B. Thorpe, "The Case of Lady Macbeth Medically Considered," *Harper's New Monthly* 8, no. 45 (Feb. 1854): 391–98. Subsequently cited by parenthetical page references in the text.
43. See Thorpe, "Case," 395–96, 397.
44. Horne ed., *Henry,* 247.
45. Knight, *Shakspere,* V 617, 629.
46. "Miss Emily Dickinson of Amherst," *Springfield Republican* 18 May 1886.
47. Messmer, *Vice,* 176.
48. See Wardrop, *Emily Dickinson's Gothic,* 46–47.
49. Sewall, *Life,* 704; and Capps, *Emily,* 66.
50. See Anderson, *Emily,* 131; Capps, *Emily,* 65.
51. Taylor, "Shakespeare," 254.
52. See Bennett, *Emily,* 98–99. In 1852, Charles Wadsworth, Dickinson's friend, insisted that the telegraph was "a lovelier and loftier creation of true poetry than . . . Shakespeare's Tempest." Quoted in Habegger, *My Wars,* 332. In a much-quoted 1858 letter to Dr. and Mrs. Holland, Dickinson presents democracy as the eradication of social distinction (L195); her letter ends with a quotation—"Lay her a-hold, a hold!"

(I i 49)—from the first scene of *The Tempest.* This summons up the loss of rank and status that accompanies the sea storm, suggesting that for Dickinson this play symbolized political and social usurpation, as well as the artist's power to create harmony by reestablishing traditional hierarchical difference.

53. "Her honour's pawn" from *The Two Gentlemen of Verona* (I iii 47); "mine honour's pawn" from *Richard II* (I i 74; IV i 55); "my honour is at pawn" from *Henry IV, part 2* (II iii 7); and "pawn mine honour for their safety" from *Cymbeline* (I vi 194).

54. Higginson, "Letter," 403.

55. See Mitchell, *Emily,* 89.

56. For Barthes's distinction between writerly and readerly texts, see Roland Barthes, *S/Z* (New York: Hill and Wang, 1974) 3–11.

57. Antony himself declares, "These strong Egyptian fetters I must break / Or lose myself in dotage" (I ii 116–17); later he realizes that "Authority melts from [him] of late" (III xiii 90).

58. Mitchell, *Emily,* 154–227.

59. Messmer, *Vice,* 115–30, 152–60.

60. Whicher, *This,* 35. See also Paglia, *Sexual,* 671.

61. See also Sewall, *Life,* 199. Thomas Johnson, *Emily Dickinson: An Interpretative Biography* (1955; Cambridge, Mass.: Belknap Press of Harvard University Press, 1966), 41. See also "Emily Dickinson's Correspondences," *Dickinson Electronic Archives* <http://jefferson.village.virginia.edu/dickinson/>.

62. Clair, "Shakespeare," *Amherst Record* 26 July 1871.

63. In October 1851, Dickinson, alluding to their ability as poets, wrote that they please themselves "with the fancy that we are the only poets, and everyone else is *prose*" (L56). In 1862, when Emily's poem "Safe in their Alabaster chambers" was published as "The Sleeping" in the *Springfield Republican,* Sue wrote, "*Has girl read Republican?* It takes as long to start our Fleet as the Burnside" (Leyda II 48). See "Writings of Susan Dickinson," *Dickinson Electronic Archives* <http://www.emilydickinson.org/susan/index/html>. Smith, *Rowing,* 157–205.

64. Bianchi, *Emily,* 29.

65. Smith, *Rowing,* 150.

66. See Jane Donahue Eberwein, ed., *An Emily Dickinson Encyclopedia* (Westport, Conn.: Greenwood, 1998), 263–65.

67. Clarke, "Shakespeare," 356.

68. Hudson, *Lectures,* I 54.

69. David Sullivan, "Suing Sue: Emily Dickinson Addressing Susan Gilbert," *Emily Dickinson Journal* 5, no. 1 (1996): 45–70.

Chapter Seven

1. Knight, *Shakspere,* VI 528–29. Scene references in this chapter are to *The Riverside Shakespeare* rather than to Knight's *Shakspere,* which omits scenes from acts three and four included in most modern editions of this play.

2. Sewall, *Lyman,* 76.

3. Knight, *Shakspere,* VI 434. See Bate ed., *Romantics,* 263.

4. Hudson, *Shakespeare,* II 395.

5. Georg Gottfried Gervinus, *Shakespeare Commentaries,* trans. F. E. Bunnett (1863; New York: Scribner, Welford & Armstrong, 1875), 724. Subsequently cited by parenthetical page references in the text. See Hudson, *Shakespeare,* II 428, 450.

6. Whipple, "Growth," 187.

7. Edward Dowden, *Shakspere: A Critical Study of His Mind and Art* (London: Routledge, 1875), 307. Subsequently cited by parenthetical page references in the text. See Hudson, *Shakespeare,* II 264.

8. Dowden, *Shakespeare,* 307, 316.

9. Gervinus, *Shakespeare,* 725–30.

10. See Patterson, *Emily,* 154.

11. Bennett, "Orient," 114; see also Patterson, *Emily,* 143–55.

12. Farr, "Emily," 232.

13. See Farr, *Passion,* 172, 174–75.

14. Sewall, *Lyman,* 76.

15. Knight, *Shakspere,* VI 490–91. See also William Shakespeare, *The Dramatic Works of William Shakespeare, illustrated: embracing a life of the poet and notes, original and selected,* 8 vols. (Boston: Phillips, Sampson, 1856), VI 160. See Farr, *Passion,* 171–72.

16. Farr, "Emily," 237, 238.

17. Smith, *Rowing,* 150.

18. Susan Dickinson, "Minstrel of the passing days." See "Writings by Susan Dickinson," *Dickinson Electronic Archives* <http://www.emilydickinson.org/susan/mins.html>. Sue's daughter, Martha, wrote a poem called "To Cleopatra's Mummy in the British Museum," which asks "do dreams recall her those poisoned slaves / Whose torments instructed her sultry charms / To walk seductive the way of graves / From Antony's pillow to Death's grim arms?" This was published in the *Atlantic Monthly* 81, no. 485 (1898): 365.

19. See the important annotation of these letters at "Emily Dickinson's Correspondences," *Dickinson Electronic Archives* <http://www.emilydickinson.org/working/nhb168.htm>. Password Protected. See also Smith, *Rowing,* 157–205.

20. See George Brandes, *William Shakespeare* (London: William Heinemann, 1898), 475.

21. See Jonathan Gil, "'Narcissus in thy face': Roman Desire and the Difference it Fakes in *Antony and Cleopatra,*" *Shakespeare Quarterly* 45, no. 4 (1994): 408–25.

22. Clair, "Shakespeare," *Amherst Record* 26 July 1871.

23. Knight, *Shakspere,* VI 434–35; VIII 421–23.

24. Oscar Fay Adams and Arthur Symons, "Antony and Cleopatra," in *The Works of William Shakespeare,* 8 vols, ed. Henry Irving and Frank Marshall (London: Blackie & Son, 1889), VI 120–24.

25. See Sharon Cameron, *Lyric Time: Dickinson and the Limits of Genre* (Baltimore: Johns Hopkins University Press, 1979), 26–55; Homans, *Women,* 176–88.

26. For example, see Páraic Finnerty, "'No Matter - now - Sweet - But when I'm Earl': Dickinson's Shakespearean Cross-Dressing," *Emily Dickinson Journal* 7, no. 2 (1998): 65–94.

27. Bianchi, *Emily,* 130–31

28. See Farr, "Emily," 236–37.

29. In 1878 she tells Sue, "Susan knows she is a Siren - and that at a word from her, Emily would forfeit Righteousness - Please excuse the grossness of this morning I was for a moment disarmed" (L554) and "I must wait a few Days before seeing you - You are too momentous. But remember it is idolatry not indifference" (L581). See Habegger, *My Wars,* 467–69, 488.

30. See Adalaide Morris, "'The Love of thee - a Prism Be': Men and Women in the Love Poetry of Emily Dickinson" *Feminist Critics Read Emily Dickinson,* ed. Suzanne Juhasz (Bloomington: Indiana University Press, 1983), 107.

31. See Comment, "Dickinson's," 167–81.

32. See Linda T. Fitz, "Egyptian Queens and Male Reviewers: Sexist Attitudes in *Antony and Cleopatra* Criticism," *Shakespeare Quarterly* 28, no. 3 (1977): 294–316.

33. Bate ed., *Romantics,* 263.

34. Dowden, *Shakspere,* 308.

35. Brandes, *William Shakespeare,* 468.

36. Irving and Marshall eds., *Works,* VI 122.

37. Irving and Marshall eds., *Works,* VI 119.

38. Charlotte Brontë, *Villette* (Harmondsworth, U.K.: Penguin, 1979), 275–82.

39. See the Houghton's inventory of books removed from the Dickinson household. See Capps, *Emily,* 94–95.

40. See Taylor, *Reinventing,* 210.

41. Julia Ward Howe, "George Sand," *Atlantic Monthly* 8, no. 49 (1861): 513.

42. Lucy Hughes-Hallett, *Cleopatra: Histories, Dreams and Distortions* (London: Bloomsbury, 1990), 213.

43. Bianchi, *Life,* 73.

44. Higginson, "Emily," 445.

45. Petrino, *Emily,* 137; Judith Farr, *The Gardens of Emily Dickinson* (Cambridge, Mass.: Harvard University Press, 2004), 70. In an 1874 letter to Higginson, she reminded him that "'Field Lilies' are Cleopatra's 'Posies,'" combining a biblical diatribe against worldliness with the most worldly of Shakespeare's heroines (L405).

46. Bingham, *Ancestor,* 166–67.

47. See Sewall, *Life,* 213–14; Paglia, *Sexual Personae,* 648, 662; Gilbert and Gubar, *Madwoman,* 613–21; Eberwein, *Dickinson,* 94–127; John Emerson Todd, *Emily Dickinson's Use of Persona* (The Hague: Mouton, 1973); Phillips, *Dickinson;* and Reynolds, *Beneath,* 414.

48. Sandra Runzo, "Dickinson, Performance, and the Homoerotic Lyric," *American Literature* 68, no. 2 (1996): 347–63 (353).

49. Pascoe, "The House," 13. Pascoe does not offer an example of Dickinson calling herself "Amherst," for a letter where Dickinson equates herself with the town (L564).

See Karen Halttunen, *Confidence Men and Painted Women: A Study of Middle-Class Culture in America* (New Haven: Yale University Press, 1982), 153–90.

50. See William Winter, *Shakespeare on the Stage,* 3rd series (New York: Moffat, York, 1911), 456–60; Charles E. L. Wingate, *Shakespeare's Heroines on the Stage,* 2 vols. (New York: Thomas Y. Crowell, 1895), II 167–74. When the play was performed it was often a version that conflated Shakespeare's play with John Dryden's *All For Love* (1677), with Shakespeare's passages that celebrate the more notorious aspects of Cleopatra's "variety" severely cut.

51. Quoted in Wingate, *Shakespeare's,* II 187.

52. Richard Madeline, ed., *Antony and Cleopatra: Shakespeare in Production* (Cambridge, U.K.: Cambridge University Press, 1998), 45–54.

53. Habegger, *My Wars,* 491.

54. "The Cleopatra of History and of Fiction," *Amherst Student* 10 September 1870, 1–2.

55. See Philips, *Dickinson,* 112–14. See also Hughes-Hallett, *Cleopatra,* 182.

56. One speaker discerns like a queen (F256); another is Queen of Calvary (F347); one is an unadorned queen (F280); another is a half-unconscious queen (F353). In other poems, the speaker is simply a queen (F596), or presents herself as the Empress of Calvary (F194). See Morris, "Love," 110–12; Todd, *Emily,* 31–55.

57. Millicent Todd Bingham, *Emily Dickinson: A Revelation* (New York: Harper & Brothers Publishers, 1954), 59.

58. Bingham, *Emily,* 23.

59. See Mary Hamer, *Signs of Cleopatra: History, Politics, Representation* (London: Routledge, 1993), xvii–xviii, 105–9.

60. See Hamer, *Signs,* 77–103. M. E. W. S., "New England Women," *Atlantic Monthly* 42, no. 250 (1878): 230–37.

61. "Cleopatra," *Amherst Student,* 2.

62. M. E. W. S., "New England Women," 236.

63. See Miller, *Emily,* 121–22.

64. See Dowden, *Shakspere,* 315–16; Brandes, *William Shakespeare,* 462–63; Irving and Marshall eds., *Works,* VI 119.

65. See Homans, *Women,* 166–69, 171.

66. Brandes, *William Shakespeare,* 462. See Smith, *Seductions,* 1–18; and Jean Baudrillard, *Seductions* (London: Macmillan, 1990), 85.

67. See Miller, *Emily;* Stonum, *Dickinson;* Karl Keller, "Notes on Sleeping with Emily Dickinson," in *Feminist Critics Read Emily Dickinson,* ed. Juhasz, 66–79.

68. The essay on Cleopatra in the *Amherst Student* suggests that Cleopatra "coquets with [Antony] as only a woman in love can do" ("Cleopatra" 2). See also Catherine Belsey, "Cleopatra's Seduction" in *Alternative Shakespeare 2,* ed. Terence Hawkes (London: Routledge, 1995), 38–62.

69. See also Prose Fragment 56.

70. See Polly Longsworth, *Austin and Mabel: The Amherst Affair & Love Letters of*

Austin Dickinson and Mabel Loomis Todd (New York, 1984; paper ed., Amherst: University of Massachusetts Press, 1999), 233–34.

71. Bingham, *Revelation,* 1–11. See Sewall, *Life,* 642. Habegger makes the important point that these drafts were given to Mabel Loomis Todd by Austin in 1890 and have "scissored deletions that tell of a deliberate act of selective preservation, the implication being that what we have is what we were *meant* to have." See Habegger, *My Wars,* 587, 589–90. See also Martha L. Werner, *Emily Dickinson's Open Folio: Scenes of Reading, Surfaces of Writing* (Ann Arbor: University of Michigan Press, 1995); Smith, *Rowing,* 29–30.

72. Bianchi, *Life,* 69.

73. For the dating of the letters between Lord and Dickinson, see Habegger, *My Wars,* 588–89, 645.

74. Thomas Wentworth Higginson, "Sunshine and Petrarch," *Atlantic Monthly* 20, no. 119 (1867): 310. He adds, "There is a vastness of transition in each, which, if recited by Fanny Kemble, would take one's breath away."

75. See Burbick, "Emily," 367, 368.

76. See Wilbur, "Sumptuous," 127–36.

77. See Anderson, *Emily,* 86–106, and Inder Nath Kher, *The Landscape of Absence: Emily Dickinson's Poetry* (New Haven: Yale University Press, 1974), 39–44.

78. Harold Bloom, *The Western Canon* (New York: Harcourt Brace, 1994), 303–7.

79. Bennett, "Orient," 113–14.

Chapter Eight

1. Lavinia's diary at the Houghton Library, Harvard. bMS Am 1118.95, box 8. See Leyda I 211.

2. For two other examples of the antitheatrical prejudice in America, see Rev. D. R Thomson, *Fashionable Amusements; with a review of Rev. Dr. Bellows' Lecture on the Theatre* (New York: M.W. Dodd, 1857), and Josiah W. Leeds, *The Theatre: An Essay upon the Non-Accordancy of Stage-plays with the Christian Profession* (Philadelphia: Walnut Street, 1884).

3. This is how the Museum is advertised in *Boston Directory for the Year of 1851:* "This Museum is the largest, most valuable, and best arranged, in the United States. It comprises no less than SEVEN DIFFERENT MUSEUMS, to which has been added, in the present year, besides the constant daily accumulation of articles, one-half of the celebrated PEALE'S PHILADELPHIA MUSEUM, swelling the already immense collection to upwards of HALF A MILLION ARTICLES, the greatest amount of objects of interest to be found together at any one place in America; and an entirely NEW HALL OF WAX STATUARY, *one hundred feet in length, completely filled with* WAX FIGURES. In addition to the attractions, and *without extra charge,* visitors are admitted to the gorgeous Exhibition Hall, where they can witness the magnificent THEATRICAL ENTERTAINMENTS given every evening, and Wednesday and Saturday afternoons, by a company

of comedians, and an orchestra of musicians, admitted to be *superior* to any before collected in this country, with the aid of STAGE AND SCENIC ARRANGEMENTS, the most grand and superb ever seen in either Europe or America! thus warranting the universal admission that the Boston Museum, besides being the most comfortable and genteel, is also the CHEAPEST PLACE OF AMUSEMENT IN THE WORLD." Quoted in Hiroko Uno, *Emily Dickinson Visits Boston* (Kyoto: Yamaguchi Publishing House, 1990), 31–32.

4. See Claire McGlinchee, *The First Decade of the Boston Museum* (Boston: Bruce Humphries, 1940), 24–26; and Kate Ryan, *Old Boston Museum Days* (Boston: Little Brown, 1915), 4–5.

5. "Boston Museum," *Boston Evening Transcript* 2 September 1843.

6. See "Boston Museum," *Boston Evening Transcript* 29 May 1850. The paper printed the following: "The great reputation of the Boston Museum for the maintenance of good order, and the strict regard always observed there in respect of the purity of language and morals submitted to public representation, induced very many to visit there, who could not, with propriety, be seen at any dramatic establishment."

7. Pascoe, "The House," 1–18.

8. Hiroko Uno suggests that Dickinson did visit the museum and must have enjoyed it (*Emily,* 32). Habegger is more skeptical, suggesting that Lavinia's diary usually indicated if she was accompanied by someone (*My Wars,* 261).

9. See McGlinchee, *First,* 79, 107–10; Ryan, *Old,* 4. Other Shakespeare plays performed at the Museum were *King Lear, Macbeth, Much Ado About Nothing,* and Garrick's version of *The Taming of the Shrew,* called *Katherine and Petruchio.*

10. Shattuck, *Shakespeare,* I 74–75; Marder, *His Exits,* 301–13; Levine, *Highbrow,* 18–19.

11. See Levine, *Highbrow,* 24; Abby Sage, "Hamlets II," 194.

12. See Whitman, *Collected,* II 597.

13. See "Boston Museum," *Boston Evening Transcript* 1, 3, 5, 11, 12 September 1851. See also McGlinchee, *First,* 99–100, 110. On 8 September, this paper reported that "Mr Booth has never better sustained his high dramatic fame than during his present performances, and the overwhelming audiences that have been in attendance are unmistakeable proof of public opinion to that effect."

14. "Boston Museum," *Boston Post* 8 September 1851.

15. "Boston Museum," *Boston Evening Transcript* 9 September 1851.

16. White, "On the Acting of Iago," 205. See Thomas R. Gould, *The Tragedian: an Essay on The Histrionic Genius of Junius Brutus Booth* (Cambridge: Riverside Press, 1868), 81–91.

17. William Winter, *Shakespeare on the Stage,* 1st ser. (New York: Moffat, Yard, 1911), 259.

18. Winter, *Shakespeare,* I 250–58. See Bate ed., *Romantics,* 160, 174–75, 200–2.

19. See Arthur Colby Sprague, *Shakespeare and the Actors: The Stage Business in His Plays 1660–1905* (Cambridge, Mass.: Harvard University Press, 1945), 185, 190, 222–23.

20. R., "The Elder Booth," *The Galaxy* 2, no. 2 (1866): 162.

21. See *Boston Evening Transcript* 9 September 1851. See also McGlinchee, *First,* 78–79.

22. See McGlinchee, *First,* 62–63, 77–78.

23. See Levine, *Highbrow,* 21–30.

24. See McGlinchee, *First,* 68–69, 80–86.

25. See Stephen M. Archer, *Junius Brutus Booth: Theatrical Prometheus* (Carbondale: Southern Illinois University Press, 1992), 187–88. See also Winter, *Shakespeare,* I 255–57. Marvin Rosenberg, *The Masks of Othello* (Berkeley: University of California Press, 1971), 61–101; Virginia Mason Vaughan, *Othello: A Contextual History* (Cambridge, U.K.: Cambridge University Press, 1994), 135–57; and Levine, *Highbrow,* 48.

26. Gould, *Tragedian,* 102–14

27. See Rosenberg, *Masks,* 70–79.

28. Prior to Kean, Othello was often presented as black. For instance, observers of David Garrick's performance of 1745 commented that his Othello seems like a "little nigger boy" (Winter, *Shakespeare,* I 245). Winter suggests that when Othello was performed on the American stage for the first time in New York in 1751, John Henry's face was black and his hair was woolly (I 262). See also Rosenberg, *Masks,* 39–42, and Ruth Cowling, "Actors, Black and Tawny in the Role of Othello—and Their Critics," *Theatre Research International* 4 (1977): 133–46.

29. F. W. Hawkins, *The Life of Edmund Kean, From Published and Original Sources,* 2 vols. (London: Tinsley Brothers, 1869), I 221.

30. Bate ed., *Romantics,* 482–83.

31. See Kris Collins, "White-Washing the Black-a-Moor: Othello, Negro Minstrelsy and Parodies of Blackness," *Journal of American Culture* 19, no. 3 (1996): 87–101.

32. Quoted in Collins, "White," 91.

33. See John Weiss, "The Horrors of San Domingo," *Atlantic Monthly* 11, no. 65 (1863): 289–306 (297). For a discussion of Dickinson's use and understanding of the term "Domingo," a word synonymous with racial conflict, rebellion, and unrest, see Ed Folsom and Kenneth Price, "Dickinson, Slavery, and the San Domingo Moment," < http://www.unl.edu/Price/dickinson/>.

34. Marder, *His Exits,* 308.

35. Quoted in Rosenberg, *Masks,* 119.

36. Bayard Taylor, "Between Europe and Asia," *Atlantic Monthly* 15, no. 87 (1865): 8–20. (16).

37. See Edward Kahn, "Creator of Compromise: William Henry Sedley Smith and the Boston Museum's *Uncle Tom's Cabin,*" *Theatre Survey* 41, no. 2 (2000): 71–82.

38. See Winter, *Shakespeare,* I 257; See Edwina Booth Grossmann, *Edwin Booth: Recollections by his Daughter* (New York: The Century, 1894), 21–22. Gould, *Tragedian,* 113–14.

39. Kahn, "Creator," 75.

40. See Ray B. Brown, "Shakespeare in America: Vaudeville and Negro Minstrelsy," *American Quarterly* 12, no. 3 (1960): 375.

41. James R. Siemon, "'Nay, that's Not Next": *Othello,* V. ii in Performance, 1760–1900," *Shakespeare Quarterly* 37, no. 1 (1986): 38–51.

42. Rosenberg, *Masks,* 31, 47–48, 55–60, 87–88, 116; and Collins, "White," 92.

43. See Collins, "White," 84–93; Vaughan, *Othello,* 160–61. See also Siemon, "Nay," 38.

44. Charles B. Lower, "Othello as Black on Southern Stages, Then and Now," in *Shakespeare in the South,* ed. Philip C. Kolin (Jackson: University Press of Mississippi, 1983), 199–228.

45. Collins, "White," 92–94; Brown, "Shakespeare," 384–88. See also Tilden G. Edelstein, "*Othello* in America: The Drama of Racial Intermarriage," *Interracialism: Black-White Intermarriage in American History, Literature, and Law* (Oxford: Oxford University Press, 2000), 363–64; See also Henry E. Jacobs and Claudia D. Johnson, *An Annotated Bibliography of Shakespearean Burlesques, Parodies, and Travesties* (New York: Garland, 1976), 104–9.

46. Collins, "White," 93–98. See Joyce Green MacDonald, "Acting Black: *Othello, Othello* Burlesques, and the Performance of Blackness," *Theatre Survey* 46, no. 2 (1994): 231–49.

47. MacDonald, "Acting," 247–48.

48. *Othello: A Burlesque* in *Nineteenth-Century Burlesque: American Shakespeare Travesties,* 5 vols., ed. Stanley Wells (London: Diploma Press, 1978), V 129.

49. Brown, "Shakespeare," 380–81.

50. Lower, "Othello," 211.

51. Brown, "Shakespeare," 387–88.

52. See Reginald Horseman, *Race and Manifest Destiny: The Origins of American Racial Anglo-Saxonism* (Cambridge, Mass.: Harvard University Press, 1981), 139–57.

53. Adams, "Misconceptions," 438.

54. John Quincy Adams, "The Character of Desdemona," *American Monthly Magazine* 1 (1836): 209–17 (210).

55. James Henry Hackett, *Notes, Criticism and Correspondence upon Shakespeare's Plays and Actors* (New York: Carleton Press, 1863), 212.

56. Richard Grant White, *Shakespeare's Scholar* (New York: D. Appleton, 1854), 432.

57. White, *Shakespeare,* 432–33.

58. White, *Shakespeare,* 435–36.

59. Knight, *Shakspere,* V 346.

60. Preston, *Studies,* 71.

61. Preston, *Studies,* 63, 67.

62. See also Reed, *Lectures,* 448–49; Horace Howard Furness, "Othello's Color," in *A New Variorum Edition of Shakespeare's Othello,* ed. Horace Howard Furness (Philadelphia: J. B. Lippincott, 1886), 391–95.

63. K., "Othello," *Ichnolite: Amherst Collegiate Magazine* 5 (January 1858), 105–11.

64. See Erkkila, "Emily," 10–11. Domhnall Mitchell, "Northern Lights: Class, Color, Culture, and Emily Dickinson," *Emily Dickinson Journal* 9, no. 2 (2000): 75–83;

Domhnall Mitchell, "Emily Dickinson and Class," in *The Cambridge Companion to Emily Dickinson,* ed. Martin, 191–214; and Paula Bernat Bennett, "'The Negor Never Knew': Emily Dickinson and Racial Typology in the Nineteenth Century," *Legacy* 19, no. 2 (2002): 53–61.

65. Vivian Pollak, "Dickinson and the Poetics of Whiteness," *Emily Dickinson Journal* 9, no. 2 (2000): 84–95.

66. Daneen Wardrop, "'The Ethiop Within': Emily Dickinson and Slavery," in *Emily Dickinson at Home, Proceedings of the Third International Conference of the Emily Dickinson International Society in South Hadley, Mount Holyoke College, 12–15 August 1999,* ed. Gundrun M. and Martina Antretter (Trier, Germany: Wissenschaftlicher Verlag Trier, 2001), 71–88. See also Folsom and Price, "Dickinson, Slavery, and the San Domingo Moment"; Daneen Wardrop, "'That Minute Domingo': Dickinson's Cooption of Abolitionist Diction and Franklin's Variorum Edition," *Emily Dickinson Journal* 8, no. 2 (1999): 72–86.

67. See *Webster's Revised Unabridged Dictionary* (G & C. Merriam, 1913), ed. Noah Porter. On-line at <http://humanities.uchicago.edu/forms_unrest/webster.form.html>

68. See Pollak, "Emily," 90.

69. Erkkila, "Emily," 11–13.

70. See Pollak, *Dickinson,* 155–56; and Farr, *Passion,* 147–50. Both Pollak and Farr argue that this poem about sexual rivalry is most likely connected with Sue (the Pearl), and Austin (the Malay). See also Capps, *Emily,* 89–90.

71. A. Dexter, "Plays," 288. See also Patterson, *Riddle,* 260–61.

72. Bianchi, *Life,* 80.

73. Of course, Dickinson's message could be read in another way: perhaps it is the others who are "possessing" Mrs. Jenkins (and her family) with the "throes of Othello." However, it is not clear why these "others" should experience such anguish and pain since they "possess" the Jenkins family. It seems more likely, within the context of this letter, that it is Dickinson and her family that are in the jealous throes of Othello. See Patterson, *Emily,* 28.

74. See Gilbert and Gubar, *Madwoman,* 613–21; Eberwein, *Dickinson,* 33–37; Farr, *Passion,* 34–37; Mitchell, "Northern," 77; Pollak, "Dickinson," 85–86.

75. See Dobson, *Dickinson,* 15–16.

76. See Novy, *Engaging,* 118–20.

77. See David H. Fennema, "The Popular Response to Tommaso Salvini in America," *Theatre History Studies* 2 (1982): 103–13.

78. David Mayers, "'Quote the Words to Prompt the Attitudes': The Victorian Performer, the Photographer, and the Photograph," *Theatre Survey* 43, no. 2 (2002): 223–51.

79. Quoted in Marvin Carlson, *The Italian Shakespearians: Performances by Ristori, Salvini and Rossi in England and America* (Washington, D.C.: Folger Shakespeare Library, 1985), 49.

80. Adam Frank, "Emily Dickinson and Photography," *Emily Dickinson Journal* 10, no. 2 (2001): 1–21; "The Soul's Distinct Connection -": Emily Dickinson, Photography,

and 19th-Century American Culture," *The Classroom Electric: Dickinson, Whitman, and American Culture* at <http://jefferson.village.virginia.edu/fdw/volume3/werner/>.

81. A picture of Salvini appeared in J. Brander Matthews, "Foreign Actors on the American Stage," *Scribner's Monthly* 21, no. 4 (1881): 533.

82. Emma Lazarus, "Tommaso Salvini," *The Century* 23, no. 1 (1881): 110–17; and Tommaso Salvini, "Impressions of Some Shakspearean Characters," *The Century* 23, no. 1 (1881): 117–25. Subsequently both are cited by parenthetical page references in the text.

83. See Carlson, *Italian,* 60–79.

84. See John Ranken Towse, *Sixty Years of the Theater* (New York, Funk & Wagnalls, 1916), 162–63.

85. See Carlton, *Italian,* 69–70.

86. Dickinson's verbal portrait of Salvini's Othello is very like his own description of his ideal Iago, who must "represent both faith and treachery, the saint and the demon, and the contrasts must be presented quickly and suddenly in order to produce the greatest effect" (124).

87. See Carlton, *Italians,* 78–79.

88. Henry James, "Tommaso Salvini," *Atlantic Monthly* 51, no. 305 (1883): 377–86. Subsequently cited by parenthetical page references in the text.

89. "Entertainments," *Boston Post* 12 April 1883.

90. For other pictorial representations of Othello, see Shattuck, *Shakespeare,* II 43, 151, 207, 230.

91. Winter, *Shakespeare,* I 289–90.

92. See Shattuck, *Shakespeare,* II 152–53.

Chapter Nine

1. See Farr, *Gardens,* 10–12; Mitchell, *Emily,* 112–53; and Petrino, *Emily,* 129–60.

2. Emerson, *Works,* I 66–67

3. Emerson, *Works,* IV 117.

4. "Hamlet," *The Indicator,* 223. Subsequently cited by parenthetical page references in the text.

5. "Hamlet," *Amherst Student,* 24 April 1875.

6. "The Character of Hamlet," *Amherst Student* 21 September 1872, 1–2.

7. "All but Death, Can be adjusted - . . . Death - unto itself - Exception - / Is exempt from Change - " (F789). "Death is the supple Suitor" of humanity "That wins at last - " (F1470). Death woos all, regardless of "Color - Caste - Denomination -"; its "large - Democratic fingers / Rub away the Brand - " (F836). Death's "Marble Disc - [is a] / Sublimer sort - than Speech - " (F422B). Death is "the Tomb / Who tells no secret" (F543). Death is always accompanied by a "sorer Robber," silence (F1315). The dead slip away into the "reportless Grave - ," they "exude away / In the recallless sea" (F1654). The dead go "Further than Guess can gallop / Further than Riddle ride - " (F1068); they have gone "past surmise" (F1706).

8. Thomas W. Ford, *Heaven Beguiles the Tired: Death in the Poetry of Emily Dickinson* (Tuscaloosa: University of Alabama Press, 1966), 14.

9. St. Armand, *Emily,* 41–52. See also Farr, *Passion,* 6; Kher, *Landscape,* 180.

10. See Habegger, *My Wars,* 616–18, 621.

11. Sewall, *Life,* 651.

12. See Habegger, *My Wars,* 587–88, 645.

13. See St. Armand, *Emily,* 137–51; Wolff, *Emily,* 260–70, 378–84; Loeffelholz, *Dickinson,* 47–80.

14. Habegger, *My Wars,* 530–31.

15. See Keiko Beppu, "'O, rare for Emily!'- Dickinson and *Antony and Cleopatra,*" in *Emily Dickinson: After a Hundred Years: Essays on Emily Dickinson* (Apollan-sha Kyoto, Japan, 1988), 175–89; Patricia Thompson Rizzo, "The Elegaic Modes of Emily Dickinson," *Emily Dickinson Journal* 11, no. 1 (2002): 104–17.

16. "The Cleopatra," *Amherst Student,* 2.

17. Wingate, *Shakespeare's,* 187.

18. Westland Marston, *Our Recent Actors: Being Recollections, of Late Distinguished Performers of Both Sexes,* 2 vols. (Boston: Roberts Brothers, 1888), II 41.

19. "Mrs. Frances Anne Kemble," *The Galaxy* 6, no. 6 (1868): 797–803. (802).

20. See Taylor, *Reinventing,* 210. See also Michael R. Booth, "Pictorial Acting and Ellen Terry," in *Shakespeare and the Victorian Stage,* ed. Richard Foulkes (Cambridge, U.K.: Cambridge University Press, 1986), 78–86.

21. Elaine Showalter, "Representing Ophelia: Women, Madness and the Responsibilities of Feminist Criticism," in *Shakespeare and the Question of Theory,* ed. Patricia Parker and Geoffrey Hartman (London: Methuen, 1985), 84–85.

22. Knight, *Shakspere,* V 206.

23. Margaret Rose, "The Figure of Desdemona in Eighteenth- and Nineteenth-Century Illustrations," in *The Renaissance Theatre: Texts, Performance, Design,* 2 vols., ed Christopher Cairns (Aldershot, U.K.: Ashgate, 1999), I 45–67.

24. Fanny Kemble, "Salvini's Othello," *Temple Bar: A London Magazine* 71 (1884): 376; Siemon, "Nay," 38–39.

25. Edgar Allan Poe, "The Philosophy of Composition," in *Edgar Allan Poe: Essays and Reviews,* ed. G. R. Thompson 19. See also Farr, *Passion,* 93; McNeil, *Emily,* 129–31.

26. See Wolff, *Emily,* 221–22; Petrino, *Emily,* 96–125; St Armand, *Emily,* 39–77; and Loeffelholz, *Dickinson,* 54–66.

27. "Hamlet," *The Indicator,* 221.

28. Ward, *Emily,* 198.

29. See "Topics of the Time," *Scribner's Monthly* 21, no. 5 (1881): 790–91.

30. Knight provides a note on "Crowner's-quest law," suggesting that the case regarded the suicide of Sir James Hales and the forfeiture of a lease to the crown; see Knight, *Shakspere,* V 235.

31. Henry James, "George Eliot's Life," *Atlantic Monthly* 55, no. 331 (1885): 677; and Edwin P. Whipple, "George Eliot's Novels," *North American Review* 141, no. 347 (1885): 701.

32. "Literary Notes," *The Critic* 15 January 1881, 1.

33. In 1856, President Stearns contrasted the miserly revenge of Shylock and the generosity of true benevolence exhibited by Antonio. Stearns, "Reading," *Hampshire and Franklin Express,* Friday, 11 January 1856.

34. Salvini, "Impressions," 124.

35. Lazarus, "Salvini," 114.

36. Sewall, *Lyman,* 47, 39–44.

37. Sewall, *Lyman* 39.

38. Sewall, *Lyman,* 78.

39. Knight, *Shakspere,* V 114.

40. Knight, *Shakspere,* V 115.

41. See Lease, *Emily,* 36–37.

42. Hudson, *Lectures,* II 86.

43. "Hamlet," *The Indicator,* 223.

44. See St. Armand, "Emily," 86–87.

45. These pages also include the almost Dickinsonian lines, "Whose whisper o'er the world's diameter, / As level as the cannon to his blank, / Transports his poison'd shot, may miss our name / And hit the woundless air" (IV i 41–44).

46. "Miss Emily Dickinson of Amherst," *Springfield Republican* 18 May 1886.

47. Kate Field, "Fechter as Hamlet," *Atlantic Monthly* 26, no. 157 (1870): 569. See Robert Hapgood, ed., *Hamlet: Shakespeare in Production* (Cambridge, U.K.: Cambridge University Press, 1999), 32.

48. E. C. Stedman, "Edwin Booth, " *Atlantic Monthly* 17, no. 103 (1866), 592; Abby Sage, "The Hamlets of the Stage II," 197–98. See also Hapgood ed., *Hamlet,* 36.

49. See Ann Douglas, *The Feminization of American Culture* (New York: Alfred A. Knopf, 1977). Charles H. Shattuck *The Hamlet of Edwin Booth* (Urbana: University of Illinois Press, 1969), 64. Stedman, "Edwin Booth," 588.

50. See Winter, *Shakespeare,* I 427–42; Taylor, *Reinventing,* 209–10; Novy, *Engaging,* 118–20; Frank W. Wadsworth, "Hamlet and Iago: Nineteenth-Century Breeches Parts," *Shakespeare Quarterly* 17, no. 2 (1966): 129–39.

51. Lisa Merrill, *When Romeo Was a Woman* (Ann Arbor: University of Michigan Press, 1999), 111. Grossmann, *Edwin,* 133–34.

52. Emma Stebbins, *Charlotte Cushman: Her Letters and Memories of Her Life* (Boston: Houghton Mifflin, 1899), 217.

53. Merrill, *When,* 132.

54. Lawrence Barrett, *Charlotte Cushman, A Lecture* (New York: Dunlap Society, 1889), 21.

55. Shattuck, *Shakespeare,* I 94.

56. John D. Stockton, "Charlotte Cushman," *Scribner's Monthly* 12 no. 3 (1876): 262–66. Subsequently cited by parenthetical page references in the text.

57. Shattuck, *Shakespeare,* I 93; Marston, *Our,* 75–76; and Stebbins, *Charlotte,* 59.

58. "Amusements," *New York Times* 16 November 1860.

59. Jill Levenson, *Romeo and Juliet: Shakespeare in Performance* (Manchester, U.K.: Manchester University Press, 1987), 32.

60. William Winter, *Shakespeare on the Stage* second series (New York: Benjamin Blom, 1916), 207–11; Shattuck, *Shakespeare,* I 92–93.

61. Levenson, *Romeo,* 34–35.

62. Quoted in Stebbins, *Charlotte,* 63.

63. Quoted in Merrill, *When,* 124. See Anne Russell, "Gender, Passion, and Performance in Nineteenth-Century Women Romeos," *Essays in Theatre* 11, no. 2 (1993): 153–66.

64. Merrill, *When,* 122, 128–30, 133.

65. See Pollak, *Dickinson,* 59–82; Smith, *Rowing,* 17, 25–30; Bennett, *Emily,* 157–68; Hart, "Encoding," 251–72.

66. See "Amusements," *Springfield Republican* 13 May 1861; Amusements," *Springfield Republican* 14 May 1861; "General New Items," *Springfield Republican* 14 May 1861; and "General New Items," *Springfield Republican* 15 May 1861.

67. Samuel Bowles to Austin and Susan Dickinson, between 1859–1861, bMS Am 1118.8 (1)–(10). By permission of the Houghton Library, Harvard University.

68. Suzanne Juhasz and Cristanne Miller, "Performances of Gender in Dickinson's Poetry," in *Cambridge Companion to Emily Dickinson,* ed. Martin, 107–28 (119).

69. This scene also involved the Friar's lament on the fickleness of love: "Young men's love then lies / Not truly in their hearts but in their eyes" (II iii 67–68). In addition, the scene may have interested Dickinson, a keen gardener, because it begins with the Friar's discussion of the medicine and poison within flowers.

70. Patterson, *Emily,* 1–29. See also Finnerty, "No Matter," 65–94.

71. See Bennett, "Gender," 94–97.

72. Nancy Johnson, "The Loaf and the Crumb: Dickinson's Aesthetics of Breadmaking," in *Emily Dickinson at Home* ed. Grabher and Antretter, 35–50 (44).

73. Farr, *Gardens,* 38, 49–74.

74. Palmer, *Stratford,* 32.

75. John E. Walsh, *This Brief Tragedy of Flesh: Unravelling the Todd-Dickinson Affair* (New York: Grove Weidenfeld, 1991), 99–100.

76. "Gloom at Northampton," *Springfield Republican* 16 April 1886; "Northampton's Grist," *Springfield Republican* 18 April 1886.

77. Levine, *Highbrow,* 13. Susan Kattwinkel, ed., *Tony Pastor Presents: Afterpieces from the Vaudeville Stage* (Westpost, Conn.: Greenwood, 1998); David L. Rinear, *The Temple of Momus: Mitchell's Olympic Theatre* (Metuchen, N.J.: Scarecrow Press, 1987); Robert C. Allen, *Horrible Prettiness: Burlesques and American Culture* (Chapel Hill: University of North Carolina Press, 1991); and Richard W. Schoch, *Not Shakespeare: Bardolatry and Burlesque in the Nineteenth-Century* (Cambridge, U.K.: Cambridge University Press, 2002).

78. "The Theater and Morality," *Amherst Student* 13 January (1877): 75–76. See Leyda II 435.

79. There is an advertisement, in the Jones Public Library, Amherst, dated 1876, that reads: "Amherst Public Library: Dramatic Entertainments, Monday & Tuesday Evenings, February 28 and 29 will be presented the celebrated Operatic Burlesque of *Capuletta or Romeo and Juliet Restored!* . . . To be followed by the Beautiful Drama, *Cricket on the Hearth.*"

80. Sewall, *Life,* 94–5, 172.

81. See also Dramatic Activities Collection, *Capuletta, or Romeo and Juliet Restored,* 1876, Archive and Special Collection, Amherst College Library. This play was performed in Amherst Public Library in 1876. Dramatic Activities Collection, Summer School Shakespeare Company, 1885, Archive and Special Collection, Amherst College Library. In 1885, a Summer School Shakespeare Company performed, in costume, scenes from *As You Like It, Hamlet, Henry V,* and *The Merchant of Venice.* Dramatic Activities Collection, *Much Ado about Nothing,* 1887–88, Archive and Special Collection, Amherst College Library. Sometime in 1887–88 there was a production of this play put on by Amherst College faculty and wives.

82. Laurence Hutton, "American Burlesque," *Harper's New Monthly* 81, no. 481 (1890): 61.

83. Schoch, *Not Shakespeare,* 12–13.

84. Dramatic Activities Collection, *Romeo and Juliet, A Travesty,* June 1881, Archive and Special Collection, Amherst College Library. This folder contains an advertisement for this play, which was to take place in College Hall on 15 June 1881 (and also on June 13). The advertisement states that "No labor or expense has been spared. The scenery is new, being designed and painted by an artist from Springfield. The Costumes for the entire Troupe, including the Chorus, were procured from Boston. Put on by Senior Dramatic Company." Also included in this folder is a version of the performed play which was reprinted by "The Class of eighty-one Amherst College as a souvenir of its 35th re-union on June 17, 1916.": *A New Travesty on Romeo and Juliet,* as originally presented before the University Club of St. Louis 16 January 1877 (St. Louis: G. I. Jones and Company, 1877). All subsequent quotations refer to this edition. See *Amherst Record* 15 June and 29 June 1881.

85. Kattwinkel ed., *Tony,* 3–4, 6.

86. Schoch, *Not,* 3–8 and Rinear, *The Temple,* 27–28.

87. Dramatic Activities Collection, *The Travesty of Hamlet* 1883, Archive and Special Collection, Amherst College Library. This folder contains an advertisement for "*The Travesty of Hamlet,* presented by The Amherst College Glee Club, Amherst College Hall, June 23 1883 (Saturday Evening). Usual Hamlet, Ophelia, Ghost, Horatio, Polonius (is a Professor), there is also an Old Lady, Guards, Courtiers, and Students, and Chorus by The Glee Club. Act 1 Hamlet's College Room in Wittenburgh University. Act 2 Exterior of Elsinore Castle. Students on guard. Act 3, 4, 5 Dining Hall and interior Elsinore Castle." The information suggests that this play was a version of *Hamlet Revamped: Modernized and set to Music* (St. Louis: G. I. Jones and Company, 1879) reprinted in Wells ed., *Burlesques,* V 156–218. All subsequent references are from Wells's edition.

88. Wells ed., *Burlesques,* V 172, 176, 200, 208.

89. See Schoch, *Not,* 60–64.

90. Mark Twain, *The Adventures of Huckleberry Finn* (New York: W. W. Norton, 1999), 152–53. See also David Reynolds, "Emily Dickinson and Popular Culture," in *Cambridge Companion to Emily Dickinson,* ed. Martin, 167–90.

91. Hutton, "American," 59.

92. See Vivian Pollak, "Emily Dickinson's Valentines," *American Quarterly* 26, no. 1 (1974): 60–78; Juhasz et al., *Comic Power,* 1–25, 103–36. See also Anderson, *Emily,* 3–33.

93. Charles Cowden-Clarke, "On the Comic Writers of England. VII.—Burlesque Writers," *Gentleman's Magazine* 5, no. 7 (1871): 557.

94. See Cartelli, *Repositioning,* 29.

INDEX

PÁRAIC FINNERTY was born in Dublin, Ireland. He received a B.A. and M.A. from University College Dublin and a Ph.D. from the University of Kent. In 2002 he was the first recipient of the Scholar in Amherst Award of the Emily Dickinson International Society, and he was a Copeland Fellow at Amherst College in 2004. Finnerty has published articles on Dickinson and Shakespeare in the *Emily Dickinson Journal.* He is currently researching transatlantic literary relations and ideas of English masculinity and has published on Dickinson and Oscar Wilde in *Symbiosis: Journal of Anglo-American Literary Relations.* He has taught English drama and American literature at the University of Kent and is currently a lecturer in English literature at the University of Portsmouth.